ACCA

PAPER P2

CORPORATE REPORTING (INTERNATIONAL)

In this June 2007 new edition

- We discuss the **best strategies** for revising and taking your ACCA exams

- We show you how to be well prepared for the **December 2007 exam**

- We give you **lots of great guidance** on tackling questions

- We show you how you can **build your own exams**

- We provide you with **three** mock exams including the **Pilot paper**

- We provide the **ACCA examiner's answers** as well as our own to key exam questions and the Pilot Paper as an additional revision aid

Our **i-Pass** product also supports this paper.

D1420082

FOR EXAMS IN DECEMBER 2007

BPP
LEARNING MEDIA

First edition June 2007

ISBN 9780 7517 3375 4

British Library Cataloguing-in-Publication Data
A catalogue record for this book
is available from the British Library

Published by

BPP Learning Media Ltd
BPP House, Aldine Place
London W12 8AA

www.bpp.com/learningmedia

Printed in Great Britain by
Page Bros
Mile Cross Lane
Norwich
NR6 6SA

All our rights reserved. No part of this publication may be reproduced, stored in a retrieval system or transmitted, in any form or by any means, electronic, mechanical, photocopying, recording or otherwise, without the prior written permission of BPP Learning Media.

We are grateful to the Association of Chartered Certified Accountants for permission to reproduce past examination questions. The answers to past examination questions have been prepared by BPP Learning Media Ltd.

Your learning materials, published by BPP Learning Media Ltd, are printed on paper sourced from sustainable, managed forests.

©
BPP Learning Media Ltd
2007

Contents

Review form & free prize draw

Question index

The headings in this checklist/index indicate the main topics of questions, but questions often cover several different topics.

Questions set under the old syllabus *Advanced Corporate Reporting* paper are included because their style and content are similar to those which appear in the P2 exam. The questions have been amended to reflect the current exam format.

BPP
LEARNING MEDIA

Mock exam 1

Questions G1 to G4

Mock exam 2

Questions G5 to G8

Mock exam 3 (Pilot paper)

Questions G9 to G12

Planning your question practice

Our guidance from page 27 shows you how to organise your question practice, either by attempting questions from each syllabus area or **by building your own exams** – tackling questions as a series of practice exams.

Topic index

Listed below are the key Paper P2 syllabus topics and the numbers of the questions in this Kit covering those topics.

If you need to concentrate your practice and revision on certain topics or if you want to attempt all available questions that refer to a particular subject, you will find this index useful.

Syllabus topic	Question numbers
Associates	D3 – D5
Cash flow statements – consolidated	D18 – D22
Consolidated balance sheet	D1
Consolidated income statement	D2
Corporate citizenship	C1
Disposals	D11, D12
Employee benefits	B7 – B9
Environmental issues	A2
Ethics	A1
Financial instruments	B14, B15
Foreign currency	D15 – D17
Impairment	B2
International issues	F1, F2
IFRS 1	ME1 Q4
IFRS 2	C5
IFRS 3	D1 – D18
Joint ventures	D5
Measurement of performance	C7
Multi-company structure	D6 – D10
Non-current assets	B1, B2
Off balance sheet finance	B1
Provisions	B3, B4
Ratio analysis	C3
Related party transactions	C8, C9, E23, E24
Share-based payment	C5, E17
Taxation	B5, B6

Using your BPP Practice and Revision Kit

Tackling revision and the exam

You can significantly improve your chances of passing by tackling revision and the exam in the right ways. Our advice is based on feedback from ACCA examiners.

- We look at the dos and don'ts of revising for, and taking, ACCA exams

- We focus on Paper P2; we discuss revising the syllabus, what to do (and what not to do) in the exam, how to approach different types of question and ways of obtaining easy marks

Selecting questions

We provide signposts to help you plan your revision.

- A full **question index**

- A **topic index** listing all the questions that cover key topics, so that you can locate the questions that provide practice on these topics, and see the different ways in which they might be examined

- **BPP's question plan** highlighting the most important questions and explaining why you should attempt them

- **Build your own exams**, showing how you can practise questions in a series of exams

Making the most of question practice

At BPP we realise that you need more than just questions and model answers to get the most from your question practice.

- Our **Top tips** provide essential advice on tackling questions, presenting answers and the key points that answers need to include

- We show you how you can pick up **Easy marks** on questions, as we know that picking up all readily available marks often can make the difference between passing and failing

- We summarise **Examiner's comments**

- We include **marking guides** to show you what the examiner rewards

- A number of questions include **Analysis** and **Helping hands** attached to show you how to approach them if you are struggling

- In a bank at the end of this Kit we include the **examiner's answers** to the Pilot paper. Used in conjunction with our answers they provide an indication of all possible points that could be made, issues that could be covered and approaches to adopt.

Attempting mock exams

There are three mock exams that provide practice at coping with the pressures of the exam day. We strongly recommend that you attempt them under exam conditions. **Mock exams 1 and 2** reflect the question styles and syllabus coverage of the exam; **Mock exam 3** is the Pilot paper. To help you get the most out of doing these exams, we not only provide help with each answer, but also guidance on how you should have approached the whole exam.

Passing ACCA exams

Revising and taking ACCA exams

To maximise your chances of passing your ACCA exams, you must make best use of your time, both before the exam during your revision, and when you are actually doing the exam.

- Making the most of your revision time can make a big, big difference to how well-prepared you are for the exam

- Time management is a core skill in the exam hall; all the work you've done can be wasted if you don't make the most of the three hours you have to attempt the exam

In this section we simply show you what to do and what not to do during your revision, and how to increase and decrease your prospects of passing your exams when you take them. Our advice is grounded in feedback we've had from ACCA examiners. You may be surprised to know that much examiner advice is the same whatever the exam, and the reasons why many students fail don't vary much between subjects and exam levels. So if you follow the advice we give you over the next few pages, you will **significantly** enhance your chances of passing **all** your ACCA exams.

How to revise

☑ Plan your revision

At the start of your revision period, you should draw up a **timetable** to plan how long you will spend on each subject and how you will revise each area. You need to consider the total time you have available and also the time that will be required to revise for other exams you're taking.

☑ Practise Practise Practise

The **more exam-standard questions** you do, the **more likely you are to pass** the exam. Practising full questions will mean that you'll get used to the time pressure of the exam. When the time is up, you should note where you've got to and then try to complete the question, giving yourself practice at everything the question tests.

☑ Revise enough

Make sure that your revision covers the breadth of the syllabus, as all topics could be examined in a compulsory question. However it is true that some topics are **key** – they are likely to appear often or are a particular interest of the examiner – and you need to spend sufficient time revising these. Make sure you also know the **basics** – the fundamental calculations, proformas and report layouts.

☑ Deal with your difficulties

Difficult areas are topics you find dull and pointless, or subjects that you found problematic when you were studying them. You mustn't become negative about these topics; instead you should build up your knowledge by reading the **Passcards** and using the **Quick Quiz** questions in the Study Text to test yourself. When practising questions in the Kit, go back to the Text if you're struggling.

☑ Learn from your mistakes

Having completed a question you must try to look at your answer critically. Always read the **Top tips guidance** in the answers; it's there to help you. Look at **Easy marks** to see how you could have quickly gained credit on the questions that you've done. As you go through the Kit, it's worth noting any traps you've fallen into, and key points in the **Top tips** or **Examiner's comments** sections, and referring to these notes in the days before the exam. Aim to learn at least one new point from each question you attempt, a technical point perhaps or a point on style or approach.

☑ Read the examiners' guidance

We refer throughout this Kit to **Examiner's comments**. As well as highlighting weaknesses, Examiner's comments often provide clues to future questions, as many examiners will test areas that are likely to cause students problems. ACCA's website also contains articles by examiners which you **must** read, as they may form the basis of questions on any paper after they've been published.

Read through the examiner's answers to key exam questions and the Pilot paper included at the back of the Kit. In general these are far longer and more comprehensive than any answer you could hope to produce in the exam, but used in conjunction with our more realistic solutions, they provide a useful revision tool, covering all possible points and approaches.

☑ Complete all three mock exams

You should attempt the **Mock exams** at the end of the Kit under **strict exam conditions**, to gain experience of selecting questions, managing your time and producing answers.

How NOT to revise

☒ Revise selectively

Examiners are well aware that some students try to forecast the contents of exams, and only revise those areas that they think will be examined. Examiners try to prevent this by doing the unexpected, for example setting the same topic in successive sittings.

☒ Spend all the revision period reading

You cannot pass the exam just by learning the contents of Passcards, Course Notes or Study Texts. You have to develop your **application skills** by practising questions.

☒ Audit the answers

This means reading the answers and guidance without having attempted the questions. Auditing the answers gives you **false reassurance** that you would have tackled the questions in the best way and made the points that our answers do. The feedback we give in our answers will mean more to you if you've attempted the questions and thought through the issues.

☒ Practise some types of question, but not others

Although you may find the numerical parts of certain papers challenging, you shouldn't just practise calculations. These papers will also contain written elements, and you therefore need to spend time practising written question parts.

☒ Get bogged down

Don't spend a lot of time worrying about all the minute detail of certain topic areas, and leave yourself insufficient time to cover the rest of the syllabus. Remember that a key skill in the exam is the ability to **concentrate on what's important** and this applies to your revision as well.

☒ Overdo studying

Studying for too long without interruption will mean your studying becomes less effective. A five minute break each hour will help. You should also make sure that you are leading a **healthy lifestyle** (proper meals, good sleep and some times when you're not studying).

How to PASS your exams

☑ Prepare for the day

Make sure you set at least one alarm (or get an alarm call), and allow plenty of time to get to the exam hall. You should have your route planned in advance and should listen on the radio for potential travel problems. You should check the night before to see that you have pens, pencils, erasers, watch, calculator with spare batteries, also exam documentation and evidence of identity.

☑ Select the right questions

You should select the optional questions you feel you can answer **best**, basing your selection on the topics covered, the requirements of the question, how easy it will be to apply the requirements and the availability of easy marks.

☑ Plan your three hours

You need to make sure that you will be answering the correct number of questions, and that you spend the right length of time on each question – this will be determined by the number of marks available. Each mark carries with it a **time allocation** of **1.8 minutes**. A 25 mark question therefore should be selected, completed and checked in 45 minutes. With some papers, it's better to do certain types of question first or last.

☑ Read the questions carefully

To score well, you must follow the requirements of the question, understanding what aspects of the subject area are being covered, and the tasks you will have to carry out. The requirements will also determine what information and examples you should provide. Reading the question scenarios carefully will help you decide what **issues** to discuss, **techniques** to use, **information** and **examples** to include and how to **organise** your answer.

☑ Plan your answers

Five minutes of planning plus twenty-five minutes of writing is certain to earn you more marks than thirty minutes of writing. Consider when you're planning how your answer should be **structured,** what the **format** should be and **how long** each part should take.

Confirm before you start writing that your plan makes **sense,** covers **all relevant points** and does not include **irrelevant material.**

☑ Show evidence of judgement

Remember that examiners aren't just looking for a display of knowledge; they want to see how well you can **apply** the knowledge you have. Evidence of application and judgement will include writing answers that only contain **relevant** material, using the material in scenarios to **support** what you say, **criticising** the **limitations** and **assumptions** of the techniques you use and making **reasonable recommendations** that follow from your discussion.

☑ Stay until the end of the exam

Use any spare time to **check and recheck** your script. This includes checking you have filled out the candidate details correctly, you have labelled question parts and workings clearly, you have used headers and underlining effectively and spelling, grammar and arithmetic are correct.

How to FAIL your exams

☒ Don't do enough questions

If you don't attempt sufficient questions on the paper, you are making it harder for yourself to pass the questions that you do attempt. If for example you don't do a 20 mark question, then you will have to score 50 marks out of 80 marks on the rest of the paper, and therefore have to obtain 63% of the marks on the questions you do attempt. Failing to attempt all of the paper is symptomatic of poor time management or poor question selection.

☒ Include irrelevant material

Markers are given detailed mark guides and will not give credit for irrelevant content. Therefore you should **NOT** braindump all you know about a broad subject area; the markers will only give credit for what is **relevant**, and you will also be showing that you lack the ability to **judge what's important.** Similarly forcing irrelevant theory into every answer won't gain you marks, nor will providing uncalled for features such as situation analyses, executive summaries and background information.

☒ Fail to use the details in the scenario

General answers or reproductions of Kit answers that don't refer to what is in the scenario in **this** question won't score enough marks to pass.

☒ Copy out the scenario details

Examiners see **selective** use of the right information as a key skill. If you copy out chunks of the scenario which aren't relevant to the question, or don't use the information to support your own judgements, you won't achieve good marks.

☒ Don't do what the question asks

Failing to provide all the examiner asks for will limit the marks you score. You will also decrease your chances by not providing an answer with enough **depth** – producing a single line bullet point list when the examiner asks for a discussion.

☒ Present your work poorly

Markers will only be able to give you credit if they can read your writing. There are also plenty of other things that will make it more difficult for markers to reward you. Examples include:

- Not using black or blue ink
- Not showing clearly which question you're attempting
- Scattering question parts from the same question throughout your answer booklet
- Not showing clearly workings or the results of your calculations

Paragraphs that are too long or which lack headers also won't help markers and hence won't help you.

Using your BPP products

This Kit gives you the question practice and guidance you need in the exam. Our other products can also help you pass:

- **Learning to Learn Accountancy** gives further valuable advice on revision

- **Passcards** provide you with clear topic summaries and exam tips

- **Success CDs** help you revise on the move

- **i-Pass CDs** offer tests of knowledge against the clock

- **Learn Online** is an e-learning resource delivered via the Internet, offering comprehensive tutor support and featuring areas such as study, practice, email service, revision and useful resources

You can purchase these products by visiting www.bpp.com/mybpp.

Visit our website www.bpp.com/acca/learnonline to sample aspects of Learn Online free of charge. Learn Online is hosted by BPP Professional Education.

Passing P2

BPP
LEARNING MEDIA

Revising P2

P2 – or its old syllabus equivalent - has the reputation of being a difficult paper. However its pass rate is usually quite high. Although the examiner, Graham Holt, sets challenging questions, the styles of question he uses are now familiar because he has been the examiner for many years. He has also provided a great deal of feedback in his examiner's reports and in the very detailed published marking schemes, many of which are included in this Kit.

Graham Holt has warned very strongly against question-spotting and trying to predict the topics that will be included in the exam. He has on occasions examined the same topic in two successive sittings. He regards few areas as off-limits for questions, and nearly all of the major areas of the syllabus can and have been tested.

Topics to revise

That said, exams over the years have shown that the following areas of the syllabus are very important, and your revision therefore needs to cover them particularly well.

*   **Group accounts.** You should not omit any aspect of group accounts, as they come up every sitting. We would advise against question spotting, but if a cash flow statement, say, has not come up for a few sittings, it might be a good bet. Group accounts will always be examined as part of the 50 mark case study question, in which you may also expect a question on some aspect of **ethics**

*   **Emerging issues.** The impact of a change in accounting standards on the financial statements is often examined.

*   **Share based payment** usually comes up as part of a question.

*   **Financial instruments** was the subject of a *Student Accountant* article, so is ripe for examination.

*   **Developments in financial reporting** , for example, the Management Commentary or the proposals on business combinations.

Question practice

Question practice under timed conditions is essential, so that you can get used to the pressures of answering exam questions in **limited time** and practise not only the key techniques but allocating your time between different requirements in each question. Our list of recommended questions includes compulsory Section A and optional Section B questions; it's particularly important to do all the Section A case-study-style questions in full as a case study involving group accounts will always come up.

Passing the P2 exam

What to expect on the paper

Of course you cannot know in advance what questions are going to come up, but you can have a fair idea of what kind of questions.

Question 1

This will always be a case study, with half or a little more than half on group accounts. It will often involve high speed number crunching. Easy marks, it cannot be said too often, will always be available for basic consolidation techniques. You cannot pass the groups part on these alone, but it can give you a foothold. Question 1 usually has a bit of a twist, for example financial instruments or pensions. This question will also contain an element of written explanation and a question on ethics or corporate social accounting. For example, the Pilot Paper had a consolidated cash flow statement; then you were asked to explain whether an investment should be consolidated and the ethics of not consolidating it.

Question 4

This question is generally on developments in financial reporting. It is usually general in nature, rather than linked to a specific accounting standard. It may cover an aspect of reporting financial performance – for example the Management Commentary. It may also cover performance measures, small company reporting, EBITDA or the environment. On the Pilot Paper, Question 4 asked for implementation issues relating to the move to IFRS, and also for a discussion of the implication of the proposals on business combinations.

While you certainly cannot bluff your way through Question 4, if you know your material it is a good way of earning marks without high speed number crunching.

Questions 2 and 3

These are very often – although not always - multi-standard, mini-case-studies, involving you in giving advice to the directors on accounting treatment, possibly where the directors have followed the wrong treatment. Being multi-standard, you may be able to answer parts, but not all of a question, so it makes sense to look through the paper to select a question where you can answer most of it. If Part (a) is on an area you are not confident about, do not dismiss the question out of hand.

The examiner is testing whether you can identify the issues. Even if you don't get the accounting treatment exactly right, you will still gain some credit for showing that you have seen what the problem is about. So do not be afraid to have a stab at something, even if you are not sure of the details.

Exam technique for P2

Do not be needlessly intimidated

There is no shortcut to passing this exam. It looks very difficult indeed, and many students wonder if they will ever pass. But most students generally do. Why is this?

Easy marks

All the questions are demanding, but there are many easy marks to be gained. Suppose, for example, you had a consolidated cash flow statement with a disposal, some foreign exchange complications and an impairment calculation. There will be easy marks available simply for the basic cash flow aspects, setting out the proforma, setting up your workings, presenting your work neatly. If you recognise, as you should, that the disposal needs to be taken into account, of course you will get marks for that, even if you make a mistake in the arithmetic. If you get the foreign exchange right, so much the better, but you could pass the question comfortably while omitting this altogether. If you're short of time, this is what you should do.

Be ruthless in ignoring the complications

Look at the question. Within reason, if there are complications – often only worth a few marks – that you know you will not have time or knowledge to do, cross them out. It will make you feel better. Than tackle the bits you can do. This is how people pass a seemingly impossible paper.

Be ruthless in allocating your time

At BPP, we have seen how very intelligent students do two almost perfect questions, one averagely good and one sketchy. The first eight to ten marks are the easiest to get. Then you have to push it up to what you think is fifteen (thirty for the case study question), to get yourself a pass.

Do your best question either first or second, and the compulsory question either first or second. The compulsory question, being on groups, will always have some easy marks available for consolidation techniques.

Exam information

Format of the exam

		Number of marks
Section A:	1 compulsory case study	50
Section B:	Choice of 2 from 3 questions (25 marks each)	50
		100

Section A will consist of one scenario based question worth 50 marks. It will deal with the preparation of consolidated financial statements including group cash flow statements and with issues in financial reporting.

Students will be required to answer two out of three questions in Section B, which will normally comprise two questions which will be scenario or case-study based and one question which will be an essay. Section B could deal with any aspects of the syllabus.

Additional information

The Study Guide provides more detailed guidance on the syllabus.

Pilot paper

Section A:

1	Cash flow statement; criteria for consolidation; ethical behaviour

Section B

2	Environmental provisional, leasing; EABSD; share-based payment
3	Deferred tax with pension scheme and financial instruments
4	Adoption of IFRS; proposals on business combinations

The Pilot paper is Mock exam 3 in this Kit.

Useful websites

The websites below provide additional sources of information of relevance to your studies for *Advanced Corporate Reporting*.

- ACCA   www.accaglobal.com
- BPP   www.bpp.com
- IASB   www.iasb.org
- Financial Times   www.ft.com
- Accountancy Foundation   www.accountancyfoundation.com
- International Federation of Accountants (IFAC)   www.ifac.org

Planning your question practice

BPP
LEARNING MEDIA

Planning your question practice

We have already stressed that question practice should be right at the centre of your revision. Whilst you will spend some time looking at your notes and Paper P2 Passcards, you should spend the majority of your revision time practising questions.

We recommend two ways in which you can practise questions.

- Use **BPP's question plan** to work systematically through the syllabus and attempt key and other questions on a section-by-section basis

- **Build your own exams** – attempt questions as a series of practice exams

These ways are suggestions and simply following them is no guarantee of success. You or your college may prefer an alternative but equally valid approach.

BPP's question plan

The BPP plan below requires you to devote a **minimum of 50 hours** to revision of Paper P2. Any time you can spend over and above this should only increase your chances of success.

Step 1   **Review your notes** and the chapter summaries in the Paper P2 **Passcards** for each section of the syllabus.

Step 2   **Answer the key questions** for that section. These questions have boxes round the question number in the table below and you should answer them in full. Even if you are short of time you must attempt these questions if you want to pass the exam. You should complete your answers without referring to our solutions.

Step 3   **Attempt the other questions** in that section. For some questions we have suggested that you prepare **answer plans or do the calculations** rather than full solutions. Planning an answer means that you should spend about 40% of the time allowance for the questions brainstorming the question and drawing up a list of points to be included in the answer.

Step 4   Attempt **Mock exams 1, 2 and 3** under strict exam conditions.

Syllabus section	2007 Passcards chapters	Questions in this Kit	Comments	Done ☑
Ethical framework	2	A1	Learn our answer. Not a typical exam question but covers many areas that will come up as part of one.	☐
Environmental, social and cultural issues	3	A2	Comes up regularly. This question covers most topics you're likely to need.	☐
Non-current assets	4, 5	B1	Prochain. A recent old syllabus question that requires you to think clearly about the issues. Do in full.	☐
Taxation	7	B5	Cohort. Answer in full.	☐
Employee benefits	6	B9	Accounting for employee benefits. Do in full. Make sure that you understand how the calculation 'works'.	☐
Leasing contracts	10	B13	AB. Leasing is always topical and practical. Make sure you can iron out the wrinkles under exam conditions.	☐
Financial instruments	8	B15	Ambush. Do in full. Very topical.	☐

Syllabus section	2007 Passcards chapters	Questions in this Kit	Comments	Done ☑
Agriculture	22	B16	Lucky Dairy. A very practical area. Do in full and sharpen your skills for the exams.	☐
Measurement of performance	12	C1	Mineral. Useful question. Answer plan.	☐
Reporting financial performance	14	C4	Rockby and Bye. Redo if necessary to make sure you have this topic well sorted for the exam.	☐
Share-based payment	15	C5	Vident. A full question on a favourite topic.	☐
Related party disclosures	15	C8	Egin Group. Useful question. Prepare an answer plan and make sure you remember the key learning points for exam purposes.	☐
Associates and joint ventures	17	D3	Status of investment. An excellent introduction to this topic.	☐
		D5	Baden. Will put you through your paces on FRS 9. Prepare a full answer.	☐
Complex groups	18	D8	Largo. A high priority question. Make sure you review your answer thoroughly. Identify areas where you require remedial action.	☐
		D9		☐
		D10	Multi-company case study questions. Do in full.	☐
Changes in group structures	19	D13	Ejoy. Good, recent question.	☐
		D14	Base group – case study questions testing changes in group structure. Do in full.	☐
Foreign currency transaction	20	D17	Memo. A useful question. Have a good stab at it.	☐
Cash flow statements	21	D21	Andash : a cash study question with a group cash flow statement. Do in full.	☐
		D22	Squire. Cash flow statements can yield sure marks. Do and redo till you can complete one quickly and accurately in an exam. This case is a study question. Do in full.	☐
Current events	24	F1	Useful coverage of range of issues. Do in full.	☐

BPP LEARNING MEDIA

Build your own exams

Having revised your notes and the BPP Passcards, you can attempt the questions in the Kit as a series of practice exams.

	Practice exams				
	1	2	3	4	5
Section A					
1	D9	D10	D14	D21	D22
Section B					
2	B5	B6	B8	B9	B3
3	B13	B11	C5	C6	C1
4	C7	E1	F1	F2	E2

Whichever practice exams you use, you must attempt **Mock exams 1, 2 and 3** at the end of your revision.

Questions

REGULATORY AND ETHICAL FRAMEWORK

Questions A1 and A2 cover Regulatory and Ethical Framework, the subject of Part A of the BPP Study Text for Paper P2.

A1 Barriers to ethical standards

(a)   Identify some common barriers to the successful adoption of ethical standards in business practice.

(11 marks)

(b)   Explain the practical steps that organisations can take towards creating an ethical framework for corporate governance.   **(14 marks)**

(Total = 25 marks)

A2 Question with answer plan: Glowball   45 mins

ACR, Pilot Paper

The directors of Glowball, a public limited company, had discussed the study by the Institute of Environmental Management which indicated that over 35% of the world's largest 250 corporations are voluntarily releasing green reports to the public to promote corporate environmental performance and to attract customers and investors. They have heard that their main competitors are applying the 'Global Reporting Initiative' (GRI) in an effort to develop a worldwide format for corporate environmental reporting. However, the directors are unsure as to what this initiative actually means. Additionally they require advice as to the nature of any legislation or standards relating to environmental reporting, as they are worried that any environmental report produced by the company may not be of sufficient quality and may detract and not enhance their image if the report does not comply with recognised standards. Glowball has a reputation for ensuring the preservation of the environment in its business activities.

Further the directors have collected information in respect of a series of events which they consider to be important and worthy of note in the environmental report but are not sure as to how they would be incorporated in the environmental report or whether they should be included in the financial statements.

The events are as follows.

(a)   Glowball is a company that pipes gas from offshore gas installations to major consumers. The company purchased its main competitor during the year and found that there were environmental liabilities arising out of the restoration of many miles of farmland that had been affected by the laying of a pipeline. There was no legal obligation to carry out the work but the company felt that there would be a cost of around $150 million if the farmland was to be restored.

(b)   Most of the offshore gas installations are governed by operating licenses which specify limits to the substances which can be discharged to the air and water. These limits vary according to local legislation and tests are carried out by the regulatory authorities. During the year the company was prosecuted for infringements of an environmental law in the USA when toxic gas escaped into the atmosphere. In 20X2 the company was prosecuted five times and in 20X1 eleven times for infringement of the law. The final amount of the fine/costs to be imposed by the courts has not been determined but is expected to be around $5 million. The escape occurred over the seas and it was considered that there was little threat to human life.

(c)   The company produced statistics that measure their improvement in the handling of emissions of gases which may have an impact on the environment. The statistics deal with:

(i)   Measurement of the release of gases with the potential to form acid rain. The emissions have been reduced by 84% over five years due to the closure of old plants.

(ii) Measurement of emissions of substances potentially hazardous to human health. The emissions are down by 51% on 20W8 levels.

(iii) Measurement of emissions to water that removes dissolved oxygen and substances that may have an adverse effect on aquatic life. Accurate measurement of these emissions is not possible but the company is planning to spend $70 million on research in this area.

(d) The company tries to reduce the environmental impacts associated with the siting and construction of its gas installations. This is done in the way that minimises the impact on wild life and human beings. Additionally when the installations are at the end of their life, they are dismantled and are not sunk into the sea. The current provision for the decommissioning of these installations is $215 million and there are still decommissioning costs of $407 million to be provided as the company's policy is to build up the required provision over the life of the installation.

Required

Prepare a report suitable for presentation to the directors of Glowball in which you discuss the following elements:

(a) Current reporting requirements and guidelines relating to environmental reporting. **(10 marks)**

(b) The nature of any disclosure which would be required in an environmental report and/or the financial statements for the events (a)-(d) above. **(15 marks)**

(The mark allocation includes four marks for the style and layout of the report.) **(Total = 25 marks)**

ACCOUNTING STANDARDS

Questions B1 to B16 cover Accounting Standards, the subject of Part B of the BPP Study Text for Paper P2.

B1 Prochain
45 mins

ACR, 6/06

Prochain, a public limited company, operates in the fashion industry and has a financial year end of 31 May 20X6. The company sells its products in department stores throughout the world. Prochain insists on creating its own selling areas within the department stores which are called 'model areas'. Prochain is allocated space in the department store where it can display and market its fashion goods. The company feels that this helps to promote its merchandise. Prochain pays for all the costs of the 'model areas' including design, decoration and construction costs. The areas are used for approximately two years after which the company has to dismantle the 'model areas'. The costs of dismantling the 'model areas' are normally 20% of the original construction cost and the elements of the area are worthless when dismantled. The current accounting practice followed by Prochain is to charge the full cost of the 'model areas' against profit or loss in the year when the area is dismantled. The accumulated cost of the 'model areas' shown in the balance sheet at 31 May 20X6 is $20 million. The company has estimated that the average age of the 'model areas' is eight months at 31 May 20X6. **(7 marks)**

Prochain acquired 100% of a sports goods and clothing manufacturer, Badex, a private limited company, on 1 June 20X5. Prochain intends to develop its own brand of sports clothing which it will sell in the department stores. The shareholders of Badex valued the company at $125 million based upon profit forecasts which assumed significant growth in the demand for the 'Badex' brand name. Prochain had taken a more conservative view of the value of the company and estimated the fair value to be in the region of $108 million to $112 million of which $20 million relates to the brand name 'Badex'. Prochain is only prepared to pay the full purchase price if profits from the sale of 'Badex' clothing and sports goods reach the forecast levels. The agreed purchase price was $100 million plus a further payment of $25 million in two years on 31 May 20X7. This further payment will comprise a guaranteed payment of $10 million with no performance conditions and a further payment of $15 million if the actual profits during this two year period from the sale of Badex clothing and goods exceed the forecast profit. The forecast profit on Badex goods and clothing over the two year period is $16 million and the actual profits in the year to 31 May 20X6 were $4 million. Prochain did not feel at any time since acquisition that the actual profits would meet the forecast profit levels. **(8 marks)**

After the acquisition of Badex, Prochain started developing its own sports clothing brand 'Pro'. The expenditure in the period to 31 May 20X6 was as follows:

Period from	Expenditure type	$m
1 June 20X5 – 31 August 20X5	Research as to the extent of the market	3
1 September 20X5 – 30 November 20X5	Prototype clothing and goods design	4
1 December 20X5 – 31 January 20X6	Employee costs in refinement of products	2
1 February 20X6 – 30 April 20X6	Development work undertaken to finalise design of product	5
1 May 20X6 – 31 May 20X6	Production and launch of products	6
		20

The costs of the production and launch of the products include the cost of upgrading the existing machinery ($3 million), market research costs ($2 million) and staff training costs ($1 million). Currently an intangible asset of $20 million is shown in the financial statements for the year ended 31 May 20X6. **(6 marks)**

Prochain owns a number of prestigious apartments which it leases to famous persons who are under a contract of employment to promote its fashion clothing. The apartments are let at below the market rate. The lease terms are short and are normally for six months. The leases terminate when the contracts for promoting the clothing terminate. Prochain wishes to account for the apartments as investment properties with the difference between the market rate and actual rental charged to be recognised as an employee benefit expense. **(4 marks)**

Assume a discount rate of 5·5% where necessary.

Required

Discuss how the above items should be dealt with in the financial statements of Prochain for the year ended 31 May 20X6 under International Financial Reporting Standards.

(Total = 25 marks)

B2 Question with helping hands: Impairment of assets 45 mins

IAS 16 *Property, plant and equipment* originally required that where there has been an impairment in the value of property, plant and equipment, the carrying amount should be written down to the recoverable amount. An asset is carried at no more than its recoverable amount if its carrying amount exceeds the amount to be recovered through use or sale of the asset. The issues of how one identifies an impaired asset, the measurement of an asset when impairment has occurred and the recognition of impairment losses are not adequately dealt with by the standard. As a result IAS 36 *Impairment of assets* was issued by the International Accounting Standards Committee in order to address the above issues.

Required

(a) (i) Describe the circumstances which indicate that an impairment loss relating to an asset may have occurred. **(7 marks)**

(ii) Explain how IAS 36 deals with the recognition and measurement of the impairment of assets.

(7 marks)

(b) AB, a public limited company, has decided to comply with IAS 36 *Impairment of assets*. The following information is relevant to the impairment review.

(i) Certain items of machinery appeared to have suffered an impairment in value. The inventories produced by the machines was being sold below its cost and this occurrence had affected the value of the productive machinery. The carrying value at historical cost of these machines is $290,000 and their fair value less costs to sell is estimated at $120,000. The anticipated net cash inflows from the machines is now $100,000 per annum for the next three years. A market discount rate of 10% per annum is to be used in any present value computations. **(4 marks)**

(ii) AB acquired a car taxi business on 1 January 20X8 for $230,000. The values of the assets of the business at that date based on fair value less costs to sell were as follows.

	$'000
Vehicles	120
Intangible assets (taxi licence)	30
Trade receivables	10
Cash	50
Trade payables	(20)
	190

On 1 February 20X8, the taxi company had three of its vehicles stolen. The fair value less costs to sell of these vehicles was $30,000 and because of non-disclosure of certain risks to the insurance company, the vehicles were uninsured. As a result of this event, AB wishes to recognise an impairment loss of $45,000 (inclusive of the loss of the stolen vehicles) due to the decline in the value in use of the cash generating unit, that is the taxi business. On 1 March 20X8 a rival taxi company commenced business in the same area. It is anticipated that the business revenue of AB will be reduced by 25% leading to a decline in the fair value less costs to sell and value in use of the business which is calculated at $150,000. The net selling value of the taxi licence has fallen to $25,000 as a result of the rival taxi operator. The fair value less costs to sell of the other assets have remained the same as at 1 January 20X8 throughout the period. **(7 marks)**

BPP
LEARNING MEDIA

Required

Describe how AB should treat the above impairments of assets in its financial statements. (In part (b)(ii) candidates should show the treatment of the impairment loss at 1 February 20X8 and 1 March 20X8.)

Please note that the mark allocation is shown after paragraph (b)(i) and (b)(ii) above.   **(Total = 25 marks)**

Helping hands

1   Part (a) is easy, memory work. Make sure you make the right number of points to get the easy marks.

2   Compares carrying value, fair value less costs to sell and value in use. Remember that if fair value less costs to sell is lower than the others, you would not sell it.

3   Recognise a loss against the stolen vehicles, and the balance against goodwill.

4   For the loss at 1 March 20X8, recognise against intangible assets and the balance against goodwill.

B3 Ryder

45 mins

ACR, 12/05

Ryder, a public limited company, is reviewing certain events which have occurred since its year end of 31 October 2005. The financial statements were authorised on 12 December 2005. The following events are relevant to the financial statements for the year ended 31 October 2005:

(a)   Ryder disposed of a wholly owned subsidiary, Krup, a public limited company, on 10 December 2005 and made a loss of $9 million on the transaction in the group financial statements. As at 31 October 2005, Ryder had no intention of selling the subsidiary which was material to the group. The directors of Ryder have stated that there were no significant events which have occurred since 31 October 2005 which could have resulted in a reduction in the value of Krup. The carrying value of the net assets and purchased goodwill of Krup at 31 October 2005 were $20 million and $12 million respectively. Krup had made a loss of $2 million in the period 1 November 2005 to 10 December 2005.   **(6 marks)**

(b)   Ryder acquired a wholly owned subsidiary, Metalic, a public limited company, on 21 January 2004. The consideration payable in respect of the acquisition of Metalic was 2 million ordinary shares of $1 of Ryder plus a further 300,000 ordinary shares if the profit of Metalic exceeded $6 million for the year ended 31 October 2005. The profit for the year of Metalic was $7 million and the ordinary shares were issued on 12 November 2005. The annual profits of Metalic had averaged $7 million over the last few years and, therefore, Ryder had included an estimate of the contingent consideration in the cost of the acquisition at 21 January 2004. The fair value used for the ordinary shares of Ryder at this date including the contingent consideration was $10 per share. The fair value of the ordinary shares on 12 November 2005 was $11 per share. Ryder also made a one for four bonus issue on 13 November 2005 which was applicable to the contingent shares issued. The directors are unsure of the impact of the above on earnings per share and the accounting for the acquisition.   **(8 marks)**

(c)   The company acquired a property on 1 November 2004 which it intended to sell. The property was obtained as a result of a default on a loan agreement by a third party and was valued at $20 million on that date for accounting purposes which exactly offset the defaulted loan. The property is in a state of disrepair and Ryder intends to complete the repairs before it sells the property. The repairs were completed on 30 November 2005. The property was sold after costs for $27 million on 9 December 2005. The property was classified as 'held for sale' at the year end under IFRS 5 *Non-current assets held for sale and discontinued operations* but shown at the net sale proceeds of $27 million. Property is depreciated at 5% per annum on the straight-line basis and no depreciation has been charged in the year.   **(6 marks)**

(d)   The company granted share appreciation rights (SARs) to its employees on 1 November 2003 based on ten million shares. The SARs provide employees at the date the rights are exercised with the right to receive cash equal to the appreciation in the company's share price since the grant date. The rights vested on 31 October 2005 and payment was made on schedule on 1 December 2005. The fair value of the SARs per share at 31 October 2004 was $6, at 31 October 2005 was $8 and at 1 December 2005 was $9. The company has recognised a liability for the SARs as at 31 October 2004 based upon IFRS 2 *Share-based payment* but the liability was stated at the same amount at 31 October 2005.   **(5 marks)**

Required

Discuss the accounting treatment of the above events in the financial statements of the Ryder Group for the year ended 31 October 2005, taking into account the implications of events occurring after the balance sheet date.

(The mark allocations are set out after each paragraph above.)   **(Total = 25 marks)**

B4 Worldwide Nuclear Fuels   45 mins

Provisions are particular kinds of liabilities. It therefore follows that provisions should be recognised when the definition of a liability has been met. The key requirement of a liability is a present obligation and thus this requirement is critical also in the context of the recognition of a provision. However, although accounting for provisions is an important topic for standard setters, it is only recently that guidance has been issued on provisioning in financial statements. IAS 37 *Provisions, contingent liabilities and contingent assets* deals with this area.

Required

(a)   (i)   Explain why there was a need for more detailed guidance on accounting for provisions.   **(7 marks)**

        (ii)   Explain the circumstances under which a provision should be recognised in the financial statements according to IAS 37 *Provisions, contingent liabilities and contingent assets*.   **(6 marks)**

(b)   Discuss whether the following provisions have been accounted for correctly under IAS 37 *Provisions, contingent liabilities and contingent assets*.

        WorldWide Nuclear Fuels, a public limited company, disclosed the following information in its financial statements for the year ending 30 November 20X9.

Provisions and long-term commitments

        (i)   Provision for decommissioning the group's radioactive facilities is made over their useful life and covers complete demolition of the facility within fifty years of it being taken out of service together with any associated waste disposal. The provision is based on future prices and is discounted using a current market rate of interest.

Provision for decommissioning costs

	$m
Balance at 1 December 20X8	675
Adjustment arising from change in price levels charged to reserves	33
Charged in the year to income statement	125
Adjustment due to change in knowledge (charged to reserves)	27
Balance at 30 November 20X9	860

        There are still decommissioning costs of $1,231m (undiscounted) to be provided for in respect of the group's radioactive facilities as the company's policy is to build up the required provision over the life of the facility.   **(7 marks)**

        (ii)   The company purchased an oil company during the year. As part of the sale agreement, oil has to be supplied to the company's former holding company at an uneconomic rate for a period of five years. As a result a provision for future operating losses has been set up of $135m which related solely to the uneconomic supply of oil. Additionally the oil company is exposed to environmental liabilities arising out of its past obligations, principally in respect of soil and ground water restoration costs, although currently there is no legal obligation to carry out the work. Liabilities for environmental costs are provided for when the group determines a formal plan of action on the closure of an inactive site. It has been decided to provide for $120m in respect of the environmental liability on the acquisition of the oil company. WorldWide Nuclear Fuels has a reputation for ensuring the preservation of the environment in its business activities. **(5 marks)**

(Total = 25 marks)

B5 Cohort

45 mins

`ACR, 6/02`

Cohort is a private limited company and has two 100% owned subsidiaries, Legion and Air, both themselves private limited companies. Cohort acquired Air on 1 January 20X2 for $5 million when the fair value of the net assets was $4 million, and the tax base of the net assets was $3.5 million. The acquisition of Air and Legion was part of a business strategy whereby Cohort would build up the 'value' of the group over a three year period and then list its existing share capital on the stock exchange.

(a)　The following details relate to the acquisition of Air, which manufactures electronic goods.

　　(i)　Part of the purchase price has been allocated to intangible assets because it relates to the acquisition of a database of key customers from Air. The recognition and measurement criteria for an intangible asset under IFRS 3 *Business combinations*/IAS 38 *Intangible assets* do not appear to have been met but the directors feel that the intangible asset of $0.5 million will be allowed for tax purposes and have computed the tax provision accordingly. However, the tax authorities could possibly challenge this opinion.

　　(ii)　Air has sold goods worth $3 million to Cohort since acquisition and made a profit of $1 million on the transaction. The inventory of these goods recorded in Cohort's balance sheet at the year end of 31 May 20X2 was $1.8 million.

　　(iii)　The balance on the retained earnings of Air at acquisition was $2 million. The directors of Cohort have decided that, during the three years to the date that they intend to list the shares of the company, they will realise earnings through future dividend payments from the subsidiary amounting to $500,000 per year. Tax is payable on any remittance or dividends and no dividends have been declared for the current year. **(13 marks)**

(b)　Legion was acquired on 1 June 20X1 and is a company which undertakes various projects ranging from debt factoring to investing in property and commodities. The following details relate to Legion for the year ending 31 May 20X2.

　　(i)　Legion has a portfolio of readily marketable government securities which are held as current assets. These investments are stated at market value in the balance sheet with any gain or loss taken to the income statement. These gains and losses are taxed when the investments are sold. Currently the accumulated unrealised gains are $4 million.

　　(ii)　Legion has calculated that it requires a specific allowance of $2 million against loans in its portfolio. Tax relief is available when the specific loan is written off.

　　(iii)　When Cohort acquired Legion it had unused tax losses brought forward. At 1 June 20X1, it appeared that Legion would have sufficient taxable profit to realise the deferred tax asset created by these losses but subsequent events have proven that the future taxable profit will not be sufficient to realise all of the unused tax loss.

The current tax rate for Cohort is 30% and for public companies is 35%. **(12 marks)**

Required

Write a note suitable for presentation to the partner of an accounting firm setting out the deferred tax implications of the above information for the Cohort Group of companies. **(Total = 25 marks)**

B6 Panel

45 mins

ACR, 12/05

The directors of Panel, a public limited company, are reviewing the procedures for the calculation of the deferred tax liability for their company. They are quite surprised at the impact on the liability caused by changes in accounting standards such as IFRS 1 *First time adoption of International Financial Reporting Standards* and IFRS 2 *Share-based payment*. Panel is adopting International Financial Reporting Standards for the first time as at 31 October 2005 and the directors are unsure how the deferred tax provision will be calculated in its financial statements ended on that date including the opening provision at 1 November 2003.

Required

(a) (i)   Explain how changes in accounting standards are likely to have an impact on the deferred tax liability under IAS 12 *Income taxes*. **(5 marks)**

(ii) Describe the basis for the calculation of the deferred taxation liability on first time adoption of IFRS including the provision in the opening IFRS balance sheet. **(4 marks)**

Additionally the directors wish to know how the provision for deferred taxation would be calculated in the following situations under IAS 12 *Income taxes*:

(i)   On 1 November 2003, the company had granted ten million share options worth $40 million subject to a two year vesting period. Local tax law allows a tax deduction at the exercise date of the intrinsic value of the options. The intrinsic value of the ten million share options at 31 October 2004 was $16 million and at 31 October 2005 was $46 million. The increase in the share price in the year to 31 October 2005 could not be foreseen at 31 October 2004. The options were exercised at 31 October 2005. The directors are unsure how to account for deferred taxation on this transaction for the years ended 31 October 2004 and 31 October 2005.

(ii) Panel is leasing plant under a finance lease over a five year period. The asset was recorded at the present value of the minimum lease payments of $12 million at the inception of the lease which was 1 November 2004. The asset is depreciated on a straight line basis over the five years and has no residual value. The annual lease payments are $3 million payable in arrears on 31 October and the effective interest rate is 8% per annum. The directors have not leased an asset under a finance lease before and are unsure as to its treatment for deferred taxation. The company can claim a tax deduction for the annual rental payment as the finance lease does not qualify for tax relief.

(iii) A wholly owned overseas subsidiary, Pins, a limited liability company, sold goods costing $7 million to Panel on 1 September 2005, and these goods had not been sold by Panel before the year end. Panel had paid $9 million for these goods. The directors do not understand how this transaction should be dealt with in the financial statements of the subsidiary and the group for taxation purposes. Pins pays tax locally at 30%.

(iv) Nails, a limited liability company, is a wholly owned subsidiary of Panel, and is a cash generating unit in its own right. The value of the property, plant and equipment of Nails at 31 October 2005 was $6 million and purchased goodwill was $1 million before any impairment loss. The company had no other assets or liabilities. An impairment loss of $1·8 million had occurred at 31 October 2005. The tax base of the property, plant and equipment of Nails was $4 million as at 31 October 2005. The directors wish to know how the impairment loss will affect the deferred tax liability for the year. Impairment losses are not an allowable expense for taxation purposes.

Assume a tax rate of 30%.

Required

(b) Discuss, with suitable computations, how the situations (i) to (iv) above will impact on the accounting for deferred tax under IAS 12 *Income taxes* in the group financial statements of Panel. **(16 marks)**

(The situations in (i) to (iv) above carry equal marks)

(Total = 25 marks)

B7 Preparation question: Defined benefit scheme

Brutus Co operates a defined benefit pension plan for its employees conditional on a minimum employment period of 6 years. The present value of the future benefit obligations and the fair value of its plan assets on 1 January 20X1 were $110 million and $150 million respectively.

In the financial statements for the year ended 31.12.X0, there were unrecognised actuarial gains of $43 million. (Brutus Co's accounting policy is to use the 10% corridor approach to recognition of actuarial gains and losses).

The pension plan received contributions of $7m and paid pensions to former employees of $10m during the year.

Extracts from the most recent actuary's report show the following:

	31 Dec 20X1
Present value of pension plan obligation	$116m
Market value of plan assets	$140m
Present cost of pensions earned in the period	$11m
Yield on high quality corporate bonds for the period	10%
Long term expected return on scheme assets for the period	12%

On 1 January 20X1, the rules of the pension plan were changed to improve benefits for plan members, vesting immediately. The actuary has advised that this will cost $20 million in total.

The average remaining working life of plan members at 31.12.X1 is 7 years. This tends to remain static as people leave and join.

Required

Produce the extracts for the financial statements for the year ended 31 December 20X1.

Assume contributions and benefits were paid on 31 December.

B8 Retirement benefits
45 mins

(a) Accounting for retirement benefits remains one of the most challenging areas in financial reporting. The values being reported are significant, and the estimation of these values is complex and subjective. Standard setters and preparers of financial statements find it difficult to achieve a measure of consensus on the appropriate way to deal with the assets and costs involved.

Required

(i) Describe four key issues in the determination of the method of accounting for retirement benefits in respect of defined benefit plans; **(6 marks)**

(ii) Discuss how IAS 19 *Employee benefits* deals with these key issues and to what extent it provides solutions to the problems of accounting for retirement benefits. **(8 marks)**

(b) A, a public limited company, operates a defined benefit plan. A full actuarial valuation by an independent actuary revealed that the value of the liability at 31 May 20X0 was $1,500 million. This was updated to 31 May 20X1 by the actuary and the value of the liability at that date was $2,000 million. The scheme assets comprised mainly bonds and equities and the fair value of these assets was as follows:

	31 May 20X0	31 May 20X1
	$m	$m
Fixed interest and index linked bonds	380	600
Equities	1,300	1,900
Other investments	290	450
	1,970	2,950

The scheme had been altered during the year with improved benefits arising for the employees and this had been taken into account by the actuaries. The increase in the actuarial liability in respect of employee service in prior periods was $25 million (past service cost). The increase in the actuarial liability resulting from employee service in the current period was $70 million (current service cost). The company had not recognised any net actuarial gain or loss in the income statement to date.

The company had paid contributions of $60 million to the scheme during the period. The company expects its return on the scheme assets at 31 May 20X1 to be $295 million and the interest on pension liabilities to be $230 million.

The average expected remaining working lives of the employees is 10 years and the net cumulative unrecognised gains at 1 June 20X0 were $247 million.

Required

Calculate the amount which will be shown as the net plan asset/plan reserve in the balance sheet of A as at 31 May 20X1 and a statement of those amounts which would be charged to operating profit.   **(11 marks)**

(Total = 25 marks)

B9 Savage

45 mins

ACR, 12/05

Savage, a public limited company, operates a funded defined benefit plan for its employees. The plan provides a pension of 1% of the final salary for each year of service. The cost for the year is determined using the projected unit credit method. This reflects service rendered to the dates of valuation of the plan and incorporates actuarial assumptions primarily regarding discount rates, which are based on the market yields of high quality corporate bonds. The expected average remaining working lives of employees is twelve years.

The directors have provided the following information about the defined benefit plan for the current year (year ended 31 October 20X5)

(a)   the actuarial cost of providing benefits in respect of employees' service for the year to 31 October 20X5 was $40 million. This is the present value of the pension benefits earned by the employees in the year.

(b)   The pension benefits paid to former employees in the year were $42 million.

(c)   Savage should have paid contributions to the fund of $28 million. Because of cash flow problems $8 million of this amount had not been paid at the financial year end of 31 October 20X5.

(d)   The present value of the obligation to provide benefits to current and former employees was $3,000 million at 31 October 20X4 and $3,375 million at 31 October 20X5.

(e)   The fair value of the plan assets was $2,900 million at 31 October 20X4 and $3,170 million (including the contributions owed by Savage) at 31 October 20X5. The actuarial gains recognised at 31 October 20X4 were $336 million.

With effect from 1 November 20X4, the company had amended the plan so that the employees were now provided with an increased pension entitlement. The benefits became vested immediately and the actuaries computed that the present value of the cost of these benefits at 1 November 20X4 was $125 million. The discount rates and expected rates of return on the plan assets were as follows:

	31 October 20X4	31 October 20X5
Discount rate	6%	7%
Expected rate of return on plan assets	8%	9%

The company has recognised actuarial gains and losses in profit or loss up to 31 October 20X4 but now wishes to recognise such gains and losses outside profit or loss in a 'statement of recognised income and expense'.

Required

(a) Show the amounts which will be recognised in the balance sheet, income statement and the statement of recognised income and expense of savage for the year ended 31 October 20X5 under IAS 19 *Employee benefits*, and the movement in the net liability in the balance sheet. (Your calculations should show the changes in the present value of the obligation and the fair value of the plan assets during the year. Ignore any deferred taxation effects and assume that pension benefits and the contributions paid were settled at 31 October 20X5.) **(21 marks)**

(b) Explain how the non-payment of contributions and the change in the pension benefits should be treated in the financial statements of Savage for the year ended 31 October 20X5. **(4 marks)**

(Total = 25 marks)

B10 Issue

45 mins

ACR, 6/03

The managing partner has asked you, on behalf of a shareholder, to prepare a report on the financial and business position of Issue, a public limited company. There has been adverse press comment on the 'aggressive management of earnings' by the company and criticism of the management. Information about Issue has been gathered by the partner and this is set out below.

Business and financial environment

Issue provides internet-based electronic hosting, delivery and marketing services. The company was formed four years ago with the Board promising to take the company into the top 10% of listed companies within five years. Management are highly motivated and are compensated in part via share/stock options. Management work in a pressurised environment.

Issue makes use of different corporate entities in order to finance its business. The company has borrowed $40 million from twenty different entities which are owned by a bank, which itself owns twenty per cent of the shares of Issue. Issue has deposited $35 million with the entities with the balance being shown as a current liability. The management of Issue say that the entities are not under their control and that because each amount borrowed is individually immaterial there is no need to disclose the relationship in the financial statements. Additionally, it appears that in previous years a common practice was for Issue to invoice the same entities in the final week of the financial year for services and reverse the invoices once the company had filed its financial statements.

Financial Statement Information extracted from the published accounts for the years ended

(a)

	31 Jan 20X3 $m	31 Jan 20X2 $m
Non-current assets at valuation		
Property	10	8
Plant and equipment	40	30
Intangibles	20	12
Current assets	230	240
Current liabilities	180	140
Share Capital – $1 ordinary shares	30	30
Reserves – revaluation surplus	30	20
Retained earnings	10	60
Non-current liabilities	50	40
Revenue	160	200
Profit before interest, tax, depreciation and amortisation	30	95
Profit/(loss) before tax	(10)	40
Extraordinary loss	(20)	(5)
Number of employees	150	250
Number of days after year end to publication of financial statements	65	25

(b) The non-current assets have been revalued by one of the directors of Issue who holds no recognised professional qualification and has used estimated realisable value as the basis of valuation. The plant and equipment is of a highly specialised nature and is constructed by the company itself and is mainly computer hardware. The intangible assets are the data purchase and data capture costs of internally developed databases and are capitalised as development expenditure and written off over four years.

(c) In the year to 31 January 20X2, a six year bond was issued by the company with a par value of $40 million for $42 million. The excess over par value was taken to the income statement. In the year to 31 January 20X3, a further six year bond with a par value of $10 million was issued for $11 million and accounted for in the same manner. The investors may request redemption after three years or if the working capital ratio falls below 1:3. The bonds bear interest at 5% per annum and are redeemable at par.

(d) Revenue represents the invoiced amount of goods sold and services provided and work undertaken during the year on long-term contracts after the deduction of trade discounts and sales related taxes.

(e) Issue has published pro-forma financial statements for the four months to 31 May 20X3 showing profit before tax to be $20 million, long term liabilities reduced to $10 million, and the working capital ratio as being 1:5.

(f) The extraordinary loss is the estimated impact of the terrorist attacks in the USA upon the business of Issue. These are sometimes referred to as the 'September 11 terrorist attacks'.

Required

Prepare a report for the managing partner on the business and financial position of Issue, setting out the implications of the financial and other information outlined above.

(25 marks)

B11 Tyre

45 mins

ACR, 6/06

Tyre, a public limited company, operates in the vehicle retailing sector. The company is currently preparing its financial statements for the year ended 31 May 20X6 and has asked for advice on how to deal with the following items.

(a) Tyre requires customers to pay a deposit of 20% of the purchase price when placing an order for a vehicle. If the customer cancels the order, the deposit is not refundable and Tyre retains it. If the order cannot be fulfilled by Tyre, the company repays the full amount of the deposit to the customer. The balance of the purchase price becomes payable on the delivery of the vehicle when the title to the goods passes. Tyre proposes to recognise the revenue from the deposits immediately and the balance of the purchase price when the goods are delivered to the customer. The cost of sales for the vehicle is recognised when the balance of the purchase price is paid. Additionally, Tyre had sold a fleet of cars to Hub and gave Hub a discount of 30% of the retail price on the transaction. The discount given is normal for this type of transaction. Tyre has given Hub a buyback option which entitles Hub to require Tyre to repurchase the vehicles after three years for 40% of the purchase price. The normal economic life of the vehicles is five years and the buyback option is expected to be exercised. **(8 marks)**

(b) The property of the former administrative centre of Tyre is owned by the company. Tyre had decided in the year that the property was surplus to requirements and demolished the building on 10 June 20X6. After demolition, the company will have to carry out remedial environmental work, which is a legal requirement resulting from the demolition. It was intended that the land would be sold after the remedial work had been carried out. However, land prices are currently increasing in value and, therefore, the company has decided that it will not sell the land immediately. Tyre uses the 'cost model' in IAS 16 *Property, plant and equipment* and has owned the property for many years. **(7 marks)**

(c) Tyre has entered into two new long lease property agreements for two major retail outlets. Annual rentals are paid under these agreements. Tyre has had to pay a premium to enter into these agreements because of the outlets' location. Tyre feels that the premiums paid are justifiable because of the increase in revenue that will occur because of the outlets' location. Tyre has analysed the leases and has decided that one is a finance lease and one is an operating lease but the company is unsure as to how to treat this premium. **(5 marks)**

(d) Tyre recently undertook a sales campaign whereby customers can obtain free car accessories, by presenting a coupon, which has been included in an advertisement in a national newspaper, on the purchase of a vehicle. The offer is valid for a limited time period from 1 January 20X6 until 31 July 20X6. The management are unsure as to how to treat this offer in the financial statements for the year ended 31 May 20X6.

(5 marks)

Required

Advise the directors of Tyre on how to treat the above items in the financial statements for the year ended 31 May 20X6.

(The mark allocation is shown against each of the above items.)

(Total = 25 marks)

B12 Preparation question: Leases

Sugar Co leased a machine from Spice Co. The terms of the lease are as follows:

Inception of lease	1 January 20X1
Lease term	4 years at $78,864 per annum payable in arrears
Present value of minimum lease payments	$250,000
Useful life of asset	4 years

Required

(a)   Calculate the interest rate implicit in the lease, using the table below.

This table shows the present value of $1 per annum, receivable or payable at the end of each year for n years.

Years (n)	Interest rates		
	6%	8%	10%
1	0.943	0.926	0.909
2	1.833	1.783	1.736
3	2.673	2.577	2.487
4	3.465	3.312	3.170
5	4.212	3.993	3.791

(b)   Prepare the extracts from the financial statements of Sugar Co for the year ended 31 December 20X1. Notes to the accounts are not required.

B13 AB

45 mins

(a)   The development of conceptual frameworks for financial reporting by accounting standard setters could fundamentally change the way in which financial contracts such as leases are accounted for. These frameworks identify the basic elements of financial statements as assets, liabilities, equity, gains and losses and set down their recognition rules. In analysing the definitions of assets and liabilities one could conclude that most leases, including non-cancellable operating leases, qualify for recognition as assets and liabilities because the lessee is likely to enjoy the future economic benefit embodied in the leased asset and will have an unavoidable obligation that results in an outflow of resources embodying economic benefits to the lessor. Because of the problems of accounting for leases, there have been calls for the capitalisation of all non-cancellable operating leases so that the only problem would be the definition of the term 'non-cancellable'.

Required

(i)   Explain how leases are accounted for in the books of the lessee under IAS 17 *Leases*.   **(7 marks)**

(ii)   Discuss the current problems relating to the recognition and classification of leases in corporate financial statements. (Candidates should give examples where necessary).   **(8 marks)**

(b)   (i)   During the financial year to 31 May 20X8, AB, a public limited company, disposed of electrical distribution systems from its electrical power plants to CD, a public limited company, for a consideration of $198m. At the same time AB entered into a long-term distribution agreement with CD whereby the assets were leased back under a 10-year operating lease. The fair value of the assets sold was $98m and the carrying value based on depreciated historical cost of the assets was $33m. The lease rentals were $24m per annum which represented twice the normal payment for leasing this type of asset.   **(5 marks)**

         (ii)   Additionally on 1 June 20X7, AB sold plant with a book value of $100m to EF, a public limited company, when there was a balance on the revaluation reserve of $30m which related to the plant. The fair value and selling price of the plant at that date was $152m. The plant was immediately leased back over a lease term of four years which is the asset's remaining useful life. The residual value at the end of the lease period is estimated to be a negligible amount. AB can purchase the plant at the end of the lease for a nominal sum of $1. The lease is non-cancellable and requires equal rental payments of $43.5m at the commencement of each financial year. AB has to pay all of the costs of maintaining and insuring the plant.

The implicit interest rate in the lease is 10% per annum. The plant is depreciated on a straight-line basis. (The present value of an ordinary annuity of $1 per period for 3 years at 10% interest is $2.49.) **(5 marks)**

Required

Show and explain how the above transactions should be dealt with in the financial statements of AB for the year ending 31 May 20X8 in accordance with IAS 17 *Leases* and the *Framework for the Preparation and Presentation of Financial Statements*. **(Total = 25 marks)**

B14 Preparation question: Financial instruments

(a) Graben Co purchases a bond for $441,014 on 1 January 20X1. It will be redeemed on 31 December 20X4 for $600,000. The bond will be held to maturity and carries no coupon.

Required

Calculate the balance sheet valuation of the bond as at 31 December 20X1 and the finance income for 20X1 shown in the income statement.

Compound sum of $1: $(1 + r)^n$

Year	2%	4%	6%	8%	10%	12%	14%
1	1.0200	1.0400	1.0600	1.0800	1.1000	1.1200	1.1400
2	1.0404	1.0816	1.1236	1.1664	1.2100	1.2544	1.2996
3	1.0612	1.1249	1.1910	1.2597	1.3310	1.4049	1.4815
4	1.0824	1.1699	1.2625	1.3605	1.4641	1.5735	1.6890
5	1.1041	1.2167	1.3382	1.4693	1.6105	1.7623	1.9254

(b) Baldie Co issues 4,000 convertible bonds on 1 January 20X2 at par. The bond is redeemable 3 years later at its par value of $500 per bond, which is its nominal value.

The bonds pay interest annually in arrears at an interest rate (based on nominal value) of 5%. Each bond can be converted at the maturity date into 30 $1 shares.

The prevailing market interest rate for three year bonds that have no right of conversion is 9%.

Required

Show the balance sheet valuation at 1 January 20X2.

Cumulative 3 year annuity factors:

5%   2.723
9%   2.531

B15 Ambush

45 mins

ACR, 12/05

Ambush, a public limited company, is assessing the impact of implementing IAS 39 *Financial instruments: recognition and measurement*. The directors realise that significant changes may occur in their accounting treatment of financial instruments and they understand that on initial recognition only certain financial assets or liabilities can be designated as one to be measured at fair value through profit or loss. There are certain issues that they wish to have explained and these are set out below.

Required

(a) Outline in a report to the directors of Ambush the following information

   (i) How financial assets and liabilities are measured and classified, briefly setting out the accounting method used for each category. (Hedging relationships can be ignored.) **(10 marks)**

   (ii) Why the 'fair value option' was initially introduced and why it caused such concern. **(5 marks)**

(b) Ambush loaned $200,000 to Bromwich on 1 December 2003. The effective and stated interest rate for this loan was 8 per cent. Interest is payable by Bromwich at the end of each year and the loan is repayable on 30 November 2007. At 30 November 2005, the directors of Ambush have heard that Bromwich is in financial difficulties and is undergoing a financial reorganisation. The directors feel that it is likely that they will only receive $100,000 on 30 November 2007 and no future interest payment. Interest for the year ended 30 November 2005 had been received. The financial year end of Ambush is 30 November 2005.

Required

   (i) Outline the requirements of IAS 39 as regards the impairment of financial assets. **(6 marks)**

   (ii) Explain the accounting treatment under IAS 39 of the loan to Bromwich in the financial statements of Ambush for the year ended 30 November 2005. **(4 marks)**

(Total = 25 marks)

Note. You need not consider the requirements of IFRS 1 *First-time adoption of International Financial Reporting Standards* in answering this question.

B16 Question with analysis: Lucky Dairy

45 mins

ACR, 6/02

The Lucky Dairy, a public limited company, produces milk for supply to various customers. It is responsible for producing twenty five per cent of the country's milk consumption. The company owns 150 farms and has inventories of 70,000 cows and 35,000 heifers which are being raised to produce milk in the future. The farms produce 2.5 million kilograms of milk per annum and normally hold an inventory of 50,000 kilograms of milk (Extracts from the draft accounts to 31 May 20X2).

> You will need to disclose cows and heifers separately

The herds comprise at 31 May 20X2:

70,000 – 3 year old cows (all purchased on or before 1 June 20X1)
25,000 – heifers (average age 1½ years old – purchased 1 December 20X1)
10,000 – heifers (average age 2 years – purchased 1 June 20X1)

There were no animals born or sold in the year. The per unit values less estimated point of sale costs were as follows.

	$
2 year old animal at 1 June 20X1	50
1 year old animal at 1 June 20X1 and 1 December 20X1	40
3 year old animal at 31 May 20X2	60
1½ year old animal at 31 May 20X2	46
2 year old animal at 31 May 20X2	55
1 year old animal at 31 May 20X2	42

> Consider whether a provision is necessary

The company has had a difficult year in financial and operating terms. The cows had contracted a disease at the beginning of the financial year which had been passed on in the food chain to a small number of consumers. **The publicity surrounding this event had caused a drop in the consumption of milk** and as a result the dairy was holding 500,000 kilograms of milk in storage.

The government had stated, on 1 April 20X2, that it was prepared to compensate farmers for the drop in the price and consumption of milk. An official government letter was received on 6 June 20X2, stating that $1.5 million will be paid to Lucky on 1 August 20X2. Additionally on 1 May 20X2, Lucky had received a letter from its lawyer saying that legal proceedings had been started against the company by the persons affected by the disease. The company's lawyers have advised them that they feel that it is probable that they will be found liable and that the costs involved may reach $2 million. The lawyers, however, feel that the company may receive additional compensation from a government fund if certain quality control procedures had been carried out by the company. **However, the lawyers will only state that the compensation payment is 'possible'.**

The company's activities are controlled in three geographical locations, Dale, Shire and Ham. The only region affected by the disease was Dale and the government has decided that it is to restrict the milk production of that region significantly. Lucky estimates that the discounted future cash income from the present herds of cattle in the region amounts to $1.2 million, taking into account the government restriction order. Lucky was not sure that the fair value of the cows in the region could be measured reliably at the date of purchase because of the problems with the diseased cattle. The cows in this region amounted to 20,000 in number and the heifers 10,000 in number. All of the animals were purchased on 1 June 20X1. Lucky has had an offer of $1 million for all of the animals in the Dale region (net of point of sale costs) and $2 million for the sale of the farms in the region. However, there was a minority of directors who opposed the planned sale and it was decided to defer the public announcement of sale pending the outcome of the possible receipt of the government compensation. The board had decided that the potential sale plan was **highly confidential but a national newspaper had published an article** saying that the sale may occur and that there would be many people who would lose their employment. The board approved the planned sale of Dale farms on 31 May 20X2.

The directors of Lucky have approached your firm for professional advice on the above matters.

Required

Advise the directors on how the biological assets and produce of Lucky should be accounted for under IAS 41 *Agriculture* and discuss the implications for the published financial statements of the above events.

(Candidates should produce a table which shows the changes in value of the cattle stock for the year to 31 May 20X2 due to price change and physical change excluding the Dale region, and the value of the herd of the Dale region as at 31 May 20X2. Ignore the effects of taxation. Heifers are young female cows.)

(25 marks)

Margin annotations:

- When is this recognised under IAS 41?
- Implications?
- Should a provision be made?

REPORTING FINANCIAL PERFORMANCE

Questions C1 to C9 cover Reporting Financial Performance, the subject of Part C of the BPP Study Text for Paper P2.

C1 Mineral

45 mins

`ACR, 12/01`

Mineral, a public limited company, has prepared its financial statements for the year ended 31 October 20X3. The following information relates to those financial statements.

	20X3	20X2
	$m	$m
Group revenue	250	201
Gross profit	45	35
Profit before interest and tax	10	9
Profit before tax	12	8
Profit for the period	5	4
Non-current assets	42	36
Current assets	55	43
Current liabilities	25	24
Non-current liabilities – long-term loans	13	9
Equity	59	46

The company expects to achieve growth in retained earnings of about 20% in the year to 31 October 20X4. Thereafter retained earnings are expected to accelerate to produce growth of between 20% and 25%. The growth will be generated by the introduction of new products and business efficiencies in manufacturing and in the company's infrastructure.

Mineral manufactures products from aluminium and other metals and is one of the largest producers in the world. Production for 20X3 increased by 18% through the acquisition of a competitor company, increased production at three of its plants and through the regeneration of old plants. There has been a recent growth in the consumption of its products because of the substitution of aluminium for heavier metals in motor vehicle manufacture. Cost reductions continued as a business focus in 20X3 and Mineral has implemented a cost reduction programme to be achieved by 20X6. Targets for each operation have been set.

Mineral's directors feel that its pricing strategy will help it compensate for increased competition in the sector. The company recently reduced the price of its products to the motor vehicle industry. This strategy is expected to increase demand and the usage of aluminium in the industry. However, in spite of the environmental benefits, certain car manufacturers have formed a cartel to prevent the increased usage of aluminium in car production.

In the period 20X3 to 20X5, Mineral expects to spend around $40 million on research and development and investment in non-current assets. The focus of the investments will be on enlarging the production capabilities. An important research and development project will be the joint project with a global car manufacturer to develop a new aluminium alloy car body.

In January 20X3, Mineral commenced a programme of acquisition of its own ordinary shares for cancellation. At 31 October 20X3, Mineral had purchased and cancelled five million ordinary shares of $1. In addition a subsidiary of Mineral had $4 million of convertible redeemable loan notes outstanding. The loan notes mature on 15 June 20X6 and are convertible into ordinary shares at the option of the holder. The competitive environment requires Mineral to provide medium and long term financing to its customers in connection with the sale of its products. Generally the financing is placed with third party lenders but due to the higher risks associated with such financing, the amount of the financing expected to be provided by Mineral itself is likely to increase.

The directors of Mineral have attempted to minimise the financial risk to which the group is exposed. The company operates in the global market place with the inherent financial risk that this entails. The management have performed a sensitivity analysis assuming a 10% adverse movement in foreign exchange rates and interest rates applied to hedging contracts and other exposures. The analysis indicated that such market movement would not have a material effect on the company's financial position.

Mineral has a reputation for responsible corporate behaviour and sees the work force as the key factor in the profitable growth of the business. During the year the company made progress towards the aim of linking environmental performance with financial performance by reporting the relationship between the eco-productivity index for basic production, and water and energy costs used in basic production. A feature of this index is that it can be segregated at site and divisional level and can be used in the internal management decision-making process.

The directors of Mineral are increasingly seeing their shareholder base widen with the result that investors are more demanding and sophisticated. As a result, the directors are uncertain as to the nature of the information which would provide clear and credible explanations of corporate activity. They wish their annual report to meet market expectations. They have heard that many companies deal with three key elements of corporate activity, namely reporting business performance, the analysis of the financial position, and the nature of corporate citizenship, and have asked your firm's advice in drawing up the annual report.

Required

Draft a report to the directors of Mineral setting out the nature of information which could be disclosed in annual reports in order that there might be better assessment of the performance of the company.

Candidates should use the information in the question and produce their report under the headings:

(a)	Reporting business performance	**(10 marks)**
(b)	Analysis of financial position	**(6 marks)**
(c)	The nature of corporate citizenship	**(5 marks)**

Marks will be awarded for the presentation and style of the report. **(4 marks)**

(Total = 25 marks)

C2 Value relevance
45 mins

ACR, 12/02

The 'value relevance' of published financial statements is increasingly being called into question. Financial statements have been said to no longer have the same relevance to investors as they had in the past. Investment analysts are developing their own global investment performance standards which increasingly do not use historical cost as a basis for evaluating a company. The traditional accounting ratio analysis is outdated with a new range of performance measures now being used by analysts.

Companies themselves are under pressure to report information which is more transparent and which includes many non-financial disclosures. At the same time the move towards global accounting standards has become more important to companies wishing to raise capital in foreign markets. Corporate reporting is changing in order to meet the investors' needs. However, earnings are still the critical 'number' in both the company and the analyst's eyes.

In order to meet the increasing information needs of investors, standard setters are requiring the use of prospective information and current values more and more with the traditional historical cost accounts and related ratios seemingly becoming less and less important.

Required

(a)   Discuss the importance of published financial statements as a source of information for the investor, giving examples of the changing nature of the performance measures being utilised by investors. **(11 marks)**

(b)   Discuss how financial reporting is changing to meet the information requirements of investors and why the emphasis on the 'earnings' figure is potentially problematic. **(8 marks)**

(c)   Discuss whether the intended use of fair values will reduce the importance of historical cost information.

(6 marks)

(Total = 25 marks)

C3 Preparation question: Financial analysis

The following five year summary relates to Wandafood Products Co, and is based on financial statements prepared under the historical cost convention.

Financial ratios			20X5	20X4	20X3	20X2	20X1
Profitability ratios							
Margin	Trading profit / Revenue	%	7.8	7.5	7.0	7.2	7.3
Return on assets	Trading profit / Net operating assets	%	16.3	17.6	16.2	18.2	18.3
Interest and dividend cover							
Interest cover	Trading profit / Net finance charges	times	2.9	4.8	5.1	6.5	3.6
Dividend cover	Earnings per ord share / Div per ord share	times	2.7	2.6	2.1	2.5	3.1
Debt to equity ratios							
	Net borrowings / Equity attributed to parent	%	65.9	61.3	48.3	10.8	36.5
	Net borrowings / Total equity	%	59.3	55.5	44.0	10.1	33.9
Liquidity ratios							
Quick ratio	Current assets less inventory / Current liabilities	%	74.3	73.3	78.8	113.8	93.4
Current ratio	Current assets / Current liabilities	%	133.6	130.3	142.2	178.9	174.7
Asset ratios							
Operating asset turnover	Revenue / Net operating assets	times	2.1	2.4	2.3	2.5	2.5
Working capital turnover	Revenue / Working capital	times	8.6	8.0	7.0	7.4	6.2
Per share							
Earnings per share	– pre-tax basis	c	23.62	21.25	17.96	17.72	15.06
	– normal basis	c	15.65	13.60	10.98	11.32	12.18
Dividends per share		c	5.90	5.40	4.90	4.60	4.10
Net assets per share		c	102.10	89.22	85.95	85.79	78.11

Net operating assets include property, plant and equipment, inventory, receivables and payables. They exclude borrowings, taxation and dividends.

Required

Prepare a report on the company, clearly interpreting and evaluating the information given. Include comments on possible effects of price changes which may limit the quality of the report.

Helping hand

1   You must get used to questions where a load of information is thrown at you.

2   You should read the information once carefully and then skim through it again, marking off the important points.

3   Produce an answer plan first, otherwise your answer will lack structure.

C4 Rockby and Bye

35 mins

ACR, 6/04, amended

Rockby, a public limited company, has committed itself before its year-end of 31 March 20X4 to a plan of action to sell a subsidiary, Bye. The sale is expected to be completed on 1 July 20X4 and the financial statements of the group were signed on 15 May 20X4. The subsidiary, Bye, a public limited company, had net assets at the year end of $5 million and the book value of related goodwill is $1 million. Bye has made a loss of $500,000 from 1 April 20X4 to 15 May 20X4 and is expected to make a further loss up to the date of sale of $600,000. Rockby was, at 15 May 20X4, negotiating the consideration for the sale of Bye but no contract has been signed or public announcement made as of that date.

Rockby expected to receive $4·5 million for the company after selling costs. The value-in-use of Bye at 15 May 20X4 was estimated at $3·9 million.

Further, the non-current assets of Rockby include the following items of plant and head office land and buildings.

(i)   **Property, plant and equipment held for use in operating leases**. At 31 March 20X4 the company has at carrying value $10 million of plant which has recently been leased out on operating leases. These leases have now expired. The company is undecided as to whether to sell the plant or lease it to customers under finance leases. The fair value less selling costs of the plant is $9 million and the value-in-use is estimated at $12 million.

Plant with a carrying value of $5 million at 31 March 20X4 has ceased to be used because of a downturn in the economy. The company had decided at 31 March 20X4 to maintain the plant in workable condition in case of a change in economic conditions. Rockby subsequently sold the plant by auction on 14 May 20X4 for $3 million net of costs.

(ii) The Board of Rockby approved the relocation of the head office site on 1 March 20X3. The head office land and buildings were renovated and upgraded in the year to 31 March 20X3 with a view to selling the site. During the improvements, subsidence was found in the foundations of the main building. The work to correct the subsidence and the renovations were completed on 1 June 20X3. As at 31 March 20X3 the renovations had cost $2·3 million and the cost of correcting the subsidence was $1 million. The carrying value of the head office land and buildings was $5 million at 31 March 20X3 before accounting for the renovation. Rockby moved its head office to the new site in June 20X3, and at the same time, the old head office property was offered for sale at a price of $10 million.

However, the market for commercial property had deteriorated significantly and as at 31 March 20X4, a buyer for the property had not been found. At that time the company did not wish to reduce the price and hoped that market conditions would improve. On 20 April 20X4, a bid of $8·3 million was received for the property and eventually it was sold (net of costs) for $7·5 million on 1 June 20X4. The carrying value of the head office land and buildings was $7 million at 31 March 20X4.

Non-current assets are shown in the financial statements at historical cost.

Required

(a) Discuss the way in which the sale of the subsidiary, Bye, would be dealt with in the group financial statements of Rockby at 31 March 20X4.

(7 marks)

(b) Discuss whether the following non-current assets should be classed as 'held for sale'.

    (i) The items of plant in the group financial statements at 31 March 20X4;

(7 marks)

    (ii) The head office land and buildings in the group financial statements at 31 March 20X3 and 31 March 20X4.

(5 marks)

(Total = 19 marks)

C5 Vident

45 mins

ACR, 6/05

The directors of Vident, a public limited company, are reviewing the impact of IFRS 2 *Share-based payment* on the financial statements for the year ended 31 May 20X5 as they wish to adopt the IFRS early. However, the directors of Vident are unhappy about having to apply the standard and have put forward the following arguments as to why they should not recognise an expense for share-based payments.

(i) They feel that share options have no cost to their company and, therefore, there should be no expense charged in the income statement.

(ii) They do not feel that the expense arising from share options under IFRS 2 actually meets the definition of an expense under the *Framework* document.

(iii) The directors are worried about the dual impact of the IFRS on earnings per share, as an expense is shown in the income statement and the impact of share options is recognised in the diluted earnings per share calculation.

(iv) They feel that accounting for share-based payment may have an adverse effect on their company and may discourage it from introducing new share option plans.

The following share option schemes were in existence at 31 May 20X5:

Director's name	Grant date	Options granted	Fair value of options at grant date $	Exercise price $	Performance conditions	Vesting date	Exercise date
J. Van Heflin	1 June 20X2	30,000	4	3·50	A	6/20X5	6/20X6
	1 June 20X3	20,000	5	4·50	A	6/20X5	6/20X6
R. Ashworth	1 June 20X4	50,000	6	6	B	6/20X7	6/20X8

The price of the company's shares at 31 May 20X5 is $12 per share and at 31 May 20X4 was $12·50 per share.

The performance conditions which apply to the exercise of executive share options are as follows:

Performance Condition A

The share options do not vest if the growth in the company's earnings per share (EPS) for the year is less than 4%.

The rate of growth of EPS was 4·5% (20X3), 4·1% (20X4), 4·2% (20X5). The directors must still work for the company on the vesting date.

Performance Condition B

The share options do not vest until the share price has increased from its value of $12·50 at the grant date (1 June 20X4) to above $13·50. The director must still work for the company on the vesting date.

No directors have left the company since the issue of the share options and none are expected to leave before June 20X7. The shares vest and can be exercised on the first day of the due month.

The directors are uncertain about the deferred tax implications of adopting IFRS 2. Vident operates in a country where a tax allowance will not arise until the options are exercised and the tax allowance will be based on the option's intrinsic value at the exercise date.

Assume a tax rate of 30%.

Required

Draft a report to the directors of Vident setting out:

(a)   The reasons why share-based payments should be recognised in financial statements and why the directors' arguments are unacceptable   **(9 marks)**

(b)   A discussion (with suitable calculations) as to how the directors' share options would be accounted for in the financial statements for the year ended 31 May 20X5 including the adjustment to opening balances   **(9 marks)**

(c)   The deferred tax implications (with suitable calculations) for the company which arise from the recognition of a remuneration expense for the directors' share options   **(7 marks)**

(Total = 25 marks)

C6 Ashlee   **45 mins**

ACR, 6/05

Ashlee, a public limited company, is preparing its group financial statements for the year ended 31 March 20X5. The company applies newly issued IFRSs at the earliest opportunity. The group comprises three companies, Ashlee, the holding company, and its 100% owned subsidiaries Pilot and Gibson, both public limited companies. The group financial statements at first appeared to indicate that the group was solvent and in a good financial position. However, after the year end, but prior to the approval of the financial statements, mistakes have been found which affect the financial position of the group to the extent that loan covenant agreements have been breached.

As a result the loan creditors require Ashlee to cut its costs, reduce its operations and reorganise its activities. Therefore, redundancies are planned and the subsidiary, Pilot, is to be reorganised. The carrying value of Pilot's net assets, including allocated goodwill, was $85 million at 31 March 20X5, before taking account of reorganisation costs. The directors of Ashlee wish to include $4 million of reorganisation costs in the financial statements of Pilot for the year ended 31 March 20X5. The directors of Ashlee have prepared cash flow projections which indicate that the net present value of future net cash flows from Pilot is expected to be $84 million if the reorganisation takes place and $82 million if the reorganisation does not take place.

Ashlee had already decided prior to the year end to sell the other subsidiary, Gibson. Gibson will be sold after the financial statements have been signed. The contract for the sale of Gibson was being negotiated at the time of the preparation of the financial statements and it is expected that Gibson will be sold in June 20X5.

The carrying amounts of Gibson and Pilot, including allocated goodwill, were as follows at the year end.

	Gibson $m	Pilot $m
Goodwill	30	5
Property, plant and equipment: cost	120	55
valuation	180	
Inventories	100	20
Trade receivables	40	10
Trade payables	(20)	(5)
	450	85

The fair value of the net assets of Gibson at the year end was $415 million and the estimated costs of selling the company were $5 million.

Part of the business activity of Ashlee is to buy and sell property. The directors of Ashlee had signed a contract on 1 March 20X5 to sell two of its development properties which are carried at the lower of cost and net realisable value under IAS 2 *Inventories*. The sale was agreed at a figure of $40 million (carrying value $30 million). A receivable of $40 million and profit of $10 million were recognised in the financial statements for the year ended 31 March 20X5. The sale of the properties was completed on 1 May 20X5 when the legal title passed. The policy used in the prior year was to recognise revenue when the sale of such properties had been completed.

Additionally, Ashlee had purchased, on 1 April 20X4, 150,000 shares of a public limited company, Race, at a price of $20 per share. Ashlee had incurred transaction costs of $100,000 to acquire the shares. The company is unsure as to whether to classify this investment as 'available for sale' or 'at fair value through profit and loss' in the financial statements for the year ended 31 March 20X5. The quoted price of the shares at 31 March 20X5 was $25 per share. The shares purchased represent approximately 1% of the issued share capital of Race and are not classified as 'held for trading'.

There is no goodwill arising in the group financial statements other than that set out above.

Required

Discuss the implications, with suitable computations, of the above events for the group financial statements of Ashlee for the year ended 31 March 20X5.

(25 marks)

C7 Financial performance

45 mins

ACR, 6/05

The International Accounting Standards Board (IASB) is currently in a joint project with the Accounting Standards Board (ASB) in the UK and the Financial Accounting Standards Board (FASB) in the USA in the area of reporting financial performance/comprehensive income. The main focus of the project is the development of a single statement of comprehensive income to replace the income statement and statement of changes in equity. The objective is to analyse all income and expenses and categorise them in a way that increases users' understanding of the results of an entity and assists in forming expectations of future income and expenditure. There seems to be some consensus that the performance statement should be divided into three components being the results of operating activities, financing and treasury activities, and other gains and losses.

Required

(a) Describe the reasons why the three accounting standards boards have decided to cooperate and produce a single statement of financial performance.
(8 marks)

(b) (i) Discuss the main factors that should be taken into account when determining how to treat gains and losses arising on property, plant and equipment in a single statement of financial performance.
(8 marks)

(ii)   Discuss whether gains and losses that have been reported initially in one section of the performance statement should be 'recycled' in a later period in another section and whether only 'realised' gains and losses should be included in such a statement.   **(9 marks)**

(Total = 25 marks)

C8 Egin Group   45 mins

ACR, 6/06

On 1 June 20X5, Egin, a public limited company, was formed out of the reorganisation of a group of companies with foreign operations. The directors require advice on the disclosure of related party information but are reluctant to disclose information as they feel that such transactions are a normal feature of business and need not be disclosed.

Under the new group structure, Egin owns 80% of Briars, 60% of Doye, and 30% of Eye. Egin exercises significant influence over Eye. The directors of Egin are also directors of Briars and Doye but only one director of Egin sits on the management board of Eye. The management board of Eye comprises five directors. Originally the group comprised five companies but the fifth company, Tang, which was a 70% subsidiary of Egin, was sold on 31 January 20X6. There were no transactions between Tang and the Egin Group during the year to 31 May 20X6. 30% of the shares of Egin are owned by another company, Atomic, which exerts significant influence over Egin. The remaining 40% of the shares of Doye are owned by Spade.

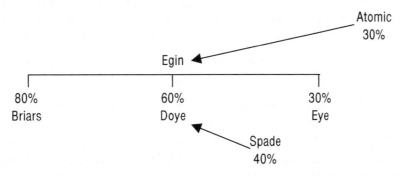

During the current financial year to 31 May 20X6, Doye has sold a significant amount of plant and equipment to Spade at the normal selling price for such items. The directors of Egin have proposed that where related party relationships are determined and sales are at normal selling price, any disclosures will state that prices charged to related parties are made on an arm's length basis.

The directors are unsure how to treat certain transactions relating to their foreign subsidiary, Briars. Egin purchased 80% of the ordinary share capital of Briars on 1 June 20X5 for 50 million euros when its net assets were fair valued at 45 million euros. At 31 May 20X6, it is established that goodwill is impaired by 3 million euros. Additionally, at the date of acquisition, Egin had made an interest free loan to Briars of $10 million. The loan is to be repaid on 31 May 20X7. An equivalent loan would normally carry an interest rate of 6% taking into account Briars' credit rating.

The exchange rates were as follows:

	Euros to $
1 June 20X5	2
31 May 20X6	2·5
Average rate for year	2·3

Financial liabilities of the group are normally measured at amortised cost.

One of the directors of Briars who is not on the management board of Egin owns the whole of the share capital of a company, Blue, that sells goods at market price to Briars. The director is in charge of the production at Briars and also acts as a consultant to the management board of the group.

Required

(a) (i) Discuss why it is important to disclose related party transactions, explaining the criteria which determine a related party relationship. **(5 marks)**

(ii) Describe the nature of any related party relationships and transactions which exists:

(1) within the Egin Group including Tang **(5 marks)**
(2) between Spade and the Egin Group **(3 marks)**
(3) between Atomic and the Egin Group **(3 marks)**

commenting on whether transactions should be described as being at 'arm's length'.

(b) Describe with suitable calculations how the goodwill arising on the acquisition of Briars will be dealt with in the group financial statements and how the loan to Briars should be treated in the financial statements of Briars for the year ended 31 May 20X6. **(9 marks)**

(Total = 25 marks)

C9 Question with helping hands: Engina

45 mins

ACR, Pilot Paper

Engina, a foreign company, has approached a partner in your firm to assist in obtaining a local Stock Exchange listing for the company. Engina is registered in a country where transactions between related parties are considered to be normal but where such transactions are not disclosed. The directors of Engina are reluctant to disclose the nature of their related party transactions as they feel that although they are a normal feature of business in their part of the world, it could cause significant problems politically and culturally to disclose such transactions.

The partner in your firm has requested a list of all transactions with parties connected with the company and the directors of Engina have produced the following summary:

(a) Every month, Engina sells $50,000 of goods per month to Mr Satay, the financial director. The financial director has set up a small retailing business for his son and the goods are purchased at cost price for him. The annual turnover of Engina is $300 million. Additionally Mr Satay has purchased his company car from the company for $45,000 (market value $80,000). The director, Mr Satay, earns a salary of $500,000 a year, and has a personal fortune of many millions of pounds.

(b) A hotel property had been sold to a brother of Mr Soy, the Managing Director of Engina, for $4 million (net of selling cost of $0.2 million). The market value of the property was $4.3 million but in the foreign country, property prices were falling rapidly. The carrying value of the hotel was $5 million and its value in use was $3.6 million. There was an over supply of hotel accommodation due to government subsidies in an attempt to encourage hotel development and the tourist industry.

(c) Mr Satay owns several companies and the structure of the group is as follows.

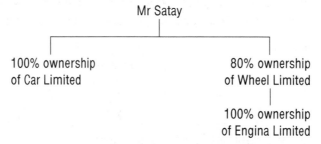

Engina earns 60% of its profits from transactions with Car and 40% of its profits from transactions from Wheel. All the above companies are incorporated in the same country.

BPP
LEARNING MEDIA

Required

Write a report to the directors of Engina setting out the reasons why it is important to disclose related party transactions and the nature of any disclosure required for the above transactions under IAS 24 *Related party disclosures*. **(25 marks)**

The mark allocation will be as follows:

		Mark
Style/layout of report		4
Reasons		8
Transaction	(a)	4
	(b)	5
	(c)	4
		25

Helping hands

1   There are four marks for style and format – make sure you get them

2   When discussing materiality – only material transactions need to be disclosed – remember that the materiality of a transaction with an individual must be judged by reference to that individual, not just the company.

3   With regard to the hotel property, the question of impairment needs to be considered

4   Engina is a wholly-owned subsidiary, but you still need to disclose transactions with Wheel because we are talking abut Engina's own financial statements.

GROUP FINANCIAL STATEMENTS

Questions D1 to D22 cover Group Financial Statements, the subject of Part D of the BPP Study Text for Paper P2.

D1 Preparation question: Simple consolidation

Alpha Co purchased 1,450,000 ordinary shares in Beta Co in 20X0, when the general reserve of Beta stood at $400,000 and there were no retained earnings.

The balance sheets of the two companies as at 31 December 20X4 are set out below.

	Alpha $'000	Beta $'000
Assets		
Non current		
Property, plant and equipment	8,868	1,787
Investment in Beta at cost	1,450	–
	10,318	1,787
Current assets		
Inventories	1,983	1,425
Receivables	1,462	1,307
Cash	25	16
	3,470	2,748
Total assets	13,788	4,535
Equity and liabilities		
Equity		
Share capital (50c ordinary shares)	5,500	1,000
General reserve	1,200	800
Retained earnings	485	100
Total equity	7,185	1,900
Non-current liabilities		
Borrowings 10%	4,000	
Borrowings 15%	–	500
Total non-current liabilities	4,000	500
Current liabilities		
Bank overdraft	1,176	840
Trade payables	887	1,077
Taxation	540	218
Total current liabilities	2,603	2,135
Total liabilities	6,603	2,635
Total equity and liabilities	13,788	4,535

At the balance sheet date the current account of Alpha with Beta was agreed at $23,000 owed by Beta. This account is included in the appropriate receivable and trade payable balances shown above. There has been no impairment of goodwill since the date of acquisition.

Required

(a) Prepare a consolidated balance sheet for the Alpha Beta Group.

(b) Show the alterations necessary to the group balance sheet if the intragroup balance owed by Beta to Alpha represented an invoice for goods sold by Alpha to Beta at a mark-up of 15% on cost, and still unsold by Beta at 31 December 20X4.

Guidance notes

1   Lay out the pro-forma balance sheet, leaving plenty of space.
2   Lay out workings for: goodwill calculation; general reserve; retained earnings; and minority interest.
3   Fill in the easy numbers given in the question.
4   Work out the more complicated numbers using the workings and then add up the balance sheet.
5   Keep all your work very neat and tidy to make it easy to follow. Cross reference all your workings.

D2 Preparation question: Consolidation

The FSR Group consists of the holding company FSR Co and two subsidiary companies, GBH Co and Short Co. FSR Co had acquired 75% of the shares in GBH Co and 80% of the shares in Short Co on 1 December 20X2. The ordinary shares in Short Co are held exclusively with a view to subsequent resale; the ordinary shares in GBH Co are held on a long-term basis. FSR Co prepares its accounts to 30 November each year.

A trainee accountant working on the consolidation for the year ended 30 November 20X3 has proposed the following adjustments.

(i)   *Treatment of profit arising from intra-group sales*

During October 20X3 GBH Co sold goods costing it $200,000 to FSR Co for $220,000. All of the goods remained in inventories as at 30 November 20X3.

Proposed to reduce the inventory and consolidated income statement by $15,000.

During September 20X3 FSR Co sold goods costing $60,000 to GBH Co for $72,000. All of the goods remained in inventory as at 30 November 20X3.

Proposed to reduce the inventories and consolidated income statement by $12,000.

(ii)   *Treatment of goodwill arising on acquisition of GBH Co*

The 75% shareholding in GBH Co was acquired on 1 December 20X2 for $3,000,000 when the fair value of the total net assets in GBH Co was estimated to be $3,000,000.

Proposed to apply the entity concept and credit the minority interest with $250,000 and record the goodwill at 1 December 20X2 at $1,000,000. This goodwill was to be written off over five years. The charge in the 20X3 accounts was to be $200,000.

Required

(a)   Describe the accounting treatment required in the consolidated accounts of the FSR Group as at 30 November 20X3 of the investment in Short Co to comply with relevant IFRSs.

(b)   Inform the trainee accountant whether the proposed consolidation adjustments in (i) and (ii) above comply with accounting standards. State any additional information which could affect the accounting treatment.

(c)   Explain briefly the reason for the accounting treatment recommended for (i) and (ii) above.

Guidance notes

1   This is basic knowledge that should act as a check on your understanding of your earlier studies.

2   If you become confused in your explanations, try jotting down the double entry of the adjustments you think should be made.

D3 Preparation question: Status of investment

International Accounting Standards make it clear that the treatment in consolidated financial statements of investments in other entities is dependent on the extent of the control or influence the investing entity is able to exercise over the other entity. Port has investments in three other entities.

(i) On 15 May 20W0, Port purchased 40 million 50c equity shares in Harbor. The issued equity share capital of Harbor on 15 May 20W0 was 50 million 50c equity shares.

(ii) On 15 June 20W1, Port purchased 30 million $1 equity shares in Inlet. The issued equity share capital of Inlet on 15 June 20W1 was 75 million $1 equity shares. The remaining equity shares in Inlet are held by a large number of investors – none with more than 5 million equity shares.

(iii) On 15 July 20W2, Port purchased 25 million 50c equity shares in Bay. The issued equity share capital of Bay on 15 July 20W2 as 80 million 50c equity shares. Another investor owns 50 million equity shares in Bay. This investor takes an active interest in directing the operating and financial decisions of Bay. On a number of occasions the investor has required Bay to follow policies that do not meet with the approval of Port.

Equity shares in all of the entities carry one vote per share at general meetings. No party can control or influence the composition of the board of directors of any of the entities other than through its ownership of equity shares. There have been no instances where shareholders in any of the entities have acted together to increase their control or influence. None of the entities has issued any additional equity shares since Port purchased its interests. All of the entities are separate legal entities.

Extracts from the income statements of the four entities for their year ended 30 June 20X1 are given below:

	Port $'000	Harbor $'000	Inlet $'000	Bay $'000
Revenue	65,000	45,000	48,000	40,000
Cost of sales	(35,000)	(25,000)	(26,000)	(19,000)
Gross profit	30,000	20,000	22,000	21,000

Note 1

Port manufactures a product that is used by Harbor and Inlet. During the year ended 30 June 20X1, sales of the product to Harbor and Inlet were:

- To Harbor – $8 million.
- To Inlet – $7.5 million.

Opening and closing inventories of this product in the financial statements of Harbor and Inlet (all purchased from Port at cost plus 25% mark up, unchanged during the year) were as follows.

Entity	Closing inventory $'000	Opening inventory $'000
Harbor	3,000	2,400
Inlet	2,500	Nil

At 30 June 20X1, there were no amounts payable by Harbor and Inlet in respect of inventories purchased from Port before 30 June 20X1.

Note 2

There was no other trading between the entities other than the payment of dividends.

Required

(a) State the alternative treatments of investments in consolidated financial statements that are set out in International Financial Reporting Standards.

(b) Identify the correct treatment of the investments in Harbor, Inlet and Bay in the consolidated financial statements of Port.

(c) Compute the consolidated revenue, cost of sales and gross profit of the Port group for the year ended 30 June 20X1. You should ensure that your computations are fully supported by relevant workings.

(d) Compute the adjustments that need to be made in respect of the transactions described in *Note 1* above when preparing the consolidated balance sheet of Port at 30 June 20X1. You should explain the rationale behind each adjustment you make.

D4 Preparation question: Associate

The balance sheets of J Co and its investee companies, P Co and S Co, at 31 December 20X5 are shown below.

BALANCE SHEETS AS AT 31 DECEMBER 20X5

	J Co $'000	P Co $'000	S Co $'000
Assets			
Non-current assets			
Freehold property	1,950	1,250	500
Plant and equipment	795	375	285
Investments	1,500	–	–
	4,245	1,625	785
Current assets			
Inventories	575	300	265
Trade receivables	330	290	370
Cash	50	120	20
	955	710	655
	5,200	2,335	1,440
Equity and liabilities			
Equity			
Share capital ($1 ordinary shares)	2,000	1,000	750
Retained earnings	1,460	885	390
	3,460	1,885	1,140
Non-current liabilities			
12% debentures	500	100	–
Current liabilities			
Bank overdraft	560		
Trade payables	680	350	300
	1,240	350	300
	5,200	2,335	1,440

Additional information

(a) J Co acquired 600,000 ordinary shares in P Co on 1 January 20X0 for $1,000,000 when the accumulated retained earnings of P Co were $200,000.

(b) At the date of acquisition of P Co, the fair value of its freehold property was considered to be $400,000 greater than its value in P Co's balance sheet. P Co had acquired the property in January 20W0 and the buildings element (comprising 50% of the total value) is depreciated on cost over 50 years.

(c) J Co acquired 225,000 ordinary shares in S Co on 1 January 20X4 for $500,000 when the retained profits of S Co were $150,000.

(d) P Co manufactures a component used by J Co only. Transfers are made by P Co at cost plus 25%. J Co held $100,000 of these components in inventories at 31 December 20X5.

(e) It is the policy of J Co to review goodwill for impairment annually. The goodwill in P Co was written off in full some years ago. An impairment test conducted at the year end revealed impairment losses on the investment in S Co of $92,000.

Required

Prepare, in a format suitable for inclusion in the annual report of the J Group, the consolidated balance sheet at 31 December 20X5.

D5 Baden   45 mins

(a)   IAS 28 *Investments in associates* and IAS 31 *Interests in joint ventures* deal with associates and joint ventures respectively. The method of accounting for interests in joint ventures depends on whether they are interests in jointly controlled operations, jointly controlled assets or jointly controlled entities.

Required

(i)   Explain the criteria which distinguish an associate from an ordinary non-current asset investment.

(5 marks)

(ii)   Explain the principal differences between a jointly controlled operation, a jointly controlled asset and a jointly controlled entity.   (5 marks)

(b)   The following financial statements relate to Baden, a public limited company.

INCOME STATEMENT
FOR YEAR ENDED 31 DECEMBER 20X8

	$m
Revenue	212
Cost of sales	(178)
Gross profit	34
Other income	12
Distribution costs	(17)
Administrative expenses	(8)
Finance costs	(4)
Profit before tax	17
Income tax expense	(5)
Profit for the period	12
Ordinary dividend – paid	4

BALANCE SHEET AT 31 DECEMBER 20X8

	$m
Property, plant and equipment	37
Current assets	31
	68
Equity	
Ordinary shares of $1	10
Share premium account	4
Retained earnings	32
	46
Non-current liabilities	10
Current liabilities	12
	68

(i)   Cable, a public limited company, acquired 30% of the ordinary share capital of Baden at a cost of $14 million on 1 January 20X7. The share capital of Baden has not changed since acquisition when the retained earnings of Baden were $9 million.

(ii) At 1 January 20X7 the following fair values were attributed to the net assets of Baden but not incorporated in its accounting records. Fair values are to be taken into account when assessing any goodwill arising on acquisition.

	$m	
Property, plant and equipment	30	(carrying value $20m)
Current assets	31	
Current liabilities	20	
Non-current liabilities	8	

(iii) Guy, an associate of Cable, also holds a 25% interest in the ordinary share capital of Baden. This was acquired on 1 January 20X8.

(iv) During the year to 31 December 20X8, Baden sold goods to Cable to the value of $35 million. The inventory of Cable at 31 December 20X8 included goods purchased from Baden on which the company made a profit of $10 million.

(v) The policy of all companies in the Cable Group is to depreciate property, plant and equipment at 20% per annum on the straight line basis.

Required

(i) Show how the investment in Baden would be stated in the consolidated balance sheet and income statement of the Cable Group under IAS 28 *Investments in associates*, for the year ended 31 December 20X8 on the assumption that Baden is an associate. **(8 marks)**

(ii) Show and explain how the treatment of Baden would change if Baden was classified as an investment in a joint venture and it utilised the proportionate consolidation method in IAS 31 *Interests in joint ventures*. **(7 marks)**

(Total = 25 marks)

D6 Preparation question: 'D'-shaped group

Below are the balance sheets of three companies as at 31 December 20X9.

	Bauble Co $'000	Jewel Co $'000	Gem Co $'000
Non-current assets			
Property, plant and equipment	720	60	70
Investments in group companies	185	100	–
	905	160	70
Current assets	175	95	90
	1,080	255	160
Equity			
Share capital – $1 ordinary shares	400	100	50
Retained earnings	560	90	65
	960	190	115
Current liabilities	120	65	45
	1,080	255	160

You are also given the following information:

(a)   Bauble Co acquired 60% of the share capital of Jewel Co on 1 January 20X2 and 10% of Gem on 1 January 20X3. The cost of the combinations were $142,000 and $43,000 respectively. Jewel Co acquired 70% of the share capital of Gem Co on 1 January 20X3.

(b)   The retained earnings balances of Jewel Co and Gem Co were:

	1 January 20X2 $'000	1 January 20X3 $'000
Jewel Co	45	60
Gem Co	30	40

3   No impairment loss adjustments have been necessary to date.

Required

(a)   Prepare the consolidated balance sheet for Bauble Co and its subsidiaries as at 31 December 20X9.

(b)   Calculate the total goodwill arising on acquisition if Bauble Co had acquired its investments in Jewel and Gem on 1 January 20X3 at a cost of $142,000 and $43,000 respectively and Jewel Co had acquired its investment in Gem Co on 1 January 20X2.

D7 Question with analysis: X Group   54 mins

What percentage? What is the status?

X, a public limited company, acquired 100 million ordinary shares of $1 in Y, a public limited company on 1 April 20X6 when the retained earnings were $120 million. Y acquired 45 million ordinary shares of $1 in Z, a public limited company, on 1 April 20X4 when the retained earnings were $10 million. On 1 April 20X4 there were no material differences between the book values and the fair values of Z. On 1 April 20X6, the retained earnings of Z were $20 million.

What is the status? What does X control?

Y acquired 30% of the ordinary shares of W, a limited company, on 1 April 20X6 for $50 million when the retained earnings of W were $7 million. Y is in a position to exercise significant influence over W and there were no material differences between the book values and the fair values of W at that date.

There had been no share issues since 1 April 20X4 by any of the group companies. The following balance sheets relate to the group companies as at 31 March 20X9.

	X $m	Y $m	Z $m	W $m
Property, plant and equipment	900	100	30	40
Intangible assets		30		
Investment in Y	320			
Investment in Z		90		
Investment in W		50		
Net current assets	640	360	75	73
	1,860	630	105	113
Share capital	360	150	50	80
Share premium	250	120	10	6
Retained earnings	1,050	210	30	17
	1,660	480	90	103
Non-current liabilities	200	150	15	10
	1,860	630	105	113

BPP
LEARNING MEDIA

<table>
<tr><td>Use tables to work out total values for X and Z at acquisition and at the balance sheet date.</td></tr>
</table>

(i) **The following fair value table sets out the book values of certain assets and liabilities of the group companies together with any accounting policy adjustments to ensure consistent group policies** at 1 April 20X6.

	Book value		Accounting policy adj.		Fair value adj.		Value after adjustments	
	$m	$m	$m	$m	$m	$m	$m	$m
	Y	Z	Y	Z	Y	Z	Y	Z
Property, plant and equipment	90	20			30	10	120	30
Intangible non-current assets	30		(30)				-	
Inventory	20	12	2		(8)	(5)	14	7
Allowance for doubtful debts	(15)				(9)		(24)	

These values had not been incorporated into the financial records. The group companies have consistent accounting policies at 31 March 20X9, apart from the non-current intangible assets in Y's books.

<table>
<tr><td>Straightforward intragroup trading.</td></tr>
</table>

(ii) During the year ended 31 March 20X9, **Z had sold goods to X and Y**. At 31 March 20X9, there were $44 million of these goods in the inventory of X and $16 million in the inventory of Y. Z had made a profit of 25% on selling price on the goods.

<table>
<tr><td>A contingent asset?</td></tr>
</table>

(iii) On 1 June 20X7, an amount of $36 million was received by Y from an arbitration award against Q. This receipt was secured as a result of an action against Q prior to Y's acquisition by X but was not included in the assets of Y at 1 April 20X6.

(iv) The group writes goodwill off immediately to reserves. However it has decided to bring its accounting policies into line with IFRSs and not local accounting policies. Thus goodwill will be capitalised under IFRS 3 *Business combinations*. At 31 March 20X6, property, plant and equipment had a remaining useful life of 10 years.

Required

(a) Prepare a consolidated balance sheet as at 31 March 20X9 for the X group. **(25 marks)**

(b) Explain how the change in accounting policy as regards goodwill should be dealt with in the financial statements of the X group under International Financial Reporting Standards. **(5 marks)**

All calculations should be rounded to the nearest million dollars. **(Total = 30 marks)**

D8 Largo

45 mins

ACR, 12/03

The following draft balance sheets relate to Largo, a public limited company, Fusion, a public limited company and Spine, a public limited company, as at 30 November 20X4:

	Largo $m	Fusion $m	Spine $m
Non-current assets			
Property, plant and equipment	329	185	64
Investment in Spine		50	
Investment in Micro	11		
	340	235	64
Current assets	120	58	40
	460	293	104
Equity			
Called up ordinary share capital of $1	280	110	50
Share premium account	30	20	10
Retained earnings	120	138	35
	430	268	95
Non-current liabilities			
Deferred tax liability	20	20	5
Current liabilities	10	5	4
	460	293	104

The following information is relevant to the preparation of the group financial statements:

(a) Largo acquired ninety per cent of the ordinary share capital of Fusion and twenty-six per cent of the ordinary share capital of Spine on 1 December 20X3 in a share for share exchange when the retained earnings were Fusion $136 million and Spine $30 million. The fair value of the net assets at 1 December 20X3 was Largo $650 million, Fusion $330 million and Spine $128 million. Any increase in the consolidated fair value of the net assets over the carrying value is deemed to be attributable to property held by the companies.

The share for share exchange on the purchase of Fusion and Spine on 1 December 20X3 has not yet been recorded in Largo's books. Largo issued 150m of its own shares to purchase Fusion and 30m to purchase Spine. There have been no new issue of shares since 1 December 20X3. On 1 December 20X3, before the share for share exchange, the market capitalisation of the companies was $644 million: Largo; $310 million: Fusion; and $130 million: Spine.

(b) In arriving at the fair value of net assets acquired at 1 December 20X3, Largo has not accounted for the deferred tax arising on the increase in the value of the property of both Fusion and Spine. The deferred tax arising on the fair valuation of the property was Fusion $15 million and Spine $9 million.

(c) Fusion had acquired a sixty per cent holding in Spine on 1 December 20X0 for a consideration of $50 million when the retained earnings reserve of Spine was $10 million. The fair value of the net assets at that date was $80 million with the increase in fair value attributable to property held by the companies. Property is depreciated within the group at five per cent per annum.

(d) Largo purchased a forty per cent interest in Micro, a limited liability investment company on 1 December 20X3. The only asset of the company is a portfolio of investments which is held for trading purposes. The stake in Micro was purchased for cash for $11 million. The carrying value of the net assets of Micro on 1 December 20X3 was $18 million and their fair value was $20 million. On 30 November 20X4, the fair value of the net assets was $24 million. Largo exercises significant influence over Micro. Micro values the portfolio on a 'mark to market' basis.

(e)   Fusion has included a brand name in its property, plant and equipment at the cost of $9 million. The brand earnings can be separately identified and could be sold separately from the rest of the business. The fair value of the brand at 30 November 20X4 was $7 million. The fair value of the brand at the time of Fusion's acquisition by Largo was $9 million.

Required

Prepare the consolidated balance sheet of the Largo Group at the year ended 30 November 20X4 in accordance with International Financial Reporting Standards. **(25 marks)**

D9 Case study question: Rod   90 mins

The following draft balance sheets relate to Rod, a public limited company, Reel, a public limited company, and Line, a public limited company, as at 30 November 20X3.

	Rod $m	Reel $m	Line $m
Non-current assets			
Property, plant and equipment	1,230	505	256
Investment in Reel	640		
Investment in Line	160	100	
	2,030	605	256
Current assets			
Inventory	300	135	65
Trade receivables	240	105	49
Cash at bank and in hand	90	50	80
	630	290	194
Total assets	2,660	895	450
Equity			
Share capital	1,500	500	200
Share premium account	300	100	50
Revaluation surplus			70
Retained earnings	625	200	60
	2,425	800	380
Non-current liabilities	135	25	20
Current liabilities	100	70	50
Total equity and liabilities	2,660	895	450

The following information is relevant to the preparation of the group financial statements.

(a)   Rod had acquired eighty per cent of the ordinary share capital of Reel on 1 December 20X0 when the retained earnings were $100 million. The fair value of the net assets of Reel was $710 million at 1 December 20X0. Any fair value adjustment related to net current assets and these net current assets had been realised by 30 November 20X3. There had been no new issues of shares in the group since the current group structure was created.

(b)   Rod and Reel had acquired their holdings in Line on the same date as part of an attempt to mask the true ownership of Line. Rod acquired forty per cent and Reel acquired twenty-five per cent of the ordinary share capital of Line on 1 December 20X1. The retained earnings of Line on that date were $50 million and those of Reel were $150 million. There was no revaluation surplus in the books of Line on 1 December 20X1. The fair values of the net assets of Line at December 20X1 were not materially different from their carrying values.

(c)   The group operates in the pharmaceutical industry and incurs a significant amount of expenditure on the development of products. These costs were formerly written off to the income statement as incurred but then reinstated when the related products were brought into commercial use. The reinstated costs are shown as 'development inventories'. The costs do not meet the criteria in

IAS 38 *Intangible assets* for classification as intangibles and it is unlikely that the net cash inflows from these products will be in excess of the development costs. In the current year, Reel has included $20 million of these costs in inventory. Of these costs $5 million relates to expenditure on a product written off in periods prior to 1 December 20X0. Commercial sales of this product had commenced during the current period. The accountant now wishes to ensure that the financial statements comply strictly with IAS/IFRS as regards this matter.

(d) Reel had purchased a significant amount of new production equipment during the year. The cost before trade discount of this equipment was $50 million. The trade discount of $6 million was taken to the income statement. Depreciation is charged on the straight line basis over a six year period.

(e) The policy of the group is now to state property, plant and equipment at depreciated historical cost. The group changed from the revaluation model to the cost model under IAS 16 *Property, plant and equipment* in the year ended 30 November 20X3 and restated all of its assets to historical cost in that year except for the property, plant and equipment of Line which had been revalued by the directors of Line 1 December 20X2. The values were incorporated in the financial records creating revaluation surplus of $70 million. The property, plant and equipment of Line were originally purchased on December 20X1 at a cost of $300 million. The assets are depreciated over six years on the straight line basis. The group does not make an annual transfer from revaluation reserves to retained earnings in respect of the excess depreciation charged on revalued property, plant and equipment. There were no additions or disposals of the property, plant and equipment of Line for the two years ended 30 November 20X3.

(f) During the year the directors of Rod decided to form a defined benefit pension scheme for the employees of the parent and contributed cash to it of $100 million. The following details relate to the scheme at 30 November 20X3.

	$m
Present value of obligation	130
Fair value of plan assets	125
Current service cost	110
Interest cost – scheme liabilities	20
Expected return on pension scheme assets	10

The only entry in the financial statements made to date is in respect of the cash contribution which has been included in Rod's trade receivables. The directors have been uncertain as how to deal with the above pension scheme in the consolidated financial statements because of the significance of the potential increase in the charge to the income statement relating to the pension scheme. They wish to recognise immediately any actuarial gain in profit or loss.

Required

(a) Show how the defined benefit pension scheme should be dealt with in the consolidated financial statements.

(5 marks)

(b) Prepare a consolidated balance sheet of the Rod Group for the year ended 30 November 20X3 in accordance with the standards of the International Accounting Standards Board. **(22 marks)**

(c) You are now advising the financial director of Rod about certain aspects of the financial statements for the year ended 30 November 20X4. The director has summarised these points as follows.

(i) **Restructuring of the group.** A formal announcement for a restructuring of the group was made after the year end on 5 December 20X4. A provision has not been made in the financial statements as a public issue of shares is being planned and the company does not wish to lower the reported profits. Prior to the year end, the company has sold certain plant and issued redundancy notices to some employees in anticipation of the formal commencement of the restructuring. The company prepared a formal plan for the restructuring which was approved by the board and communicated to the trade union representatives prior to the year end. The directors estimate the cost of the restructuring to be $60 million, and it could take up to two years to complete the restructuring. The estimated cost of restructuring includes $10 million for retraining and relocating existing employees, and the directors feel that costs of $20 million (of which $5 million is relocation expenses) will have been incurred by the time the financial statements are approved. **(7 marks)**

(ii) **Fine for illegal receipt of a state subsidy**. The company was fined on 10 October 20X4 for the receipt of state subsidies that were contrary to a supra-national trade agreement. The subsidies were used to offset trading losses in previous years. Rod has to repay to the government $300 million plus interest of $160 million. The total repayment has been treated as an intangible asset which is being amortised over twenty years with a full year's charge in the current year. **(5 marks)**

The financial director wishes to prepare a report for submission to the Board of Directors which discusses the above accounting treatment of the key points in the financial statements.

(d) Rod spends many millions of pounds on research in innovative areas. Often the research and development expenditure does not provide a revenue stream for many years. The company has gained a significant expertise in this field and is frustrated by the fact that the value which is being created is not shown on the balance sheet, but the cost of the innovation is charged to the profit and loss account. The knowledge gained by the company is not reported in the financial statements.

Advise the directors on the current problems of reporting financial performance in the case of a 'knowledge led' company such as Rod. **(8 marks)**

(e) In many organisations, bonus payments related to annual profits form a significant part of the total remuneration of all senior managers, not just the top few managers. The directors of Rod feel that the chief internal auditor makes a significant contribution to the company's profitability, and should therefore receive a bonus based on profit.

Advise the directors as to whether this is appropriate. **(3 marks)**

(Total marks = 50)

D10 Case study question: Exotic   90 mins

The Exotic Group carries on business as a distributor of warehouse equipment and importer of fruit into the country. Exotic was incorporated in 20X1 to distribute warehouse equipment. It diversified its activities during 20X3 to include the import and distribution of fruit, and expanded its operations by the acquisition of shares in Melon in 20X5 and in Kiwi in 20X7.

Accounts for all companies are made up to 31 December.

The draft income statements for Exotic, Melon and Kiwi for the year ended 31 December 20X9 are as follows.

	Exotic	Melon	Kiwi
	$'000	$'000	$'000
Revenue	45,600	24,700	22,800
Cost of sales	18,050	5,463	5,320
Gross profit	27,550	19,237	17,480
Distribution costs	3,325	2,137	1,900
Administrative expenses	3,475	950	1,900
Finance costs	325	–	–
Profit before tax	20,425	16,150	13,680
Income tax expense	8,300	5,390	4,241
Profit for the period	12,125	10,760	9,439
Dividends paid and declared for the period	9,500	–	–

The draft balance sheets as at 31 December 20X9 are as follows.

	Exotic $'000	Melon $'000	Kiwi $'000
Non-current assets			
Property, plant and equipment (NBV)	35,483	24,273	13,063
Investments			
Shares in Melon	6,650		
Shares in Kiwi		3,800	
	42,133	28,073	13,063
Current assets	1,568	9,025	8,883
	43,701	37,098	21,946
Equity			
$1 ordinary shares	8,000	3,000	2,000
Retained earnings	22,638	24,075	19,898
	30,638	27,075	21,898
Current liabilities	13,063	10,023	48
	43,701	37,098	21,946

The following information is available relating to Exotic, Melon and Kiwi.

(a) On 1 January 20X5 Exotic acquired 2,700,000 $1 ordinary shares in Melon for $6,650,000 at which date there was a credit balance on the retained earnings of Melon of $1,425,000. No shares have been issued by Melon since Exotic acquired its interest.

(b) On 1 January 20X7 Melon acquired 1,600,000 $1 ordinary shares in Kiwi for $3,800,000 at which date there was a credit balance on the retained earnings of Kiwi of $950,000. No shares have been issued by Kiwi since Melon acquired its interest.

(c) During 20X9, Kiwi had made intragroup sales to Melon of $480,000 making a profit of 25% on cost and $75,000 of these goods were in inventories at 31 December 20X9.

(d) During 20X9, Melon had made intragroup sales to Exotic of $260,000 making a profit of 331/3% on cost and $60,000 of these goods were in inventories at 31 December 20X9.

(e) On 1 November 20X9 Exotic sold warehouse equipment to Melon for $240,000 from inventories. Melon has included this equipment in its property, plant and equipment. The equipment had been purchased on credit by Exotic for $200,000 in October 20X9 and this amount is included in its current liabilities as at 31 December 20X9.

(f) Melon charges depreciation on its warehouse equipment at 20% on cost. It is company policy to charge a full year's depreciation in the year of acquisition to be included in the cost of sales.

(g) An impairment test conducted at the year end did not reveal any impairment losses.

Required

Prepare for the Exotic Group:

(a) A consolidated income statement for the year ended 31 December 20X9   **(16 marks)**

(b) A consolidated balance sheet as at that date   **(12 marks)**

(c) The following year, Exotic acquired the whole of the share capital of Zest Software, a public limited company and merged Zest Software with its existing business. The directors feel that the goodwill ($10 million) arising on the purchase has an indefinite economic life. Additionally, Exotic acquired a 50% interest in a joint venture which gives rise to a net liability of $3 million. The reason for this liability is the fact that the negative goodwill ($6 million) arising on the acquisition of the interest in the joint venture was deducted from the interest in the net assets ($3 million). Exotic is proposing to net the liability of $3 million against a loan made to the joint venture by Exotic of $5 million, and show the resultant balance in property, plant and equipment. The equity method of accounting has been used to account for the interest in the joint venture. It is proposed to treat negative goodwill in the same manner as the goodwill on the purchase of Zest Software and leave it in the balance sheet indefinitely. **(11 marks)**

(d) Advise the directors of Exotic on the issues relating to the reporting of environmental information in financial statements and the current reporting requirements in the UK. **(11 marks)**

(Total marks= 50)

D11 Preparation question: Part disposal

Angel Co bought 70% of the share capital of Shane Co for $120,000 on 1 January 20X6. At that date Shane Co's retained earnings stood at $10,000.

The balance sheets at 31 December 20X8, summarised income statements to that date and movement on retained earnings are given below:

	Angel Co $'000	Shane Co $'000
BALANCE SHEETS		
Non-current assets		
Property, plant and equipment	200	80
Investment in Shane Co	120	–
	320	80
Current assets	890	140
	1,210	220
Equity		
Share capital – $1 ordinary shares	500	100
Retained earnings	400	90
	900	190
Current liabilities	310	30
	1,210	220
SUMMARISED INCOME STATEMENTS		
Profit before interest and tax	110	30
Income tax expense	(40)	(12)
Profit for the period	70	18
MOVEMENT IN RETAINED EARNINGS		
Balance at 31 December 20X7	330	72
Profit for the period	70	18
Balance at 31 December 20X8	400	90

Angel Co sells one half of its holding in Shane Co for $160,000 on 30 June 20X8, and the remaining holding is to be dealt with as an associate. This does not represent a discontinued operation.

No entries have been made in the accounts for the above transaction.

Assume that profits accrue evenly throughout the year.

Required

Prepare the consolidated balance sheet, income statement and a reconciliation of movement in retained earnings for the year ended 31 December 20X8.

Ignore income taxes. No impairment losses have been necessary to date.

D12 Preparation question: Plans

X, a public limited company, owns 100 per cent of companies Y and Z which are both public limited companies. The X group operates in the telecommunications industry and the directors are considering two different plans to restructure the group. The directors feel that the current group structure is not serving the best interests of the shareholders and wish to explore possible alternative group structures.

The balance sheets of X and its subsidiaries Y and Z at 31 May 20X1 are as follows:

	X	Y	Z
	$m	$m	$m
Property, plant and equipment	600	200	45
Cost of investment in Y	60		
Cost of investment in Z	70		
Net current assets	160	100	20
	890	300	65
Share capital – ordinary shares of $1	120	60	40
Retained earnings	770	240	25
	890	300	65

X acquired the investment in Z on 1 June 20W5 when the company retained earnings balance was $20 million. The fair value of the net assets of Z on 1 June 20W5 was $60 million. Company Y was incorporated by X and has always been a 100 per cent owned subsidiary. The fair value of the net assets of Y at 31 May 20X1 is $310 million and of Z is $80 million. The fair values of the net current assets of both Y and Z are approximately the same as their book values.

The directors are unsure as to the impact or implications that the following plans are likely to have on the individual accounts of the companies and the group accounts.

Local companies legislation requires that the amount at which share capital is recorded is dictated by the nominal value of the shares issued and if the value of the consideration received exceeds that amount, the excess is recorded in the share premium account. Shares cannot be issued at a discount. In the case of a share for share exchange, the value of the consideration can be deemed to be the book value of the investment exchanged.

The two different plans to restructure the group are as follows.

Plan 1

Y is to purchase the whole of X's investment in Z. The directors are undecided as to whether the purchase consideration should be 50 million $1 ordinary shares of Y or a cash amount of $75 million.

Plan 2

The assets and trade of Z are to be transferred to Y. Company Z would initially become a non trading company. The assets and trade are to be transferred at their book value. The consideration for the transfer will be $60 million which will be left outstanding on the intercompany account between Y and Z.

Required

Discuss the key considerations and the accounting implications of the above plans for the X group. Your answer should show the potential impact on the individual accounts of X, Y and Z and the group accounts after each plan has been implemented.

D13 Ejoy

45 mins

ACR, 6/06

Ejoy, a public limited company, has acquired two subsidiaries. The details of the acquisitions are as follows:

Company	Date of acquisition	Ordinary share capital of $1 $m	Reserves at acquisition $m	Fair value of net assets at acquisition $m	Cost of investment $m	Ordinary share capital of $1 acquired $m
Zbay	1 June 20X4	200	170	600	520	160
Tbay	1 December 20X5	120	80	310	216	72

The draft income statements for the year ended 31 May 20X6 are:

	Ejoy $m	Zbay $m	Tbay $m
Revenue	2,500	1,500	800
Cost of sales	(1,800)	(1,200)	(600)
Gross profit	700	300	200
Other income	70	10	–
Distribution costs	(130)	(120)	(70)
Administrative expenses	(100)	(90)	(60)
Finance costs	(50)	(40)	(20)
Profit before tax	490	60	50
Income tax expense	(200)	(26)	(20)
Profit for the period	290	34	30
Profit for year 31 May 20X5	190	20	15

The following information is relevant to the preparation of the group financial statements.

(a) Tbay was acquired exclusively with a view to sale and at 31 May 20X6 meets the criteria of being a disposal group. The fair value of Tbay at 31 May 20X6 is $300 million and the estimated selling costs of the shareholding in Tbay are $5 million.

(b) Ejoy entered into a joint venture with another company on 31 May 20X6. The joint venture is a limited company and Ejoy has contributed assets at fair value of $20 million (carrying value $14 million). Each party will hold five million ordinary shares of $1 in the joint venture. The gain on the disposal of the assets ($6 million) to the joint venture has been included in 'other income'.

(c) On acquisition, the financial statements of Tbay included a large cash balance. Immediately after acquisition Tbay paid a dividend of $40 million. The receipt of the dividend is included in other income in the income statement of Ejoy. Since the acquisition of Zbay and Tbay, there have been no further dividend payments by these companies.

(d) Zbay has a loan asset which was carried at $60 million at 1 June 20X5. The loan's effective interest rate is six per cent. On 1 June 20X5 the company felt that because of the borrower's financial problems, it would receive $20 million in approximately two years time, on 31 May 20X7. At 31 May 20X6, the company still expects to receive the same amount on the same date. The loan asset is classified as 'loans and receivables'.

(e) On 1 June 20X5, Ejoy purchased a five year bond with a principal amount of $50 million and a fixed interest rate of five per cent which was the current market rate. The bond is classified as an 'available for sale' financial asset. Because of the size of the investment, Ejoy has entered into a floating interest rate swap. Ejoy has designated the swap as a fair value hedge of the bond. At 31 May 20X6, market interest rates were six per cent. As a result, the fair value of the bond has decreased to $48·3 million. Ejoy has received $0·5 million in net interest payments on the swap at 31 May 20X6 and the fair value hedge has been 100% effective in the period, and you should assume any gain/loss on the hedge is the same as the gain/loss on the bond. No entries have been made in the income statement to account for the bond or the hedge.

(f)   No impairment of the goodwill arising on the acquisition of Zbay had occurred at 1 June 20X5. The recoverable amount of Zbay was $630 million and that of Tbay was $290 million at 31 May 20X6. Impairment losses on goodwill are charged to cost of sales.

(g)   Assume that profits accrue evenly throughout the year and ignore any taxation effects.

Required

Prepare a consolidated income statement for the Ejoy Group for the year ended 31 May 20X6 in accordance with International Financial Reporting Standards.

(25 marks)

D14 Case study question: Base Group

90 mins

(a)   Base, a public limited company, acquired two subsidiaries, Zero and Black, both public limited companies, on 1 June 20X1. The details of the acquisitions at that date are as follows.

Subsidiary	Ordinary Share capital of $1 $m	Reserves $m	Fair value of net assets at acquisition $m	Cost of Investment $m	Ordinary share capital acquired $m
Zero	350	250	770	600	250
Black	200	150	400	270	120

The draft income statements for the year ended 31 May 20X3 are:

	Base $m	Zero $m	Black $m
Revenue	3,000	2,300	600
Cost of sales	(2,000)	(1,600)	(300)
Gross profit	1,000	700	300
Distribution costs	(240)	(230)	(120)
Administrative expenses	(200)	(220)	(80)
Finance cost: interest expense	(20)	(10)	(12)
Investment income receivable (including intragroup dividends paid May 20X3)	(100)	–	–
Profit before tax	640	240	88
Income tax expense	(130)	(80)	(36)
Net profit after tax	510	160	52
Reserves 1 June 20X2	1,400	400	190

The following information is relevant to the preparation of the group financial statements.

(i)   On 1 December 20X2, Base sold 50 million $1 ordinary shares in Zero for $155 million. The only accounting entry made by Base was to record the receipt of the cash consideration in the cash account and in a suspense account.

(ii)   On 1 March 20X3, Black issued 100 million ordinary shares of $1 at a price of $2·65 per share. It was fully subscribed and paid up on that day. Base decided not to subscribe for the shares but the directors of Base had significant influence over the decision to issue the shares. The directors of Black had prepared financial information as at 28 February 20X3 for the purpose of the new issue of shares showing the carrying values of the net assets of Black to be $480 million.

(iii)   Black had sold $150 million of goods to Base on 30 April 20X3. There was no opening inventory of intragroup goods but the closing inventories of these goods in Base's financial statements was $90 million. The profit on these goods was 30% on selling price.

(iv)   Base has implemented in full IAS 19 *Employee benefits* in its financial statements. The directors have included the following amounts in the figure for cost of sales.

	$m
Current service cost	5
Actuarial deficit on obligation	4
Interest cost	3
Actuarial gain on assets	(2)
Charged to cost of sales	10

The accounting policy in respect of these accounts is recognition in the income statement using the 100% corridor approach. The fair value of the plan assets at 31 May 20X2 was $48 million and the present value of the defined benefit obligation was $54 million at that date. The net cumulative unrecognised actuarial loss at 31 May 20X2 was $3 million and the expected remaining working lives of the employees was ten years.

(v)   Base issued on 1 June 20X2 in a redeemable debt instrument at a cost of $20 million. The debt is repayable in four years at $24.7 million. Base has included the redeemable debt in its balance sheet at $20 million. The effective interest cost on the bond is 5.4%.

(vi)   Base had carried out work for a group of companies (Drum Group) during the financial year to 31 May 20X2. Base had accepted one million share options of the Drum Group in full settlement of the debt owed to them. At 1 June 20X2 these share options were valued at $3 million which was the value of the outstanding debt. The following table gives the prices of these shares and the fair value of the option.

	Share price	Fair value of option
31 May 20X2	$13	$3
31 May 20X3	$10	$1

The options had not been exercised during the year and remained at $3 million in the balance sheet of Base. The options can be exercised at any time after 31 May 20X5 for $8·50 per share.

(vii)   Base had paid a dividend of $50 million in the year and Zero had paid a dividend of $70 million in May 20X3.

(viii)   The post acquisition income statement effect of the fair value adjustments has been incorporated into the subsidiaries' records. Goodwill is reviewed for impairment annually. At 1 June 20X2 the group had recognised impairment losses of $10 million relating to Zero and $6 million relating to Black. No further impairment losses were necessary during the year ending 31 May 20X3.

(ix)   Ignore the tax implications of any capital gains made by the Group and assume profits accrue evenly throughout the year.

Required

Prepare a consolidated income statement for the Base Group for the year ended 31 May 20X3 in accordance with International Accounting Standards/International Financial Reporting Standards.   **(26 marks)**

(b)   The revenue of the group results mainly from the sale of software under licences which provide customers with the right to use these products. Base has stated that it follows emerging best practice in terms of its revenue recognition policy which it regards as US GAAP. It has stated that the International Accounting Standards Board has been slow in revising its current standards and the company has therefore adopted the US standard SAB101 *Revenue Recognition in Financial Statements.* The group policy is as follows.

(i)   If services are essential to the functioning of the software (for example setting up the software) and the payment terms are linked, the revenue for both software and services is recognised on acceptance of the contract.

(ii)   Fees from the development of customised software, where service support is incidental to its functioning, are recognised at the completion of the contract.   **(6 marks)**

(c)   The directors of the Base group feel that their financial statements do not address a broad enough range of users' needs. They have reviewed the published financial statements and have realised that there is very little information about the corporate environmental governance. Base discloses the following environmental information in the financial statements.

(i)   The highest radiation dosage to a member of the public
(ii)   Total acid gas emissions and global warming potential

Contribution to clean air through emissions savings

Required

(i)   Explain the factors which provide encouragement to companies to disclose social and environmental information in their financial statements, briefly discussing whether the content of such disclosure should be at the company's discretion.   **(11 marks)**

(ii)   Describe how the current disclosure by the Base Group of 'corporate environmental governance' could be extended and improved.   **(7 marks)**

               (Total marks=50)

D15 Hyperinflation   45 mins

IAS 21 *The effects of changes in foreign exchange rates* states that where an entity has foreign operations, such as overseas subsidiaries, branches, joint ventures or associates, it should determine the functional currency of that foreign operation. The functional currency is the currency of the primary economic environment in which the entity operates. Where a foreign operation has a functional currency that is different from that of the reporting entity, it will be necessary to translate the financial statements of the foreign operation into the currency in which the reporting entity presents its financial statements.

However, where the foreign operation is located in a country with a high rate of inflation, the translation process may not be sufficient to present fairly the financial position of the foreign operation. Some adjustment for inflation should be undertaken to the local currency financial statements before translation. IAS 29 *Financial reporting in hyper-inflationary economies* deals with this issue.

Required

(a)   Explain the factors which should be taken into account in determining whether or not the functional currency of a foreign operation is the same as that of its parent.   **(10 marks)**

(b)   Discuss the effects that hyper-inflation can have on the usefulness of financial statements, and explain how entities with subsidiaries that are located in hyper-inflationary economies should reflect this fact in their consolidated financial statements. You should restrict your discussion to financial statements that have been prepared under the historical cost convention.   **(7 marks)**

(c)   On 30 November 20X3 Gold Co set up a subsidiary in a foreign country where the local currency is effados. The principal assets of this subsidiary were a chain of hotels. The value of the hotels on this date was 20 million effados. The rate of inflation for the period 30 November 20X3 to 30 November 20X7 has been significantly high. The following inflation is relevant to the economy of the foreign country.

	Effados in exchange for $	Consumer price index in foreign country
30 November 20X3	1.34	100
30 November 20X7	17.87	3,254

There is no depreciation charged in the financial statements as the hotels are maintained to a high standard.

Required

(i)   Calculate the value at which the hotels would be included in the group financial statements of Gold Co on the following dates.

(1)   At 30 November 20X3 and 30 November 20X7.
(2)   At 30 November 20X7 after adjusting for current price levels.   **(4 marks)**

(ii) Discuss the results of the valuations of the hotels, commenting on the validity of the different bases outlined above.   **(4 marks)**

(Total = 25 marks)

D16 Question with helping hands: Zetec

45 mins

ACR, 12/01

Zetec, a public limited company, owns 80% of the ordinary share capital of Aztec, a public limited company which is a foreign operation. Zetec acquired Aztec on 1 November 20X1 for $44 million when the retained earnings of Aztec were 98 million Krams (Kr). Aztec has not issued any share capital, nor revalued any assets since acquisition. The following financial statements relate to Zetec and Aztec.

BALANCE SHEET AT 31 OCTOBER 20X2

	Zetec $m	Aztec Kr'm
Non-current assets		
Tangible assets (including investments)	180	380
Investment in Aztec	44	
Intangible assets		12
Net current assets	146	116
	370	508
Capital and reserves		
Ordinary shares of $1/1Kr	65	48
Share premium	70	18
Revaluation surplus		12
Retained earnings	161	110
	296	188
Non-current liabilities	74	320
	370	508

INCOME STATEMENTS FOR THE YEAR ENDED 31 OCTOBER 20X2

	Zetec $m	Aztec Kr'm
Revenue	325	250
Cost of sales	(189)	(120)
Gross profit	136	130
Distribution and administrative expenses	(84)	(46)
Interest payable	(2)	(20)
Profit before taxation	50	64
Income tax expense	(15)	(30)
Profit on ordinary activities after taxation	35	34
Extraordinary items	–	(22)
Retained profit for the year	35	12

The directors of Zetec have not previously had the responsibility for the preparation of consolidated financial statements and are a little concerned as they understand that the financial statements of Aztec have been prepared under local accounting standards which are inconsistent in some respects with International Financial Reporting

Standards (IFRS). They wish you to prepare the consolidated financial statements on their behalf and give you the following information about the financial statements of Aztec.

(a)   Under local accounting standards, Aztec had capitalised 'market shares' under intangible assets. Aztec acquired a company in the year to 31 October 20X2 and merged its activities with its own. The acquisition allowed the company to obtain a significant share of a specific market and, therefore, the excess of the price paid over the fair value of assets is allocated to 'market shares'. The amount capitalised was Kr12 million and no amortisation is charged on 'market shares'.

Further, under local accounting standards, from 1 November 20X1 Aztec classified revaluation gains and losses and the effects of changes in accounting policies as extraordinary items. During the year, the amounts classified as extraordinary items were as follows:

Revaluation loss

A non-current asset was physically damaged during the year and an amount of Kr9 million was written off its carrying value as an impairment loss. This asset had been revalued on 31 October 20X0 and a credit of Kr6 million still remains in revaluation surplus in respect of this asset.

Changes in accounting policy

A change in the accounting policy for research expenditure has occurred during the period, in an attempt to bring Aztec's policies into line with IFRS. Prior to November 20X1, research expenditure was capitalised and amortised. The amount included in extraordinary items as a prior year adjustment was Kr13 million.

(b)   The fair value of the net assets of Aztec at the date of acquisition was Kr240 million after taking into account any changes necessary to align the financial statements with IFRS. The directors do not know how to calculate the amount of goodwill. The increase in the fair value of Aztec over the net assets' carrying value relates to a stock market portfolio (included in tangible assets) held by Aztec. The value of these investments (in Krs) has not changed materially since acquisition.

(c)   Zetec sold $15 million of components to Aztec and these goods were shipped free on board (fob) on 31 May 20X2. The goods were received by Aztec on 30 June 20X2 as there had been a problem in the shipping of the goods. Zetec made a profit of 20% on selling price on the components. All of the goods had been utilised in the production process at 31 October 20X1 but none of the finished goods had been sold at that date. Aztec had paid for the goods on 31 July 20X2. This was the only intragroup transaction in the year. Foreign exchange gains/losses on such transactions are included in cost of sales by Aztec.

(d)   The following exchange rates are relevant to the financial statements.

	Krams to the $
31 October 20X0	5
1 November 20X1	6
1 April 20X2	5.3
31 May 20X2	5.2
30 June 20X2	5.1
31 July 20X2	4.2
31 October 20X2	4
Weighted average for year to 31 October 20X2	5

(e)   A dividend of $4 million has been paid by Zetec during the financial year.

Required

Prepare a consolidated income statement for the year ended 31 October 20X2 and a balance sheet as at that date for the Zetec group.

(Candidates should show any exchange gains or losses arising in the consolidated financial statements.)

(25 marks)

Helping hands

1   Learn our format for translation of the income statement and balance sheet.

2   It is best to do workings for property, plant and equipment and net current assets on the face of the I/S and balance sheet with reference to supporting workings where appropriate.

3   Remember that goodwill is translated at the closing rate, which means that there will be an exchange difference. The best and neatest way to calculate this difference is to set out your goodwill working as we have done.

D17 Memo

45 mins

ACR, 6/04

Memo, a public limited company, owns 75% of the ordinary share capital of Random, a public limited company which is situated in a foreign country. Memo acquired Random on 1 May 20X3 for 120 million crowns (CR) when the retained profits of Random were 80 million crowns. Random has not revalued its assets or issued any share capital since its acquisition by Memo. The following financial statements relate to Memo and Random:

BALANCE SHEETS AT 30 APRIL 20X4

	Memo $m	Random CRm
Property, plant and equipment	297	146
Investment in Random	48	–
Loan to Random	5	–
Current assets	355	102
	705	248
Equity		
Ordinary shares of $1/1CR	60	32
Share premium account	50	20
Retained earnings	360	95
	470	147
Non current liabilities	30	41
Current liabilities	205	60
	705	248

INCOME STATEMENTS FOR YEAR ENDED 30 APRIL 20X4

	Memo $	Random CRm
Revenue	200	142
Cost of sales	(120)	(96)
Gross profit	80	46
Distribution and administrative expenses	(30)	(20)
Profit from operations	50	26
Interest receivable	4	–
Interest payable	–	(2)
Profit before taxation	54	24
Income tax expense	(20)	(9)
Profit after taxation	34	15

The following information is relevant to the preparation of the consolidated financial statements of Memo.

(a)   Goodwill is reviewed for impairment annually. At 30 April 20X4, the impairment loss on recognised goodwill was Kr4.2m.

(b) During the financial year Random has purchased raw materials from Memo and denominated the purchase in crowns in its financial records. The details of the transaction are set out below:

	Date of transaction	Purchase price $m	Profit percentage on selling price
Raw materials	1 February 20X4	6	20%

At the year end, half of the raw materials purchased were still in the inventory of Random. The intragroup transactions have not been eliminated from the financial statements and the goods were recorded by Random at the exchange rate ruling on 1 February 20X4. A payment of $6 million was made to Memo when the exchange rate was 2·2 crowns to $1. Any exchange gain or loss arising on the transaction is still held in the current liabilities of Random.

(c) Memo had made an interest free loan to Random of $5 million on 1 May 20X3. The loan was repaid on 30 May 20X4. Random had included the loan in non-current liabilities and had recorded it at the exchange rate at 1 May 20X3.

(d) The fair value of the net assets of Random at the date of acquisition is to be assumed to be the same as the carrying value.

(e) The functional currency of Random is the Crown.

(f) The following exchange rates are relevant to the financial statements:

	Crowns to $
30 April/1 May 20X3	2·5
1 November 20X3	2·6
1 February 20X4	2
30 April 20X4	2·1
Average rate for year to 30 April 20X4	2

(g) Memo has paid a dividend of $8 million during the financial year and this is not included in the income statement.

Required

Prepare a consolidated income statement for the year ended 30 April 20X4 and a consolidated balance sheet at that date in accordance with International Financial Reporting Standards.

(Candidates should round their calculations to the nearest $100,000.)   **(25 marks)**

D18 Preparation question: Cash flow statement

The summarised financial statements of Charmer for the year to 30 September 20X1, together with a comparative balance sheet, are as follows.

INCOME STATEMENT

	$'000
Revenue	7,482
Cost of sales	(4,284)
Gross profit	3,198
Operating expenses	(1,479)
Interest payable	(260)
Investment income	120
Profit before tax	1,579
Income tax expense	(520)
Profit for the period	1,059

BPP LEARNING MEDIA

BALANCE SHEET AS AT:

	30 September 20X1			30 September 20X0		
	Cost/ valuation $'000	Depreciation $'000	NBV $'000	Cost/ valuation $'000	Depreciation $'000	NBV $'000
Assets						
Non-current assets						
Property, plant and equipment	3,568	1,224	2,344	3,020	1,112	1,908
Investment			690			nil
			3,034			1,908
Current assets						
Inventories			1,046			785
Trade receivables			935			824
Short term treasury bills			120			50
Bank			nil			122
			2,101			1,781
Total assets			5,135			3,689
Equity and liabilities						
Equity						
Ordinary shares of $1 each			1,400			1,000
Share premium			460			60
Revaluation surplus			90			40
Equity component of 10% convertible loan stock			nil			20
Retained earnings						
Retained earnings b/d		192			177	
Profit for period		1,059			65	
Dividends paid		(180)			(50)	
Retained earnings c/d			1,071			192
			3,021			1,312
Non-current liabilities						
Deferred tax liability			439			400
Government grants			275			200
10% convertible loan stock			nil			380
			714			980
Current liabilities						
Trade payables			644			760
Interest payable			40			25
Provision for negligence claim			nil			120
Current tax payable			480			367
Government grants			100			125
Overdraft			136			nil
			1,400			1,397
Total equity and liabilities			5,135			3,689

The following information is relevant.

QUESTIONS

(a) *Non-current assets*

Property, plant and equipment is analysed as follows.

| | 30 September 20X1 | | | 30 September 20X0 | | |
	Cost/ valuation $'000	Depreciation $'000	NBV $'000	Cost/ valuation $'000	Depreciation $'000	NBV $'000
Land and buildings	2,000	760	1,240	1,800	680	1,120
Plant	1,568	464	1,104	1,220	432	788
	3,568	1,224	2,344	3,020	1,112	1,908

On 1 October 20X0 Charmer recorded an increase in the value of its land of $150,000.

During the year an item of plant that had cost $500,000 and had accumulated depreciation of $244,000 was sold at a loss (included in cost of sales) of $86,000 on its carrying value.

(b) *Government grant*

A credit of $125,000 for the current year's amortisation of government grants has been included in cost of sales.

(c) *Share capital and loan stock*

The increase in the share capital during the year was due to the following events.

(i) On 1 January 20X1 there was a bonus issue (out of the revaluation reserve) of one bonus share for every 10 shares held.

(ii) On 1 April 20X1 the 10% convertible loan stock holders exercised their right to convert to ordinary shares. The terms of conversion were 25 ordinary shares of $1 each for each $100 of 10% convertible loan stock.

(iii) The remaining increase in the ordinary shares was due to a stock market placement of shares for cash on 12 August 20X1.

(d) *Dividends*

The directors of Charmer always declare a final dividend (if the company has made a profit) in the week following the company's year end. It is paid after the annual general meeting of the shareholders.

(e) *Provision for negligence claim*

In June 20X1 Charmer made an out of court settlement of a negligence claim brought about by a former employee. The dispute had been in progress for two years and Charmer had made provisions for the potential liability in each of the two previous years. The unprovided amount of the claim at the time of settlement was $30,000 and this was charged to operating expenses.

(f) *Short term treasury bills*

The treasury bills mature on 31 July 20X2.

Required

Prepare a cash flow statement for Charmer for the year to 30 September 20X1 in accordance with IAS 7 Cash Flow Statements using the indirect method.

Notes to the cash flow statement are not required.

BPP
LEARNING MEDIA

D19 Preparation question: Consolidated cash flow statement

On 1.9.20X5 Swing Co acquired 70% of Slide Co for $5,000,000 comprising $1,000,000 cash and 1,500,000 $1 shares.

The balance sheet of Slide Co at acquisition was as follows:

	$'000
Property, plant and equipment	2,700
Inventories	1,600
Trade receivables	600
Cash	400
Trade payables	(300)
Income tax payable	(200)
	4,800

The consolidated balance sheet of Swing Co as at 31 December 20X5 was as follows:

	20X5	20X4
Non-current assets	$'000	$'000
Property, plant and equipment	35,000	25,000
Goodwill	1,400	–
	36,400	25,000
Current assets		
Inventories	16,000	10,000
Trade receivables	9,800	7,500
Cash	2,400	1,500
	28,200	19,000
	64,600	44,000
Equity attributable to equity holders of the parent		
Share capital	12,300	10,000
Share premium	5,800	2,000
Retained earnings	32,100	21,900
	50,200	33,900
Minority interest	1,600	–
	51,800	33,900
Current liabilities		
Trade payables	7,600	6,100
Income tax payable	5,200	4,000
	12,800	10,100
	64,600	44,000

The consolidated income statement of Swing Co for the year ended 31 December 20X5 was as follows:

	20X5
	$'000
Profit before tax	16,500
Income tax expense	(5,200)
Profit for the period	11,300
Attributable to:	
Equity holders of the parent	11,100
Minority interest	200
	11,300

Notes:

1   Depreciation charged for the year was $5,800,000. The group made no disposals of property, plant and equipment.

2   Dividends paid by Swing Co amounted to $900,000.

Required

Prepare the consolidated cash flow statement of Swing Co for the year ended 31 December 20X5. Only the note relating to the acquisition of the subsidiary is required.

D20 Portal

45 mins

ACR, Pilot Paper

Portal Group, a public limited company, has prepared the following group cash flow statement for the year ended 31 December 20X0.

PORTAL GROUP
GROUP STATEMENT OF CASH FLOWS
FOR THE YEAR ENDED 31 DECEMBER 20X0 (DRAFT)

	$m	$m
Cash generated from operations		875
Interest paid	(9)	
Income taxes paid	31	22
Net cash from operating activities		897
Cash flows from investing activities		
Disposal of subsidiary	(25)	
Purchase of property, plant and equipment	(380)	
Disposal and transfer of property, plant and equipment at carrying value	1,585	
Purchase of interest in joint venture	(225)	
Interest received	26	
Net cash used in investing activities		981
Cash flows from financing activities		
Increase in short term deposits	(143)	
Minority interest	(40)	
Net cash used in financing activities		(183)
Net increase in cash and cash equivalents		1,695

The accountant has asked your advice on certain technical matters relating to the preparation of the group cash flow statement. Additionally the accountant has asked you to prepare a presentation for the directors on the usefulness and meaning of cash flow statements generally and specifically on the group cash flow statements of Portal.

The accountant has informed you that the actual change in cash and cash equivalents for the period is $185 million, which does not reconcile with the figure in the draft group cash flow statement above of $1,695 million. The figures for cash and cash equivalents were $600 million at 1 January 20X0 and $785 million at 31 December 20X0.

The accountant feels that the reasons for the difference are the incorrect treatment of several elements of the cash flow statement of which he has little technical knowledge. The following information relates to these elements:

(a)   Portal has disposed of a subsidiary company, Web, during the year. At the date of disposal (1 June 20X0) the following balance sheet was prepared for Web:

		$m	$m
Property, plant and equipment:	valuation		340
	depreciation		(30)
			310
Inventory		60	
Trade receivables		50	
Cash		130	
			240
			550
Share capital			100
Retained earnings			320
			420
Current liabilities (including taxation $25 million)			130
			550

The loss on the sale of the subsidiary in the group accounts comprised:

		$m
Sale proceeds:	ordinary shares	300
	cash	75
		375
Net assets sold (80% of 420)		(336)
Goodwill		(64)
Loss on sale		(25)

The accountant was unsure as to how to deal with the above disposal and has simply included the above loss in the cash flow statement without any further adjustments.

(b) During the year, Portal has transferred several of its items of property, plant and equipment to a newly created company, Site, which is owned jointly with another company.

The following information related to the accounting for the investment in Site:

		$m
Purchase cost:	property, plant and equipment transferred	200
	cash	25
		225
Dividend received		(10)
Profit for year on joint venture after tax		55
Revaluation of property, plant and equipment		30
Closing balance per balance sheet – Site		300

The cash flow statement showed the cost of purchasing a stake in Site of $225 million. Site is accounted for using the equity accounting approach rather than by proportional consolidation.

(c) The taxation amount in the cash flow statement is the difference between the opening and closing balances on the taxation account. The charge for taxation in the income statement is $171.

(d) Included in the cash flow figure for the disposal of property, plant and equipment is the sale and leaseback, on an operating basis, of certain land and buildings. The sale proceeds of the land and buildings were $1,000 million in the form of an 8% loan note receivable by Portal in 20X2. The total profit on the sale of tangible non-current assets, including the land and buildings, was $120 million.

(e) The minority interest figure in the statement comprised the difference between the opening and closing balance sheet totals. The profit attributable to the minority interest for the year was $75 million.

(f) The cash generated from operations is the profit before taxation adjusted for the balance sheet movement in inventory, trade receivables and current liabilities and the depreciation charge for the year. The interest receivable credited to the income statement was $27 million and the interest payable was $19 million.

Required

(a) Prepare a revised group cash flow statement for Portal, taking into account notes (a) to (f) above, and using the format set out in the question. **(18 marks)**

(b) Prepare a brief presentation on the usefulness and information content of group cash flow statements generally and specifically on the group cash flow statement of Portal. **(7 marks)**

(Total = 25 marks)

D21 Cash study question: Andash

90 mins

(a) The following draft group financial statements relate to Andash, a public limited company.

ANDASH
DRAFT GROUP BALANCE SHEETS AS AT

	20X6 $m	20X5 $m
Assets		
Non-current assets		
Property, plant and equipment	5,170	4,110
Goodwill	120	130
Investment in associate	60	–
	5,350	4,240
Current assets		
Inventories	2,650	2,300
Trade receivables	2,400	1,500
Cash and cash equivalents	140	300
	5,190	4,100
Total assets	10,540	8,340
Equity and liabilities		
Equity attributable to equity holders of parent		
Share capital	400	370
Other reserves	120	80
Retained earnings	1,250	1,100
	1,770	1,550
Minority interest	200	180
Total equity	1,970	1,730
Non-current liabilities		
Long term borrowings	3,100	2,700
Deferred tax	400	300
Total non-current liabilities	3,500	3,000
Current liabilities		
Trade payables	4,700	2,800
Interest payable	70	40
Current tax payable	300	770
Total current liabilities	5,070	3,610
Total liabilities	8,570	6,610
Total equity and liabilities	10,540	8,340

BPP
LEARNING MEDIA

ANDASH
DRAFT GROUP INCOME STATEMENT FOR THE YEAR ENDED 31 OCTOBER 20X6

	$m
Revenue	17,500
Cost of sales	(14,600)
Gross profit	2,900
Distribution costs	(1,870)
Administrative expenses	(490)
Finance costs – interest payable	(148)
Gain on disposal of subsidiary	8
Profit before tax	400
Income tax expense	(160)
Profit after tax	240
Attributable to equity holders of parent	200
Attributable to minority interest	40
	240

ANDASH
DRAFT STATEMENT OF CHANGES IN EQUITY OF THE PARENT FOR THE YEAR ENDED 31 OCTOBER 20X6

	Share capital $m	Other reserves $m	Retained earnings $m	Total $m
Balance at 31 October 20X5	370	80	1,100	1,550
Profit for period			200	200
Dividends			(50)	(50)
Issue of share capital	30	30		60
Share options issued		10		10
Balance at 31 October 20X6	400	120	1,250	1,770

The following information relates to the draft group financial statements of Andash.

(i)   There had been no disposal of property, plant and equipment during the year. The depreciation for the period included in cost of sales was $260 million. Andash had issued share options on 31 October 20X6 as consideration for the purchase of plant. The value of the plant purchased was $9 million at 31 October 20X6 and the share options issued had a market value of $10 million. The market value had been used to account for the plant and share options.

(ii)   Andash had acquired 25 per cent of Joma on 1 November 20X5. The purchase consideration was 25 million ordinary shares of Andash valued at $50 million and cash of $10 million. Andash has significant influence over Joma. The investment is stated at cost in the draft group balance sheet. The reserves of Joma at the date of acquisition were $20 million and at 31 October 20X6 were $32 million. Joma had sold inventory in the period to Andash at a selling price of $16 million. The cost of the inventory was $8 million and the inventory was still held by Andash at 31 October 20X6. there was no goodwill arising on the acquisition of Joma.

(iii)   Andash owns 60% of a subsidiary Broiler, a public limited company. The goodwill arising on acquisition was $90 million. The carrying value of Broiler's identifiable net assets (excluding goodwill arising on acquisition) in the group consolidated financial statements is $240 million at 31 October 20X6. The recoverable amount of Broiler is expected to be $260 million and no impairment loss has been recorded up to 31 October 20X5.

(iv)   On 30 April 20X6 a wholly owned subsidiary, Chang was disposed of Chang prepared interim financial statements on that date which are as follows:

	$m
Property, plant and equipment	10
Inventories	8
Trade receivables	4
Cash and cash equivalents	5
	27

Share capital	10
Retained earnings	4
Trade payables	6
Current tax payable	7
	27

The consolidated carrying values of the assets and liabilities at that date were the same as above. The group received cash proceeds of $32 million and the carrying amount of goodwill was $10 million.

(Ignore the taxation effects of any adjustments required to the group financial statements and round all calculations to the nearest $million.)

BPP note: Assume no dividend was paid by Joma during the period.

Required

Prepare a group cash flow statement using the indirect method for the Andash Group for the year ended 31 October 20X6 in accordance with IAS 7 *Cash flow statements* after making any necessary adjustments required to the draft group financial statements of Andash as a result of the information above.

(Candidates are not required to produce the adjusted group financial statements of Andash.)   **(25 marks)**

(b)   Andash manufactures mining equipment and extracts natural gas. You are advising the directors on matters relating to the year ended 31 October 20X7.

The directors are uncertain about the role of the IASB's *Framework for the Preparation and Presentation of Financial Statements* (the *Framework*) in corporate reporting. Their view is that accounting is based on the transactions carried out by the company and these transactions are allocated to the company's accounting periods by using the matching and prudence concepts. The argument put forward by the directors is that the *Framework* does not take into account the business and legal constraints within which companies operate. Further they have given two situations which have arisen in the current financial statements where they feel that the current accounting practice is inconsistent with the *Framework*.

Situation 1

Andash has recently constructed a natural gas extraction facility and commenced production one year ago (1 November 20X6). There is an operating licence given to the company by the government which requires the removal of the facility and rectification of the damage caused by extraction of natural gas at the end of its life, which is estimated at 20 years. Depreciation is charged on the straight line basis. The cost of the construction of the facility was $200 million and the net present value at 1 November 20X6 of the future costs to be incurred in order to return the extraction site to its original condition are estimated at $50 million (using a discount rate of 5% per annum). 80 per cent of these costs relate to the removal of the facility and 20% relate to the rectification of the damage caused through the extraction of the natural gas. The auditors have told the company that a provision for decommissioning has to be set up.

Situation 2

Andash purchased a building on 1 November 20X6 for $10 million. The building qualified for a grant of $2 million which has been treated as a deferred credit in the financial statements. The tax allowances are reduced by the amount of the grant. There are additional temporary differences of $40 million in respect of deferred tax liabilities at the year end. Also the company has sold extraction equipment which carries a five year warranty. The directors have made a provision for the warranty of $4 million at 31 October 20X7 which is deductible for tax when costs are incurred under the warranty. In addition to the warranty provision the company has unused tax losses of $70 million. The directors of the company are unsure as to whether a deferred tax liability is required.

(Assume that the depreciation of the building is straight line over ten years, and tax allowances of 25% on the reducing balance basis can be claimed on the building. Tax is payable at 30%.)

Required

(i) Explain the importance of the *Framework* to the reporting of corporate performance and whether it takes into account the business and legal constraints placed upon companies. **(6 marks)**

(ii) Explain with reasons and suitable extracts/computations the accounting treatment of the above two situations in the financial statements for the year ended 31 October 20X7. **(14 marks)**

(iii) Discuss whether the treatment of the items in the situations above appears consistent with the *Framework*. **(5 marks)**

(Total = 50 marks)

D22 Case study question: Squire   90 mins

(a) The following draft financial statements relate to Squire, a public limited company.

SQUIRE
DRAFT GROUP BALANCE SHEET
AT 31 MAY 20X2

	20X2 $m	20X1 $m
Non-current assets		
Property, plant and equipment	2,630	2,010
Intangible assets	105	65
Investment in associate	535	550
	3,270	2,625
Retirement benefit asset	22	16
Current assets		
Inventories	1,300	1,160
Trade receivables	1,220	1,060
Cash at bank and in hand	90	280
	2,610	2,500
Total assets	5,902	5,141
Equity attributable to equity holders of the parent		
Share capital	200	170
Share premium account	60	30
Revaluation surplus	92	286
Retained earnings	533	505
	885	991
Minority interest	522	345
Total equity	1,407	1,336
Non-current liabilities	1,675	1,320
Deferred tax liability	200	175
Current liabilities	2,620	2,310
Total liabilities	4,495	3,805
Total equity and liabilities	5,902	5,141

SQUIRE
DRAFT GROUP INCOME STATEMENT
FOR THE YEAR ENDED 31 MAY 20X2

	$m
Revenue	8,774
Cost of sales	(7,310)
	1,464
Distribution and administrative expenses	(1,005)
Exchange difference on payment for purchase of non-current assets	(9)
Finance costs	(75)
Share of profit of associate	45
Profit before tax	420
Income tax expense	(205)
Profit for the period	215

	$m
Attributable to	
Equity holders of the parent	123
Minority interests	92
	215

SQUIRE
DRAFT GROUP STATEMENT OF CHANGES IN EQUITY
FOR THE YEAR ENDED 31 MAY 20X2

	$m
Balance at 1 June 20X1	1,336
Foreign exchange difference of associate	(10)
Impairment losses on non-current assets offset against revaluation surplus	(194)
Net income recognised directly in equity	(204)
Profit for the period	215
Minority interest acquired on acquisition of subsidiary	90
Total recognised income and expenses for the period	101
Dividends (parent and minority interest)	(90)
Issue of share capital	60
Balance at 31 May 20X2 carried forward	1,407

The following information relates to Squire.

(i)   Squire acquired a seventy per cent holding in Hunsten Holdings, a public limited company, on 1 June 20X1. The fair values of the net assets acquired were as follows.

	$m
Property, plant and equipment	150
Inventories and work in progress	180
Provisions for onerous contracts	(30)
	300

The purchase consideration was $200 million in cash and $50 million (discounted value) deferred consideration which is payable on 1 June 20X3. The provision for the onerous contracts was no longer required at 31 May 20X2 as Squire had paid compensation of $30 million in order to terminate the contact on 1 December 20X1. The intangible asset in the group balance sheet comprises goodwill only. The difference between the discounted value of the deferred consideration ($50m) and the amount payable ($54m) is included in 'finance costs'.

(ii)   There had been no disposals of property, plant and equipment during the year. Depreciation for the period charged in cost of sales was $129 million.

(iii)   Current liabilities comprised the following items.

	20X2	20X1
	$m	$m
Trade payables	2,355	2,105
Interest payable	65	45
Taxation	200	160
	2,620	2,310

(iv) Non-current liabilities comprised the following.

	20X2	20X1
	$m	$m
Deferred consideration – purchase of Hunsten	54	
Liability for the purchase of non-current assets	351	
Loans repayable	1,270	1,320
	1,675	1,320

(v) The retirement benefit asset comprised the following.

	$m
Movement in year:	
Surplus at 1 June 20X1	16
Current and past service costs charged to income statement	(20)
Contributions paid to retirement benefit scheme	26
Surplus at 31 May 20X2	22

Required

Prepare a group cash flow statement using the indirect method for Squire group for the year ended 31 May 20X2 in accordance with IAS 7 *Cash flow statements*.

The note regarding the acquisition of the subsidiary is not required. **(27 marks)**

You have been asked to conduct an environmental audit for the Squire Group to assess how 'green' it is in terms of energy consumption, use of renewable resources, and employee awareness of these issues.

(b) Describe the information you would seek when planning the audit. **(8 marks)**

(c) Explain how would you test for employee awareness, and how would you involve all employees in the initiative. **(6 marks)**

(d) Discuss the reasons why companies wish to disclose environmental information in their financial statements. Discuss whether the content of such disclosure should be at the company's discretion.

(9 marks)
(Total = 50 marks)

> **SPECIALISED ENTITIES**
>
> Questions E1 and E2 cover Regulatory and Ethical Framework, the subject of Part E of the BPP Study Text for Paper P2.

E1 IFRSs and SMEs

45 mins

`ACR, 6/06`

International Financial Reporting Standards (IFRSs) are primarily designed for use by publicly listed companies and in many countries the majority of companies using IFRSs are listed companies. In other countries IFRSs are used as national Generally Accepted Accounting Practices (GAAP) for all companies including unlisted entities. It has been argued that the same IFRSs should be used by all entities or alternatively a different body of standards should apply to small and medium entities (SMEs).

Required

(a)   Discuss whether there is a need to develop a set of IFRSs specifically for SMEs.   **(7 marks)**

(b)   Discuss the nature of the following issues in developing IFRSs for SMEs.

     (i)   The purpose of the standards and the type of entity to which they should apply.   **(7 marks)**

     (ii)   How existing standards could be modified to meet the needs of SMEs.   **(6 marks)**

     (iii)   How items not dealt with by an IFRS for SMEs should be treated.   **(5 marks)**

(Total = 25 marks)

E2 Seejoy

`ACR, 12/06`

Seejoy is a famous football club but has significant cash flow problems. The directors and shareholders wish to take steps to improve the club's financial position. The following proposals had been drafted in an attempt to improve the cash flow of the club. However, the directors need advice upon their implications.

(a)   **Sale and leaseback of football stadium (excluding the land element)**

The football stadium is currently accounted for using the cost model in IAS 16 *Property, plant and equipment*. The carrying value of the stadium will be $12 million at 31 December 20X6. The stadium will have a remaining life of 20 years at 31 December 20X6, and the club uses straight line depreciation. It is proposed to sell the stadium to a third party institution on 1 January 20X7 and lease it back under a 20 year finance lease. The sale price and fair value are $15 million which is the present value of the minimum lease payments. The agreement transfers the title of the stadium back to the football club at the end of the lease at nil cost. The rental is $1.2 million per annum in advance commencing on 1 January 20X7. The directors do not wish to treat this transaction as the raising of a secured loan. The implicit interest rate on the finance in the lease is 5.6%.   **(9 marks)**

(b)   **Player registrations**

The club capitalises the unconditional amounts (transfer fees) paid to acquire players.

The club proposes to amortise the cost of the transfer fees over ten years instead of the current practice which is to amortise the cost over the duration of the player's contract. The club has sold most of its valuable players during the current financial year but still has two valuable players under contract.

Player	Transfer fee capitalised $m	Amortisation to 31 December 20X6 $m	Contract commenced	Contract expires
A Steel	20	4	1 January 20X6	31 December 20Y0
R Aldo	15	10	1 January 20X5	31 December 20X7

If Seejoy win the national football league, then a further $5 million will be payable to the two players' former clubs. Seejoy are currently performing very poorly in the league. **(5 marks)**

(c) **Issue of bond**

The club proposes to issue a 7% bond with a face value of $50 million on 1 January 20X7 at a discount of 5% that will be secured on income from future ticket sales and corporate hospitality receipts, which are approximately $20 million per annum. Under the agreement the club cannot use the first $6 million received from corporate hospitality sales and reserved tickets (season tickets) as this will be used to repay the bond. The money from the bond will be used to pay for ground improvements and to pay wages to players.

The bond will be repayable, both capital and interest, over 15 years with the first payment of $6 million due on 31 December 20X7. it has an effective interest rate of 7.7%. There will be no active market for the bond and the company does not wish to use valuation models to value the bond. **(6 marks)**

(d) **Player trading**

Another proposal is for the club to sell its two valuable players, Aldo and Steel. It is thought that it will receive a total of $16 million for both players. The players are to be offered for sale at the end of the current football season on 1 May 20X7. **(5 marks)**

Required

Discuss how the above proposals would be dealt with in the financial statement of Seejoy for the year ending 31 December 20X7, setting out their accounting treatment and appropriateness in helping the football club's cash flow problems.

(Candidates do not need knowledge of the football finance sector to answer this question.)

(Total = 25 marks)

EVALUATING CURRENT DEVELOPMENTS

Questions F1 and F2 cover Evaluating Current Developments, the subject of Part F of the BPP Study Text for Paper P2.

F1 Handrew

45 mins

`ACR, 6/05`

Handrew, a public limited company, is adopting International Financial Reporting Standards (IFRS) in its financial statements for the year ended 31 May 20X5. The directors of the company are worried about the effect of the move to IFRS on their financial performance and the views of analysts. The directors have highlighted some 'headline' differences between IFRS and their current local equivalent standards and require a report on the impact of a move to IFRS on the key financial ratios for the current period.

Differences between local Generally Accepted Accounting Practice (GAAP) and IFRS

Leases

Local GAAP does not require property leases to be separated into land and building components. Long-term property leases are accounted for as operating leases in the financial statements of Handrew under local GAAP. Under the terms of the contract, the title to the land does not pass to Handrew but the title to the building passes to the company.

The company has produced a schedule of future minimum operating lease rentals and allocated these rentals between land and buildings based on their relative fair value at the start of the lease period. The operating leases commenced on 1 June 20X4 when the value of the land was $270 million and the building was $90 million. Annual operating lease rentals paid in arrears commencing on 31 May 20X5 are land $30 million and buildings $10 million. These amounts are payable for the first five years of the lease term after which the payments diminish. The minimum lease term is 40 years.

The net present value of the future minimum operating lease payments as at 1 June 20X4 was land $198 million and buildings $86 million. The interest rate used for discounting cash flows is 6%. Buildings are depreciated on a straight line basis over 20 years and at the end of this period, the building's economic life will be over. The lessor intends to redevelop the land at some stage in the future. Assume that the tax allowances on buildings are given to the lessee on the same basis as the depreciation charge based on the net present value at the start of the lease, and that operating lease payments are fully allowable for taxation.

Plant and equipment

Local GAAP requires the residual value of a non-current asset to be determined at the date of acquisition or latest valuation. The residual value of much of the plant and equipment is deemed to be negligible. However, certain plant (cost $20 million and carrying value $16 million at 31 May 20X5) has a high residual value. At the time of purchasing this plant (June 20X3), the residual value was thought to be approximately $4 million. However the value of an item of an identical piece of plant already of the age and in the condition expected at the end of its useful life is $8 million at 31 May 20X5 ($11 million at 1 June 20X4). Plant is depreciated on a straight line basis over eight years.

Investment properties

Local GAAP requires investment property to be measured at market value and gains and losses reported in equity. The company owns a hotel which consists of land and buildings and it has been designated as an investment property. The property was purchased on 1 June 20X4. The hotel has been included in the balance sheet at 31 May 20X5 at its market value on an existing use basis at $40 million (land valuation $30 million, building $10 million). A revaluation gain of $5 million has been recognised in equity. The company could sell the land for redevelopment for $50 million although it has no intention of doing so at the present time. The company wants to recognise holding

 BPP LEARNING MEDIA

gains/losses in profit and loss. Local GAAP does not require deferred tax to be provided on revaluation gains and losses.

The directors have calculated the following ratios based on the local GAAP financial statements for the year ended 31 May 20X5.

Return on capital employed

$$\frac{\text{Profit before interest and tax}}{\text{Share capital, reserves and non - current liabilities}} \quad \frac{\$130m}{\$520m} \times 100\% \text{ ie } 25\%$$

Gearing ratio

$$\frac{\text{Non - current liabilities}}{\text{Share capital and reserves}} \quad \frac{\$40m}{\$480m} \times 100\% \text{ ie } 8.3\%$$

Price Earnings ratio

$$\frac{\text{Market price per share}}{\text{Earnings per share}} \quad \frac{\$6 \text{ per share}}{\$0.5 \text{ per share}} \text{ ie } 12$$

The issued share capital of Handrew is 200 million ordinary shares of $1. There is no preference capital. The interest charge and tax charge in the income statement are $5 million and $25 million respectively. Interest and rental payments attract tax allowances in this jurisdiction when paid. Assume taxation is 30%.

Required

Write a report to the directors of Handrew:

(a) Discussing the impact of the change to IFRS on the reported profit and balance sheet of Handrew at 31 May 2005. **(18 marks)**

(b) Calculate and briefly discuss the impact of the change to IFRS on the three performance ratios. **(7 marks)**

(Candidates should show in an appendix calculations of the impact of the move to IFRS on profits, taxation and the balance sheet. Candidates should not take into account IFRS 1 *First time adoption of International Financial Reporting Standards* when answering this question.)

(Total = 25 marks)

F2 Guide

ACR, 12/04

Guide, a public limited company, is a leading international provider of insurance and banking services. It currently prepares its financial statements using a National GAAP which is not based upon International Financial Reporting Standards. It is concerned about the impact of the change to International Financial Reporting Standards (IFRS) which is required by local legislation.

The company is particularly worried about the impact of IFRS in the following areas.

(a) The practical factors it will need to consider in implementing the change to IFRS **(10 marks)**
(b) Debt covenants **(5 marks)**
(c) Performance related pay **(5 marks)**
(d) The views of financial analysts **(5 marks)**

Required

Draft a report to the directors of Guide setting out your views and advice on the potential impact in each of the above four areas of a move to reporting under International Financial Reporting Standards. **(Total = 25 marks)**

Answers

BPP LEARNING MEDIA

A1 Barriers to ethical standards

> **Top tips.** This question requires thought; the important elements of the answer are the problems of coming up with a clear definition, how much cultural factors should be allowed to influence ethical thinking and the need for the ethical framework to be more than a superficial gloss. The compatibility of ethical and commercial concerns is also an important issue to raise.

(a) **Problems with ethical framework**

Over the past few years the topic of business ethics has been examined and debated by many writers and academics. Although many organisation world-wide have adopted or redefined their business with ethics in mind, there are many people both in business and who study the area who see many barriers to businesses implementing an ethical framework.

What constitutes ethics

Defining 'what we mean by ethics' is for the most part easy to understand (inappropriate gifts, accepting money, environmental protection are all ethical issues). More **contentious issues** are topics such as workplace safety, product safety standards, advertising content and whistle-blowing which are areas where some businesses have been considered less ethical.

Necessity for action

Actions speak **louder than words.** Ethics are guidelines or rules of conduct by which we aim to live by. It is the actual conduct of the people in the organisation that, collectively, determines the organisation's standards – in other words it is not what the organisations 'says', but rather what it 'does' which is the real issue. It is no good having a code of ethics that is communicated to the outside world, but is ignored and treated with disdain by those inside the organisation.

Varying cultures

Globalisation and the resultant need to operate within different ethical frameworks has **undermined the idea** that ethical guidance can be defined in simple absolute terms. It may be culturally acceptable to promote by merit in one country, or by seniority in another. Paying custom officials may be acceptable in some cultures, but taboo in others.

Ethical versus commercial interests

Ethical and commercial interests have, it is argued, always diverged to some extent. Some organisations have seen for example the issues of **'being seen to be ethical'** as a good business move. However this viewpoint is pragmatic rather than idealistic; being ethical is seen as a means towards the end of gaining a better reputation and hence increasing sales.

Policies of others

Modern commercialism places great demands on everyone in organisations to succeed and provide the necessary revenues for the future growth and survival of the business. Acting with social responsibility can be hard, as not everyone plays by the same rules.

(b) **Need for practical steps**

If organisations are to **achieve a more ethical stance** they **need to put into place a range of practical steps** that will achieve this. Developing an ethical culture within the business will require the organisation to communicate to its workforce the 'rules' on what is considered to be ethical and is not. Two approaches have been identified to the management of ethics in organisations.

Rules-based approach

This is primarily designed to ensure that the organisation acts within the letter of the law, and that violations are **prevented, detected and punished.** This is very much the case in the US, where legal compliance is very much part of the business environment. The problem here is that legislation alone will not have the desired effect, particularly for those businesses who operate internationally and therefore may not be subject to equivalent legislation in other jurisdictions.

Integrity-based programmes

Here the concern is not for any legal control, but with developing an **organisational culture.** The task of ethics management is to define and give life to an organisation's **defining values** and to create an environment that supports ethical behaviour and to instil a sense of **shared accountability** among all employees. Integrity-based programmes require not just words or statements, but on seeing and doing and action. The purpose with this approach is not to exact revenge through legal compliance but the develop within the workforce a **culture of ethics** that has **value and meaning** for those in it.

The integrity-based approach encompasses all aspects of the business – **behavioural assumptions** of what is right or is wrong; staffing, education and training, audits and activities that promote a social responsibility across the workforce.

Organisations can also take further steps to reinforce their values by adopting **ethical committees** who are appointed to rule on misconduct and to develop ethical standards for the business.

Kohlberg's framework

Kohlberg's ethical framework demonstrates how individuals advance through different levels of moral development, their advance relating to how their **moral reasoning develops.** Kohlberg's framework goes from individuals who see ethical decisions solely in terms of the good or bad consequences for themselves through to individuals who choose to follow universal ethical principles, even if these conflict with the values of the organisation for which they are working.

The importance of different components of an organisation's ethical framework can indicate the level of moral reasoning that staff are in effect expected to employ.

Pre-conventional reasoning

A rules-based framework that sets out **expected behaviour** in detail and has strong provisions for punishing breaches implies that staff are at the lowest stage of development – they define right or wrong solely in terms of expected rewards or punishments. An emphasis on bureaucratic controls, including the reporting of all problems that occur with staff, would be designed to prevent 'You scratch my back, I scratch yours' behaviour that is also part of moral reasoning at this level.

Conventional reasoning

An emphasis on a **strong ethical culture** would indicate staff are expected to adopt the intermediate stage of Kohlberg's framework. **Peer pressure**, also the concepts that managers should set an **example**, are features of this sort of ethical approach; if also the organisation appears to be responding to **pressures from outside** to behave ethically, this suggests higher level reasoning within this stage

Post-conventional reasoning

An ethical approach based on staff using post-conventional reasoning would be likely to emphasise adherence to an ethical code. A detailed code based on rights and values of society would imply ethical reasoning based on the idea of the organisation **enforcing a social contract.** Higher-level reasoning would be expected if the code was framed in terms of more abstract principles such as justice or equality.

A2 Question with answer plan: Glowball

Top tips. This is a comprehensive question covering most aspects of environmental reporting that are likely to come up. Learn our answer and apply it to many questions on this topics

Answer plan

Current disclosures – mention

Current disclosures are voluntary

Guidelines and Codes of Practice – list a few especially the Global Reporting Initiative

Environmental events:

(a)   IAS 37.
        No legal obligation but may be a constructive obligation.

(b)   Set up as provision for fine.
        Put in context in the environmental report.

(c)   Emphasise accurate but fair reporting.
        No provision.

(d)   Environmental report to mention steps taken to rectify the problem.
        Provision must be made in full.

Marking scheme

			Marks
(a)	Current reporting requirements		10
(b)	Restoration		5
	Infringement of law		4
	Emissions		4
	Decommissioning activities		4
	Report		4
		Available	31
		Maximum	25

REPORT

To: The Directors
        Glowball

From: Ann Accountant

Date: 8 June 20X3

Environmental Reporting

Introduction

The purpose of this report is to provide information about current reporting requirements and guidelines on the subject of environmental reporting, and to give an indication of the required disclosure in relation to the specific events which you have brought to my attention. We hope that it will assist you in preparing your environmental report.

Current reporting requirements and guidelines

Most businesses have generally ignored environmental issues in the past. However, the use and **misuse** of **natural resources** all lead to environmental costs generated by businesses, both large and small.

There are very few rules, legal or otherwise, to ensure that companies disclose and report environmental matters. Any **disclosures tend to be voluntary**, unless environmental matters happen to fall under standard accounting principles. Environmental matters may be reported in the accounts of companies in the following areas.

*   Contingent liabilities
*   Exceptional charges
*   Operating and financial review comments/management discussion and analysis
*   Profit and capital expenditure focus

The **voluntary approach** contrasts with the position in the **United States**, where the **SEC/FASB accounting standards** are **obligatory**.

While nothing is compulsory, there are a number of **published guidelines** and **codes of practice**, including:

*   The Global Reporting Initiative
*   The Valdez Principles
*   The Confederation of British Industry's guideline *Introducing Environmental Reporting*
*   The ACCA's *Guide to Environment and Energy Reporting*
*   The Coalition of Environmentally Responsible Economies (CERES) formats for environmental reports
*   The Friends of the Earth *Environmental Charter for Local Government*
*   The Eco Management and Audit Scheme Code of Practice

The question arises as to verification of the environmental information presented. Companies who adopt the Eco Management and Audit Scheme must have the report validated by an external verifier. In June 1999, BP Amoco commissioned KPMG to conduct an independent audit of its greenhouse gas emissions in the first ever **environmental audit**.

Comments on 'environmental events'

(a)   Of relevance to the farmland restoration is IAS 37 *Provisions, contingent liabilities and contingent assets.* Provisions for environmental liabilities should be recognised where there is a **legal or constructive obligation** to rectify environmental damage or perform restorative work. The mere existence of the restorative work does not give rise to an obligation and there is no legal obligation. However, it could be argued that there is a constructive obligation arising from the company's approach in previous years, which may have given rise to an **expectation** that the work would be carried out. If this is the case, a provision of $150m would be required in the financial statements. In addition, this provision and specific examples of restoration of land could be included in the environmental report.

(b)   The treatment of the **fine** is straightforward: it is an obligation to transfer economic benefits. An estimate of the fine should be made and a **provision** set up in the financial statements for $5m. This should be mentioned in the environmental report. The report might also **put the fines in context** by stating how many tests have been carried out and how many times the company has passed the tests. The directors may feel that it would do the company's reputation no harm to point out the fact that the number of prosecutions has been falling from year to year.

(c)   These statistics are good news and need to be covered in the environmental report. However, the emphasis should be on **accurate factual reporting** rather than boasting. It might be useful to provide target levels for comparison, or an industry average if available. The emissions statistics should be split into three categories:

*   Acidity to air and water
*   Hazardous substances
*   Harmful emissions to water

As regards the aquatic emissions, the $70m planned expenditure on **research** should **be mentioned in the environmental report**. It shows a commitment to benefiting the environment. However, **IAS 37 would not permit a provision** to be made for this amount, since an obligation does not exist and the **expenditure is avoidable**. Nor does it qualify as development expenditure under IAS 38.

(d)   The environmental report should mention the steps the company is taking to minimise the harmful impact on the environment in the way it sites and constructs its gas installations. The report should also explain the policy of dismantling the installations rather than sinking them at the end of their useful life.

Currently the company builds up a provision for decommissioning costs over the life of the installation. However, IAS 37 does not allow this. Instead, the **full amount must be provided** as soon as there is an **obligation** arising as a result of **past events**, the **settlement** of which is **expected** to result in an **outflow of resources**. The obligation exists right at the beginning of the installation's life, and so the full $407m must be provided for. A corresponding asset is created.

B1 Prochain

Top tips. This question was a case study that dealt with the accounting issues for an entity engaged in the fashion industry. The areas examined were fundamental areas of the syllabus: non-current assets, intangible assets, determination of the purchase consideration for the subsidiary, and research and development expenditure. Tricky bits to get right were:

(a)   A provision for dismantling the 'model areas' would need to be set up and discounted back to the present.
(b)   Contingent consideration that is not probable would not be included in the cost of acquisition.
(c)   Investment properties do not include properties owned and occupied by the entity.

When discussing the development expenditure, the criteria for capitalisation may be remembered using the mnemonic PIRATE.

Easy marks. Stating the obvious – that the model areas are items of property, plant and equipment and need to be depreciated will earn you easy marks, as will mentioning the basic distinction between research and development expenditure and listing the criteria when talking about the brand.

Examiner's comment. Generally, candidates answered the question quite well, obtaining a pass mark, although accounting for the non-current assets did confuse some candidates.

Marking scheme

	Marks
Model areas	7
Purchase of Badex	8
Research and Development	6
Apartments	4
maximum/available	25

Model areas

IAS 16 *Property, plant and equipment* is the relevant standard here. The model areas are held for use in the supply of goods and are used in more than one accounting period. The company should recognise the costs of setting up the model areas as **tangible non-current assets** and should **depreciate** the costs over their useful lives. **Subsequent measurement should be based on cost**. In theory the company could measure the model areas at fair value if the revaluation model of IAS 16 was followed, but it would be difficult to measure their fair value reliably.

IAS 16 states that the initial cost of an asset **should include** the initial estimate of the **costs of dismantling and removing the item and restoring the site** where the entity has an obligation to do so. A **present obligation appears to exist**, as defined by IAS 37 *Provisions, contingent liabilities and contingent assets* and therefore the entity should also **recognise a provision** for that amount. The provision should be **discounted to its present value** and the unwinding of the discount recognised in the income statement.

At 31 May 20X6, the entity should recognise a non-current asset of $15.7 million (cost of $23.6 million (W) less accumulated depreciation of $7.9 million (W)) and a provision of $3.73 million (W).

Working

	$m
Cost of model areas	20.0
Plus provision ($20 \times 20\% \times \dfrac{1}{1.055^2}$ (= 0.898)	3.6
Cost on initial recognition	23.6
Less accumulated depreciation ($23.6 \times 8/24$)	(7.9)
Net book value at 31 May 20X6	15.7
Provision: on initial recognition ($20 \times 20\% \times 0.898$)	3.6
Plus unwinding of discount ($3.6 \times 5.5\% \times 8/12$)	0.13
Provision at 31 May 20X6	3.73

Purchase of Badex

IFRS 3 *Business Combinations* states that the cost of a business combination is the **aggregate** of the **fair values of the consideration** given plus any **directly attributable costs**. Fair value is measured at the date of exchange. Where any of the consideration is **deferred,** the amount should be **discounted to its present value**. Where there may be an adjustment to the final cost of the combination **contingent on one or more future events**, the amount of the adjustment is included in the cost of the combination at the acquisition date **only if payment is probable** and the amount **can be measured reliably**.

The purchase consideration consists of **$100 million paid on the acquisition date** plus a **further $25 million payable on 31 May 20X7**, including **$15 million payable only if profits exceed forecasts**. At the acquisition date it appeared that **profit forecasts would not be met** and that therefore payment of the contingent consideration of $15 million was **not probable**. This situation had not changed by 31 May 20X6. Therefore the **cost of the combination** at both dates is **$109 million** (100 + 10 × 0.898).

A further issue concerns the valuation and treatment of the 'Badex' brand name. The brand name is an internally generated intangible asset of Badex, and therefore it will not be recognised in the balance sheet of Badex. However, **IFRS 3 requires intangible assets** of an acquiree to be **recognised if they meet the identifiability criteria** in IAS 38 *Intangible assets* and their fair value can be **measured reliably**. For an intangible asset to be identifiable the asset must be separable or it must arise from contractual or other legal rights. It appears that these **criteria have been met** (a brand is **separable**) and the brand has also been **valued at $20 million** for the purpose of the sale to Prochain. Therefore the 'Badex' brand will be **separately recognised in the consolidated balance sheet.**

Development of own brand

IAS 38 *Intangible assets* divides a development project into a research phase and a development phase. In the research phase of a project, an entity cannot yet demonstrate that the expenditure will generate probable future economic benefits. Therefore expenditure on **research** must be **recognised as an expense when it occurs.**

Development expenditure is capitalised when an entity demonstrates **all** the following.

(a)   The **technical feasibility** of completing the project

(b)   Its **intention to complete** the asset and use or sell it

(c)   Its **ability to use or sell** the asset

(d)   That the asset will generate **probable future economic benefits**

(e)   The availability of **adequate technical, financial and other resources** to complete the development and to use or sell it

(f)   Its ability to **reliably measure** the expenditure attributable to the asset.

Assuming that all these criteria are met, the cost of the development should comprise **all directly attributable costs** necessary to **create the asset** and to make it **capable of operating in the manner intended by management**. Directly attributable costs **do not include selling or administrative costs,** or **training costs** or market research. The **cost of upgrading** existing machinery can be recognised as **property, plant and equipment**. Therefore the expenditure on the project should be treated as follows:

	Expense (income statement)	Recognised in balance sheet Intangible Assets	Property, plant and equipment
	$m	$m	$m
Research	3		
Prototype design		4	
Employee costs		2	
Development work		5	
Upgrading machinery			3
Market research	2		
Training	1		
	6	11	3

Prochain should **recognise $11 million** as an intangible asset.

Apartments

The apartments are leased to persons who are under contract to the company. Therefore they **cannot be classified as investment property**. IAS 40 *Investment property* specifically states that **property occupied by employees** is not investment property. The apartments must be treated as **property, plant and equipment**, carried at cost or fair value and depreciated over their useful lives.

Although the rent is below the market rate the difference between the actual rent and the market rate is simply **income foregone** (or an opportunity cost). In order to recognise the difference as an employee benefit cost it would also be necessary to **gross up rental income** to the market rate. The financial statements would **not present fairly** the financial performance of the company. Therefore the company **cannot recognise the difference** as an employee benefit cost.

B2 Question with helping hands: Impairment of assets

Top tips. You may not have got all the indicators in part (a) (i) below. However you should have been able to identify at least seven in order to earn the seven marks.

(a)   (i)   Indicators will include the following.

External factors

- A **significant decrease** in the **market** value of an asset in excess of **normal passage of time**.

- Significant **adverse changes** in the **markets** or **business** in which the asset is used.

- Adverse changes to the **technological, economic** or **legal environmental** of the business.

- Increase in **market interest rates** likely to affect the **discount rate** used in calculating **value in use**.

- Where **interest rates increase**, adversely affecting **recoverable amounts**.

- The **carrying amount** of an entity's **assets** exceeding its **market capitalisation**.

Internal factors

- **Adverse changes** to the **method** of **use** of the **asset**.

- Indications suggest the **economic performance** of the asset will be **worse** than expected.

- **Physical damage** or **obsolescence** has occurred.

- For new assets, **cost increases** adversely affect profitability.

- Where **actual cash flows are less than estimated** cash flows if an asset is valued in terms of 'value in use'.

- Where the **management** intend to **reorganise** the **entity**.

(ii) **Recognition and measurement of impairment**

IAS 36 states that if an **asset's value** is **higher than** its **recoverable amount**, an **impairment loss** has occurred. The impairment loss should be **written off against profits**.

The **recoverable amount** is **defined** as the **higher** of the **asset's fair value less costs to sell** and its **value in use**. If the recoverable amount is less than the carrying amount, then the resulting impairment loss should be charged as an expense in the income statement. When an **impairment loss occurs** for a **revalued asset**, the **impairment loss** should be charged to the **revaluation surplus**, any **excess** is then charged to the **income statement**.

Where it is not possible to measure impairment for individual assets, the loss should be measured for a cash generating unit. **Impairment losses** for **cash generating units** should be **allocated initially** to **goodwill, then** to all **other assets** on a **pro rata basis**. Impairment losses should only be reversed if there has been a change in the estimates used to determine the asset's recoverable amount since the last impairment loss was recognised.

After impairment losses have been recognised, the depreciation charge should be revised.

(b) **Recommended treatments of impairments**

(i) An impairment review will be carried out because of the losses and the taxi business problems.

For the productive machinery

	$m
Carrying value	290,000
Fair value less costs to sell	120,000
Value in use (100,000 × 3, discounted at 10%)	248,600

An impairment loss of $41,400 (290,000 – 248,600) will be recognised in the income statement.

(ii) *At 1 February 20X8*

	1.1.X8 $'000	Impairment loss $'000	1.2.X8 $'000
Goodwill (230 – 190)	40	(15)	25
Intangible assets	30		30
Vehicles	120	(30)	90
Sundry net assets	40		40
	230	(45)	185

An impairment loss is recognised for the stolen vehicles. The balance of $15,000 is allocated to goodwill in the cash generating unit.

At 1 March 20X8

	_1.2.X8_	_Impairment loss_	_1.3.X8_
	$'000	$'000	$'000
Goodwill	25	(25)	
Intangible assets	30	(5)	25
Vehicles	90		90
Sundry net assets	40		40
	185	(30)	155

A further impairment loss of $30,000 is recognised. The recoverable amount falls to the higher of fair value less costs to sell (155) or value in use (150). There is no indication that other tangible assets are impaired. The loss is applied initially to the intangible assets and then to goodwill.

B3 Ryder

Top tips. This is a mixed standard question, of the kind that the examiner generally likes.

Easy marks. Parts (a) and (b) are fairly straightforward. You should be familiar with IAS 10 and 36, even if you missed the IFRS 5 aspect.

Examiner's comment. This question was generally well answered. The question was quite discriminating as there was in most cases a correct answer rather than an issue to discuss. Surprisingly many candidates did not know how to deal with contingent consideration on the purchase of subsidiary. Candidates dealt well with the property intended for sale but many candidates did not realise that cash settled share based payments (share appreciation rights) are remeasured to fair value at each reporting date. There was some confusion in candidate's answers over what constitutes 'grant date' and 'vesting date' and the importance for the share based payment transactions. The question was quite discriminating as there was in most cases a correct answer rather than an issue to discuss. Surprisingly many candidates did not know how to deal with a proposed dividend or how to deal with contingent consideration on the purchase of subsidiary. Candidates dealt well with the property intended for sale but many candidates did not realise that cash settled share based payments (share appreciation rights) are remeasured to fair value at each reporting date. There was some confusion in candidate's answers over what constitutes 'grant date' and 'vesting date' and the importance for the share based payment transactions.

(a) **Disposal of subsidiary**

The issue here is the value of the subsidiary at 31 October 20X5. The directors have stated that there has been no significant event since the year end which could have resulted in a reduction in its value. This, taken together with the loss on disposal, indicates that the subsidiary had **suffered an impairment at 31 October 20X5**. IAS 10 requires the sale to be treated as an **adjusting event** after the balance sheet date as it provides **evidence of a condition that existed at the balance sheet date.**

The assets of Krup should be **written down to their recoverable amount**. In this case this is the eventual sale proceeds. Therefore the value of the net assets and purchased goodwill of Krup should be **reduced by $11 million** (the loss on disposal of $9 million plus the loss of $2 million that occurred between 1 November 2005 and the date of sale). IAS 36 _Impairment of assets_ states that an impairment loss should be allocated to goodwill first and therefore the **purchased goodwill of $12 million is reduced to $1 million**. The impairment loss of $11 million is **recognised in the income statement**.

Because there was no intention to sell the subsidiary at 31 October 20X5, **IFRS 5 _Non current assets held for sale and discontinued operations_ does not apply**. The disposal is **disclosed** in the notes to the financial statements in accordance with IAS 10.

(b) **Issue of shares**

IFRS 3 *Business combinations* requires contingent consideration to be **included in the cost of the combination** at the acquisition date if (as in this case) the payment is **probable** and the amount can be **measured reliably**. Ryder has **correctly included** an estimate of the amount of consideration in the cost of the acquisition on 21 January 20X4. This would have been based on the fair value of its ordinary shares at that date, which has since **increased from $10 per share to $11 per share**. Therefore the **cost of combination must be adjusted**, with a corresponding **adjustment to goodwill**. As a result, **goodwill increases by $300,000** (300,000 × 11 – 10). Because the acquisition took place **more than twelve months before** the share issue, the adjustment is treated as a **change of accounting estimate** in accordance with IAS 8 *Accounting policies, changes in accounting estimates and errors* and the change is **recognised in the current period.**

The value of the contingent shares should be included in a **separate category of equity** in the balance sheet at 31 October 20X5. They should be transferred to share capital and share premium after the actual issue of the shares on 12 November 20X5.

The other matter is whether the share issue and the bonus issue affect the calculation of earnings per share for the year ended 31 October 20X5. IAS 33 *Earnings per share* states that contingently issuable shares should be included in the calculation of basic earnings per share only from the date that all conditions are met. As the conditions were met at 31 October 20X5, the shares should be included in the calculation from that date, even though the shares were not issued until after the year end. In the case of diluted earnings per share, IAS 33 requires contingently issue shares to be included from the beginning of the period in which all conditions are met, ie from 1 September 20X4. IAS 33 also states that if there is a bonus share issue after the year end but before the financial statements are authorised for issue, the bonus shares should be included in the calculation (and in the calculation of earnings per share for all previous periods presented).

Both IAS 10 and IAS 33 require **disclosure of all material share transactions** or potential share transactions entered into after the balance sheet date, excluding the bonus issue. Therefore **details of the issue of the contingent shares should be disclosed** in the notes to the financial statements.

(c) **Property**

The property appears to have been **incorrectly classified** as 'held for sale'. Although the company had always intended to sell the property, IFRS 5 states that in order to qualify as 'held for sale' an asset must be **available for immediate sale in its present condition**. Because **repairs were needed** before the property could be sold and these were **not completed until after the balance sheet date**, this was clearly **not the case at 31 October 20X5.**

In addition, even if the property had been correctly classified, it has been **valued incorrectly**. IFRS 5 requires assets held for sale to be valued at **the lower of their carrying amount or fair value less costs to sell**. The property **should have been valued at its carrying amount of $20 million**, not at the eventual sale proceeds of $27 million.

The property **must be included within property, plant and equipment** and must be **depreciated**. Therefore its **carrying amount at 31 October 20X5 is $19 million** ($20 million less depreciation of $1 million). The **gain of $7 million** that the company has previously recognised **should be reversed**.

Although the property cannot be classified as 'held for sale' in the financial statements for the year ended 31 October 2005, it **will qualify for the classification after the balance sheet date**. Therefore details of the sale should be **disclosed** in the notes to the financial statements.

(d) **Share appreciation rights**

The granting of share appreciation rights is a **cash settled share based payment transaction** as defined by IFRS 2 *Share based payment*. IFRS 2 requires these to be **measured at the fair value of the liability** to pay cash. The liability should be **re-measured at each reporting date and at the date of settlement**. Any **changes in fair value** should be **recognised in profit or loss** (the income statement) for the period.

However, the company has **not remeasured the liability since 31 October 20X4**. Because IFRS 2 requires the expense and the related liability to be recognised over the two-year vesting period, the rights should be measured as follows:

	$m
At 31 October 20X4: ($6 × 10 million × ½)	30
At 31 October 20X5 ($8 × 10 million)	80
At 1 December 20X5 (settlement date) ($9 × 10 million)	90

Therefore at 31 October 20X5 the liability **should be re-measured to $80 million** and an **expense of $50 million** should be recognised in the income statement for the year.

The additional expense of $10 million resulting from the remeasurement at the settlement date is not included in the financial statements for the year ended 31 October 20X5, but is recognised the following year.

B4 Worldwide Nuclear Fuels

> **Top tips**. This is a thorough testing of your knowledge of IAS 37. However remember that other standards may also apply. In particular IAS 16 in part b (i).

(a)   (i)   **Need for guidance on accounting for provisions**

The IASB is keen to ensure that **only liabilities** as **defined** in its *Framework* **appear** on the **balance sheet**.

Provisions are 'liabilities of uncertain timing or amount' and in particular the IASB wishes to **prevent companies providing for future operating losses**. Provisions can be difficult to differentiate from liabilities and reclassification is common with the passage of time and clarification of events. Provisions are often subject to disclosures which do not apply to other payables, eg movements on provisions during a year. Many companies pay little regard to disclosures by utilising a heading 'other provisions'.

Once a provision has been set up, it becomes possible to charge expenses directly to it and so bypass the income statement. Companies have engaged in **creative accounting devices** by setting up **large provisions** and subsequently releasing them back to the income statements; provisions then became 'income smoothing' devices.

There is concern over the ways in which provisions have been recognised. In many cases provisions have been **set up where there is no obligation** and in **other cases** companies have **failed to set up provisions where obligations do exist**. So there is scope for income and profit smoothing and **inconsistent reporting between companies**.

Users expect that a provision is recognised and measured on a consistent basis and disclosure occurs of the details of the provision to understand its nature, timing and amount.

(ii)   **Criteria for recognising provisions**

Under IAS 37, provisions must be recognised in the following circumstances.

(1)   There is a **legal** or **constructive obligation** to transfer benefits as a result of past events.

(2)   It is probable an **outflow of economic resources** will be required to **settle** the **obligation**.

(3)   A **reasonable estimate** of the amount required to settle the obligation can be made.

(4)   If a company **can avoid expenditure by its future action**, **no provision** should be recognised.

Constructive obligations emerge when an entity is committed to certain expenditures because of a pattern of behaviour which the public at large would expect to continue. Any alternative course of action which would conceal the constructive obligation could be very onerous. (An example would be a practice of giving customer refunds to preserve goodwill, where there is no legal obligation to do so.)

A constructive obligation for restructuring only exists when the criteria in IAS 37 are satisfied.

If an entity has an **onerous contract**, the **present obligation** should be **recognised** and **measured**.

No provisions for future operating losses should be recognised.

IAS 37 therefore takes a **balance sheet perspective** of provisions. It ensures that all **proper liabilities** exist, rather than recognising expenses in the income statement.

(b) **Assessment of accounting treatments**

(i) The company is building up the provision over the life of the asset using the 'units of production' method.

IAS 37 requires a provision to be the **best estimate** of the expenditure required to **settle** the **obligation** at the **balance sheet date**. The provision should be capitalised as an **asset** if the expenditure provides access to **future economic benefits**; **otherwise** it should be immediately charged to the **income statement**.

IAS 16 *Property, plant and equipment* has been amended to cater for debits set up when assets are created as a result of provisions. Such assets are **written off over** the **life** of the facility and **normal impairment rules** will apply. The decommissioning costs of $1,231m (undiscounted) not yet provided for will be included as a provision (at the discounted amount) in the balance sheet and a corresponding asset created.

The discounting method used is inconsistent. IAS 37 requires the use of a pre tax rate reflecting current market assessments of the time value of money and risks. The **discount rate** should **not reflect risks** which have been **included by adjusting future cash flows**.

The company also makes reserve adjustments for changes in price levels. This adjustment comprises two elements chargeable to the income statement not reserves:

(1) **Adjustments** to the provision caused by changes in **discount rates**.

(2) An **interest element** representing the **'unwinding' of the discount**, which should be classified as part of interest expenses in the income statement.

Any subsequent change in the provision should be recognised in the income statement; whereas the company is treating the adjustment of $27m as a movement on reserves.

(ii) **No provisions** for **future operating losses** should be set up according to IAS 37. If the company has an 'onerous contract' then a provision may be established. (An onerous contract is one where the costs of completing the contract exceed the revenues and where compensation is payable if the contract is not completed.) As the losses of $135m appear to arise from an onerous contract, the provision of $135m can remain and will be part of the fair value exercise and goodwill calculation.

Provisions for **environmental liabilities** should be **recognised** when a **legal** or **constructive obligation** exists, where a company has **no option** but to carry out remedial work. There is no current obligation in this case, but the company's conduct could create a valid expectation that it will clean up the environment. This is a very **subjective exercise** which the directors and auditors will have to argue through. Example 2B in IAS 37 appears to act as a guide for a similar situation which would require a provision.

B5 Cohort

Top tips. This question required a knowledge of deferred tax (IAS 12). The question focused on the key areas of the Standard and required an understanding of those areas. It did not require detailed computational knowledge but the ability to take a brief outline scenario and advise the client accordingly. Rote knowledge would be of little use in this situation.

Examiner's comment. Some candidates scored quite well on the question but again guessing at the answer was a fruitless exercise. The key areas were intragroup profit in inventory, unremitted earnings of subsidiaries, revaluation of securities, general provisions and tax losses. Basically an appreciation was required of how to deal with each of these areas but unfortunately most candidates struggled to deal with the issues involved.

Marking scheme

		Marks
Air	– acquisition	5
	– intangible asset	3
	– intra group profit	3
	– unremitted earnings	3
Legion	– long term investments	4
	– loan provision	4
	– deferred tax asset	4
	Available	26
	Maximum	25

Acquisition of the subsidiaries – general

Fair value adjustments have been made for consolidation purposes in both cases and these will **affect the deferred tax charge for the year**. This is because the deferred tax position is viewed **from the perspective of the group** as a whole. For example, it may be possible to recognise deferred tax assets which previously could not be recognised by individual companies, because there are now sufficient tax profits available within the group to utilise unused tax losses. Therefore a **provision** should be made for **temporary differences between fair values of the identifiable net assets acquired and their carrying values** ($4 million less $3.5 million in respect of Air). **No provision should be made for the temporary difference** of $1 million **arising on goodwill** recognised as a result of the combination with Air.

Future listing

Cohort plans to seek a listing in three years time. Therefore it will become a **public company** and will be subject to a **higher rate of tax**. IAS 12 states that deferred tax should be measured at the **average tax rates expected to apply in the periods in which the timing differences are expected to reverse**, based on current enacted tax rates and laws. This means that Cohort may be paying tax at the higher rate when some of its timing differences reverse and this should be taken into account in the calculation.

Acquisition of Air

(a) The directors have calculated the tax provision on the assumption that the intangible asset of $0.5 million will be allowed for tax purposes. However, this is not certain and the directors **may eventually have to pay the additional tax**. If the directors cannot be persuaded to adjust their calculations **a liability for the additional tax should be recognised**.

113

(b) The intra-group transaction has resulted in an **unrealised profit** of $0.6 million in the group accounts and this will be **eliminated on consolidation**. The tax charge in the group income statement includes the tax on this profit, for which **the group will not become liable to tax until the following period. From the perspective of the group, there is a temporary difference**. Because the temporary difference arises in the financial statements of Cohort, **deferred tax should be provided** on this difference (an asset) using the rate of tax payable by Cohort.

(c) **Deferred tax should be recognised on the unremitted earnings of subsidiaries** unless the parent is able to **control the timing of dividend payments** and it is **unlikely that dividends will be paid for the foreseeable future**. Cohort controls the dividend policy of Air and this means that there would normally be no need to make a provision in respect of unremitted profits. However, the profits of Air **will be distributed** to Cohort over the next few years and **tax will be payable** on the dividends received. Therefore a **deferred tax liability should be shown.**

Acquisition of Legion

(a) A **temporary difference arises** where non-monetary assets are **revalued upwards** and the **tax treatment of the surplus is different from the accounting treatment**. In this case, the revaluation surplus has been **recognised in the income statement** for the current period, rather than in equity but no corresponding adjustment has been made to the tax base of the investments because the gains will be taxed in future periods. Therefore the company **should recognise a deferred tax liability on the temporary difference of $4 million**.

(b) A temporary difference arises when the provision for the loss on the loan portfolio is first recognised. The general allowance is expected to increase and therefore it is unlikely that the temporary difference will reverse in the near future. However, a **deferred tax liability should still be recognised**. The temporary difference gives rise to a **deferred tax asset**. IAS 12 states that **deferred tax assets should not be recognised unless it is probable that taxable profits will be available** against which the taxable profits can be utilised. **This is affected by the situation in point (c) below**.

(c) In theory, unused tax losses give rise to a deferred tax asset. However, IAS 12 states that **deferred tax assets should only be recognised to the extent that they are regarded as recoverable**. They should be regarded as recoverable to the extent that on the basis of all the evidence available it is **probable that there will be suitable taxable profits against which the losses can be recovered**. The future taxable profit of Legion **will not be sufficient to realise all the unused tax loss. Therefore the deferred tax asset is reduced to the amount that is expected to be recovered**.

This reduction in the deferred tax asset implies that it was **overstated at 1 June 20X1**, when it was acquired by the group. As these are the first post-acquisition financial statements, **goodwill should also be adjusted**.

B6 Panel

Top tips. This is a single topic question, which is a departure from the examiner's usual mixed standard question. The IFRS 1 aspects are likely to become less frequent over time.

Easy marks. Part (b) (iii) and (iv) are easier than (i) and (ii), though they carry the same number of marks.

Examiner's comment. Part (a) was quite well answered albeit often in a very general way. Part (b) was answered far better than when this area was tested in June 2005. The other three areas were a leasing transaction, an inter company sale and an impairment of property plant and equipment. These elements of the question were quite well answered although the discussion of the topic areas was generally quite poor whilst the computations were quite good. Deferred tax is a key area and must be understood.

(a) (i) **The impact of changes in accounting standards**

IAS 12 *Income taxes* is based on the idea that all **changes in assets and liabilities** have unavoidable **tax consequences**. Where the recognition criteria in IFRS are different from those in tax law, the **carrying amount of an asset or liability in the financial statements is different from the amount at which it is stated for tax purposes (its 'tax base')**. These differences are known as **'temporary differences'**. The practical effect of these differences is that a transaction or event occurs in a different accounting period from its tax consequences. For example, income from interest receivable is recognised in the financial statements in one accounting period but it is only taxable when it is actually received in the following accounting period.

IAS 12 requires a company to make **full provision** for the tax effects of temporary differences. Where a change in an accounting standard results in a change to the carrying value of an asset or liability in the financial statements, the **amount of the temporary difference** between the carrying value and the tax base **also changes**. Therefore the amount of the deferred tax liability is affected.

(ii) **Calculation of deferred tax on first time adoption of IFRS**

IFRS 1 *First time adoption of International Financial Reporting Standards* requires a company to **prepare an opening IFRS balance sheet** and to **apply IAS 12 to temporary differences** between the carrying amounts of assets and liabilities and their tax bases at that date. Panel prepares its opening IFRS balance sheet **at 1 November 20X3**. The carrying values of its assets and liabilities are **measured in accordance with IFRS 1** and **other applicable IFRSs** in force at 31 October 20X5. The deferred tax provision is based on **tax rates that have been enacted or substantially enacted by the balance sheet date**. Any **adjustments** to the deferred tax liability under previous GAAP are **recognised directly in equity (retained earnings)**.

(b) (i) **Share options**

Under IFRS 2 *Share based payment* the company **recognises an expense** for the employee services received in return for the share options granted over the vesting period. The related tax deduction **does not arise until the share options are exercised**. Therefore a **deferred tax asset arises**, based on the difference between the intrinsic value of the options and their carrying amount (normally zero).

At 31 October 20X4 the tax benefit is as follows:

	$m
Carrying amount of share based payment	–
Less: tax base of share based payment (16 ÷ 2)	(8)
Temporary difference	(8)

The **deferred tax asset is $2.4 million** (30% × 8). This is recognised at 31 October 20X4 provided that taxable profit is available against which it can be utilised. Because the tax effect of the remuneration expense is greater than the tax benefit, the tax benefit is **recognised in the income statement.** (The tax effect of the remuneration expense is 30% × $40 million ÷ 2 = $6 million.)

At 31 October 20X5 there is **no longer a deferred tax asset** because the options have been exercised. The **tax benefit receivable is $13.8 million** (30% × $46 million). Therefore the deferred tax asset of $2.4 million is no longer required.

(ii) **Leased plant**

An asset leased under a finance lease is **recognised as an asset** owned by the company and the **related obligation** to pay lease rentals is **recognised as a liability**. Each instalment payable is treated partly as interest and partly as repayment of the liability. The **carrying amount** of the plant for accounting purposes is the **net present value of the lease payments less depreciation**. Because the lease rentals attract tax relief, its **tax base is the amount of the obligation** to pay lease rentals. Therefore at 31 October 20X5 a **temporary difference** arises as follows:

	$m	$m
Carrying value in financial statements:		
Net present value of future lease payments at inception of lease	12	
Less: depreciation (12 ÷ 5)	(2.4)	
		9.6
Less: tax base		
Liability at inception of lease	12	
Interest (8% × 12)	0.96	
Lease rental	(3)	
		(9.96)
Temporary difference		0.36

A **deferred tax asset of $108,000** (30% × 360,000) arises.

Note. It is possible to argue that the tax base of a finance lease is nil, because no asset or liability is recognised in the financial statements as a result. If this approach is taken, the carrying value of the lease is the net amount at which the lease is measured in the financial statements, ie the outstanding obligation less the net book value of the asset. This gives the same answer: a temporary difference of $360,000 and a deferred tax asset of $108,000.

(iii) **Intra-group sale**

Pins has **made a profit of $2 million** on its sale to Panel. Tax is **payable on the profits of individual companies**. Pins is liable for tax on this profit in the current year and will have provided for the related tax in its individual financial statements. However, **from the viewpoint of the group** the profit **will not be realised until the following year**, when the goods are sold to a third party and must be **eliminated** from the consolidated financial statements. Because the group **pays tax before the profit is realised** there is a **temporary difference of $2 million** and a **deferred tax asset of $600,000** (30% × $2 million).

(iv) **Impairment loss**

The impairment loss in the financial statements of Nails **reduces the carrying value** of property, plant and equipment, but is **not allowable for tax**. Therefore the **tax base** of the property, plant and equipment **is different from its carrying value** and there is a **temporary difference**.

Under IAS 36 *Impairment of assets* the impairment loss is allocated first to goodwill and then to other assets:

	Goodwill	Property, plant and equipment	Total
	$m	$m	$m
Carrying value at 31 October 20X5	1	6.0	7.0
Impairment loss	(1)	(0.8)	(1.8)
	–	5.2	5.2

IAS 12 states that **no deferred tax should be recognised on goodwill** and therefore **only the impairment loss relating to the property, plant and equipment affects the deferred tax position.**

The effect of the impairment loss is as follows:

	Before impairment	After impairment	Difference
	$m	$m	$m
Carrying value	6	5.2	
Tax base	(4)	(4)	
Temporary difference	2	1.2	0.8
Tax liability (30%)	0.6	0.36	0.24

Therefore the impairment loss reduces deferred the tax liability by $240,000.

B7 Preparation question: Defined benefit scheme

Income statement note

Defined benefit expense recognised in profit or loss

	$'m
Current service cost	11
Interest cost (10% × (110 + 20))	13
Expected return on plan assets (12% × 150)	(18)
Recognised actuarial gains (Working)	(4)
Past service cost	20
	22

Balance sheet notes

Net defined benefit liability recognised in the balance sheet

	$'m
Present value of pension obligation	116
Fair value of plan assets	(140)
	(24)
Unrecognised actuarial gains/(losses) (Working)	42
	18

Changes in the present value of the defined benefit obligation

	$'m
Opening defined benefit obligation	110
Interest cost (10% × (110 + 20))	13
Current service cost	11
Benefits paid	(10)
Past service cost	20
Actuarial gain (balancing figure)	(28)
Closing defined benefit obligation	116

Changes in the fair value of plan assets

	$'m
Opening fair value of plan assets	150
Expected return on plan assets (12% × 150)	18
Contributions	7
Benefits paid	(10)
Actuarial loss (balancing figure)	(25)
Closing fair value of plan assets	140

Working

Recognised/Unrecognised actuarial gains and losses

	$'m	$'m
Corridor limits, greater of:		
10% of pension obligation b/d (10% × 110)	11	
10% of plan assets b/d (10% × 150)	15	
⇒ Corridor limit	15	
Unrecognised gains b/d		43
Gain recognised in I/S [(43 – 15)/7]		(4)
Gain on obligation in the year		28
Loss on assets in the year		(25)
Unrecognised gains c/d		42

B8 Retirement benefits

(a)   (i)   There are many key issues in determining how accounting for retirement benefits in respect of a defined benefit plan is carried out:

       (1)   The two main alternative approaches are what might be called the **income statement approach** or the **balance sheet approach**. Under the income statement approach the pension cost is seen as an operating cost and under the accruals or matching concept the attempt is made to spread the total pension cost over the service lives of the employees. The balance sheet approach however concentrates on the valuation of the assets and liabilities of the plan and the cost to the income statement is the change in value of the plan net assets or liabilities.

       (2)   Regarding the assets of the defined benefit plan there are two issues, **whether or not they should be included** on the balance sheet of the company and **how** they would be **valued**. Alternative valuation methods such as cost, market value and fair value are available.

       (3)   How should scheme liabilities be valued? Should they be valued using an **actuarial valuation or a market value**? Usually actuarial techniques will have to be used as there is no market value for such liabilities but then there is an issue over which actuarial method should be used.

       (4)   Should **discounting** be used when valuing the scheme liabilities in order to take account of the time value of money?

       (5)   If **actuarial gains and losses** occur where should they be **recognised** – in the incomes statement or in a secondary statement? Should such gains and losses be recognised immediately or spread over the remaining service lives of the employees? Or should the actuarial gains and losses only be recognised in the income statement if they exceed a predetermined amount? The problem that faces standard setters is how to deal with the volatility of actuarial gains and losses.

       (6)   **How often** should **actuarial valuations** take place? In theory they should take place at each year end but the costs and practicalities of this makes it difficult and onerous.

       (7)   If there are **changes to the defined benefit plan** such as improvement of benefits or addition of new benefits in relation to past service how should these be accounted for? The alternatives are to recognise the cost immediately in the income statement, spread it over the remaining service lives of employees or to offset it against any surplus in the scheme.

       Note. Candidates are only required to describe **four** of the above.

    (ii)   IAS 19 *Employee benefits* follows a **balance sheet approach** to accounting for defined benefit schemes. The liabilities of the scheme are to be valued on an actuarial basis using the **projected unit credit method** and the liabilities should be discounted to reflect the time value of money and the particular characteristics of the liability. The discount rate to be used is the market rate of return on high quality corporate bonds of equivalent currency and term as the scheme liabilities being valued. The plan assets are valued at fair value.

       The net amount of the fair value of the assets and the discounted value of the liabilities appears in the balance sheet as a **surplus or a deficit**. Actuarial valuations should take place with sufficient regularity to ensure that the financial statement amounts do not differ materially from the amounts that would be determined at the balance sheet date.

       If the balance sheet amount is an asset then this asset cannot exceed the **net total** of:

       (1)   Any unrecognised actuarial losses and past service cost

       (2)   The present value of any available funds from the plan or reduction in future contributions to the plan

Gains and losses are measured at the year end and recognised in the subsequent year. Any net gain or loss is recognised in the income statement if it is **in excess of 10% of the greater of the defined benefit obligation or the fair value** of the **plan** assets. The period of amortisation must not exceed the average remaining service period.

Past service costs for active employees are recognised in the income statement on **a straight line basis** over the average remaining vesting period. If the past service costs relate to former employees they should be recognised immediately.

IAS 19 offers a choice of treatments of how to deal with profits or losses not recognised in the income statement. Actuarial gains or losses can be deferred if the cumulative amount remains within the 10% limit or corridor and any amount outside the corridor can be amortised over any period shorter than the working lives of the employees or even written off to the income statement immediately. Alternatively all actuarial gains and losses can be recognised in the income statement provided that the treatment is consistent.

(b) **Net plan asset as at 31 May 20X1**

	$m
Fair value of plan assets	2,950
Actuarial valuation of liabilities	(2,000)
Pension scheme surplus	950
Unrecognised actuarial gains (W1)	(692)
Net plan asset	258

A test must be carried out to ensure that the net plan asset does not exceed the future economic benefit that it represents for the company.

Charge to profit or loss

	$m
Current service cost	70
Past service cost	25
Interest on liabilities	230
Actuarial gain recognised (W2)	(5)
Return on scheme assets	(295)
	25

Workings

1 *Unrecognised actuarial gains*

	$m
Unrecognised actuarial gains at 1 June 20X0	247
Actuarial loss on obligation (W3)	(175)
Actuarial gain on plan assets (W4)	625
	697
Actuarial gain recognised (W2)	(5)
Unrecognised actuarial gain at 31 May 20X1	692

2 *Actuarial gain recognised in income statement*

The 10% limits will be the greater of 10% of $1,500m and 10% of $1,970m.

	$m
Net unrecognised gain	247
10% corridor (10% × $1,970)	(197)
	50
Amortisation over 10 years (50/10)	5

3   *Present value of obligation*

	$m
Present value of obligation at 1 June 20X0	1,500
Interest cost	230
Current service cost	70
Past service cost	25
	1,825
Actuarial loss (balancing figure)	175
Present value of obligation at 31 May 20X1	2,000

4   *Fair value of plan assets*

	$m
Fair value of plan assets at 1 June 20X0	1,970
Return on plan assets	295
Contributions	60
	2,325
Actuarial gain (balancing figure)	625
Fair value of plan assets at 31 May 20X1	2,950

B9 Savage

Top tips. A lot of the information is given to you in the question. You need to know how to present it.

Easy marks. Part (b), a test of knowledge is a source of easy marks.

Examiner's comment. In theory, this question should have had the highest average mark on the paper. In practice it was the poorest answered. The question was on employee benefits. The main problem for candidates is not the accounting process but understanding the terminology and what that means for the accounting process. An article has been prepared for *student accountant* which hopefully will help candidates.

Candidates had to calculate the expense recognised in profit or loss, the amount recognised in the balance sheet and the statement of recognised income and expense for the employee benefit transactions in the year. Candidates had very few calculations to make. Basically the only calculations were the interest cost and the expected return on the plan assets. The remainder of the question simply required candidates to enter the various transactions into the relevant accounts, but because of the problem of understanding the nature of the items, this proved to be a difficult exercise. Hopefully the article will help.

Part (b) of the question required candidates to explain how the non-payment of the contributions and change in the pension benefits should be treated. Many candidates did not attempt this part of the question which is not a good strategy even though the part only carried four marks.

(a)   AMOUNTS RECOGNISED IN THE BALANCE SHEET

	31 October 20X5 $m	31 October 20X4 $m
Present value of obligation	3,375	3,000
Less: fair value of plan assets (3,170 – 8)	(3,162)	(2,900)
Liability	213	100

EXPENSE RECOGNISED IN INCOME STATEMENT FOR YEAR ENDED 31 OCTOBER 20X5

	$m
Current service cost	40
Interest cost	188
Expected return on assets	(232)
Past service cost	125
	121

AMOUNT RECOGNISED IN STATEMENT OF RECOGNISED INCOME AND EXPENSE
FOR YEAR ENDED 31 OCTOBER 20X5

	$m
Actuarial loss on obligation	64
Actuarial gain on plan assets	(52)
Net actuarial loss recognised	(12)

CHANGES IN THE PRESENT VALUE OF THE OBLIGATION

	$m
Present value of obligation at 1 November 20X4	3,000
Past service cost	125
Interest cost (6% × 3,125)	188
Current service cost	40
Benefits paid	(42)
Actuarial loss on obligation (balancing figure)	64
Present value of obligation at 31 October 20X5	3,375

Note: the past service costs of $125 million are recognised immediately because the benefits vest on 1 November 20X4. They are also included in opening scheme liabilities for the purpose of calculating interest.

CHANGES IN THE FAIR VALUE OF PLAN ASSETS

	$m
Fair value of plan assets at 1 November 20X4	2,900
Expected return on plan assets (8% × 2,900)	232
Contributions	20
Benefits paid	(42)
Actuarial gain on plan assets (balancing figure)	52
Fair value of plan assets at 31 October 20X4 (3,170 – 8)	3,162

(b) At 31 October 20X5, contributions of $8 million remain unpaid. IAS 19 *Employee benefits* states that **plan assets do not include unpaid contributions**. However, contributions payable of $8 million should be disclosed in the notes to the accounts of Savage at 31 October 20X5. This amount is payable to the Trustees.

IAS 19 also states that where there are changes to a defined benefit plan, **past service costs** should be **recognised immediately if the benefits have already vested**. The benefits vested on 1 November 20X4 and therefore past service costs of $125 million should be recognised in the income statement for the year ended 31 October 20X5.

B10 Issue

Top tips. This question required you to discuss the business and financial position of a company. It is not a ratio analysis question, but it involves the evaluation of the financial position taking into account all the available information.

Easy marks. There is a lot of information in the question, which you should make full use of in order to gain easy marks.

Examiner's comment. Some candidates' answers were quite narrow, showing that they had not seen the implications of the information provided. Others wasted time calculating ratios.

	Marks
Environment – business	3
Special purpose entities	4
Related party and immateriality	3
Reversal of invoices	1
Non-current assets	2
Intangibles	2
Liquidity	4
Revenue recognition	2
Extraordinary items	2
Pro-forma information	2
Ratios	2
Conclusion: employees	1
publication lag	1
other	4
Report – style	1
Available	34
Maximum	25

REPORT

To: Managing Partner
From:
Subject: Financial and business position of Issue
Date: June 20X3

As requested, I report below on the business and financial position of Issue and on the implications of the financial information and the other information provided.

General business environment

Issue operates in a sector that has recently suffered an **economic downturn** and Issue's performance and financial position should be interpreted in this context.

There has been adverse press comment about **'aggressive earnings management'**. The company certainly operates under conditions that could **provide an incentive to adopt dubious accounting practices.** Management are partly **remunerated by means of share options**; this means that they personally **benefit from any increase in the share price**. In addition, the Board has promised to take the company into the top 10% of listed companies within its first five years; this period is now almost up. The company is **vulnerable** because it has issued bonds which are **redeemable if the working capital ratio falls below 1.3**. This means that **management may be under pressure to achieve unrealistic targets.**

There is evidence that management has adopted several **questionable accounting policies**.

Specific accounting policies

Special purpose entities

The company has borrowed $40 million from 20 different entities, all of which are owned by a bank. It has deposited $35 million of this with the entities, so that only $5 million is shown as actual debt in the financial statements. These entities are **Special Purpose Entities** (sometimes called quasi-subsidiaries or vehicle companies) which **appear to have been used to hide the true level of the company's indebtedness** from users of the financial statements. The economic substance of the arrangement is that the entities are **probably subsidiaries of Issue** rather than of the bank and if so,

consolidated financial statements should have been prepared (although in practice these might not have provided much better information because intra-group balances would have been eliminated on consolidation).

It is necessary to **examine the detail of the arrangement** to determine whether the entities are subsidiaries of Issue or of the bank. If the bank controls the entities then the **long-term borrowings of Issue are understated by $35 million.**

Management **claims that each individual transaction is immaterial** and does not have to be disclosed. This is **incorrect** as **transactions of the same nature should be considered in aggregate**, rather than individually. In addition, because the bank owns 20% of the shares of Issue, it is **likely to be a related party** under IAS 24 *Related party disclosures*. This is a **further suggestion that the entities are vehicle companies.**

Issue has invoiced the entities for 'services' at each year end and has subsequently reversed the invoices after the company has filed its financial statements. Therefore it seems to be **using the entities to increase earnings (and possibly working capital ratios) artificially.**

Valuation of non-current assets

The valuation of the property, plant and equipment and intangible assets has been performed by one of the directors of Issue who is **not professionally qualified**. This **casts doubt on the legitimacy** of the valuation. It should be noted that the **revaluation reserve has increased by $10 million** during the year; an unexpectedly large amount, given that many of the assets are of a **specialised nature**.

In addition, the **basis for valuing the plant and equipment appears to be incorrect**. IAS 16 *Property, plant and equipment* states that **fair value is normally market value**, not net realisable value. Where, as in this case, **assets are specialised** so that there is unlikely to be a reliable market value, **depreciated replacement cost should be used**. Revaluations of plant and equipment are **unusual** and there is no obvious reason for this one other than strengthening the balance sheet.

The intangible assets are data purchase and data capture costs of internally generated databases. IAS 38 *Intangible assets* states that **development costs should only be recognised as assets if the company can demonstrate that they will generate cash inflows in excess of the cash outflows**. Given the nature of the costs, this is **unlikely** and it appears that they **should have been written off** as they were incurred. However, further investigation of the reason for adopting this policy is needed.

Six year bonds

At first sight the accounting treatment adopted for the two bond issues **appears to be incorrect**. Under IAS 39 *Financial instruments: recognition and measurement*, this type of financial instrument is **normally measured at amortised cost**. This means that the finance credits of $2 million and $1 million **should not be recognised in the income statement immediately**, but over the **shortest period** that the investor can require redemption (three years in this case). However, it could be argued that **there is a case for recognising the finance credits immediately**, because the holders can demand payment immediately if the working capital ratio falls below 1.3.

Revenue recognition

IAS 18 *Revenue* **does not deal adequately** with the type of transactions likely to be undertaken by information technology businesses. In practice these businesses use **a variety of different policies**, some acceptable and some not. Issue **has long-term contracts**, but it is **unclear exactly when amounts are invoiced and revenue recognised.** Is revenue recognised on completion, or in stages as the contract progresses? It should be noted that because there is **little adequate guidance**, many software companies have adopted **'aggressive earnings management'** by **invoicing and recognising revenue as early in a transaction as possible**, well before the company has performed any work under the contract. However, it is **not certain** that Issue has done this.

Extraordinary items

Issue has recognised an **extraordinary item** in the income statement: losses caused by the terrorist attacks on New York on 11 September 20X1. IAS 1 *Presentation of financial statements* has now been amended so that it **prohibits**

the recognition of extraordinary items. This is very clearly an attempt to manipulate the earnings figure and therefore **operating profit is actually $20 million lower** than reported.

The financial position

Like many other businesses in the same sector, the company is **clearly facing difficulties**. In the year ended 31 January 20X3 **revenue fell by 20%** and it **reported earnings** before interest, tax, depreciation and amortisation **of $10 million** (adjusted for the extraordinary item) **compared with $90 million the previous year**. It is possible that these figures are **considerably overstated**. **Return on shareholders' equity is now a negative figure of 42.9%** (compared with a positive figure of 31.8% the previous year). Staff numbers have **reduced by 40%,** indicating that the company has been **forced to cut costs.**

A further problem is the **level of indebtedness**. Gearing has **risen from 27% to 42%** and it is **possible that it should be still higher**, because of the $35 million debt that may be 'off balance sheet'. **Liquidity has also worsened**; the working capital (current) ratio fell from 1.71 in 20X2 to 1.28 in 20X3. Not only might this cause problems in itself, but **as the working capital ratio has fallen below 1.3 the bonds of $50 million may have to be repaid.** This would **probably be disastrous** as it is unlikely that the company has sufficient funds available to make the payments.

A further thing to note is the **increasing length of time** between the year-end and the publication of the financial statements. This suggests that in 20X3 the company **might have had to spend additional time finalising** the financial statements and **devising ways of making the company's performance appear better than it was.**

Issue has **published pro-forma information** for the four months to 31 May 20X3. This seems to indicate that **the situation has improved dramatically** and in particular that **gearing has reduced**. The working capital ratio has increased to 1.5. However, pro-forma financial statements should always be **interpreted with caution** as they are **notoriously unreliable**. Issue has probably provided this additional information in an **attempt to restore investor confidence** or to **prevent the redemption of the bonds**. Given the company's use of special purpose entities and its other questionable accounting policies, **there has to be a degree of suspicion** about the way in which the improvement has been managed.

Conclusion

There appear to be a **number of problems**, both with Issue's **management culture** and with the **financial information provided. Many of the company's accounting policies require further investigation.** It is possible that the figures for **revenue, property, plant and equipment and intangible assets are all overstated** and that the figures **for current liabilities and long-term borrowings are significantly understated.** Even the figures as they stand suggest that the company's revenues and profits are falling, that liquidity is decreasing and gearing is increasing and that the company is in difficulties.

Given these problems, we **cannot recommend that you continue to invest in this company**.

Appendix

	20X3	20X2
Return on shareholders' equity (adjusted for extraordinary item)	$\frac{(30)}{70} = (42.9)\%$	$\frac{35}{110} = 31.8\%$
Working capital ratio	$\frac{230}{180} = 1.28$	$\frac{240}{140} = 1.71$
Gearing ratio	$\frac{50}{120} = 42\%$	$\frac{40}{150} = 27\%$

B11 Tyre

> **Top tips.** This question required candidates to deal with issues surrounding revenue recognition: accounting for non-current assets, provisions for environmental costs, accounting for lease premiums, and provisioning under IAS 37 *Provisions, contingent liabilities and contingent assets*. Make sure that you recognise the operating lease nature of the transaction.
>
> **Easy marks.** Although this is mainly about application of knowledge, there are easy marks for showing that you know what is going on. Credit will be given for different but sensible interpretations, for example, if you argued for a provision being made for the potential cost of the free car accessories.
>
> **Examiner's comment.** The question was quite well answered, particularly the revenue recognition aspects.

Marking scheme

	Marks
Revenue recognition	8
Administrative building	7
Lease agreements	5
Car accessories	5
available/maximum	25

(a) **General sales to customers**

IAS 18 *Revenue* states that revenue from the sale of goods **should not be recognised unless** the following conditions have been met:

- the entity has **transferred the significant risks and rewards** of ownership to the buyer

- the entity **does not retain** continuing managerial **involvement or control** associated with ownership of the goods

- the amount of revenue and costs can be **measured reliably**

- it is **probable** that the **economic benefits** associated with the transaction will **flow to the entity**.

These conditions **have not been met**, because **ownership has not been transferred** and there is a possibility that the deposit might have to be returned if Tyre does not perform its part of the contract. In addition, the appendix to the standard states that where partial payment is received in advance of delivery, **revenue should only be recognised when goods are delivered to the buyer**.

Therefore the deposit should be treated as a **liability** until the vehicle has been delivered to the customer. Only then should revenue be recognised. If the customer cancels the order, the deposit should be recognised as revenue at the date of cancellation.

Sale of car fleet to Hub

The buyback option is **expected to be exercised**. Therefore it is clear that the significant **risks and rewards** associated with ownership **have not been transferred** to Hub, because Tyre **retains an interest** in the residual value of the fleet.

The **substance** of the transaction is that Tyre has **leased the vehicles**, rather than sold them. The **risks and rewards of ownership** have not been transferred. Tyre **will only receive 60%** of the (heavily discounted) purchase price of the vehicles, meaning that the **present value** of the **minimum lease payments** will be considerably **less than their fair value**. In addition, Tyre will buy the vehicles back well **before the end** of their **economic life**. All these factors indicate that the lease is an **operating lease**.

The fleet of vehicles will therefore be included as property, plant and equipment and **depreciated** over their useful lives in accordance with IAS 16 *Property, plant and equipment*. Because the discount is normal for this type of transaction, the fair value of the vehicles will be measured at their actual purchase price, not the discounted price. **Income from the lease** should be **recognised over the lease term** on a straight line basis.

The **buyback option** may meet the definition of a **financial liability** under IAS 39 *Financial instruments: Recognition and measurement*. If this is the case, the liability should be **measured initially at its fair value** and subsequently at **amortised cost**.

(b)   **Former administrative centre**

The land and the building must be considered separately. The decision to demolish the building was taken **during the year** and this indicates that it was **impaired** at 31 May 20X6. The **recoverable amount** of the building is **zero** and therefore it should be written down to that amount, and the **impairment loss recognised in the income statement** for the year ended 31 May 20X6.

The **demolition costs** must be **charged** to the income statement **in the period in which they occur** (the year ended 31 May 20X7). **No provision** for remedial environmental work **should be recognised at 31 May 20X6**, because the company **did not have an obligation** to incur costs at that date (the building had not yet been demolished).

Although the company has decided to sell the land, it **does not meet the definition** of an asset **'held for sale'** under IFRS 5 *Non-current assets held for sale and discontinued operations*. In order to be treated as 'held for sale' the land would have to be **actively marketed** and **available for immediate sale in its present condition**. Remedial work must be carried out and the directors have decided to delay the sale to take advantage of rising prices. Therefore **the criteria have clearly not been met**.

The land is measured at **cost** as Tyre uses the cost model of IAS 16. It was acquired many years ago and prices are rising, so it **cannot be impaired**. When the remedial work has been completed, it may be possible to treat the land as an **investment property** using the **fair value model** in IAS 40 *Investment Property*. **Subsequent gains or losses** in value could then be **recognised in profit and loss** each period.

(c)   **Lease premiums**

Because one lease is a **finance lease** and the other is an **operating lease** the two lease premiums must be **treated differently**.

IAS 17 *Leases* states that costs that are **directly attributable to a finance lease** should be **added to the amount recognised as an asset**. Therefore the **amount capitalised** at the start of the finance lease should **include the premium**, which will then be **depreciated** over the lease term or the property's useful life (whichever is the shorter). The premium is also **included in the liability** for future payments under the lease.

The premium paid to enter into the **operating lease** is treated as **part of the lease rentals**. In effect, this is a prepayment of rent. Therefore the premium is **recognised as an expense** over the lease term on a **straight line basis** (unless some other systematic basis is more appropriate).

(d)   **Car accessories**

The main issue here is whether the company has **incurred an obligation** to supply the free car accessories at 31 May 20X6 and therefore whether a **provision** should be recognised in the financial statements.

IAS 37 *Provisions, contingent liabilities and contingent assets* states that a provision should only be recognised if:

- there is a **present obligation** as the result of a **past event**
- an **outflow of resources embodying economic benefits is probable**; and
- a **reliable estimate** of the amount can be made.

The accessories can only be obtained by presenting a coupon when a vehicle is purchased. The **purchase of the car is the obligating event** and an **outflow of resources embodying economic benefits occurs at the same time**. The company does not have an obligation to provide free goods relating to sales that have not yet happened. **No provision should be recognised.**

The cost of the accessories is included in the **cost of sales**. The **revenue recognised should be the actual amount received** from the customer; the sales price of the car only, not grossed up to include the value of the accessories.

B12 Preparation question: Leases

(a)   Interest rate implicit in the lease

PV = annuity × cumulative discount factor

250,000   = 78,864 × CDF

$$\therefore \text{CDF} \quad = \frac{250,000}{78,864}$$

= 3.170

∴ Interest rate is 10%

(b)   *Property, plant and equipment*

Net book value of assets held under finance leases is $187,500.

Non-current liabilities

	$
Finance lease liabilities (W)	136,886

Current liabilities

	$
Finance lease liabilities (W) (196,136 – 136,886)	59,250

Income statement

	$
Depreciation on assets held under finance leases	62,500
Finance charges	25,000

Working

		$
Year ended 31 December 20X1:		
1.1.20X1	Liability b/d	250,000
1.1.20X1 – 31.12.20X1	Interest at 10%	25,000
31.12.20X1	Instalment in arrears	(78,864)
31.12.20X1	Liability c/d	196,136
Year ended 31 December 20X2:		
1.1.20X2 – 31.12.20X2	Interest at 10%	19,614
31.12.20X2	Instalment in arrears	(78,864)
31.12.20X2	Liability c/d	136,886

B13 AB

Top tips. Much of this question is on discussion rather than calculation. Learn our answer carefully.

(a)   (i)   **Approach to lease accounting**

IAS 17 *Leases* differentiates between operating and finance leases.

A finance lease

(1)   Transfers substantially all of the **risks and rewards** incident to **ownership** of an asset to a lessee.

(2)   Should be **capitalised** in the accounts at the **fair value** of the leased asset or, if lower, the **PV** of **minimum lease payments** over the lease term using the **interest rate implicit in the lease** (otherwise the lessee's marginal borrowing rate may be used). Any **residual payments** guaranteed by the lessee should also be **included**.

(3)   The capitalised asset is **depreciated** over the **shorter** of the **lease term** or **useful life**.

(4)   Interest and principal components of each payment must be identified and allocated to accounting periods, thus reducing the lease liability.

(5)   **Finance charges** are calculated as the difference between the total of the minimum lease payments and value of the liability to the lessor. Finance charges are applied to produce a constant periodic rate of charge on the liability in the income statement.

An operating lease

(1)   Is any lease which is **not a finance lease**.

(2)   **Lease rentals** are charged to the **income statement** on a **systematic basis** which represents the **pattern** of the **benefits derived by the user** from the leased asset.

(ii)   **Recognition and classification problems**

Current standards do not adequately deal with leases. The problems are as follows.

(1)   The rights and obligations under operating leases are not recognised in the lessee's accounts. IAS 17 takes the view that if risks and rewards of ownership are *not* substantially transferred to a lessee then the lease is classified as an operating lease.

(2)   The **issue** lies with the definition of 'substantial', which has been judged against **quantitative not qualitative factors**. If a lease is non cancellable and the PV of the minimum lease payments is greater than or substantially equal to the asset's fair value or the lease term covers the major part of the asset's life, then the lease is usually treated as a finance lease.

(3)   '**Substantially equal**' has been taken to be in **excess of 90% of the fair value** of the leased asset and the figure of 75% of the life has typically been used, but these terms are not defined in IAS 17.

(4)   However, many leases have been designed which are in *substance* **finance leases** but, when **judged in quantitative terms**, are **classified as operating leases**.

(5)   Factors such as relative responsibilities of lessor/lessee for maintenance, insurance and bearing losses have also blurred the distinction and classification of leases.

(6)   **Long term finance leases** have often been **packaged as operating leases** in order to represent a source of **'off balance sheet finance'**.

(7)   Specific measures are used to enable classification as operating leases. These include **contingent rentals** which are excluded from the calculation of minimum lease payments;

making the **implicit interest rate impossible to calculate**, so the lessee uses an estimated rate which could reduce the PV of minimum lease payments. Also for leases of land and buildings, it is expected that the risks and rewards of ownership of land cannot pass without legal transfer of ownership. Companies may allocate as much as possible to the land element, thus ensuring the buildings element is also treated as an operating lease by reducing the PV of the minimum lease payments.

(b)   **Recommended accounting treatments**

(i)   *Electrical distribution system*

Where a **lessee** enters a **sale and leaseback transaction** resulting in an **operating lease**, then the **original** asset should be **treated as sold**. If the transaction is at fair value then immediate recognition of the profit/loss should occur.

If the transaction is above fair value, then the profit based on fair value of $65m (98 – 33) should be recognised. The balance in excess of fair value of $100m (198 – 98) should be deferred and amortised over the period for which the asset is expected to be used (10 years) ie $10m pa.

If the sales value is not at fair value, the operating lease rentals of $24m are likely to have been adjusted for the excess price paid. For AB the sales value is more than twice the fair value and the use of the *Framework* dictates the **substance of a transaction** is essentially one of **sale and a loan back equal to the deferred income element** ($100m). The company may have shown the excess over fair value as a loan and part of the costs of the operating lease will essentially be repayment of capital and interest ($12m pa).

(ii)   *Sale and leaseback of plant*

This appears to create a **finance lease** because the **lease term** is for the **major part** of the **asset's remaining life** and the PV of the **minimum lease payments** is **substantially equal to the fair value** ($43.5 + ($43.5m × 2.49))= $151.82m, compared to fair value $152m). The lease also contains a bargain purchase option. AB seems to enjoy all the risks and rewards of ownership.

Under IAS 17, where a sale and leaseback transaction results in a finance lease, any excess of sale proceeds over the carrying amount should be deferred and recognised over the lease term. Therefore the excess proceeds $52m (152 – 100) will be amortised over four years at $13m pa. The asset and the lease obligation are recorded at the sale value of $152m. Depreciation is charged on the new asset value and if the revaluation reserve is transferred to revenue reserves, this will also occur over the four year lease term.

B14 Preparation question: Financial instruments

(a)   INCOME STATEMENT

	$
Finance income	
(441,014 × (W1) 8%)	35,281
BALANCE SHEET	
Non-current assets	
Financial asset (441,014 + 35,281)	476,295

Working: Effective interest rate

$$\frac{600,000}{441,014} = 1.3605$$

∴ from tables interest rate is 8%

(b) **Compound instrument**

Presentation

	$
Non-current liabilities	
Financial liability component of convertible bond (Working)	1,797,467
Equity	
Equity component of convertible bond (2,000,000 – (Working) 1,797,467)	202,533

Working

	$
Fair value of equivalent non-convertible debt	
Present value of principal payable at end of 3 years	1,544,367

$$(4,000 \times \$500 = \$2m \times \frac{1}{(1.09)^3})$$

Present value of interest annuity payable annually in arrears	
for 3 years [(5% × $2m) × 2.531]	253,100
	1,797,467

B15 Ambush

Top tips. A whole question on IAS 39 may appear daunting, but in fact this question is quite fair.

Easy marks. These are available for the discursive aspects, which are most of the question.

Examiner's comment. The first part of the question was well answered but candidates' answers on the fair value option and impairment were of poorer quality. Candidates often set out the requirement for the impairment of non current assets rather than financial instruments. There are some similarities but the conditions are different. The problems of the fair value option are well documented and some candidates answered this part of the question very well. However many candidates offered little in the way of logical argument as to why it has caused concern. Overall however the question was well answered.

REPORT

To: Directors of Ambush
From:
Subject: IAS 39 *Financial instruments: Recognition and measurement*
Date: December 20X5

As requested, this report outlines the way in which financial instruments are measured and classified and explains why the fair value option was initially introduced.

(a) (i) **How financial assets and liabilities are measured and classified**

IAS 39 states that all financial assets and liabilities should be **measured at fair value when they are first recognised.** This is normally their cost (the fair value of the consideration given or received). Fair value **includes transaction costs** unless the instrument is **classified as 'at fair value through profit or loss'**, in which case transaction costs are **recognised in the income statement.**

The way in which an instrument is measured subsequently **depends on its classification**. There are **four categories**:

- Financial assets and liabilities at fair value through profit or loss
- Held to maturity investments
- Loans and receivables
- Available-for-sale financial assets

Financial assets and liabilities **at fair value through profit or loss** includes all items **held for trading** and all **derivative financial instruments**. Until recently it was possible to designate any financial asset or liability as 'at fair value through profit or loss'. However, as a result of the problems explained below **IAS 39 has now been amended to restrict the use of 'the fair value option'.** Unless this classification is required it can now only be used if it **results in more relevant information**, because either:

(1) It **eliminates or significantly reduces inconsistencies** that would otherwise arise from measuring assets or liabilities or recognising the gains and losses on them on different bases; or

(2) A group of financial assets, financial liabilities or both is **managed** and its **performance is evaluated** on a **fair value basis**, in accordance with a documented risk management or investment strategy.

Held to maturity investments have **fixed or determinable payments** and **fixed maturity.** The company must have the **positive intention and ability** to **hold them to maturity**. There are a number of detailed conditions that must be met before an instrument can be classified in this way. Equity instruments cannot be held to maturity investments.

Loans and receivables have **fixed or determinable payments** and are **not quoted in an active market.**

Available for sale financial assets are all **items that do not fall into the other categories**. Financial instruments not required to be classified as at fair value through profit or loss can be designated as available for sale.

IAS 39 **restricts reclassifications** between categories. Instruments cannot be reclassified into or out of 'at fair value through profit or loss'. There are penalties if held to maturity investments are reclassified or sold; a company cannot use this category again for two years.

Most financial assets are measured at fair value. Exceptions are **held to maturity investments** and **loans and receivables**, which are measured at **amortised cost**, using the **effective interest rate method**. This involves adjusting the cost of an instrument to reflect interest and repayments. The interest is allocated to accounting periods so as to achieve a **constant rate on the carrying amount** over the term of the instrument. Investments in **unquoted equity instruments** for which there is no reliable market value are measured at **cost**.

Financial **liabilities at fair value through profit or loss** are measured at **fair value. Other financial liabilities** are measured at **amortised cost**.

The way in which **gains and losses on remeasurement** are treated also depends upon the classification of the instruments. Gains and losses relating to instruments at **fair value through profit or loss** are **recognised in the income statement**, even if they are unrealised. Gains and losses relating to changes in the fair value of **available for sale financial assets** are **recognised in equity** and 'recycled' to the income statement when the asset is sold. Changes in **amortised cost** are recognised in the **income statement**.

(ii)   **Financial instruments held at fair value**

The main advantage of holding financial instruments of fair value is that **fair value provides more relevant information** than historic cost. Fair value also has **specific advantages**. It eliminates the burden of **separating embedded derivatives** and it **eliminates volatility** in the income statement where matched positions of financial assets and financial liabilities are not measured consistently.

However, in practice fair value has **disadvantages**. It can be **used inappropriately**. For example:

- Companies could apply fair value to financial instruments whose fair value is **not verifiable**. Because the valuation is **subjective**, they would then have scope to **manipulate profit or loss**.

- Use of fair values **could increase volatility** in profit and loss if the option were applied **selectively**.

- If **financial liabilities were held at fair value**, a company might recognise gains and losses as a result of **changes in its own creditworthiness**.

For those reasons, IAS 39 **restricts use of fair value to certain financial instruments and not others**.

(b)   (i)   **Impairment of financial assets**

IAS 39 states that **at each balance sheet date**, an entity should **assess** whether there is any **objective evidence that a financial asset or group of assets is impaired**. **Indications** of impairment include **significant financial difficulty** of the issuer; the probability that the borrower will **enter bankruptcy**; a **default** in interest or principal payments; or (for available for sale financial assets) a significant and prolonged **decline in fair value** below cost.

Where there is objective evidence of impairment, the entity should **determine the amount** of any impairment loss, which should be **recognised immediately in profit or loss**. Only losses relating to **past events** can be recognised. **Two conditions** must be met before an impairment loss is recognised:

- There is **objective evidence** of impairment as a result of one or more events that **occurred after the initial recognition** of the asset; and

- The **impact on the estimated future cash flows** of the asset can be **reliably estimated.**

For financial assets **carried at amortised cost** (held to maturity investments and loans and receivables) the impairment loss is the **difference** between the asset's **carrying amount** and its **recoverable amount**. The asset's recoverable amount is the **present value of estimated future cash flows**, discounted at the financial instrument's **original** effective interest rate.

For financial assets **carried at cost** because their fair value cannot be reliably measured, the impairment loss is the **difference** between the asset's **carrying amount** and the **present value of estimated future cash flows**, discounted at the **current market rate of return for a similar financial instrument.**

For **available for sale** financial assets, the impairment loss is the **difference** between the **acquisition cost** (net of any principal repayment and amortisation) and **current fair value** (for equity instruments) or **recoverable amount** (for debt instruments).

Assets at **fair value through profit or loss** are **not subject to impairment testing**, because changes in fair value are automatically recognised immediately in profit or loss.

(ii)   **Loan to Bromwich**

The **financial difficulties** and **reorganisation** of Bromwich are **objective evidence of impairment**. The impairment loss is the **difference** between the **carrying amount** of the loan at 30 November 2005 and the **present value of the estimated future cash flows**, $100,000 on 30 November 2007, discounted at the **original effective interest rate of 8%**.

This is **$85,730** (100,000 × 0.8573). Therefore **the impairment loss is $114,270** (200,000 – 85,730) and this is **recognised immediately in the income statement**.

B16 Question with analysis: Lucky Dairy

Top tips. In this question you were required to deal with a scenario that had as its main theme IAS 41 *Agriculture*. You should not, however, make the mistake of thinking that this question is just about IAS 41; it required a knowledge of several other standards including IAS 37 and IFRS 5.

Examiner's comment. Some candidates had not studied the area and guessed at the answer which generally led to poor marks. However many candidates produced excellent answers although some seemed to think that the question was solely on IAS 41.

The dairy herd

The dairy herd is a **biological asset** as defined by IAS 41 *Agriculture*. IAS 41 states that a biological asset should be **measured at fair value less estimated point of sale costs** unless its fair value cannot be measured reliably. **Gains and losses** arising from a change in fair value should be **included in profit or loss** for the period.

In this case, fair value is based on market price and point of sale costs are the costs of transporting the cattle to the market. Cattle stock for the Ham and Shire regions is valued on this basis.

IAS 41 encourages companies to **analyse the change in fair value** between the movement due to **physical changes** and the movement due to **price changes** (see the table below). It also encourages companies to provide a quantified description of each group of biological assets. Therefore the value of the cows and the value of the heifers should be **disclosed separately** in the balance sheet.

Valuing the dairy herd for the Dale Region is less straightforward as its **fair value cannot be measured reliably at the date of purchase**. In this situation IAS 41 requires the herd to be valued at **cost less any impairment losses**. The standard also requires companies to provide an explanation of why fair value cannot be measured reliably and the **range of estimates** within which fair value is likely to fall.

Valuation of cattle stock, excluding Dale region

	Cows $'000	Heifers $'000	Total $'000
Fair value of herd at 1 June 20X1 (50,000 × 50)	2,500		2,500
Purchase 1 December 20X1 (25,000 × 40)		1,000	1,000
Increase in fair value less estimated point of sale costs due to price change:			
(50,000 × (55 – 50)/25,000 × (42 – 40))	250	50	300
Increase in fair value less estimated point of sale costs due to physical change:			
(50,000 × (60 – 55)/25,000 × (46 – 42))	250	100	350
Fair value less estimated point of sale costs at 31 May 20X2 (50,000 × 60/25,000 × 46)	3,000	1,150	4,150

ANSWERS

Valuation of cattle stock in Dale Region

	$'000
Cost at 1 June 20X1	
Cows (20,000 × 50)	1,000
Heifers (10,000 × 40)	400
	1,400
Less impairment loss	(200)
	1,200

Note. The herd is impaired because its recoverable amount is $1.2 million. This is the higher of fair value less costs to sell of $1 million (the amount that the Lucky Dairy has been offered) and value in use of $1.2 million (discounted value of the milk to be produced).

	$'000
Estimated fair value at 31 May 20X2 (for disclosure only):	
Cows (20,000 × 60)	1,200
Heifers (10,000 × 55)	550
	1,750

Milk

The milk is **agricultural produce** as defined by IAS 41 and should normally be measured at **fair value less estimated point of sale costs at the time of milking**. In this case the company is holding ten times the amount of inventory that it would normally hold and it is probable that much of this milk is unfit for consumption. The company should estimate the amount of milk that will not be sold and **write down** the inventory accordingly. The write down should be disclosed separately in the income statement as required by IAS 1 *Presentation of financial statements.*

Government grant

Under IAS 41, the government grant should be recognised as income **when it becomes receivable**. As it was only on 6 June 20X2 that the company received official confirmation of the amount to be paid, the income **should not be recognised in the current year**. The amount may be sufficiently material to justify disclosure as a non-adjusting event after the balance sheet date.

Legal proceedings and additional compensation

The lawyers have indicated that the company will probably be found liable for passing on the disease to consumers. There is a **present obligation as the result of a past obligating event** and therefore a **provision for $2 million should be recognised,** as required by IAS 37 *Provisions, contingent liabilities and contingent assets.*

IAS 37 states that **reimbursement** should only be recognised when it is **virtually certain** to be received. It is **only possible** that the company will receive compensation for the legal costs and therefore this **cannot be recognised**. However, the compensation should be disclosed as a contingent asset in the financial statements.

Planned sale of Dale farms

The Board of Directors has **approved the planned closure**, but there has **not yet been a public announcement**. Despite the fact that a local newspaper has published an article on the possible sale, the company **has not created a valid expectation** that the sale will take place and in fact **it is not certain** that the sale will occur. Therefore there is no **'constructive obligation'** and under IAS 37 **no provision should be made** for redundancy or any other costs connected with the planned sale.

Under IFRS 5 *Non-current assets held for sale and discontinued operations* Dale must be treated as a **continuing operation** for the year ended 31 May 20X2 as the sale has not taken place. As management are not yet fully committed to the sale **neither the operation as a whole nor any of the separate assets of Dale can be classified as 'held for sale'**.

C1 Mineral

Top tips. This question required candidates to discuss the nature of information, which could be disclosed in annual reports in order to better assess the performance of a company.

The question was case study based although many candidates ignored the information in the question. This type of question will arise regularly.

Where you are required to write a report, develop a plan or structure. Identify headings and sub-headings before you begin writing that will help you stick to the question requirements.

Examiner's comment. Too often candidates simply wrote about environmental reporting, or produced a ratio analysis type answer, or assessed the current performance of the company. The question was about the information content of published financial statements and how this might be improved. This was clearly set out in the question.

Answers were often wide-ranging and irrelevant and candidates sometimes spent a disproportionate amount of time on this question. However, generally speaking the layout and style of the reports were quite good and marks were awarded accordingly.

Marking scheme

		Marks
Reporting business performance:	Strategy and targets	3
	Operating performance	2
	Risks	2
	Investment	2
Analysis of financial position:	Long term capital structure	2
	Liquidity	2
	Treasury management	2
Corporate citizenship:	Corporate governance	2
	Ethics	1
	Employee reports	1
	Environment	1
Use of information in question		4
Style and layout		4
	Available	28
	Maximum	25

REPORT

To:	The Directors, Mineral
From:	Accountant
Date:	12 November 20X1

Information to improve assessment of corporate performance

In addition to the main financial statements, annual reports need to contain information about **key elements of corporate activity**. This report focuses on three main areas.

- Reporting business performance
- Analysis of the financial position
- Nature of corporate citizenship

(a)   **Reporting business performance**

A report on business performance may include a ratio analysis, with a year on year comparison. The ratios commonly selected are those concerned with **profitability and liquidity:**

Profitability

	20X1	20X0
Return on capital employed	$\dfrac{10}{59+13} = 13.9\%$	$\dfrac{9}{46+9} = 16.4\%$
$\dfrac{\text{Gross profit}}{\text{Sales}}$	$\dfrac{45}{250} = 18\%$	$\dfrac{35}{201} = 17.4\%$
$\dfrac{\text{PBIT}}{\text{Sales}}$	$\dfrac{10}{250} \times 100\% = 4\%$	$\dfrac{9}{201} \times 100\% = 4.5\%$

Long– and short-term liquidity

$\dfrac{\text{Current assets}}{\text{Current liabilities}}$	$\dfrac{55}{25} = 2.2$	$\dfrac{43}{24} = 1.8$
$\dfrac{\text{Long - term liabilities}}{\text{Equity}}$	$\dfrac{13}{59} \times 100\% = 22\%$	$\dfrac{9}{46} \times 100\% = 19.6\%$

These ratios raise a number of questions.

Use of ratios

(i)   **Gross profit margin** has **risen**, while **operating profit margin** and **return on capital employed** have **fallen**. Possible problems with **control of overheads?**

(ii)   **Short-term liquidity** has **improved**, but **gearing** has **deteriorated**. Is the company using long-term loans to finance expansion? The company has **expanded**, both in revenue and non-current assets.

(iii)   **Standard ratios** are a useful tool, but must be discussed in relation to the **specific circumstances of the company.**

- The **impact of the increase in production** through the **acquisition** of the **competitor company** and the **regeneration** of **old plants** needs to be taken into account when considering revenue and non-current asset ratios and other comments in the report.

- When considering profit ratios, the **effectiveness of the cost control programme** might be assessed.

(iv)   As well as **year on year comparison**, a report on business performance might usefully **compare actual performance against targets**. To enhance the usefulness of the information, the targets should be industry specific, measurable and realistic.

- The targets set for growth in retained earnings are 20% for 20X2 and between 20% to 25% thereafter. Reporting on actual performance would be informative.

- An objective is to generate the growth by the introduction of new products and improved efficiency. The actual performance in these areas might also be worthy of comment.

(v)   The discussion of **business performance** also takes into consideration the **risks** that the business faces. In the context of Mineral, such a discussion would cover:

- The proposed $40m **expenditure on research and development and investment in non-current assets.** Are the directors justified in assuming the **predicted growth** in **retained earnings** that this **large expenditure** is meant to bring about?

BPP)))
LEARNING MEDIA

- The **joint project** to develop a new aluminium car body will be very lucrative if successful, but is the risk v return decision appropriate?

- The company's pricing strategy and projected increase in demand should be discussed.

(vi) **Knowledge management** is also an important issue where new processes and products are being developed.

(vii) As modern investors become more sophisticated, they are also likely to want to learn about the company's **strategic objectives** including the maintenance and development of **income and profit streams**, future projects and capital expenditure projects.

(b) **Analysis of the financial position**

(i) Annual reports should contain a review of the company's **financing arrangements** and **financial position** as well as a review of its **operating activities**.

(ii) In the case of Mineral plc, such a review is likely to note that:

- **Gearing has increased, but it is still low**, so the expenditure on research and development could be financed by borrowing, if not by retained earnings.

- Of the long-term loans of $13m, debentures of $4m could be converted into shares or redeemed.

- Should the debentures be **converted**, the **existing shareholders' interest will be diluted**, and they should be made aware of this.

- Current assets are comfortably in excess of current liabilities (by $30m), so the company should have little problem in redeeming the debentures.

(iii) The report will need to disclose information about the **treasury management policies** of the company. This would cover such issues as the potential adverse movement in **foreign exchange risk** and details of the use of **financial instruments** for **hedging**.

(iv) **Currency risk and interest rate risk** need to be **managed and minimised**, and the report needs to disclose the **company's approach** for dealing with this.

(v) **Credit risk** is also an **important issue**, particularly as the company operates in the **global market place**.

(vi) A **cash flow statement** will be provided as part of the financial statements, but the annual report should also indicate the **maturity profile of borrowings**.

(vii) Finally, the financial analysis might benefit from the use of techniques such as **SWOT analysis,** covering **potential liquidity problems** and **market growth**. Reference would be made to the **cartel** of car manufacturers aiming to prevent the increased use of aluminium in the car industry.

(c) **Nature of corporate citizenship**

(i) Increasingly businesses are expected to be **socially responsible as well as profitable**.

(ii) **Strategic decisions** by businesses, particularly global businesses nearly always have wider **social consequences**. It could be argued, as Henry Mintzburg does, that a company produces two outputs:

- goods and services
- the social consequences of its activities, such as pollution.

(iii) One **major development** in the area of corporate citizenship is the **environmental report.**

- This is not a legal requirement, but a large number of UK FTSE 100 companies produce them.

- Worldwide there are around 20 award schemes for environmental reporting, notably the ACCA's.

(iv) Mineral shows that it is responsible with regard to the environment by disclosing the following information.

- The use of the **eco-productivity index** in the financial performance of sites and divisions. This **links environmental and financial performance**

- The **regeneration of old plants**

- The development of **eco-friendly cars**. Particularly impressive, if successful, is the project to develop a new aluminium alloy car body. Aluminium is rust-free, and it is also lighter, which would reduce fuel consumption.

(v) Another environmental issue which the company could consider is **emission levels** from factories. Many companies now **include details** of this in their **environmental report**.

(vi) The other main aspect of corporate citizenship where Mineral plc scores highly is in its **treatment of its workforce.** The company sees the workforce as the **key factor** in the **growth** of its business. The car industry had a reputation in the past for **restrictive practices,** and the annual report could usefully discuss the extent to which these have been eliminated.

(vii) **Employees** of a businesses are **stakeholders** in that business, along with shareholders and customers. A company wishing to demonstrate good corporate citizenship will therefore be concerned with **employee welfare**. Accordingly, the annual report might usefully contain information on details of **working hours**, **industrial accidents** and **sickness of employees**.

(viii) In conclusion, it can be seen that the annual report can, and should go **far beyond the financial statements** and traditional ratio analysis.

C2 Value relevance

Top tips. This question required candidates to discuss the importance of published financial statements as a source of information, how financial reporting is changing to meet various needs, the problem of reliance on the earnings figure and the use of fair values. Part (c) of the question required a discussion about 'fair value' accounting.

Examiner's comment. The question was quite well answered but many candidates' answers were quite narrow, relying on traditional advantages and disadvantages of published financial statements. Again there was evidence of a lack of knowledge of current thinking and practice. Many candidates simply discussed the benefits of ratio analysis which is not sufficient for a Part 3 paper. Candidates would benefit from reading the scenario at the beginning of the question, as it often contains some guidance as regards the nature of the answer required. Part (c) was not well answered and candidates struggled to find examples of the use of 'fair value' accounting.

Marking scheme

		Marks
(a)	Subjective	11
(b)	Subjective	8
(c)	Subjective	6
		25

(a) **The importance of published financial statements**

The objective of published financial statements is to satisfy the information needs of users. Some types of user will always need financial statements as their main source of information about a company. **Companies are normally required to file financial statements with the regulatory authorities** so that a certain amount of information is available to the general public. The government uses financial statements in order to assess taxation and to regulate the activities of businesses.

Financial reporting has evolved to meet the needs of investors in large public companies and their advisers. Yet **published financial statements have serious limitations**: they are based on historic information and they only reflect the financial effects of transactions and events. **Investors need to predict a company's future performance**, including changes in shareholder value. These are affected by the development of new products, the quality of management, the use of new technology and the economic and political environment.

Traditional financial statements are **only one of many sources of information used by investors**. Other sources include **market data, product information, quarterly earnings announcements, press conferences and other briefings given by the directors to institutional investors, analysts and financial journalists**.

Traditional ratio analysis is becoming outdated. The Association for Investment Management and Research (AIMR) has developed global investment performance standards. These are based on 'total return', which includes realised and unrealised gains and income and rates of return that are adjusted for daily-weighted cash flows. **Earnings per share and the price earnings ratio continue to be important, but analysts now calculate a range of other measures. These include cash flow per share, market value per share and 'consensus earnings per share', which predicts future performance.**

Free cash flow is a key performance measure used by analysts to value a company. Free cash flow is cash revenues less cash expenses, taxation paid, cash needed for working capital and cash required for routine capital expenditure. **This can be compared with the cost of capital employed to assess whether shareholder value has increased or decreased**. It can also be projected and discounted to provide an approximate market value.

(b) **How financial reporting is changing**

Financial reporting practice develops over time in response to changes in the business environment. For example, because businesses are entering into more sophisticated transactions, financial reporting **standards are now based on principles rather than rules**. Businesses increasingly operate across national boundaries and so there is an **emphasis on international convergence of accounting standards**. These developments improve the transparency and comparability of the information available to investors and other users of the financial statements.

Businesses increasingly recognise the **limitations of traditional financial statements** and **non-financial information is now routinely included in the annual report**. Companies disclose information about **risks and opportunities, long term goals, products, human resources, intangible assets and research and development activities**. They may also report the effects of their operations on the **natural environment** and on the **wider social community**. These disclosures reflect a growing awareness that **an entity's performance goes far beyond its earnings for the year**.

Despite this, **many users and preparers of financial statements still focus narrowly on the earnings figure**. As a result, earnings before interest, tax, depreciation and amortisation **(EBITDA) has been developed as a key performance measure. 'Aggressive earnings management' (inappropriate methods of revenue recognition) and other forms of 'creative accounting' may be used in an attempt to enhance EBITDA.** Emphasis on profits means that quite small changes in earnings can bring about major fluctuations in a company's share price.

(c) **The use of fair values**

Financial statements should provide information that helps users to predict the future performance of a company. Fair values are more relevant than historic costs for this purpose. In theory fair values reflect the present value of future cash flows and the fair value of an asset shows its potential contribution to future cash flows.

However, **there will always be a difference between the overall value of a company and the aggregate fair values of its assets and liabilities**. (This difference is often described as goodwill.) There may not be a direct relationship between future cash flows and the assets and liabilities on the balance sheet. In addition, **investors and others may use financial statements for purposes other than predicting future performance and cash flows**.

It can be difficult to arrive at a fair value for an asset or liability because there may not always be a reliable market price. If this is the case, (in theory) fair values are based on the company's own predictions of future cash flow and can only be subjective.

Historic cost accounting has the advantages of being **objective and reliable**. It is **based on actual transactions which can be verified**. Therefore **traditional historic cost financial statements may better meet the needs of users than financial statements based on fair values**.

C3 Preparation question: Financial analysis

Top tips. This is a straightforward question on interpretation of accounts, of a manageable size and providing you with all the ratios you need. You should, as with all interpretation questions, spend some time *thinking* about the ratios before you start writing. Mark what you think are the significant trends shown in the question and make brief notes which will serve as an answer plan. Then proceed to discuss each area, using sensible headings to break your report up, and including a brief introduction and conclusion.

WANDAFOOD PRODUCTS
FIVE YEAR SUMMARY: 20X1 TO 20X5

Prepared by: An Accountant
Date: 28 February 20X6

Introduction

This report discusses the trends shown in the five year summary prepared from the published accounts for the five years ended 31 December 20X5. It also considers how price changes over that period may have limited the usefulness of the historical cost data provided.

Profitability

The net profit margin has remained fairly constant, although it dropped in 20X3. Operating asset turnover has decreased over the five years, pulling back a little in 20X4. Return on assets, the primary ratio produced by combining these two secondary ratios, has therefore decreased over the period but was at its lowest in 20X3.

These findings seem to indicate that **assets** are being **used inefficiently** and that this has caused the decrease in return on assets. Inflation may be responsible for increases in revenue which would mask even worse **decreases in efficiency**.

Interest and dividend cover

Interest cover improved markedly between 20X1 and 20X2, falling back a little in 20X3 and 20X4 but now below the 20X1 level, indicating increases in debt and/or interest rates. Dividend cover, however, after dropping below 20X1 levels, has now recovered some lost ground. In both cases cover was adequate, even at the lowest points. However, since there has been a substantial increase in gearing, interest cover ought to be watched carefully. **Profits** may be available to cover interest and dividends, but this must be **matched by good cash flow**.

Debt to equity

Debt to equity fell dramatically in 20X2 but has steadily increased until in 20X5 it was almost double its 20X1 level. Minority interests appear to have remained a relatively insignificant element in the group's funding. It is more likely that debt has increased than equity has decreased (for example, because of a purchase or redemption of own shares). Interest cover has fallen in line with this increase in borrowing as a proportion of long-term capital.

Liquidity

Both the current and the quick ratios have declined over the period, except for 20X2 when they both improved. However, they have been fairly constant between 20X3 and 20X5 and are quite high, although comments on the adequacy of these ratios are of very limited utility in the absence of **information** about the **company's activities and industry averages**.

The reduction may have been planned to reduce the costs involved in maintaining high levels of inventories and allowing **generous credit to customers**. From the differential between the quick and current ratios it would seem that inventories are a significant asset here. However, current liabilities must not be allowed to increase to the extent that current assets (and especially liquid assets) are insufficient to cover them, as this can lead to a liquidity crisis. Worsening liquidity ratios can be an **indicator of overtrading**; but this most often arises when expansion is funded from short-term borrowings, whereas new long-term debt appears to have been found in this case.

Assets

As working capital has fallen in size, it is now being used more efficiently, generating more revenue from a reduced base. It would seem likely, given the slight fall in operating asset turnover, that non-current asset turnover has worsened considerably and that the improvement in working capital turnover has compensated for this in calculating return on assets. It may be that long-term borrowings have financed capital expenditure which has not yet affected operations. (An increase in the amount of non-current assets would decrease non-current asset turnover if revenue did not increase correspondingly.)

Investors' ratios

Earnings, dividends and net assets per share have all increased over the period. There has, therefore, been no need to increase dividends regardless of fluctuations in earnings.

The increase in net assets per share seems to indicate either that **retained profits** and **borrowings** have been **used** to increase **non-current asset expenditure** or (less likely) that assets have been revalued each year.

Inflation

Historical cost accounts do not show the effect on the **group's operating capacity** of rising prices over a period. The modest increases in EPS and dividend do not suggest that profit has increased sufficiently to compensate for more than a very low level of inflation. It is also possible that the value of assets is understated, so that ROCE and asset turnover measures are all understated. The **underlying trends** in **real terms** may be very much worse than those shown in historical cost terms.

Conclusion

The group would appear, from this superficial analysis, to be a steady performer but not expanding fast. This may be an advantage in times of recession: debt is probably not so high as to cause liquidity problems nor have shareholders come to expect a **high payout ratio**. However, inflation may be eroding its profits. The possible recent expansion of non-current assets may help it to grow in future, as will its improved working capital management.

C4 Rockby and Bye

Top tips. This question required candidates to have knowledge of IFRS 5 and discontinued operations. The question has been amended to reflect the publication of a full IFRS, rather than the original exposure draft. In part (b), you had to discuss whether certain assets would be considered to be 'held for sale'.

Easy marks. The obvious easy marks are for Part (a), which is straight out of your Study Text. But as the examiner said, 'Often in questions of this nature, candidates assume certain facts about the scenario. If the assumptions are reasonable, due regard is taken and credit given.'

Examiner's comment. This question was well answered, though candidates did not use the facts of the question in formulating their answer as much as they should have done.

				Marks
(a)	Discussion – IAS			3
	Impairment – IAS			5
(b)	(i)	Operating lease		4
		Plant		3
	(ii)	Property		6
			Available	21
			Maximum	19

(a) **Sale of the subsidiary**

IFRS 5 *Non-current assets held for sale and discontinued operations* requires an asset or disposal group to be classified as held for sale where it is **available for immediate sale** in its **present condition** subject only to **terms that are usual** and customary and the sale is **highly probable**. For a sale to be highly probable:

- Management must be **committed** to the sale.
- An **active programme to locate a buyer** must have been initiated.
- The **market price** must be **reasonable** in relation to the asset's current fair value.
- The sale must be **expected to be completed within one year** from the date of classification.

The proposed sale of Bye **appears to meet these conditions**. Although the sale had not taken place by the time that the 20X4 financial statements were approved, **negotiations were in progress** and the sale is expected to take place on 1 July 20X4, well **within a year** after the decision to sell. Rockby had **committed** itself to the sale **before its year-end of 31 March 20X4.**

Where a subsidiary is held for sale it **continues to be included** in the consolidated financial statements, but it is **presented separately** from other assets and liabilities in the balance sheet and its assets and liabilities should not be offset. If Bye represents a **separate major line of business or geographical area** of operations it will also qualify as a **discontinued operation**, which means that on the **face of the income statement** the group must disclose a single amount comprising the **total of its post-tax loss for the year** and **any post-tax gain or loss recognised on its remeasurement. Further analysis is required in the notes** and the notes must also disclose a description of the facts and circumstances leading to the expected disposal and the expected manner and timing of the disposal.

Bye must be **reviewed for impairment** immediately before its classification as 'held for sale'. The calculation is as follows:

	$'000
Net assets at 31 March 20X4	5,000
Goodwill	1,000
	6,000
Value in use at 15 May 20X4	3,900
Add losses incurred from 1 April 20X4 to 15 May 20X4	500
Value in use at 31 March 20X4	4,400
Fair value less costs to sell	4,500

Recoverable amount is the **higher of fair value less costs to sell** and **value in use**. In this case, recoverable amount **is fair value less costs to sell** and so there is an **impairment loss of $1.5 million.** IFRS 5 requires items held for sale to be measured at the **lower of carrying amount and fair value less costs to sell** and therefore Bye will be carried **at $4.5 million** in the balance sheet and the loss of $1.5 million will be recognised in the income statement.

(b)   **Items of plant**

If the items of plant are to be classified as 'held for sale', management must be **committed** to the sale and the sale must be **highly probable** and **expected to take place within one year**. The operating leases **do not appear to qualify** as the company is **undecided** as to whether to sell or lease the plant under finance leases. Therefore the company should **continue to treat them as non-current assets** and to depreciate them. The value in use of the items is greater than their carrying value and so they are **not impaired**.

The other items of plant will also **not be classified as 'held for sale'**. Although they were no longer in use at 31 March 20X4 and were sold subsequently, a **firm decision** to sell them **had not been made by the year-end**. IFRS 5 **prohibits retrospective use** of the 'held for sale' classification if, as in this case, assets are sold after the year end but before the financial statements are authorised for issue, although the sale should be **disclosed as an event after the balance sheet date**. IFRS 5 also requires **disclosure** of the **facts and circumstances** of the sale and a **description** of the items, together with the segment in which they are presented under IAS 14 *Segment reporting* (if applicable).

Head office land and buildings

In order to qualify as 'held for sale' an asset must be **available for immediate sale** in its **present condition**, subject to the usual terms. Although the company had taken the decision to sell the property at 31 March 20X3, the **subsidence** would have meant that a buyer was **unlikely to be found** for the property until the renovations had taken place. Therefore the property **did not qualify as 'held for sale' at 31 March 20X3**.

At 31 March 20X4 the property **had been on the market for nine months** at the price of $10 million. **No buyer** had yet been found. Despite the fact that the **market had deteriorated significantly** the company had **not reduced the price**. The property was eventually sold for $7.5 million on 1 June 20X4. To qualify as being held for sale at the year-end the **market price must be reasonable** in relation to the asset's current fair value. It appears that the market price of $10 million is **not reasonable when compared with the eventual selling price** of $7.5 million, the **offer** of $8.3 million received on 20 April or the **carrying value** of $7 million. Therefore the property **should not be classified as 'held for sale' at 31 March 20X4**.

C5 Vident

Top tips. This question examined the topic of share-based payment. The first part of the question dealt with the reasons why a standard was needed in this area. This type of question will often appear when a new standard is issued. The other elements dealt with the accounting for a shared-based payment transaction, and the deferred tax implications.

Easy marks. Part (a) is very straightforward and can be reproduced from the BPP Study Text. And nine marks is generous for a straightforward bit.

Examiner's comment. Candidates did not seem to know IFRS 2 very well. Candidates managed to discuss the reasons behind the standard quite well but generally found it difficult to account for a transaction. The actual calculation of the expense/equity to be recognised was at a basic level, but candidates did not seem to be able to achieve the desired result – a discussion, and calculation, of the way a share-based transaction should be accounted for. Similarly, the deferred tax implications were generally not understood by candidates. The deferred tax aspect is important for companies adopting the standard, as in many regions a significant deferred tax asset may be created.

		Marks
(a)	Discussion	9
(b)	Computation and discussion	9
(c)	Computation and discussion	7
	Available/maximum	25

REPORT

To: Directors of Vident
From:
Subject: IFRS 2 Share based payment
Date: June 20X5

As requested, this report explains why share based payments should be recognised in the financial statements. It also explains how the directors' share options should be accounted for in the financial statements for the year ended 31 May 20X5.

(a) **Why share based payments should be recognised in the financial statements**

IFRS 2 *Share based payment* applies to **all share option schemes granted after 7 November 2002**. The directors have put forward several arguments for not recognising the expense of remunerating directors in this way.

Share options have no cost to the company

When shares are **issued for cash** or in a business acquisition, **an accounting entry is needed** to **recognise the receipt of cash** (or other resources) as consideration for the issue. Share options (the right to receive shares in future) **are also issued in consideration for resources**: services rendered by directors or employees. These resources are **consumed by the company** and it would be **inconsistent not to recognise an expense**.

Share issues do not meet the definition of an expense in the IASB Framework

The *Framework* defines an expense as a **decrease in economic benefits** in the form of **outflows of assets** or **incurrences of liabilities**. It is not immediately obvious that employee services meet the definition of an asset and therefore **it can be argued that consumption of those services does not meet the definition of an expense**. However, share options **are issued for consideration in the form of employee services** so that **arguably there is an asset**, although it is **consumed at the same time that it is received**. Therefore the recognition of an expense relating to share based payment is **consistent with the *Framework***.

The expense relating to share options is already recognised in the diluted earnings per share calculation

It can be argued that to recognise an expense in the income statement **would have the effect of distorting diluted earnings per share** as diluted earnings per share would then **take the expense into account twice**. This is not a valid argument. There are **two events** involved: **issuing the options**; and **consuming the resources** (the directors' services) received as consideration. The diluted earnings per share calculation **only reflects the issue of the options**; there is **no adjustment to basic earnings**. Recognising an expense reflects the consumption of services. There is **no 'double counting'**.

BPP
LEARNING MEDIA

Accounting for share based payment may discourage the company from introducing new share option plans

This is quite **possibly true**. Accounting for share based payment **reduces earnings**. However, it **improves the information provided** in the financial statements, as these now make users aware of the **true economic consequences** of issuing share options as remuneration. The economic consequences are the reason why share option schemes may be discontinued. IFRS 2 simply **enables management and shareholders** to **reach an informed decision** on the best method of remuneration.

(b) **Accounting for share options in the financial statements for the year ended 31 May 20X5**

The basic principle of accounting for share options is that **an expense is recognised** for the **services rendered** by the directors and a **corresponding amount is credited to equity**. The transaction is **measured at the fair value of the options granted at the grant date** and fair value is taken to be the **market price**. Where (as is usual) options vest only after staff have completed a specified period of service, the expense is **allocated to accounting periods over this period of service.**

Options granted to J. Van Heflin on 1 June 20X3

The **performance conditions have been met** and the director is **still working for the company** at 31 May 20X5. As the **number of shares** that will vest is **fixed**, the expense is **allocated on a straight line basis to the two years ended 31 May 20X5.**

Options granted to R. Ashworth on 1 June 20X4

The **performance conditions** (the increase in the share price to $13.50) **have not yet been met**. However, the director is **still working for the company** and **must work for the company for three years** before the options vest, so the **expense is recognised**. Again, the **number of shares is fixed**, so the expense is **allocated on a straight line basis over the three years to 31 May 20X7.**

The expense to be recognised is calculated as follows:

	At 1 June 20X4 $	*Year ended 31 May 20X5* $
J. Van Heflin (20,000 × $5 × ½)	50,000	50,000
R. Ashworth (50,000 × $6 × 1/3)		100,000
	50,000	150,000

At 1 June 20X4 the **opening balance of retained earnings is reduced by $50,000** and a **separate component of equity is increased by $50,000**.

An **expense of $150,000 is recognised** in the income statement for the year ended 31 May 20X5. **Equity** (the same separate component as before) is **credited with $150,000**.

(c) **Deferred tax implications of the recognition of an expense for directors' share options**

The company will **recognise an expense** for the consumption of employee services given in consideration for share options granted, **but will not receive a tax deduction until the share options are actually exercised.** Therefore a **temporary difference arises** and IAS 12 *Income taxes* requires the recognition of deferred tax.

A **deferred tax asset** (a deductible temporary difference) results from the **difference** between the **tax base of the services received** (a tax deduction in future periods) and the **carrying value of zero**. IAS 12 requires the **measurement** of the deductible temporary difference to be based on the **intrinsic value of the options at the year end**. This is the **difference** between the **fair value of the share** and the **exercise price of the option**.

If the amount of the **estimated future tax deduction exceeds the amount of the related cumulative remuneration expense**, the tax deduction relates not only to the remuneration expense, but to equity. If this is the case, the **excess should be recognised directly in equity.**

ANSWERS

At 1 June 20X4

Deferred tax asset:

	$
Fair value (20,000 × $12.50 × 1/2)	125,000
Exercise price of option (20,000 × $4.50 × ½)	(45,000)
Intrinsic value (estimated tax deduction)	80,000
Tax at 30%	24,000

The cumulative remuneration expense is $50,000, which is less than the estimated tax deduction. Therefore:

- A deferred tax asset of $24,000 is recognised in the opening balance sheet.
- Opening retained earnings are increased by $15,000 (50,000 × 30%).
- The excess of $9,000 (30,000 × 30%) goes to equity.

The comparative is re-stated for the options granted on 1 June 20X3.

Year to 31 May 20X5

Deferred tax asset:

	$
Fair value:	
(20,000 × $12)	240,000
(50,000 × $12 × 1/3)	200,000
	440,000
Exercise price of options	
(20,000 × $4.50)	(90,000)
(50,000 × $6 × 1/3)	(100,000)
Intrinsic value (estimated tax deduction)	250,000
Tax at 30%	75,000
Less previously recognised	(24,000)
	51,000

The cumulative remuneration expense is $200,000, which is less than the estimated tax deduction. Therefore:

- A deferred tax asset of $75,000 is recognised in the balance sheet at 31 May 20X5.
- There is potential deferred tax income of $51,000 for the year ended 31 May 20X5.
- Of this, $6,000 (50,000 × 30% – 9,000) goes directly to equity.
- The remainder ($45,000) is recognised in the income statement for the year.

I hope that the above explanations and advice are helpful. Please do not hesitate to contact me should you require any further assistance.

LEARNING MEDIA

C6 Ashlee

Top tips. This question was a case study which described mistakes or problems occurring in the financial statements of a company. Candidates had to discuss the implications for the financial statements. The case study dealt with going concern, reorganisation provisions, discontinuance, revenue recognition, impairment, financial instruments, and breach of loan covenants. The answer required a discussion of the implications of the events, together with relevant computations. In the answer, it is important to set out the basic principles relating to the event, then quantify (if possible) the impact on the financial statements and, finally, to discuss the implications/solutions to the problem.

Easy marks. There are no obviously easy marks in this question, which does not specify a mark allocation for each item. It is best to assume that marks are allocated equally.

Examiner's comment. The question was quite well-answered but candidates do not seem to be able to apply their knowledge to the case study. Instead, rote knowledge was set out in answers and not application of that knowledge. This is a continuing problem. In addition, the areas covered by this question appear frequently in this paper and yet the standard of answers is not really improving.

Marking scheme

		Marks
Introduction		3
Pilot		9
Gibson		8
Ashlee		6
	Available	26
	Maximum	25

General

The **mistakes** which have been found in the financial statements **must be adjusted** before the financial statements are approved by the directors and published.

Loan covenants have been breached. This means that **the directors should determine whether the company continues to be a going concer**n. If this is not the case, the financial statements for the year ended 31 March 20X5 should not be prepared on a going concern basis. The company appears to have come to an arrangement with the loan creditors and this suggests that **in practice it will be able to carry on trading** at least in the short term. Any **material uncertainties** that **cast doubts on the company's ability to continue as a going concern** should be **disclosed** in the notes to the financial statements, as required by IAS 1 *Presentation of financial statements*.

The fact that the loan covenants have been breached suggests that **the assets of the group may have become impaired**. An **impairment review should be carried out** in accordance with IAS 36 *Impairment of assets* and **any impairment loss should be recognised** in the financial statements for the year ended 31 March 20X5.

Pilot

IAS 37 *Provisions, contingent liabilities and contingent assets* states that **a provision for reorganisation costs cannot be recognised** unless the entity had a **constructive obligation** to carry out the reorganisation at the year end. The **decision** to reorganise Pilot **was not taken until after the year end.** Therefore the reorganisation costs of $4 million **cannot be recognised** in the financial statements for the year ended 31 March 20X5. The financial statements should **disclose** details of the planned reorganisation in the notes as it is a **non-adjusting event** as defined by IAS 10 *Events after the balance sheet date*.

A major reorganisation indicates that **the assets of Pilot may be impaired** and so an **impairment review is required**. Because the **reorganisation costs** cannot be recognised, these **should not be included in any calculation of recoverable amount**. The **recoverable amount** (value in use) of Pilot is **$82 million** without the reorganisation, this is **less than the carrying value of $85 million** and therefore the company should **recognise an impairment loss of $3 million**. This reduces the carrying value of Pilot's **goodwill**. IAS 36 **prohibits** any **subsequent reversal** of impairment losses **relating to goodwill.**

Gibson

The **decision** to sell Gibson was **made before the year end**. Therefore **IFRS 5** *Non-current assets held for sale and discontinued operations* **may apply.** The contract for sale **was being negotiated** at the time of preparation of the financial statements and the sale **appears to be certain**. Therefore Gibson **meets the definition of a 'disposal group'**: a group of assets to be disposed of in a single transaction.

A disposal group is **measured at the lower of its carrying amount and fair value less costs to sell**. The **carrying amount is $450 million** and **fair value less costs to sell is $410 million** ($415 million less selling costs of $5 million) and therefore **an impairment loss of $40 million is recognised**. The loss is **allocated as set out in IAS 36**: first to goodwill, then to the other non-current assets on a pro-rata basis.

Impairment calculation:

	Before impairment $m	Impairment loss $m	After impairment $m
Goodwill	30	(30)	–
Property, plant and equipment at cost	120	(4)	116
Property, plant and equipment at valuation	180	(6)	174
Inventory	100	–	100
Net current assets	20	–	20
	450	(40)	410

(An impairment review would have been required even if there had been no plans to sell Gibson, because of the reorganisation.)

A disposal group is **separately disclosed on the face of the balance sheet** and **details** of the disposal **are disclosed in the notes** to the financial statements.

Revenue recognition

IAS 18 *Revenue* states that **where properties are sold**, sales **revenue should be recognised when title passes**. Ashlee has followed this policy in previous years and **the change seems questionable**. Therefore the **profit of $10 million on sale should not be recognised** in the income statement and the properties should **continue to be recognised at their carrying value in the balance sheet.**

Financial instruments

IAS 39 *Financial instruments: Recognition and measurement* allows some financial assets to be designated as 'at fair value through profit or loss'. The shares are **neither derivatives, nor held for trading** and so they are **not required to be classified as 'at fair value through profit or loss'**. Investments in equity instruments that **do not have a quoted market price** in an active market and **whose fair value cannot be reliably measured cannot be designated in this way**. A recent amendment to IAS 39 **restricts the use of the fair value option** to situations where a group of financial assets is **managed and its performance evaluated on a fair value basis** or where **use of the fair value option eliminates or significantly reduces a measurement or recognition inconsistency** that would otherwise arise. It is **unclear whether either of these situations applies**.

If the shares are **designated as 'at fair value through profit or loss'** the shares are **initially valued at $3 million** (150,000 × $20). **Transaction costs are charged to the income statement**. At 31 March 2005 the shares are **revalued to their fair value of $3.75 million** (150,000 × $25) and a **gain of $750,000 is recognised in the income statement.**

BPP
LEARNING MEDIA

If the shares are **classified as 'available for sale'** they are **also valued on a fair value basis**, except that **transaction costs are included in the initial measurement**. Therefore the shares are **initially valued at $3.1 million**. At the year end they are **remeasured to $3.75 million as before**. The **gain of $650,000 is recognised in equity**, rather than as part of the profit for the year. When the shares are eventually **sold**, the cumulative **gains and losses on remeasurement are 'recycled'** from equity to the income statement.

It should be emphasised that **use of the fair value option is now restricted** and the directors should consider very carefully whether the shares actually qualify for this designation. Given **the company's present circumstances** and the fact that the **financial statements are open to particular scrutiny**, it may be **prudent to classify the shares as 'available for sale'**.

C7 Financial performance

Top tips. The question required candidates to set out why a single statement of performance was being developed. Additionally, candidates had to discuss the issues surrounding the treatment of gains and losses on tangible non-current assets, and the recycling of gains and losses. Remember that it is the characteristics of the gains and losses that determines the accounting treatment.

Easy marks. Part (a) has some easy marks for listing arguments that will be in your text book. Likewise Part (b)(ii)

Examiner's comment. The question was quite well-answered but the answers demonstrated that many candidates do not read very widely. Many candidates did not have an understanding of the different nature of gains/losses. Many candidates did not understand the issues surrounding the recognition of a profit in the performance statement on more than one occasion. Examples of recycling were not often discussed in candidates' answers.

Marking scheme

				Marks
(a)		Reasons 2 marks per point	Maximum	8
(b)	(i)	Factors 2 marks per point	Maximum	8
	(ii)	Discussion		9
			Maximum/available	25

(a) There are several reasons why the three accounting standards boards believe that a single statement of financial performance is needed. Most of these are a response to the problems of reporting performance under current accounting standards.

   (i) It is **difficult to compare** the financial performance of **entities in different countries**, because a variety of different formats are used. There are also a variety of different requirements relating to comparative information.

   (iii) Business practice is becoming more sophisticated and as a result **many see traditional performance measures such as profit before tax as too simplistic**. There is evidence that the **use of the traditional performance measures is decreasing**. The financial statements should provide users with the information that they need to arrive at key performance measures. Because the key measures used are changing and evolving it can be argued that increasingly they do not do this.

   (iii) There are a number of **different views** as to **how** an entity's **financial performance should be defined**. This means that there is no agreement on what the key performance measures should be and therefore no agreement about the information that should be provided in the financial statements

(iv)   There is often **too much aggregation** of financial information. This prevents users from analysing an entity's performance effectively.

(v)   Information is often **inconsistently classified** within and outside totals and subtotals.

(vi)   **Some relevant items are not included in profit and loss.** For example, many countries require gains and losses on the retranslation of the net investment in a foreign operation to be recognised in equity, rather than the income statement. In contrast, **some questionable items may be included in profit and loss.** Some countries require proposed dividends to be shown on the face of the income statement, although they are not an expense, but a transaction with the owners of the business.

(vii)   Current financial reporting uses a **mixed measurement model** in which some items are measured at historic cost and some at fair value. Therefore users of the financial statements **need to be able to distinguish between items measured at historic cost and items measured at fair value** and to distinguish between **operating gains** and **revaluation gains**. Some countries, such as the UK, now use an additional performance statement to record revaluation gains and losses, but reporting is inconsistent and sometimes confusing to users.

(viii)   Financial instruments have caused particular problems. It is often **difficult for users to understand the effects of financial instruments on performance**, because the way in which gains and losses are reported depends upon the classification of the instrument.

(ix)   Some countries permit the **'recycling'** of certain gains and losses from equity to the income statement so that they are **effectively recognised twice**. Others prohibit it. These **inconsistencies are unhelpful to users**.

(b)   (i)   Determining how and where to report gains and losses arising on tangible non-current assets presents particular problems. Some assets are measured at historic cost while others are measured at current value or fair value. Gains and losses take a number of different forms: revaluation gains and losses, gains and losses on disposal, depreciation and impairment.

Revaluation gains and losses are **part of an entity's performance, but not part of its operating activities.** Users need to be able to appreciate this difference and therefore there is a need to **report them separately from operating activities**. There is also an argument that as they are **not certain until the asset is sold** they should be **reported outside the main performance statement** or in a separate section of it ('other gains and losses').

It is generally accepted that **depreciation** is not a loss in market value, but an **application of the accruals concept**. Depreciation reflects the consumption of an asset by the entity and for this reason it is **reported in operating activities**.

There are two possible views of **impairment**. One is that it is a form of **depreciation**; it arises because the **economic benefits relating to an asset have been consumed**. This type of impairment is clearly an **operating loss**. The other view of impairment is that it is a **holding loss** and this **should not be reported in operating activities**. Impairment that is effectively a holding loss may arise where an asset that has previously been revalued upwards becomes impaired. Under current accounting standards, the **impairment is set off against the revaluation surplus** relating to the asset. Any excess is treated as consumption of economic benefits and is reported in operating activities. There is an **argument that** because an asset is impaired if its carrying amount is above its recoverable amount, *all* impairment losses represent consumption of economic benefits and all impairment losses should be reported within operating activities.

Gains and losses on disposal are calculated as the difference between the sale proceeds and the asset's carrying amount. There are **several arguments** for **reporting these outside operating activities**. Selling assets is **not normally part of an entity's trading operations**. Where a gain or a loss is material, users of the financial statements need to be made aware that it will not recur (although this issue is partly one of separate presentation, rather than where to report particular gains and losses in the performance statement). Where a **gain** arises **on an asset that has been revalued**, that gain is a **holding gain, rather than an operating gain**.

BPP
LEARNING MEDIA

There are also **arguments for reporting gains and losses on disposal within operating activities**. Where an asset is carried at historical cost, the gain or loss is **effectively an adjustment to depreciation** (for example, because the rate has been underestimated) and depreciation is an operating expense. The **same argument applies** where a loss on disposal has arisen **because the asset is impaired**. However, many would still take the view that there is such a thing as a holding loss (caused by a fall in market value) as distinct from an impairment loss (caused by consumption of economic benefits). A **holding loss should not be included in operating activities**. On the other hand it would **be difficult to clearly distinguish between a holding loss and an impairment loss** and this ambiguity would provide companies with a means of manipulating their operating profits.

One objective of a single performance statement is to enable users to **appreciate the various components of financial performance**. This will be achieved if **gains and losses with similar characteristics are reported together.** This will also improve the comparability of the financial statements.

(ii)   **Recycling** occurs where an item of financial performance is **reported in more than one accounting period.** An item that is recycled is recognised in the financial statements twice. For example, current accounting standards require gains and losses on the retranslation of the net investment in a foreign operation to be reported in equity when they occur and then to be reported again in the income statement (profit and loss) when the operation is eventually sold.

The main **argument for recycling** is that **all items are ultimately part of the operating or financing activities of an entity.** Therefore **all items should pass through the main performance statement** or be reported as part of earnings at some point in time, even if they have previously been recognised in equity. It has also been argued that when unrealised items become realised they should be reported again and when uncertain measurements become certain they should be reported again.

The **argument against recycling** is that **an item should only be recognised in the statement(s) of financial performance once**, regardless of whether it is realised or unrealised. If an item is recognised in the financial statements it is assumed that there is reasonable **certainty that it exists** and that it can be **measured reliably.** There is **no justification** for **recognising it in equity/'other gains and losses' in one period** and **recognising it again in profit and loss/operating activities in a subsequent period.**

The idea that an item should only be reported in profit or loss if it is **realised** (almost certain to result in a present or future inflow or outflow of cash) has **become outdated**. In many countries, **realisation is a legal concept**. Unrealised gains, such as revaluation gains, are subjective. **Only realised gains can be recognised in distributable profits** because they are **certain.** However, given the **increasing complexity of the business environment** and the **widespread use of financial instruments**, the distinction between realised and unrealised profits is **no longer a particularly useful basis** for **classifying elements of financial performance.** In practice, the effect of realised gains and losses is **shown in the cash flow statement. Unrealised items often form an important part of** an entity's **overall financial performance** and there is **no longer any real case for excluding them** from the performance statement.

C8 Egin Group

Top tips. This question dealt with the importance of the disclosure of related party transactions and the criteria determining a related party. Additionally, it required candidates to identify related parties, and to account for goodwill and a loan made to one of the related parties which was an foreign subsidiary. Don't forget, from your group accounting knowledge, that goodwill relating to the foreign subsidiary is treated as a foreign currency asset and translated at the closing rate of exchange.

Easy marks. Part (a) should earn you five very easy marks, as it is basic knowledge. Part (b) is application, but very straightforward. This leaves only nine marks for the more difficult aspects.

Examiner's comment. The importance of related parties and their criteria was quite well answered, although candidates often quoted specific examples rather than the criteria for establishing related parties. The identification of related party relationships was well answered, but the accounting for the goodwill of the foreign subsidiary (and the loan made to it) were poorly answered.

Marking scheme

			Marks
(a)	(i)	Reasons and explanation	5
	(ii)	Egin	5
		Spade	3
		Atomic	3
(b)		Goodwill	5
		Loan	5
		Available	26
		Maximum	25

(a)   (i)   Why it is important to disclose related party transactions

The directors of Egin are correct to say that related party transactions are a normal feature of business. However, where a company **controls** or can exercise **significant influence** over another the **financial performance and position of both companies can be affected**. For example, one group company can sell goods to another at artificially low prices. Even where there are no actual transactions between group companies, **a parent normally influences the way in which a subsidiary operates**. For example, a parent may instruct a subsidiary not to trade with particular customers or suppliers or not to undertake particular activities.

In the absence of other information, users of the financial statements **assume that a company pursues its interests independently** and undertakes transactions on an **arm's length basis** on terms that could have been obtained in a transaction with a third party. Knowledge of related party relationships and transactions affects the way in which users assess a company's operations and the risks and opportunities that it faces. Therefore **details of an entity's controlling party and transactions with related parties should be disclosed.** Even if the company's transactions and operations have not been affected by a related party relationship, **disclosure puts users on notice that they may be affected in future.**

IAS 24 *Related party disclosures* states that a party is related to another if:

(1)   –   the party **controls**, is **controlled** by, or is under **common control** with the entity or

      –   has an interest in the entity that gives it **significant influence** over the entity or

–   has **joint control** over the entity

(2)   the party is an **associate** of the entity or a **joint venture**

(3)   the party is a member of the **key management personnel** of the entity or its parent

(4)   the party is a **close family member** of anyone referred to in (a) or (c) above

(5)   the party is **controlled, jointly controlled** or **significantly influenced** by any individual in (c) or (d) above

Control is the **power to govern the financial and operating policies of an entity** so as to obtain benefits from its activities. Significant influence is the **power to participate** in the financial and operating policy decisions of the entity but is not control over those policies. Significant influence may be gained by share ownership, statute or agreement.

(ii)   **Nature of related party relationships**

Within the Egin Group

Briars and Doye are related parties of Egin because they are **controlled** by Egin. **Eye is also a related party of Egin** because Egin has **significant influence** over it. **Briars and Doye** are also **related parties of each other** because they are under **common control**.

Briars and Doye may not be related parties of Eye, as there is only one director in common and IAS 24 states that entities are not necessarily related simply because they have a director in common. A related party relationship probably exists if this director **actually exercises control** or **significant influence** over the policies of the companies in practice.

Although Tang was sold several months before the year end it was a **related party of Egin, Briars and Doye until then**. Therefore the related party relationship between Tang and the Egin group **should be disclosed** even though there were no transactions between them during the period.

Blue is a related party of Briars as a **director of Briars controls it**. Because the director is not on the management board of Egin it is **not clear whether Blue is also a related party of Egin group**. This would depend on whether the director is considered key management personnel at a group level. The director's services as a consultant to the group may mean that a related party relationship exists.

Between Spade and the Egin Group

Spade is a related party of Doye because it holds **significant voting power** in Doye. This means that the **sale** of plant and equipment **to Spade must be disclosed**. **Egin is not necessarily a related party of Spade** simply because both have an investment in Doye. A related party relationship will only exist if one party **exercises influence** over another **in practice.**

The directors have proposed that disclosures should state that prices charged to related parties are set on an **arm's length basis**. Because the transaction took place **between related parties** by definition it **cannot have taken place on an arm's length basis** and this description would be **misleading**. Doye sold plant and equipment to Spade at **normal selling prices** and this is the information that should be disclosed.

Between Atomic and the Egin Group

Atomic is a related party of Egin because it can exercise **significant influence** over it. It is **also a related party of Briars and Doye** because **Egin controls Briars and Doye**. It is **unlikely that Eye is a related party of Atomic** because Eye is an associate of an associate. Atomic would have to be able to **exercise significant influence in practice** for a related party relationship to exist.

(b)   **Goodwill arising on the acquisition of Briars**

IAS 21 *The effect of changes in foreign exchange rates* states that goodwill arising on the acquisition of a foreign subsidiary should be expressed in the functional currency of the foreign operation and **retranslated at the closing rate at each year-end**. Goodwill is calculated and translated as follows:

	Euros m	Rate	$m
Cost of combination	50	2	25.0
Less: fair value of identifiable net assets acquired (80% × 45)	(36)	2	(18.0)
Goodwill at acquisition	14		7.0
Impairment	(3)	2.5	(1.2)
Exchange loss (balancing figure)			(1.4)
At 31 May 20X6	11	2.5	4.4

Goodwill is measured at **$4.4 million** in the balance sheet. An impairment loss of **$1.2 million** is **recognised in the income statement** and an **exchange loss of $1.4 million** is **recognised in equity** (taken to the translation reserve).

Loan to Briars

The loan is a **financial liability measured at amortised cost**. The loan is measured at **fair value** on initial recognition. Fair value is the amount for which the liability could be settled between **knowledgeable, willing parties on an arm's length basis**. This would normally be the actual transaction price. However, Egin and Briars are **related parties** and the transaction **has not taken place on normal commercial terms**.

IAS 39 *Financial instruments: Recognition and measurement* states that it is necessary to **establish what the transaction price would have been** in an arm's length exchange motivated by normal business considerations. The amount that will eventually be repaid to Egin is $10 million and the normal commercial rate of interest is 6%. Therefore the fair value of the loan is its **discounted present value**, which is **retranslated at the closing rate** at each year-end.

Therefore the loan is measured at the following amounts in the balance sheet:

	$'000	Rate	Euros000
At 1/6/20X5 $(10 \times \frac{1}{1.06^2})$	8,900	2	17,800
Interest (unwinding of discount) (8,900 × 6%)	534	2.3	1,228
Exchange loss			4,557
At 31/5/20X6 $(10 \times \frac{1}{1.06})$	9,434	2.5	23,585

The **unwinding of the discount** is recognised as a **finance cost** in the income statement and the **exchange loss** is also **recognised in the income statement**.

Note. it would also be possible to calculate the finance cost for the year ended 31 May 20X6 at the closing rate. This would increase the exchange loss and the total expense recognised in profit and loss would be the same.

C9 Question with helping hands: Engina

Marking scheme

	Marks
Style of letter/report	4
Reasons	8
Goods to directors	4
Property	5
Group	4
Maximum	25

BPP LEARNING MEDIA

REPORT

To: The Directors
        Engina Co
        Zenda
        Ruritania

From: Ann Accountant

Date: 12 May 20X3

Related Party Transactions

The purpose of this report is to explain why it is necessary to **disclose related party transactions**. We appreciate that you may regard such disclosure as politically and culturally **sensitive**. However, there are **sound reasons why International Financial Reporting Standards require such disclosures**. It should be emphasised that related party transactions are a **normal part of business** life, and the disclosures are required to give a **fuller picture** to the users of accounts, rather than because they are problematic.

Prior to the issue of IAS 24, disclosures in respect of related parties were concerned with directors and their relationship with the group. The **IASB extends this definition and also the required disclosures**. This reflects the objective of the IASB to provide **useful data for investors**, not merely for companies to report on stewardship activities.

Unless investors know that transactions with related parties have not been carried out at **'arm's length'** between independent parties, they may fail to ascertain the **true financial position**.

Related party transactions typically take place on **terms which are significantly different** from those undertaken on normal commercial terms.

IAS 24 requires all material related party transactions to be disclosed.

It should be noted that related party transactions are not necessarily fraudulent or intended to deceive. Without proper disclosures, investors may be disadvantaged – IAS 24 seeks to remedy this.

Sale of goods to the director

(a)   **Disclosure** of related party transactions is only necessary when the transactions are material. For the purposes of IAS 24, however, transactions are material when their disclosure might reasonably be **expected to influence decisions made by users of the financial statements, irrespective of their amount**.

(b)   The **materiality** of a related party transaction with an individual, for example a director, must be **judged by reference to that individual** and not just the company. In addition, **disclosure of contracts** of **significance** with **directors** is required by most **Stock Exchanges**.

(c)   Mr Satay has purchased $600,000 (12 × $50,000) worth of goods from the company and a car for $45,000, which is just over half its market value.

(d)   The transactions are not material to the company, and because Mr Satay has considerable personal wealth, they are not material to him either.

(e)   However, IAS 24 confirms that directors are related parties and transactions with directors should be disclosed. In addition, IAS 24 requires disclosure of **compensation** paid to directors. Compensation includes subsidised goods and benefits in kind. **Details of the transaction should be disclosed**, including the amount of the transactions and any outstanding balances.

Hotel property

(a) The hotel property sold to the Managing Director's brother is a **related party transaction**, and it appears to have been undertaken at **below market price**.

(b) IAS 24 envisages disclosure of the substance of the transaction.

(c) IAS 24 requires disclosure of 'information about the **transaction** and **outstanding balances** necessary for an understanding of the **potential effect of the relationship upon the financial statements**'.

(d) Not only must the transaction itself be disclosed, but the question of **impairment** needs to be **considered**. The value of the hotel has become impaired due to the **fall in property prices**, so the **carrying value needs to be adjusted** in accordance with IAS 36 *Impairment of assets*. The hotel should be shown at the lower of carrying value ($5m) and the recoverable amount. The recoverable amount is the higher of fair value less costs to sell ($4.3m – $0.2m = $4.1m) and value in use ($3.6m). Therefore the hotel should be shown at $4.1m.

The sale of the property was for $100,000 below this impaired value, and it is this amount which needs to be disclosed. This would highlight the nature of the transactions within the existing property market conditions.

Group structure

(a) Local companies legislation and the Stock Exchange often require **disclosure of directors' interests** in a company's share capital. IAS 24 requires disclosure of the 'ultimate controlling party'. Mr Satay controls Engina as a result of his ownership of 80% of the share capital of Wheel.

(b) IAS 24 requires disclosure of the **related party relationship** between Engina and Wheel and also of **transactions** between the two companies, despite the fact that Engina is a wholly owned subsidiary.

(c) Engina's transactions with Car Ltd will also need to be disclosed. IAS 24 states that companies under **common control** are related parties, and the two companies are under the common control of Mr Satay.

D1 Preparation question: Simple consolidation

Top tips. This is a simpler question than any you will meet with in the examination. It is designed as a gentle introduction to the basic principles of consolidation, illustrating the calculation and accounting treatment of goodwill.

(a) ALPHA
CONSOLIDATED BALANCE SHEET AS AT 31 DECEMBER 20X4

	$'000
Assets	
Non-current	
Property, plant and equipment	10,655.0
Goodwill (W1)	435.0
	11,090.0
Current assets	
Inventories	3,408.0
Receivables (1,462 + 1,307 – 23)	2,746.0
Cash	41.0
	6,195.0
Total assets	17,285.0

	$'000
Equity and liabilities	
Equity attributable to equity shareholders of the parent	
Share capital (50c ordinary shares)	5,500.0
General reserve (W2)	1,490.0
Retained earnings (W3)	557.5
	7,547.5
Minority interest (W4)	522.5
Total equity	8,070.0
Non current liabilities	
Borrowings	4,500.0
Current liabilities	
Overdraft	2,016.0
Trade payables (887 + 1,077 – 23)	1,941.0
Taxation	758.0
Total current liabilities	4,715.0
Total liabilities	9,215.0
Total equity and liabilities	17,285.0

(b) Alpha has made a profit of 15/115 × $23,000 = $3,000 on its sale of goods to Beta. Beta has not yet sold goods to an outside party and the profit is therefore unrealised as far as the group is concerned. An adjustment is necessary to reduce the balance of retained earnings, and the value of inventory by $3,000.

Workings

1 *Goodwill*

	$'000	$'000
Cost of combination		1,450
Fair value of identifiable net assets acquired		
Share capital	1,000	
General reserve	400	
	1,400	
Group share (72½%)		1,015
		435

2 *General reserve*

	Alpha	Beta
	$'000	$'000
Per question	1,200	800
At acquisition	–	(400)
	1,200	400
Share of post acquisition reserves		
of Beta (72½% × 400)	290	
	1,490	

3 *Retained earnings*

	Alpha	Beta
	$'000	$'000
Per question	485.0	100
At acquisition	–	–
	485.0	100
Share of post acquisition profits		
of Beta (72½ % × 100)	72.5	
	557.5	

4   *Minority interest*

	$'000
Share capital	1,000
Reserves (800 + 100)	900
	1,900
Minority interest (27½%)	522.5

D2 Preparation question: Consolidation

(a)   Accounting treatment

IAS 27 *Consolidated and separate financial statements* states that consolidated financial statements **must include all subsidiaries** of the parent. This means that Short Co must be **consolidated**, despite the fact that the group's interest in the subsidiary is held **exclusively** with a view to **subsequent resale**.

The reasoning behind the treatment of the investment is that all assets held by the group **should be treated in the same way**. However, IFRS 5 *Non-current assets held for sale and discontinued* operations requires the subsidiary to be **classified as 'held for sale'**, provided that the company is available for immediate sale and that the sale is highly probable and expected to take place within one year from the date of acquisition. The identifiable assets and liabilities of the company are **measured at fair value less costs to sell** and must be **presented separately** on the face of the consolidated balance sheet.

IFRS 5 also states that a subsidiary acquired exclusively with a view to resale should be treated as a **discontinued operation**. The consolidated income statement should show a **single amount representing the post-tax profit or loss of Short Co** for the period. IFRS 5 requires other disclosures about Short Co in the notes. In this way, **users** of the financial statements **are made aware** that Short Co **will not contribute to the continuing activities** of the group.

(b)   (i)   Profit from inter group sales

IAS 27 requires that profits or losses on any intra-group transaction should be eliminated in full. This elimination should be set against the group's interest and minority interest in proportion to their respective interests.

For sales made to FSR Co from GBH Co the full $20,000 profit should be eliminated from inventory, consolidates retained earnings reduced by $15,000 and the minority interest reduced by $5,000.

The sales from FSR Co to GBH Co have been correctly treated.

(ii)   Goodwill arising on combination

Goodwill recognised in a business combination represents the goodwill acquired by the parent, based on the parent's ownership interest in the net fair value of the subsidiary's identifiable assets and liabilities (as required by IFRS 3 *Business Combinations*). Goodwill attributable to a minority interest is not recognised in the parent's consolidated financial statements. Therefore the goodwill arising on the holding in GBH is as follows.

	$'000
Cost of combination	3,000
Share of identifiable net assets acquired (75% × $3,000,000)	2,250
Goodwill	750

The goodwill should not be amortised. IFRS 3 states that goodwill acquired in a business combination should be measured at cost less any accumulated impairment losses.

(c)   Reasons for recommended accounting treatment

(i)   The profit arising on the intra-group transaction is eliminated because it has not arisen for the group as a whole but merely for the individual company. The purpose of the **consolidated financial statements** is to present information about the **group as a single economic unit**.

The elimination is made in full even though there are minority interests because the transactions involve assets entirely within the group's control, even if they are not wholly owned.

(ii)   The reason that goodwill attributable to the minority interest is not recognised is that, whilst it may be possible to estimate by extrapolation or valuation an amount attributable to the minority when a subsidiary is acquired, this figure would be hypothetical as the minority is not a party to the transaction.

D3 Preparation question: Status of investment

> **Top tips.** Watch the treatment of the various investments. In the exam, many students treated Bay as an associate despite lack of control. Many students also did badly in parts (b) and (c). Make sure you know how to deal with unrealised profit.

(a)   International Accounting Standards (IASs) set out **four alternative ways** in which investments can be treated.

(i)   Where the **investor controls the investee**, the controlling entity (the parent) and the controlled entity (the subsidiary) form a group. **Consolidated financial statements** are prepared for the group. The gains, losses, assets, liabilities and cash flows of the parent and the subsidiary are aggregated in order to present the financial performance and position of the group as a **single economic entity**. This treatment is required by IFRS 3 *Business combinations* and IAS 27 *Consolidated and separate financial statements*.

(ii)   Where the **investor does not have control but exerts significant influence** over the investee's operating and financial policies the investee is an associate and **the equity method is used**, as required by IAS 28 *Investments in associates*. The investor's share of the results and net assets of the investee are not combined with the investor's own activities and resources, but are brought into its financial statements on a single line in the income statement and balance sheet respectively. This treatment recognises the investor's share of the results and net assets, but does not misrepresent the extent of its influence over the investee.

(iii)   Where the investor **shares control over the investee** with others the investee is a joint venture and is **proportionately consolidated**, as required by IAS 31 *Financial reporting of interests in joint ventures*. The investor's share of each of the assets, liabilities, income and expenses of a jointly controlled entity is combined with similar items in the investor's own financial statements. The **equity method may also be used**. Like the equity method, proportionate consolidation recognises the investor's share of the results and net assets, but does not misrepresent the extent of its influence over the investee.

(iv)   Where the investor **does not exercise control, joint control or significant influence**, the only amounts recognised in the consolidated financial statements are the **investment at fair value** (as required by IAS 39 *Financial instruments: Recognition and measurement*) and **any investment income**.

(b)   *Harbor*

Port owns 80% of the equity share capital of Harbor. Therefore Port clearly **controls** Harbor and Harbor is a **subsidiary** and should be consolidated.

Inlet

Port owns 40% of the equity share capital of Inlet. This is **not sufficient to control** Inlet, but the fact that there are no other major shareholdings indicates that Port **can exercise significant influence** over the policies adopted by Inlet. Therefore Inlet is **an associate** of Port and should be accounted for using the equity method.

Bay

Port owns 31.25% of the equity share capital of Bay. Where an investor holds 20% or more of the voting rights normally it is normally presumed that the investor can exercise significant influence (and therefore has an associate). However, **another investor holds 62.5% of the equity share capital and clearly exercises control in practice** (by making Bay adopt policies that do not meet with the approval of Port). Therefore Bay is a simple **non-current asset investment** recognised at fair value.

(c)

	Port $'000	Harbor $'000	Adjustments $'000	Consolidated $'000
Revenue (W1)	65,000	45,000	(8,000)	102,000
Cost of sales (W1)	(35,000)	(25,000)	8,000	
(W2)			(120)	(52,120)
Gross profit	30,000	20,000	(120)	49,880

Workings

1   *Intra-group sales*

		$'000	$'000
DEBIT	Revenue	8,000	
CREDIT	Cost of sales		8,000

Elimination of the sales made by Port to Harbor

2   *Provision for unrealised profit*

Inventory relating to intra-group sales have increased by $600,000 (3,000 – 2,400)

Provision for unrealised profit is $120,000 (600 × 25/125).

(d)   **Adjustments to the consolidated balance sheet**

(i)

		$'000	$'000
DEBIT	Consolidated retained earnings	600	
CREDIT	Inventories		600

Unrealised profit eliminated from the inventory of Harbor (3,000 × 25/125).

This adjustment is needed because the consolidated financial statements must present the activities of the group as a **single economic entity**. Port has made a profit of 25% of cost on its sales to Harbor. Harbor has not yet sold all these goods to third parties and so part of the profit made by Port plc has **not yet been realised by the group** and must be eliminated from the consolidated financial statements.

(ii)

		$'000	$'000
DEBIT	Consolidated retained earnings	200	
CREDIT	Investment in associate		200

Group share of unrealised profit eliminated from the net assets of Inlet (40% × 2,500 × 25/125).

The rationale behind this adjustment is similar to the rationale behind adjustment (i). Some of the goods sold by Port to Inlet remain in inventory and therefore the inventory of Inlet must be **adjusted to eliminate the unrealised profit**. Because Inlet is an associate rather than a subsidiary, the consolidated balance sheet does not include the individual assets and liabilities of Inlet. Instead the cost of investment plus group share of post acquisition retained earnings of Inlet are reported in a single line within non-current assets. **Therefore only the group share of the unrealised profit is eliminated**.

BPP LEARNING MEDIA

D4 Preparation question: Associate

J GROUP CONSOLIDATED BALANCE SHEET AS AT 31 DECEMBER 20X5

	$'000
Assets	
Non-current assets	
Freehold property (1,950 + 1,250 + 370 (W2))	3,570
Plant and equipment (795 + 375)	1,170
Investment in associate (W8)	480
	5,220
Current assets	
Inventories (575 + 300 – 20 (W3))	855
Trade receivables (330 + 290))	620
Cash at bank and in hand (50 + 120)	170
	1,645
	6,865
Equity and liabilities	
Equity attributable to equity holders of the parent	
Issued share capital	2,000
Retained earnings	1,781
	3,781
Minority interests (W6)	894
Total equity	4,675
Non-current liabilities	
12% debentures (500 + 100)	600
Current liabilities	
Bank overdraft	560
Trade payables (680 + 350)	1,030
	1,590
Total liabilities	2,190
	6,865

Workings

1 Group structure

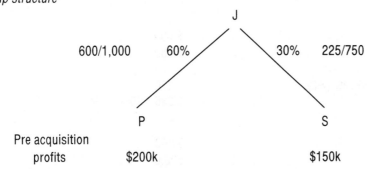

2 Fair value adjustment table

	At acquisition $'000	Movement $'000	At balance sheet date $'000
Land	200		200
Buildings	200	(30)	170 (200 × 34/40)
	400	(30)	370

3 Unrealised profit on inventories

P Co ⟶ J Co $100k × 25/125 = $20,000

4   *Goodwill*

	P Co	
	$'000	$'000
Cost of investment		1,000
Net assets acquired:		
Share capital	1,000	
Retained earnings at acquisition	200	
Fair value adjustment (W2)	400	
	1,600	
Group share	60%	(960)
		40
Impairments to date		40
Year-end value		–

5   *Retained earnings*

	J Co	P Co	S Co
	$'000	$'000	$'000
Retained earnings per question	1,460	885	390
Unrealised profit (W3)		(20)	
Retained earnings profits at acquisition		(200)	(150)
Fair value adjustment			
movement (W2)		(30)	
		635	240
P Co: share of post acquisition profits			
60% × 635	381		
S Co: share of post acquisition profits			
30% × 240	72		
Goodwill impairments to date			
(40 + 92) (W4)	(132)		
	1,781		

6   *Minority interest*

	$'000
Net assets per question	1,885
Unrealised profit (W3)	(20)
Fair value adjustment at B/S date (W2)	370
	2,235 × 40% = 894

7   *Investment in associate*

	$'000
Cost of associate	500.0
Share of post acquisition retained reserves	
((390 – 150) × 30%)	72.0
Less impairment of investment in associate	(92.0)
	480.0

D5 Baden

> **Top tip**. A thorough testing of the different treatments for associates and joint ventures under IAS 28 and IAS 31.

(a) (i) **Associate v ordinary non-current asset investment**

An **investor** will take a **relatively passive role** in an ordinary non current asset investment; whereas an **associate** is a **vehicle** for the conduct of business since the investor can **exercise significant influence** over the financial and operational **policies** of the investee company.

Under IAS 28, a holding of **20% or more of voting rights** suggests the investor has **significant influence**. The **attitude** of the investor towards **dividends**, is important. For an investment, the investor will press for high dividends, but for an associate the investor will be keen to see profits reinvested.

IAS 28 indicates that board representation plus at least 20% voting rights will indicate associate status. Significant influence can also be exercised by intra company trading, exchange of key staff or providing technical support or information.

(ii) **Principal differences: jointly controlled operation/asset/entity**

Under IAS 31, **jointly controlled operations** utilise assets and resources from the venturers and are **not separate entities**. A **venturer** will **recognise** the **assets** it **controls**, the **liabilities** incurred, the **expenses** incurred and the **share of income** in its **consolidated accounts**.

A **jointly controlled asset** occurs when there is **no separate entity**. The venturer will **recognise** its **share** of the **asset**, any **liabilities** incurred and its share of any **joint liabilities** in **its accounts**.

A **jointly controlled entity** is a **separate entity** in which **each venturer** has an interest. **Proportionate consolidation** is used to account for these on an **aggregate or line by line basis**. **IAS 31 permits** the use of **equity accounting** in group accounts for jointly controlled entities **as well**.

(b) (i) At 1 January 20X7, goodwill is calculated as follows.

	$m	$m
Cost of investment		14.0
Property, plant and equipment	30.00	
Current assets	31.00	
Current liabilities	(20.00)	
Non-current liabilities	(8.00)	
Fair value of net assets	33.00	
30% thereof		9.9
Goodwill		4.1

Carrying value 31.12.20X8 in the balance sheet

	$m
Investment cost	14.0
30% post acquisition profit	
(32 – 9)	6.9
Fair value adjustment for depreciation	
(2 × 20% × (30 – 20) × 30%)	(1.2)
	19.7

The following would appear in the consolidated income statement.

	$m
Share of profit of associate	–
((30% × 12) – inter co profit 3.0 – depreciation 0.6)	

Intragroup profit on the inventory will be treated as follows.

- Deducted from share of associate profit.
- Deduct from inventory as the asset subject to the transaction is held by the parent.

(ii) **Change in treatment**

Jointly controlled entities are accounted for using **proportionate consolidation**, as required by IAS 31 *Interests in joint ventures*. The venture can aggregate its share of joint assets, liabilities, income or expenses with similar items in the **consolidated accounts** on a **line by line basis or include as separate items**.

All the items (except the dividend) would be multiplied by 30% and consolidated in the income statement:

BADEN
CONSOLIDATED INCOME STATEMENT

	$m
Revenue (212 – 35) × 30 %	53.1
Cost of sales ((178 – 35) × 30%)+ 3 + 0.6))	(46.5)
Other income	3.6
Distribution costs	(5.1)
Administration expenses	(2.4)
Finance costs	(1.2)
Income tax expense	(1.5)
Profit for the period	0.0

The balance sheet would include:

	$m
Non current assets	12.9
(30% × 37 + fair value adjustment (10 × 30% – depreciation 1.2))	
Goodwill	4.1
Current assets (30% × 31)	9.3
	26.3
Non current liabilities (30% × 10)	(3.0)
Current liabilities (30% × 12)	(3.6)
	19.7

D6 Preparation question 'D'-shaped group

(a) BAUBLE GROUP
CONSOLIDATED BALANCE SHEET AS AT 31 DECEMBER 20X9

	$'000
Non-current assets	
Property, plant and equipment (720 + 60 + 70)	850
Goodwill (W2)	126
	976
Current assets (175 + 95 + 90)	360
	1,336
Equity attributable to equity holders of the parent	
Share capital – $1 ordinary shares	400
Retained earnings (W4)	600
	1,000
Minority interest (W3)	106
	1,106
Current liabilities (120 + 65 + 45)	230
	1,336

Workings

1   *Group Structure*

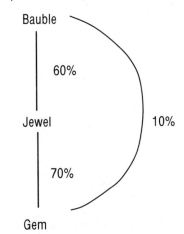

Bauble

60%

Jewel

10%

70%

Gem

Bauble interest in Gem

– direct	10%
– indirect (60% × 70%)	42%
	52%

Minority interest in Gem	48%

2   *Goodwill*

	B in J		B in G		J in G	
	$'000	$'000	$'000	$'000	$'000	$'000
Cost of combination		142		43		100
Share of net assets acquired as represented by						
Share capital	100		50		50	
Ret'd earnings	45		40		40	
	145		90		90	
Group share	60%		10%		70%	
		87		9		63
Goodwill		55		34		37
Total goodwill = $126,000						

3   *Minority interest*

	Jewel	Gem
	$'000	$'000
Net assets per question	190	115
Goodwill (W2)	37	
Less: cost of investment in Gamma	(100)	
	127	115
Minority share	× 40%	× 48%
	50.8	55.2

106.0

4   *Consolidated retained earnings*

	B	J	G
	$'000	$'000	$'000
Per Q	560	90	65
Less: pre-acquisition ret'd earnings		(45)	(40)
		45	25
J – share of post acquisition ret'd earnings (45 × 60%)	27		
G – share of post acquisition ret'd earnings (25 × 52%)	13		
	600		

(b) **Goodwill**

	$'000	$'000
Cost of combination		142.0
Fair value of identifiable net assets acquired:		
Jewel Share capital	100.0	
Retained earnings	60.0	
Cost of investment – Gem	(100.0)	
	60.0 × 60%	(36.0)
Gem Share capital	50.0	
Retained earnings (1 January 20X3)	40.0	
	90.0 × 42% EI	(37.8)
		68.2
Bauble in Gem (per part (a))		34.0
		102.2

D7 Question with analysis: X Group

> **Top tips**. This is a complicated question. However, you should be able to answer it if you work logically and methodically through the information given.

Marking scheme

		Marks
(a)	Property, plant and equipment	3
	Goodwill and investment in W	8
	Net current assets	2
	Non current liabilities	1
	Minority interest	7
	Capital and reserves	5
		25
(b)	Subjective	5
	Maximum	30

(a) X GROUP
BALANCE SHEET AS AT 31 MARCH 20X9

	$m
Property, plant and equipment (W3)	1,058
Goodwill (W5)	79
Investment in associate (W4)	53
Net current assets 640 + 360 + 75 − 15 (W6)	1,060
	2,250
Equity	360
Share premium	250
Retained earnings (W8)	1,114
Minority interest (W7)	161
	1,885
Non current liabilities 200 + 150 + 15	365
	2,250

Workings

1   *Group structure*

		Holding	Date acquired	Retained earnings 1.4.X4	Retained earnings 1.4.X6
	X				
$66^2/_3\%$ Y		$\dfrac{100m}{150m} =$	1.4.X6	N/A	$120m
	90%	$66^2/_3\%$			
30%	Z	$\dfrac{45m}{50m} = 90\%$	1.4.X4	$10m	$20m
W		30%	1.4.X6	–	$7m

2   *Fair value adjustments and other adjustments to net assets*

Y	Acquisition	At balance sheet date
	$'m	$'m
Property, plant and equipment	30	30
Amortisation (30 × 10% × 3)		(9)
Non-current intangible assets	(30)	(30)
Inventory (2 − 8)	(6)	
Allowance for doubtful debts	(9)	
	(15)	(9)

Z	Acquisition	At balance sheet date
	$'m	$'m
Property, plant and equipment	10	10
Amortisation (10 × 10% × 3)		(3)
Inventory	(5)	
	5	7

Note

The amount received as a result of the arbitration award was a contingent asset at the date of acquisition and is therefore not recognised as a fair value adjustment. IFRS 3 only requires recognition of contingent liabilities.

3   *Property, plant and equipment*

	X	Y	Z
	$m	$m	$m
Per question	900	100	30
Fair value adjustments (W2)	–	30	10
Amortisation (W2)	–	(9)	(3)
	900	121	37
Y	121		
Z	37		
	1,058		

4   *Investment in W – associate*

	$m
Cost	50
Add 30% post acquisition profit (17 – 7)	3
	53

5   *Goodwill*

	X	
	|	2/3
	Y	
	|	90%
	Z	

	Y	Z
Investment by X	2/3	60% (2/3 of 90%)
Minority interest	1/3	40%

	$m	$m
Cost of Y and Z		320
Fair value of identifiable net assets acquired in Y:		
Share capital	150	
Share premium	120	
Reserves	120	
Fair value adjustments (W2)	(15)	
Investment in Z	(90)	
	285	
2/3		(190)
Fair value of identifiable net assets acquired in Z:		
Share capital	50	
Share premium	10	
Reserves	20	
Fair value adjustments (W2)	5	
60%	85	
		(51)
		79

6   *Unrealised profit*

	$m
On sales to X	44
On sales to Y	16
	60

Unrealised profit 25% × 60 = $15m

BPP
LEARNING MEDIA

7   *Minority interests*

	$m	$m
Y		
Net assets at balance sheet date per question	480	
Fair value adjustments (W2)	(9)	
Cost of investment in Z	(90)	
Cost of investment in associate	(50)	
Investment in associate (W4)	53	
1/3	384	128
Z		
Net assets at balance sheet date per question	90	
Fair value adjustments (W2)	7	
Intragroup profit in inventories (44 + 16 × 25%)	(15)	
40%	82	33
		161

8   *Consolidated retained earnings*

	X	Y	Z	W
	$m	$m	$m	$m
Per question	1,050	210	30	17
Intragroup profit in inventories (W8)			(15)	
Fair value adjustments (W2)	–	6	2	–
Retained earnings at acquisition (W5)	–	(120)	(20)	(7)
	1,050	96	(3)	10
Post-acquisition profits of Y (2/3 × 96)	64			
Post-acquisition profits of Z (60% × (3))	(2)			
Post-acquisition profits of W (20% × 10)	2			
	1,114			

(b)   **Change of policy re goodwill**

IFRS 1 *First time adoption of International Financial Reporting Standards* is relevant as the company appears to be adopting IFRSs for the first time.

IFRS 1 requires retrospective adoption of all IFRSs in force at the reporting date for the first IFRS financial statements (31 March 20X9). Assuming that the company presents comparative figures for one year only (the minimum required by IFRS 1), it will prepare an opening IFRS balance sheet at 1 April 20X7, which will be the date of transition to IFRSs. As all its investments were acquired before this date, it must recognise the goodwill arising as an intangible asset.

Retrospective application means that X should adjust opening retained earnings for the effect of the change. X must also test the goodwill for impairment at the date of transition.

IFRS 1 contains an exemption from applying IFRS 3 retrospectively. However, the group wishes to account for the change in policy retrospectively and therefore is not claiming the exemption.

D8 Largo

Top tips. In this question you had to prepare a consolidated balance sheet of a group where there were multiple shareholdings. You had to determine the date at which control was gained for the purpose of the group accounts. Since the question was set, IFRS 3 has outlawed the pooling of interests method, so the purchase method had to be used. You were also required to deal with deferred tax arising on the fair value of the tangible non-current assets and the impairment of a brand name.

Easy marks. As always, there are easy marks for basic consolidation techniques and for determining the group structure. If you did not correctly value the consideration given, this would not result in a significant loss of marks as it was only one element of the goodwill calculation.

Examiner's comment. This question was well answered in most cases. However, many candidates did not charge the additional depreciation on the fair value increase on the property of the subsidiaries, and failed to treat the brand name correctly on acquisition.

Marking scheme

	Marks
Discussion of method of accounting for shareholdings	3
Equity of Fusion	6
Equity of Spine	5
Fair value calculation – assets	3
Fair value of consideration	3
Brand name	2
Property, plant and equipment	3
Group reserves	2
Micro	3
Available	30
Maximum	25

LARGO
CONSOLIDATED BALANCE SHEET AT 30 NOVEMBER 20X4

	$m
Assets	
Non current assets	
Property, plant and equipment (329 + 185 + (W2) + 60.8 + 64 + (W2) 36.1 – 9 brand)	665.9
Goodwill (W3)	80.3
Other intangible assets	7.0
Investment in associate (W4)	12.6
	765.8
Current assets (120 + 58 + 40)	218.0
	983.8
Equity and liabilities	
Equity attributable to equity holders of the parent	
Share capital (280 + 150 + 30)	460.0
Share premium [30 + (150 × $1.30) + (30 × $1.30)]	264.0
Retained earnings (W6)	122.2
	846.2
Minority interest (W5)	50.8
	897.0

	$m
Non-current liabilities	
Deferred tax liability (20 + 20 + (W2) 14.25 + 5 + (W2) 8.55)	67.8
Current liabilities (10 + 5 + 4)	19.0
	983.8

Workings

1   *Group structure*

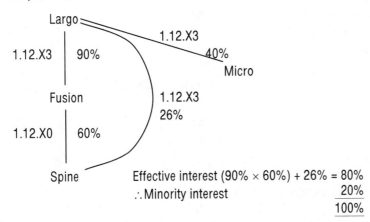

Effective interest (90% × 60%) + 26% = 80%
∴ Minority interest   20%
                      100%

2   *Fair value adjustments*

	At acq'n 1.12.X3	Movement (5%)	At B/S date 30.11.X4
Fusion	$m	$m	$m
Property (330 – 110 – 20 – 136)	64	(3.2)	60.8
Deferred tax liability	(15)	0.75	(14.25)
	49	(2.45)	46.55
Spine			
Property (128 – 50 – 10 – 30)	38	(1.9)	36.1
Deferred tax liability	(9)	0.45	(8.55)
	29	(1.45)	27.55

Goodwill

	Largo in Fusion Group $m	$m	Largo in Spine $m	$m
Cost of combination (150 × $2.30*)/(30 × $2.30*)		345		69
Fair value of net assets acquired:				
Fusion				
Share capital	110			
Share premium	20			
Retained earnings (1.12.X3)	136			
Fair value adjustments: Property (W2)	64			
Deferred tax liability	(15)			
Cost of investment in Spine	(50)			
	265			
Group share	90%	(238.5)		
Spine				
Share capital	50		50	
Share premium	10		10	
Retained earnings (1.12.X3)	30		30	
Fair value adjustments: Property (W2)	38		38	
Deferred tax liability	(9)		(9)	
	119		119	
Group share	54%	(64.26)	26%	(30.94)
		42.24		38.06
			80.30	

Note. IFRS 3 requires goodwill arising on a business combination to be tested annually for impairment. There is no information as to whether the goodwill is impaired hence no adjustment for impairment is necessary.

*The market price of the shares is calculated by reference to the market capitalisation of Largo: $644 million ÷ 280 million shares = $2.30 per share. Therefore the premium on each share is $1.30.

4   *Investment in associate*

	$m
Cost of associate	11.0
Share of post acquisition retained reserves ((24 − 20) × 40%)	1.6
	12.6

5   *Minority interest*

	Fusion $m	Spine $m
Net assets at balance sheet date per question	268	95
Fair value adjustments (W2)	46.55	27.55
Cost of investment in Spine	(50)	
Impairment of brand (9 − 7)	(2)	–
	262.55	122.55
MI share (10%/20% effective interest (W1))	26.26	24.51
		50.77

BPP
LEARNING MEDIA

6   *Retained earnings*

	Largo $m	Fusion $m	Spine $m
Per question	120	138.00	35.00
Fair value change (W2)		(2.45)	(1.45)
Impairment loss		(2.00)	–
		133.55	33.55
At acquisition		(136.00)	(30.00)
		(2.45)	3.55
Group share of Fusion ((2.45) × 90%)	(2.21)		
Group share of Spine (3.55 × 80%)	2.84		
Share of profit of associate ((24 – 20) × 40%)	1.60		
	122.23		

D9 Case study question: Rod

Top tips. This question required candidates to prepare a consolidated balance sheet of a complex group. Candidates were given a basic set of data – information concerning current accounting practices – which required adjustment in the financial statements, and information about the implementation of 'new' accounting standards. This type of question will appear regularly on this paper (obviously with different group scenarios and different accounting adjustments). Candidates had to deal with adjustments relating to tangible non-current assets, inventory and defined benefit pension schemes. Part (c) is a practical question on key issues. In part (d), do not be tempted to waffle. Part (e) concerns ethics, a topic new to this syllabus.

Examiner's comment. Generally speaking, candidates performed quite well on this question but often struggled with the accounting for the defined benefit pension scheme. Many candidates treated one of the subsidiaries as an associate. In this situation, where the relationship between the companies has been incorrectly determined, marks are awarded for the methodology used in the question.

Marking scheme

			Marks
(a)		Defined benefit pension scheme	5
(b)		Shareholding	3
		Equity – Line	6
		Non current assets – Line	4
		Equity – Reel	8
		Fair value adjustment	2
		Group properties, plant and equipment	2
		Group retained earnings	3
		Trade receivables	1
		Inventory	1
(c)	(i)	Provision: current practice	4
		acceptability	2
	(ii)	Fine: intangible asset	3
		acceptability	2

(d)	1 mark per valid point	10
(e)	For	2
	Against	2
	Conclusion	1
	Available	59
	Maximum	50

(a) **Defined benefit pension scheme**

The defined benefit pension scheme is treated in accordance with IAS 19 *Employee benefits*.

The pension scheme has a deficit of liabilities over assets:

	$m
Fair value of scheme assets	125
Less present value of obligation	(130)
	(5)

The deficit is reported as a liability in the balance sheet.

The income statement for the year includes:

	$m
Current service cost	110
Interest cost	20
Expected return on plan assets	(10)
Actuarial gain	(15)
	105

There is an actuarial gain of $15 million on the defined benefit pension scheme assets (W). Under IAS 19 the unrecognised gains and losses at the end of the **previous** reporting period can be recognised in the income statement using the '10% corridor' approach or any other systematic approach including immediate recognition, either in retained earnings or in the income statement. Here, the directors have chosen to recognise the gain immediately in the income statement.

Adjustment to the group accounts:

	$m	$m
DEBIT Retained earnings	105	
CREDIT Trade receivables		100
CREDIT Defined benefit pension scheme		5

Workings

1 *Income statement*

	$m
Current service cost	110
Interest cost	20
Expected return on plan assets	(10)
Actuarial gain recognised immediately in profit or loss	(15)
	105

2 *Balance sheet*

	$m
Fair value of scheme assets	125
Preset value of obligation	(130)
Liability	(5)

(b)   ROD
CONSOLIDATED BALANCE SHEET AT 30 NOVEMBER 20X2

	$m
Non-current assets	
Property, plant and equipment (W5)	1,930
Goodwill (W2)	137
	2,067
Current assets	
Inventories (300 + 135 + 65 – 20)	480
Receivables (240 + 105 + 49 – 100)	294
Cash at bank and in hand	220
	994
	3,061
Equity attributable to equity holders of the parent	
Share capital	1,500
Share premium	300
Retained earnings (W4)	586
	2,386
	270
	2,656
Minority interest (W3)	180
Non-current liabilities	
Pension scheme	5
Other	220
Current liabilities	405
	3,061

Workings

1   *Group structure*

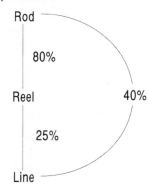

Rod's total holding in Line is 60% (40% direct + 80% × 25% indirect).

2 *Goodwill*

	Rod in Reel		Reel in Line		Rod in Line	
	$m	$m	$m	$m	$m	$m
Cost of investment		640		100		160
Net assets acquired						
Share capital	500		200		200	
Share premium	100		50		50	
Retained earnings	100		50		50	
Fair value adjustment	10		–		–	
	710		300		300	
Group share	80%		25%		40%	
		(568)		(75)		(120)
		72		25		40

Total goodwill: $72m + $25m + $40m = $137m

3 *Minority interests*

	Reel	Line
	$m	$m
Net assets per question	800	380
Investment in Line	(100)	–
Development costs written off	(20)	–
Trade discount on PPE less depreciation	(5)	–
Goodwill in Line (W2)	25	–
Elimination of revaluation reserve (W6)	–	(70)
Adjustment for excess depreciation (W6)	–	14
	700	324
	× 20%	× 40%
	140	129.6
	269.6	

4 *Retained earnings*

	Rod	Reel	Line
	$m	$m	$m
Per question	625.0	200	60
Fair value adjustment realised		(10)	
Development costs written off		(20)	
Trade discount on tangible assets less depreciation		(5)	
Adjustment for excess depreciation (W6)			14
At acquisition		(100)	(50)
	625.0	65	24
Group share of Reel (80% × 65)	52.0		
Group share of Line (60% × 24)	14.4		
Less defined benefit pension scheme (part (a))	(105.0)		
	586.4		

Note. The development costs do not meet the recognition criteria in IAS 38 and they cannot be treated as inventory because they have previously been written off as incurred. They were reinstated after acquisition, so they must be written off post-acquisition reserves.

BPP LEARNING MEDIA

5 *Property, plant and equipment*

	$m
Rod	1,230
Reel	505
Line	256
	1,991
Less adjustment to PPE of Line (W6)	(56)
Reel: trade discount net of depreciation (6 × 5/6)	(5)
	1,930

Note. IAS 16 states that the cost of a item of PPE should be measured net of trade discounts. The trade discount must be deducted from Reel's tangible assets.

6 *Adjustment to property, plant and equipment of Line*

An adjustment must be made to re-state the PPE of Line from their revalued amount to depreciated historical cost, in line with group accounting policies.

The revaluation took place after acquisition, so the adjustment does not affect goodwill.

	Valuation	Depreciated historic cost
	$m	$m
Cost at 1 December 20X1 (date of acquisition by Rod)	300	300
Depreciation (300/6)	(50)	(50)
NBV at 30 November 20X2	250	250
Revaluation	70	–
Revalued amount	320	
Depreciation (320/5)	(64)	(50)
NBV at 30 November 20X3	256	200

Adjustment required to the group accounts:	$m	$m
DEBIT Revaluation surplus	70	
CREDIT Retained earnings (64 – 50)		14
CREDIT Property, plant and equipment (256 – 200)		56

(c) (i) **Restructuring of the group**

IAS 37 *Provisions, contingent liabilities and contingent assets* **contains specific requirements** relating to **restructuring provisions**. The general recognition criteria apply and IAS 37 also states that **a provision should be recognised** if an entity has a **constructive obligation** to carry out a restructuring. A constructive obligation exists where **management has a detailed formal plan** for the restructuring and has also raised a **valid expectation** in those affected that it will carry out the restructuring. In this case, the company made a **public announcement** of the restructuring **after the year end**, but it had actually **drawn up the formal plan and started to implement it before the year end**, by communicating the plan to trade union representatives. Although the plan is **expected to take two years to complete**, it appears that the company **had a constructive obligation to** restructure at the year end. Therefore **a provision should be recognised**.

IAS 37 states that a restructuring provision should include **only the direct expenditure** arising from the restructuring. Costs that relate to the **future conduct of the business**, such as training and relocation costs, **should not be included**. Measuring the provision is likely to be difficult in practice, given that the restructuring will take place over two years. IAS 37 requires the provision to be the **best estimate** of the expenditure required to settle the present obligation at the balance sheet date, **taking all known risks and uncertainties into account**. There **may be a case for providing $50 million** (total costs of $60 million less relocation costs of $10 million) and the company **should**

certainly provide at least $15 million ($20 million incurred by the time the financial statements are approved less $5 million relocation expenses). IAS 37 requires **extensive disclosures** and these **should include an indication of the uncertainties** about the amount or timing of the cash outflows.

(ii) **Fine for illegal receipt of a state subsidy**

IAS 38 *Intangible assets* defines an **intangible asset** as a **resource controlled by the company** as a result of **past events** and **from which economic benefits are expected to flow**. The fine **does not meet this definition**. The subsidy was used to offset trading losses, not to generate future income. The fine should be **charged as an expense** in the income statement for the year ended 30 November 20X4. As it is **material** it should be **separately disclosed.**

(d) Rod spends considerable amounts of money on research that ultimately creates economic benefits and enhances shareholder value. However, this **research does not meet the criteria for deferral** under IAS 38 *Intangible assets* because of the time lag between the expenditure and the revenue that it generates. Therefore the company's activities **appear to reduce profits, rather than increase them.** The company's expertise is **part of its inherent goodwill** and cannot be valued reliably at a monetary amount. Therefore it is **not recognised** on the balance sheet.

There is a strong argument that traditional financial reporting is **inadequate to deal with 'knowledge led' companies** such as Rod. It is possible that the capital markets will undervalue the company because the financial statements **do not reflect the 'true' effect of the company's research activities.** The economy is becoming more 'knowledge based' and many companies find themselves in this situation.

The market value of a company is **based on the market's assessment of its future prospects**, based on available information. Analysts have developed **alternative measures of performance such as Economic Value Added (EVA).** These take factors such as expenditure on research and development expenditure into account, so that they attempt to assess estimated future cash flows. **There is a growing interest in ways of measuring shareholder value as opposed to earnings**.

Analysts and other users of the financial statements now **recognise the importance of non-financial information about a company.** Many Stock Exchanges require companies to present an Operating and Financial Review (sometimes called Management Discussion and Analysis) and some large companies do so voluntarily. This normally includes a description of the business, its objectives and its strategy. It is current best practice to analyse the **main factors and influences that may have an effect on future performance** and to comment on how the directors have sought to **maintain and improve future performance.** In this way the directors of Rod can make the markets aware of its research activities and the way in which they give rise to future income streams and enhance shareholder value.

(e) **Internal auditor bonus**

For

The chief internal auditor is an employee of Rod, which pays a salary to him or her. As part of the internal control function, he or she is helping to **keep down costs and increase profitability**. It could therefore be argued that the chief internal auditor should have a reward for adding to the profit of the business.

Against

Conversely, the problem remains that, if the chief internal auditor receives a bonus based on results, he or she may be **tempted to allow certain actions, practices or transactions which should be stopped**, but which are increasing the profit of the business, and therefore the bonus.

Conclusion

On balance, it is **not advisable** for the chief internal auditor to receive a bonus based on the company's profit.

D10 Case study question: Exotic

> **Top tips**. The consolidation section of this question is quite straightforward as long as you remember how to calculate the MI of a sub-subsidiary. Points to watch in this question are the treatment of intragroup transactions and the calculation of minority interest.
>
> Part (c) required candidates to advise a client about the acceptability of certain accounting practices used by that client. These related to joint ventures and intangibles. Part (d) required candidates to discuss the issues surrounding environmental reporting.
>
> **Easy marks**. With complex groups, remember to sort out the group structure first. There are enough straightforward marks available here if you remember your basic rules for consolidations. The consolidation is quite straightforward as long as you remember how to calculate the MI of a sub-subsidiary.

(a)   EXOTIC GROUP
       CONSOLIDATED INCOME STATEMENT FOR THE YEAR ENDED 31 DECEMBER 20X9

	$'000
Revenue (W4)	92,120
Cost of sales (W5)	(27,915)
Gross profit	64,205
Distribution costs (3,325 + 2,137 + 1,900)	(7,362)
Administrative expenses (3,475 + 950 + 1,900)	(6,325)
Finance costs	(325)
Profit before tax	50,193
Income tax expense (8,300 + 5,390 + 4,241)	(17,931)
Profit for the period	32,262

Attributable to:	
Equity holders of the parent	28,549
Minority interest (W6)	3,713
	32,262

Dividends paid and declared for the period	9,500

(b)   EXOTIC GROUP
       CONSOLIDATED BALANCE SHEET AS AT 31 DECEMBER 20X9

	$'000
Non-current assets	
Property, plant and equipment (35,483 + 24,273 + 13,063 − (W3) 40 + (W3) 8)	72,787
Goodwill (W7)	4,107
	76,894
Current assets (1,568 + 9,025 + 8,883 − (W2) 15 − (W2) 15)	19,446
	96,340
Equity attributable to equity holders of the parent	
Share capital	8,000
Retained earnings (W9)	56,609
	64,608
Minority interest (W8)	8,597
	73,206
Current liabilities (13,063 + 10,023 + 48)	23,134
	96,340

Workings

1   *Group structure*

Exotic
| 90%
Melon
| 80%

Kiwi	Effective interest (90% × 80%)	72%
	∴ Minority interest	28%
		100%

2   *Intragroup trading*

(i)   Cancel intragroup sale/purchase:

DEBIT group revenue (260 + 480) $740,000
CREDIT group cost of sales $740,000

(ii)   Unrealised profit

	$'000
Melon ($60 \times 33\frac{1}{3}/133\frac{1}{3}$)	15
Kiwi ($75 \times 25/125$)	15

Adjust in books of seller:

DEBIT Cost of sales/retained earnings
CREDIT Group Inventories

3   *Intragroup transfer of equipment*

(i)   Cancel intragroup sale/purchase:

DEBIT group revenue $240,000
CREDIT group cost of sales $240,000

(ii)   Unrealised profit on intragroup sale of equipment

	$'000
$(240,000 - 200,000)$	40

Adjust in books of seller (Exotic):

DEBIT Cost of sales/retained earnings $40,000
CREDIT Group property, plant and equipment $40,000

(iii)   Excess depreciation

	$'000
$(240,000 - 200,000) \times 20\%$	8

Adjust in books of seller (Exotic):

DEBIT Property, plant and equipment $8,000
CREDIT Cost of sales/retained earnings $8,000

4   *Revenue*

	$'000
Exotic	45,600
Melon	24,700
Kiwi	22,800
Less intragroup sales (W2)	(740)
Less intragroup transfer of equipment (W3)	(240)
	92,120

BPP LEARNING MEDIA

5   *Cost of sales*

	$'000
Exotic	18,050
Melon	5,463
Kiwi	5,320
Less intragroup purchases (W2)	(740)
Less intragroup transfer of equipment (at transfer price) (W3)	(240)
Add unrealised profit on transfer of equipment (W3)	40
Less excess depreciation $(240 - 200) \times 20\%$	(8)
Add PUP (W2): Melon	15
Kiwi	15
	27,915

6   *Minority interest (income statement)*

	$'000
Melon $((10,760 - (W2)\ 15) \times 10\%)$	1,074
Kiwi $((9,439 - (W2)\ 15) \times (W1)\ 28\%)$	2,639
	3,713

7   *Goodwill on acquisition*

	Exotic in Melon		Melon in Kiwi	
	$'000	$'000	$'000	$'000
Cost of combination		6,650		3,800
Share of net assets acquired:				
Share capital	3,000		2,000	
Retained earnings at acquisition	1,425		950	
	4,425		2,950	
Group share	90%	3,983	80%	2,360
		2,667		1,440

4,107

8   *Minority interest (balance sheet)*

	Melon	Kiwi
	$'000	$'000
Net assets per question	27,075	21,898
Less: PUP (W2)	(15)	(15)
Less: Cost of investment in Kiwi	(3,800)	
Goodwill (W7)	1,440	
	24,700	21,883
	$\times 10\%$	$\times 28\%$
	2,470	6,127

8,597

9   *Retained earnings*

	Exotic $'000	Melon $'000	Kiwi $'000
Retained earnings per question	22,638	24,075	19,898
Less: PUP (W2)		(15)	(15)
Transfer of equipment (W3): PUP	(40)		
excess dep'n	8		-
Pre-acquisition retained earnings		(1,425)	(950)
		22,635	18,933
Share of Melon (22,635 × 90%)	20,372		
Share of Kiwi (18,933 × (W1) 72%)	13,631		
	56,609		

(c)   **Goodwill arising on acquisition of Zest Software**

The company believes that this goodwill has an **indefinite economic life** and therefore it will be **retained in the balance sheet** indefinitely. IFRS 3 *Business combinations* states that goodwill arising on a business combination should be **recognised as an intangible asset and is not amortised**. However, goodwill must be **reviewed for impairment annually** and impairment losses charged to the income statement where necessary. It should be noted that s**oftware products generally have short lives and the sector is not noted for stability.** This suggests that in practice the goodwill is **likely to suffer impairment** within a reasonably short time.

Interest in joint venture

Although the main standard dealing with joint ventures is IAS 31 *Interests in joint ventures,* the company uses the equity method to account for its interest. IAS 31 **allows the use of the equity method** and IAS 28 *Investments in associates* deals with its application.

IAS 28 states that **if an investor's share of the losses** of an associate **equals its interest** in the associate, it discontinues recognising its share of further losses. The investment **is reported at nil value**. In theory, IAS 28 does not prevent the company from including the loan to the joint venture as part of its investment, particularly if it is a long-term loan. Therefore **the net liability in the joint venture should not be offset against the loan.** (However, IAS 1 *Presentation of financial statements* prohibits offsetting unless required or permitted by a standard.)

This leaves a **net liability of $3 million** (the company's share of the net assets of the joint venture of $3 million less negative goodwill of $6 million). In this case the **net liability arises from negative goodwill**, rather than net liabilities in the joint venture itself. IAS 28 states that where there is negative goodwill this should be **excluded** from the carrying amount of the investment and should be **immediately recognised in the income statement** (as a gain). This treatment of negative goodwill is also required by IFRS 3.

Therefore the net interest in the joint venture should be reported in the balance sheet as a **non-current asset investment** (the **usual treatment** for an investment in a joint venture accounted for using the equity method at a value of $3 million and the negative goodwill of $6 million recognised in the income statement).

(d)   **Environmental reporting**

At present, most companies are **not specifically required to report any information about the way in which their activities affect the environment**.

Some accounting standards require disclosure of **specific environmental information**:

- **IAS 1** *Presentation of financial statements* requires details of **material items** recognised in the income statement; these may include environmental costs.

- **IAS 37** *Provisions, contingent liabilities and contingent assets* requires **disclosure of information about provisions and contingent liabilities relating to environmental matters.**

In addition, many companies, particularly listed companies, may present an Operating and Financial Review or Management Discussion and Analysis. It is best practice to describe business risks related to environmental issues, and to disclose details of potential environmental liabilities and environmental protection costs.

Apart from this, companies can disclose as much or as little information as they wish in whatever way that they wish.

In practice companies often present information **selectively or in such a general way that it is meaningless.** This means that it is difficult to compare the performance of different companies. However, many large companies publish extensive and extremely informative 'environmental reports' that are completely separate from the financial statements themselves. Because most environmental disclosures **do not have to be audited, users cannot yet rely on the environmental information included in the financial statements.**

Progas's operations clearly do have an impact on the environment and the company **should seriously consider disclosing environmental information** in its financial statements. By acknowledging its responsibility for the environment, a company **can enhance its reputation and distinguish itself from competitors.** Information that would be useful to users of the financial statements might include the following.

(i)   Details of **emissions**, including **reductions/increases from the previous year**;
(ii)   The **impact of gas emissions** on the environment and **action taken** to minimise this impact;
(iii)   **Expenditure on restoring the countryside** after pipelines have been laid;
(iv)   Details of any **infringement of environmental laws/guidelines** including details of any **fines**.

There are a number of **codes of practice** which companies may follow, for example, the *Sustainability Reporting Guidelines* published by the Global Reporting Initiative (GRI). The company may also consider signing up to the Eco Management and Audit Scheme (EMAS). This would involve agreeing to a specific code of practice with the environmental report being validated by an accredited independent verifier.

D11 Preparation question: Part disposal

ANGEL GROUP
CONSOLIDATED BALANCE SHEET AS AT 31 DECEMBER 20X8

	$'000
Non-current assets	
Property, plant and equipment	200
Investment in Shane (W3)	88
	288
Current assets (890 + 160)	1,050
	1,338
Equity attributable to equity holders of the parent	
Share capital	500
Retained earnings (W4)	528
	1,028
Current liabilities	310
	1,338

ANGEL GROUP
CONSOLIDATED INCOME STATEMENT FOR THE YEAR ENDED 31 DECEMBER 20X8

	$'000
Profit before interest and tax [110 + (30 × 6/12)]	125.00
Profit on disposal of shares in subsidiary (W6)	75.15
Share of profit of associate (18 × 35% × 6/12)	3.15
Profit before tax	203.30
Income tax expense [40 + (12 × 6/12)]	(46.00)
Profit for the period	157.30

Attributable to:	
Equity holders of the parent	154.6
Minority interest (18 × 6/12 × 30%)	2.7
	157.3

ANGEL GROUP
CONSOLIDATED RECONCILIATION OF MOVEMENT IN RETAINED EARNINGS

	$'000
Balance at 31 December 20X7 (W7)	373.4
Profit for the period	154.6
Balance at 31 December 20X8 (W4)	528.0

Workings

1   *Timeline*

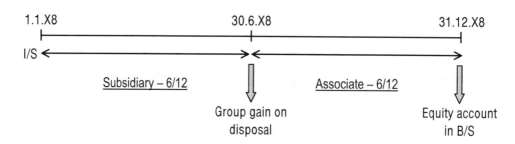

2   *Profit on disposal of Shane in Angel's separate financial statements*

	$'000
Sale proceeds	160
Less: cost of Shane (120 × ½)	(60)
	100

3   *Investment in associate (Shane)*

	$'000
Cost of associate (120 × ½)	60
Share of post acquisition retained reserves [(90 – 10) × 35%]	28
	88

4   *Retained earnings*

	Angel	Shane
	$'000	$'000
Per Q	400	90
Add: profit on disposal (W2)	100	
Less: Pre-acquisition retained earnings		(10)
	500	80
Shane – Share of post acquisition ret'd earnings (80 × 35%)	28	
	528	

BPP
LEARNING MEDIA

5   *Goodwill - Shane*

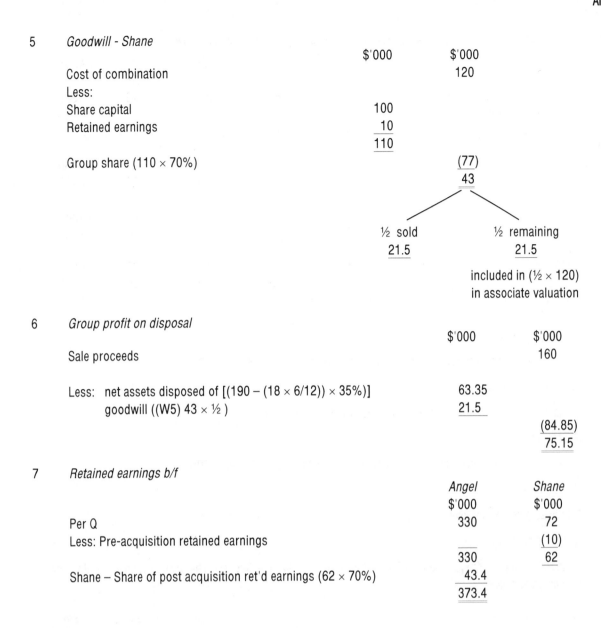

	$'000	$'000
Cost of combination		120
Less:		
Share capital	100	
Retained earnings	10	
	110	
Group share (110 × 70%)		(77)
		43

½ sold
21.5

½ remaining
21.5

included in (½ × 120)
in associate valuation

6   *Group profit on disposal*

	$'000	$'000
Sale proceeds		160
Less: net assets disposed of [(190 − (18 × 6/12)) × 35%)]	63.35	
goodwill ((W5) 43 × ½)	21.5	
		(84.85)
		75.15

7   *Retained earnings b/f*

	Angel $'000	Shane $'000
Per Q	330	72
Less: Pre-acquisition retained earnings		(10)
	330	62
Shane – Share of post acquisition ret'd earnings (62 × 70%)	43.4	
	373.4	

D12 Preparation question: Plans

Key considerations and accounting impacts

There are a number of reasons why a group may re-organise.

- To **reduce gearing** by floating a business
- Companies may be transferred to another business during a **divisionalisation process**
- To **create efficiencies** of group structure for **tax purposes**

The impact of each of the proposed structures is discussed below.

Plan 1

The implications of this plan will be different, depending on the choice of purchase consideration.

Share for share exchange

If the purchase consideration is in the form of shares, then a share premium account will need to be set up in the books of Y. This share premium account must comprise the minimum premium value, which is the excess of the book value of the investment over the nominal value of the shares issued: $70m − $50m = $20m.

The impact on the individual company accounts and on the group accounts is as follows.

	Note	X $m	Y $m	Z $m	Group $m
Property, plant and equipment		600	200	45	845
Intangible assets: goodwill					10
Cost of investment in Y	1	130			
Cost of investment in Z	2		70		
Net current assets		160	100	20	280
		890	370	65	1,135

	Note	X	Y	Z	Group
Share capital	3	120	110	40	120
Share premium	4		20		
Retained earnings	5	770	240	25	1,015
		890	370	65	1,135

Notes

1   *Cost of investment in Y*

This is increased by the total value of the shares issued: $50m + $20m = $70m.

2   *Cost of investment in Z*

Transferred to Y. The book value of the investment is preserved.

3   *Share capital*

Y's share capital is increased by the nominal value of the shares issued, $50m.

4   *Share premium*

This is as discussed above.

5   *Retained earnings*

Goodwill arising on the purchase of Z is $10m ($70m − ($40m + $20m)). The group retained earnings are calculated as follows.

	X $m	Y $m	Z $m
Per question	770	240	25
Retained earnings at acquisition		−	(20)
	770	240	5
Share of post-acquisition profits of Y (100%)	240		
Share of post-acquisition profits of Z (100%)	5		
	1,015		

Cash purchase

The group accounts are not affected by the change as the reorganisation is internal. It has no impact on the group as a single entity.

If the purchase consideration is in the form of cash, a gain or loss on the sale of Z will arise in the books of X. This does not count as a distribution as the cash price of $75m is not in excess of the fair value of the net assets of Z, $80m. The effect on the accounts would be as follows.

	Note	X $m	Y $m	Z $m	Group $m
Property, plant and equipment		600	200	45	845
Goodwill					10
Cost of investment in Y		60			
Cost of investment in Z	1		75		
Net current assets	2	235	25	20	280
		895	300	65	1,135
Share capital		120	60	40	120
Retained earnings	3	775	240	25	1,015
		895	300	65	1,135

Notes

1 Cost of investment in Z

This is the cash consideration of $75m.

2 Net current assets

X's cash increases by $75m and Y's cash decreases by $75m.

3 Retained earnings

X's retained earnings have been increased by $5m, being the profit on the sale of the investment in Z. This is eliminated on consolidation as it is an intra-group transaction. The consolidated retained earnings are calculated in exactly the same way as in the share for share exchange.

Plan 2

This restructuring plan is a rationalisation, aimed at simplifying the group structure. An important point to take into account is that the investment in Z in the books of X may be impaired. Z was originally purchased for $70m, with goodwill of $10m arising, but the assets have been transferred to Y at book value of $60m. Z will be a shell company with a net asset value of $60m and this will be shown as an intercompany account with Y. The cost of X's investment in Z should be reduced to $60m, with a corresponding charge to the revenue reserves. The accounts would appear as follows.

	Note	X $m	Y $m	Z $m	Group $m
Goodwill					10
Property, plant and equipment		600	245		845
Cost of investment in Y		60			
Cost of investment in Z	1	60			
Net current assets	2	160	60	60	280
		880	305	60	1,135
Share capital		120	60	40	120
Revaluation surplus	3		5		
Retained earnings	4	760	240	20	1,015
		880	305	60	1,135

Notes

1 Cost of investment in Z

	$m
Per question	70
Less impairment	(10)
	60

2   *Net current assets*

Y's net current assets are $100m + $20m less intragroup payable $60m.

Note that this calculation is based on the assumption that the $10m loss in X's books, the revaluation gain in Y's books and the loss on the transfer of assets to Y in Z's books are intragroup items and can be ignored.

3   *Revaluation surplus*

This is the gain on the purchase of the assets from Z: $65m − $60m.

4   *Retained earnings*

X's individual retained earnings are $770m less the impairment of $10m, which gives $760m.

The group retained earnings are calculated as follows.

	X $m	Y $m	Z $m
Per question	770	240	25
Retained earnings at acquisition	–	–	(20)
	770	240	5
Share of post-acquisition profits of Y (100%)	240		
Share of post-acquisition profits of Z (100%)	5		
	1,015		

Z's retained earnings are $20m, ie $25m less $5m loss on transfer of assets.

Summary and conclusion

There are advantages and disadvantages to each of the three plans. Before we could make a recommendation we would need more information about why the group wishes to restructure.

Plan 1 does not change the group financial statements. From an internal point of view it results in a closer relationship between Y and Z. This may be advantageous if Y and Z are close geographically or in terms of similarity of business activities. Alternatively, it might be advantageous for tax reasons.

Plan 2 is an example of divisionalisation: the assets and trade of Z are transferred to Y and Z becomes a shell company. This could result in cost savings overall. Furthermore, Z becomes a non-trading company and this could be used for some other purpose.

D13 Ejoy

Top tips. This question required the production of a consolidated income statement of a group. Candidates were expected to calculate and impairment test the investment in a subsidiary, to account for a joint venture, to deal with impairment and hedging of financial assets, and account for a pre-acquisition dividend and a discontinued operation.

Easy marks. Do not spend too long on the discontinued operation. You would not be penalised too heavily if you got this wrong and there are easy marks to be gained for adding across and other basic consolidation aspects.

Examiner's comment. Overall the question was quite well answered, with the majority of candidates achieving a pass mark. However, candidates answered the financial instruments part of the question quite poorly. The main problem seemed to be the application of knowledge; candidates could recite the principles of accounting for financial instruments but could not deal with the practical application thereof. The calculation of the goodwill was done well, as was the accounting for the pre-acquisition dividend. However, the impairment testing of the investment in the subsidiary was poorly answered. Candidates need to understand this procedure as it will be a regular feature of future papers.

	Marks
Goodwill	7
Joint venture	2
Financial assets	7
Dividend	2
Income statement	7
Tbay	4
Minority interest	2
Available	31
Maximum	25

EJOY: CONSOLIDATED INCOME STATEMENT FOR THE YEAR ENDED 31 MAY 20X6

	$m
Continuing operations	
Revenue (2,500 + 1,500)	4,000
Cost of sales (1,800 + 1,200 + 26 (W8))	(3,026)
Gross profit	974
Other income (70 + 10 – 3 (W11) – 24 (W2))	53
Distribution costs (130 + 120)	(250)
Administrative expenses (100 + 90)	(190)
Finance income (W5)	6
Finance costs (W6)	(134)
Profit before tax	459
Income tax expense (200 + 26)	(226)
Profit for period from continuing operations	233
Discontinued operations	
Profit for the period from discontinued operations ((30 × 6/12) – 2 (W8))	13
Profit for the period	246
Attributable to:	
Equity holders of the parent	241
Minority interest (W12)	5
	246

Workings

1   *Group structure*

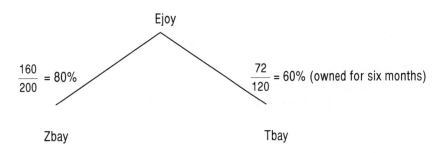

$\frac{160}{200} = 80\%$ Ejoy $\frac{72}{120} = 60\%$ (owned for six months)

Zbay   Tbay

Tbay is a discontinued operation (IFRS 5).

Timeline

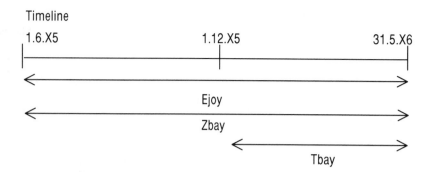

2 *Pre-acquisition dividend income*

Pre-acquisition dividend income (Tbay)

	$m	$m
Dividend treated as a reduction in cost of investment (60% × 40)		24
DEBIT Dividend income	24	
CREDIT Cost of investment in Tbay (W7)		24

3 *Loan asset held by Zbay*

	$m
Carrying value of loan at 1.6.X5 (a financial asset)	60.0
Impairment loss (balancing figure)	(42.2)
Present value of expected future cash flows (20 × $\dfrac{1}{1.06^2}$ at 1.6.X5 (note)	17.8
Interest income (6% × 17.8)	1.1
At 31.5.X6	18.9

Note. The $20 million is expected to be received on 31 May 20X7, ie. in two years' time.

4 *Hedged bond (Ejoy)*

	$m
1.6.X5	50.0
Interest income (5% × 50)	2.5
Fair value loss (balancing figure)	(1.7)
Fair value at 31.5.X6 (per question)	48.3

Because the interest rate swap is 100% effective as a fair value hedge, it exactly offsets the loss in value of $1.7 million on the bond. The bond is an 'available for sale' item (per IAS 39) and therefore the loss would normally be taken to equity, but because hedge accounting is adopted both the gain on the swap and the loss on the bond are recognised in profit and loss as income and expense. The net effect on profit and loss is nil.

5 *Finance income*

	$m
Interest income on loan asset held by Zbay (W3)	1.1
Interest receivable on bond held by Ejoy (W4)	2.5
Interest received on interest rate swap held by Ejoy	0.5
Fair value gain on interest rate swap	1.7
	5.8

BPP
LEARNING MEDIA

6   *Finance costs*

	$m
Per draft income statements (50 + 40)	90.0
Impairment loss (loan asset held by Zbay) (W3)	42.2
Fair value loss on hedged land (W4)	1.7
	133.9

7   *Goodwill*

	Zbay		Tbay	
	$m	$m	$m	$m
Cost of business contribution		520		216
Less pre-acquisition dividend (W2)				(24)
Fair value of net assets at acquisition	600		310	
Group share (W1)	80%		60%	
		(480)		(186)
		40		6

8   *Impairment losses*

	Zbay	Tbay
	$m	$m
Notional goodwill (40 × 100/80) (6 × 100/5) (W7)	50.0	10.0
Carrying amount of net assets (W9)/(W10)	612.9	285.0
	662.9	295.0
Recoverable amount 630/(300 − (5 × 100/60))	(630.0)	(291.7)
Impairment loss: gross	32.9	3.3
Impairment loss recognised: all allocated to goodwill		
(80% × 32.9)/(60% × 3.3)	26.3	2.0

9   *Carrying amount of net assets at 31 May 20X6 (Zbay)*

	$m
Fair value of identifiable assets and liabilities acquired (1 June 20X4)	600.0
Profit for year to 31 May 20X5	20.0
Profit for year to 31 May 20X6 per draft income statement	34.0
Less impairment loss (loan asset) (W3)	(42.2)
Interest income (loan asset) (W3)	1.1
	612.9

10   Carrying amount of net assets *(Tbay)*

	$m
Carrying value of investment in Tbay at 31 May 20X6:	
Fair value of net assets at acquisition (1 December 20X5)	310
Post acquisition profit (30 × 6/12)	15
Less dividend	(40)
	285

11   *Joint venture*

	$m	$m
Elimination of other venturer's share of gain on disposal (50% × 6)		3
DEBIT Other income	3	
CREDIT Investment in joint venture		3

12   *Minority interest*

	Zbay $m	Tbay $m
Profit for period per question	34.0	
× 6/12		15
Less impairment loss on loan asset (W3)	(42.2)	
Interest income on loan asset (W3)	1.1	
	(7.1)	15
	× 20%	× 40%
	(1.4)	6
	4.6	

D14 Case study question: Base Group

Top tips. This question required a consolidated income statement.. This included the calculation of the profit/loss on a disposal of shares/deemed disposal, adjustments for inter company profit, retirement benefits, convertible debt instruments and share options as well as dealing with accounting for associates, minority interests and goodwill. The question included a deemed disposal. However, if you missed this, you would only be penalised once for this mistake. Part (b) deals with revenue recognition. In part (c) there are easy marks to be had for backing up your arguments.

Easy marks. There are a lot of easy marks here for basic consolidation technique, which, even if you missed complications like the deemed disposal, you could still gain.

Examiner's comment. In general this question was well answered. However, some candidates used proportional consolidation for the subsidiary, and few treated the share options correctly.

Marking scheme

		Marks
(a)	Revenue	1
	Cost of sales	4
	Distribution/administration	1
	Interest expense	2
	Investment income	1
	Taxation	1
	Goodwill	3
	Inter-company profit	2
	Retirement benefit – explanation	2
	Debt – explanation	2
	Share options – explanation	2
	Associate	4
	Minority interest	2
	Deemed disposal	3
	Disposal of shares	2
(b)	Revenue recognition	6

(c) (i)   Strategic issue   1
            Sustainable performance   1
            Transparency   1
            Best practice   1
            Responsible ownership   1
            Performance   1
            Reduction of risks   1
            Reputation   1
            Exploitation   1
            Governments   1
            External awards   1
            Cultural/social pressures   1

                                              Maximum

     (ii)   1 mark per point up to a maximum   7
                                                                            ──
                                                                            50

(a)   BASE GROUP
       CONSOLIDATED INCOME STATEMENT FOR THE YEAR ENDED 31 MAY 20X3

                                                                            $m
       Revenue (3,000 + 2,300 + (600 × 9/12))   5,750
       Cost of sales (W2)   (3,822)
       Gross profit   1,928
       Distribution costs (240 + 230 + (120 × 9/12))   (560)
       Administrative expenses (200 + 220 + (80 × 9/12))   (480)
       Profit on disposal of shares in subsidiaries (W3)   6
       Finance costs (W4)   (43)
       Investment income receivable (100 − (200/350 × 70))   60
       Share of loss of associate (W5)   (6)
       Profit before tax   905
       Income tax expense (130 + 80 + 27)   (237)
       Profit for the year   668

       Attributable to
         Equity holders of the parent   595
         Minority interests (W8)   73
                                                                            668

Workings

1   *Group structure*

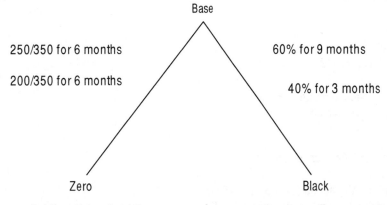

Zero was a subsidiary throughout the year.

Black became an associate on 1 March 20X3; the share issue reduced Base's shareholding, resulting in a deemed disposal.

2   *Cost of sales*

	$m
Base	2,000
Zero	1,600
Black (300 × 9/12)	225
	3,825
Retirement benefit (W7)	(5)
Share options (3 – 1)	2
	3,822

Note. The loss in the value of the share options is included in cost of sales because the options were received in exchange for trade receivables.

3   *Profit on disposal of shares in subsidiaries*

Zero

	$m	$m
Sale proceeds		155
Less net assets disposed of:		
Share capital	350	
Retained earnings at start of year	400	
Profit for current year (160 × 6/12)	80	
Fair value adjustment (770 – 350 – 250)	170	
	1,000	
Share disposed of (50/350)		(143)
Goodwill not yet written off (50/250 × 40) (W6)		(8)
		4

Black

	$m	$m
Carrying value of net assets after the new issue:		
At date of issue	480	
Proceeds of issue (100 × 2.65)	265	
	745	
Group share (40%)		298
Less: group share of net assets before issue (60% × 480)		(288)
Gain		10
Goodwill not yet written off (20/60 × 24) (W6)		(8)
		2

Total profit on disposal is $8.5 million (rounded to $9 million).

4   *Finance costs*

	$m
Base	20
Zero	10
Black (12 × 9/12)	9
	39
Redeemable debt (20 × 5.4%)	1.1
Retirement benefit plan	3
	43.1

5   *Share of loss of associate*

	$m
Profit for the period (52 × 3/12 × 40%)	5.2
Provision for unrealised profit (90 (W9))	(10.8)
	(5.6)

6   *Goodwill*

	Zero $m	Black $m
Cost of combination	600	270
Less: fair value of net assets acquired:		
(250/350 × 770)	(550)	
(60% × 400)		(240)
	50	30
Impairment losses to 1 June 20X2	(10)	(6)
Goodwill not yet written off at date of disposal/deemed disposal	40	24

7   *Retirement benefits*

	$m
Amount originally included in cost of sales	10
Amount that should be included (current service cost only)	(5)
Adjustment (reduction)	5

10% 'corridor' (based on amounts at 31 May 20X2)

10% of present value of defined benefit obligation ($54m) $5.4m

10% of fair value of plan assets ($48 m) $4.8 m

The unrecognised actuarial loss is only $3 million and therefore no loss is recognised during the year.

8   *Minority interests*

	$m
Zero to 1 December 20X2 (160 × 6/12 × 100/350)	23
Zero to 31 May 20X3 (160 × 6/12 × 150/350)	34
Black to 1 March 20X3 (52 × 9/12× 40%)	16
	73

9   *Provision for unrealised profit*

$90 × 30%	= $25m
Group share: 40%	= £10.8m

(b)   **Revenue from the sale of software under licences**

At present the company must comply with **IAS 18** *Revenue*, although this standard **only sets out general principles**. There have recently been several high profile cases in which companies have been criticised for adopting questionable revenue recognition policies. As a result, **many companies have turned to US GAAP where this provides further guidance** on reporting specific types of transaction. In itself, **this does not contravene IAS 18**.

However, IAS 18 does require that where a transaction consists of **more than one distinct element**, each element should be **accounted for separately**. An Appendix to IAS 18 states that where the selling price of the product includes an identifiable amount for subsequent servicing, that amount, including a profit element, should be **deferred and recognised as revenue over the period during which the service is performed**. Alternatively, it could be argued that the provision of the software and the services are **linked** and should be **treated as one transaction**. The correct accounting treatment **depends on the economic substance** of the transactions.

The Appendix to IAS 18 also states that fees from the development of customised software should be recognised **by reference to the stage of completion of the development**. At present the company only recognises revenue at the completion of the contract and therefore **this accounting policy should be changed**.

(c)   (i)   There are a number of factors which encourage companies to disclose social and environmental information in their financial statements.

Public interest in corporate social responsibility is steadily increasing. Although financial statements are primarily intended for investors and their advisers, there is growing recognition that companies actually have **a number of different stakeholders**. These include **customers, employees and the general public,** all of whom are **potentially interested** in the way in which a company's operations affect the natural environment and the wider community. These stakeholders can have a **considerable effect on a company's performance**. As a result many companies now deliberately attempt to build a **reputation for social and environmental responsibility**. Therefore the disclosure of environmental and social information is essential. There is also growing recognition that **corporate social responsibility is actually an important part of an entity's overall performance.** Responsible practice in areas such as reduction of damage to the environment and recruitment **increases shareholder value**. Companies that act responsibly and make social and environmental disclosures are **perceived as better investments** than those that do not.

Another factor is **growing interest by governments and professional bodies**. Although there are **no IFRSs** that specifically require environmental and social reporting, it may be required by **company legislation**. There are now a number of **awards for environmental and social reports** and high quality disclosure in financial statements. These provide further encouragement to disclose information.

At present companies are normally able to disclose **as much or as little information as they wish in whatever manner that they wish**. This causes a number of **problems**. Companies tend to disclose information **selectively** and it is difficult for users of the financial statements to **compare the performance of different companies**. However, there are **good arguments** for continuing to allow companies a certain amount of freedom to determine the information that they disclose. If detailed rules are imposed, **companies are likely to adopt a 'checklist' approach** and will **present information in a very general and standardised way**, so that it is of very little use to stakeholders.

   (ii)   The Base Group could improve its disclosure of 'Corporate Environmental Governance' by including the following information in its financial statements:

(1)   a general description of its **policies** relating to the environment

(2)   descriptions of the **ways in which the company seeks to manage and minimise environmental risks**

(3)   **details** of any **serious pollution incidents** that have occurred during the year and details of any **fines** imposed for environmental offences

(4)   a report on the company's **environmental performance** including **details of acid gas and other emissions** and details of how the company's activities affect the natural environment in other ways. The report should include **narrative information** (descriptions of how the risks are reduced) and **numerical information** if this is verifiable

(5)   details of the company's **targets (key performance indicators)** for reducing emissions and other forms of pollution and whether these have been met; **historical data** should be included here if this is practicable

There exist a number of **guidelines** that set out the information that should be disclosed in an environmental report (for example, the Global Reporting Initiative (GRI) framework of performance indicators). The guidance is **non-mandatory, but represents best practice**. Ideally, the environmental information should be **audited.**

BPP
LEARNING MEDIA

D15 Hyperinflation

(a) A foreign operation normally has the same functional currency of its parent when:

    (i) The foreign company is merely an **extension** of the **investing company** operations overseas.

    (ii) The foreign company is **dependent** upon the investing company for financing.

    (iii) The foreign company **cash flows** have a **material impact** on those of the investing company.

    (iv) The majority of the **transactions** are denominated in the **investing company currency**.

A foreign operation normally has a different functional currency from is parent when:

    (i) The foreign operation is **separate** or **independent**.

    (ii) The normal operations are denominated in the **local currency**.

    (iii) The normal operations are (at least partially) **financed locally**.

    (iv) The foreign operation has a management team committed to maximisation of the **local currency profits**.

    (v) The **financial statements** of the **foreign operation** are be **expressed** in the **local currency** as the **best indicator** of the **performance locally**.

Factors which may be taken into account in determining the **functional currency** include the following.

    (i) **Pricing** and **market conditions**. Are they determined locally or by the investing company?

    (ii) Does the foreign operation buy **goods and services locally** or rely on imports?

    (iii) How is the foreign operation **financed**? Locally or by the investing company?

    (iv) What is the extent of **inter company trading**?

(b) **The effects of hyper-inflation on the financial statements**

Hyper-inflation can **reduce the usefulness** of financial statements in the following ways:

- The amounts at which assets are stated in the balance sheet are **unlikely to reflect their current values.**

- The **level of profit** for the year may be **misleading**. Income appears to increase rapidly, while expenses such as depreciation may be based on out of date costs and are artificially low.

- It is therefore difficult to make any **meaningful assessment** of an entity's performance as **assets are understated** and **profits are overstated**.

These are well known disadvantages of basing financial statements on historic cost and they affect most entities. However, where there is hyper-inflation these problems are exacerbated. In addition, where an entity's financial statements are translated into dollars, hyper-inflation often gives rise to **significant exchange differences** which may **absorb reserves**.

How hyper-inflation should be dealt with in the financial statements

IAS 29 **does not provide a definition** of hyper-inflation. However, it does include guidance as to characteristics of an economic environment of a country in which hyper-inflation may be present. These include, but are not limited to, the following.

- The general population prefers to keep its wealth in **non-monetary assets** or in a relatively **stable foreign currency**

- Interest rates, wages and prices are **linked to a price index**

- The cumulative **inflation rate** over three years is **approaching, or exceeds, 100%**

IAS 29 states that the financial statements of an entity that reports in the currency of a hyper-inflationary economy should be **restated in terms of the measuring unit current at the balance sheet date.** This involves remeasuring assets and liabilities by **applying a general price index.** The **gain or loss on the net monetary position is included in net income** and **separately disclosed.** The fact that the financial statements have been restated should also be disclosed, together with details of the index used.

IAS 21 *The effects of changes in foreign exchange rates* states that where there is hyper-inflation, the financial statements of a foreign operation **should be restated** in accordance with the requirements of IAS 29 **before they are translated into the currency of the reporting entity.** In this way users are made aware of the effect of hyper-inflation on the results and net assets of the entity.

(c)   (i)

(1)

	Value (E million)	Exchange rate	$m
30 November 20X3	20	1.34	14.93
30 November 20X7	20	17.87	1.12

(A material reduction in value)

(2)

	Value E million	Index	Exchange rate	$m
30 November 20X7	20 ×	3,254/100	17.87	36.42

(ii)   In example (1) the tremendous reduction is due to **severe exchange rate movements** and has nothing at all to do with trading performance from the assets.

In example (2) a paper gain emerges simply as **a result of revaluation locally**, again this has little to do with trading performance and reflects an unrealised holding gain measured locally. However, this method does eliminate the 'disappearing assets' problem and IAS 29 requires restatement using this method where there is hyperinflation.

D16 Question with helping hands: Zetec

Top tips. This question required candidates to produce a consolidated income statement and balance sheet for a parent company and its foreign subsidiary. Adjustments had to be made before consolidation to bring the subsidiary's financial statements into line with 'local' accounting standards.

Examiner's comment. Candidates generally made good attempts at the translation of the foreign subsidiary and the calculation of goodwill, inter company profit in inventory, and the gain in translation. At the same time, there were problems with the 'extraordinary' items and surprisingly with the rates of exchange to be used in translating the income statement and balance sheet of the subsidiary. However, generally the performance on this question was good.

Marking scheme

	Marks
Consolidated income statement	13
Consolidated balance sheet	12
Maximum	25

ZETEC GROUP
CONSOLIDATED BALANCE SHEET AS AT 31 OCTOBER 20X2

	$m
Non-current assets: 180 + 95 (W1) + 19.3 (W3)	294
Goodwill: (3 + 18) (W1, W7)	21
Net current assets: 146 + 29 (W1) – 3 (W4)	172
	487

Equity attributable to the equity holders of the parent	
Ordinary shares of $1	65
Share premium	70
Retained earnings (W9)	162
Translation reserve (W10)	23
	320
Minority interest (W8)	13
Non-current liabilities: 74 + 80 (W1)	154
	487

ZETEC GROUP
CONSOLIDATED INCOME STATEMENT FOR THE YEAR ENDED 31 OCTOBER 20X2

	$m
Revenue: 325 + 50 (W2) – 15 (W4)	360
Cost of sales: 189 + 24.6 (W2) – 15 (W4) + 3 (W4)	(202)
Gross profit	158
Distribution and administrative expenses: 84 + 9 (W2)	(93)
Finance costs: 2 + 4 (W2)	(6)
Profit before tax	59
Income tax expense: 15 + 6 (W2)	(21)
Profit for the period	38

Attributable to:	
Equity holders of the parent	37
Minority interest: 6.2 (W2) × 20%	1
	38

Workings

1   *Translation of subsidiary's balance sheet/adjustment to IFRS*

	Per qu Kr'm	Adjustments	Note/ Working	Total	Rate (Note 1)	$m
Non-current assets	380			380	4	95.0
Goodwill	12		2	12	4	3.0
Net current assets	116			116	4	29.0
	508			508		127.0
Equity						
Ordinary shares: 1 kr	48			48	6	8.0
Share premium	18			18	6	3.0
Pre-acq'n reserves:						
Revaluation surplus	12			12	6	2.0
Retained earnings	98	(13)	(W6)	85	6	14.2
	176			163		27.2
Post-acq'n reserves:						
Profit (excl extraord item)	34	(3)		31	5	6.2
'Extraordinary' item	(22)	3 + 6 + 13	(W6)	-		-
Revaluation surplus		(6)	(W6)	(6)	5	(1.2)
Translation reserve	-			-	balance	14.8
	188			188		47.0
Long-term liabilities	320			320	4	80.0
	508			508		127.0

Notes

1   Translate assets and liabilities at the rate ruling at the balance sheet date, and share capital and pre-acquisition reserves at the historic rate. Post-acquisition reserves are as calculated above. The translation reserve is the balancing figure.

2   Aztec has allocated the excess of the price paid for its acquisition of a company over the fair value of the company's net assets to 'market share'. However, this should be re-classified as goodwill.

2   *Translation of Aztec income statement*

	Kr'm	Rate	$m
Revenue	250	5	50.0
Cost of sales (120 – 3 (W6))	(123)	5	24.6
Gross profit	127		25.4
Distribution and administrative expenses	(46)	5	(9.2)
Interest payable	(20)	5	(4.0)
Profit before tax	61		12.2
Income tax expense	(30)	5	6.0
Profit for the period	31		6.2

3   *Fair value adjustment*

	Acquisition	Movement	Exchange differences	B/S date
	Kr'm	Kr'm	Kr'm	Kr'm
Stock market portfolio (240 – (W1) 163)	77	-	-	77
Exchange rate	6	5	-	4
Translated	12.8	-	6.5	19.3

4   *Unrealised profit in inventories*

Although the goods sold by Zetec to Aztec have been consumed in the manufacturing process, they have not been sold and are included in closing finished goods inventories. Hence, the unrealised profit must be eliminated on consolidation. The profit sits in Zetec's (the parent) books and must therefore be adjusted in full against its profits.

Goods transferred from Zetec at selling price	$ 15m
Percentage profit on selling price	× 20%
Unrealised profit sitting in Zetec	$3m

5   *Settlement of debt from inventory transfer*

A gain would be made by Aztec, calculated as follows:

	Kr'm
Liability arising on transfer of the goods at 31 May 20X2: 15m × 5.2	78
Settlement on 31 July 20X2: 15m × 4.2	63
Gain	15

This would have already been included in Aztec's income statement (in cost of sales) and is therefore recorded in Aztec's income statement in the amount of Kr 15 million in cost of sales and included in the group accounts accordingly.

6   *Elimination of extraordinary item*

The extraordinary items figure of Kr 22m in the income statement of Aztec has been eliminated in Working 1 as follows.

	Kr'm
Accounting policy adjustment to opening reserves *	13
Impairment of non-current asset charged to revaluation surplus **	6
Impairment of non-current asset charged to cost of sales (9 – 6)	3
	22

BPP LEARNING MEDIA

*Aztec has written the prior year adjustment of Kr 13m off to the current period's income statement. Under IAS 8, it should be treated as a prior year adjustment and charged against opening reserves, ie deducted from pre-acquisition profits and added back to post-acquisition profits.

**This would result in a debit balance on the post acquisition revaluation surplus. Consequently, on consolidation the translated figure of 1.2 (6 ÷ 5 from Working 1) will have to be offset against group retained earnings (see Working 9 below).

7   *Goodwill arising on acquisition of Aztec*

	Kr'm	Kr'm	Rate	$m
Cost of business combination ($44m × 6)		264		
Less fair value of net assets acquired	240			
Group share: 80%		192		
		72	6	12
FX gain		–	β	6
		72	4	18

8   *Minority interest*

	$m
Net assets at balance sheet date [47.0 (W1) + 19.3 (W3)]	66.3
Minority share	× 20%
	13.3

9   *Retained earnings*

	$m
Zetec per question	161
Aztec post acquisition [(6.2 (W1) – 1.2 (W1, W6 note)) × 80%]	4
Unrealised profit (W4)	(3)
	162

10   *Translation reserve*

	$m
Total exchange differences recognised in translation reserve	
on translation of financial statements (14.8 (W1) × 80%)	11.8
on fair value adjustments [(W3) 6.5 × 80%]	5.2
on goodwill (W7)	6.0
	23.0

11   *Proof of movement on retained earnings*

	$m
Retained earnings at 1 November 20X1 [161 – 35 + 4]	130
Profit for the period	37
Dividends paid	(4)
Impairment of non-current asset charged to rev'n surplus (1.2 (W1, W6 note) × 80%)	(1)
Retained earnings as at as at 31 October 20X2	162

Analysis of exchange gain (specifically asked for in the requirement)

	$m
Closing net assets at closing rate (W1)	47.0
Opening net assets at opening rate (W1)	(27.2)
Increase in net assets	19.8
Less: profit for year (W1)	(6.2)
Add back: charge to revaluation surplus in the year (W1)	1.2
Therefore, translation reserve for the year (and c/f as only 1 year) (agrees to W1 bal figure)	14.8
Included in group translation reserve (80%)	11.8
Included in minority interest (20%)	3.0
	14.8

D17 Memo

> **Top tips.** In this question, you had to produce a consolidated income statement and balance sheet for a parent company and its foreign subsidiary. Adjustments had to be made for intragroup items such as loans and inventory, and candidates had to deal with the treatment of goodwill as a foreign currency asset. Exchange gains and losses had to be recognised in the financial statements.
>
> **Easy marks.** Just setting out the proforma and doing the mechanics of translation will earn you easy marks, even if you struggle with more difficult aspects.
>
> **Examiner's comment.** This question was well answered. Candidates generally made good attempts at the translation of the foreign subsidiary, the calculation of goodwill, intragroup profit in inventory, and the gain on translation. At the same time, there were problems with the treatment of goodwill as a foreign currency asset, and the exchange gain on the intra group loan.

Marking scheme

	Marks
Consolidated balance sheet	6
Translation of sub-balance sheet	4
Goodwill	1
Minority interest	1
Post acquisition reserves	5
Consolidated income statement	5
Unrealised profit	4
Loan	3
Available	29
Maximum	25

(Movement on reserves and exchange gain analysis not asked for)

MEMO
CONSOLIDATED BALANCE SHEET AT 30 APRIL 20X4

	$m
Assets	
Property, plant and equipment	367
Goodwill (W4)	8
Current assets (355 + 48.6 – 0.6) (W7)	403
	778
Equity and liabilities	
Equity attributable to equity holders of the parent:	
Share capital	60
Share premium	50
Retained earnings (W5)	363
Translation reserve (W9)	9
	482
Minority interests (W6)	18
	500
Non-current liabilities (30 + 18.6 – 5)	44
Current liabilities	234
	778

BPP LEARNING MEDIA

MEMO
CONSOLIDATED INCOME STATEMENT FOR THE YEAR ENDED 30 APRIL 20X4

	$m
Revenue (200 + 71 – 6)	265
Cost of sales (120 + 48 – 6 + 0.6 (W7)	(163)
Gross profit	102
Distribution costs and administrative expenses	(40)
Impairment of goodwill (W4)	(2)
Finance costs	(1)
Interest receivable	4
Exchange gains (W7)	1
Profit before tax	64
Income tax expense	(24)
Profit for the year	40
Attributable to	
Equity holders of the parent	38
Minority interests (25% × 7.9) (W3)	2
	40

Workings

1   *Group structure*

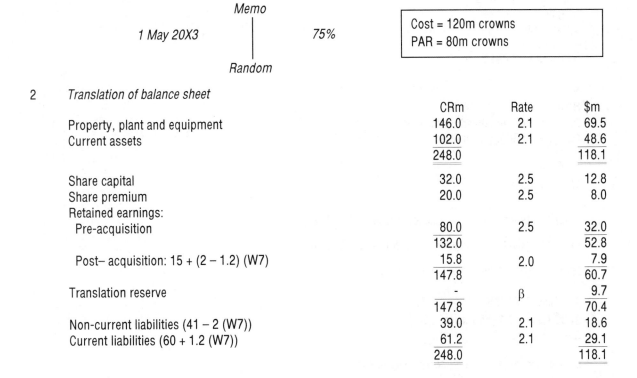

2   *Translation of balance sheet*

	CRm	Rate	$m
Property, plant and equipment	146.0	2.1	69.5
Current assets	102.0	2.1	48.6
	248.0		118.1
Share capital	32.0	2.5	12.8
Share premium	20.0	2.5	8.0
Retained earnings:			
Pre-acquisition	80.0	2.5	32.0
	132.0		52.8
Post– acquisition: 15 + (2 – 1.2) (W7)	15.8	2.0	7.9
	147.8		60.7
Translation reserve	-	β	9.7
	147.8		70.4
Non-current liabilities (41 – 2 (W7))	39.0	2.1	18.6
Current liabilities (60 + 1.2 (W7))	61.2	2.1	29.1
	248.0		118.1

3   *Translation of income statement*

	CRm	Rate	$m
Revenue	142	2	71
Cost of sales	(96)	2	(48)
Gross profit	46	2	23
Distribution and administrative expenses	(20)	2	(10)
Interest payable	(2)	2	(1)
Exchange gain (2 – 1.2) (W7)	0.8	2	0.4
Profit before tax	24.8	2	12.4
Income tax expense	(9)	2	(4.5)
Profit for the year	15.8	2	7.9

4   *Goodwill*

	CRm	CRm	Rate	$m
Cost of investment		120.0		
Less fair value of net assets acquired				
Share capital	32			
Share premium	20			
Retained earnings	80			
	132			
Group share (75%)		(99.0)		
		21.0	2.5	8.4
Impairment losses		(4.2)	2.1	(2.0)
FX gain		–	β	1.6
At 30.4.X4		16.8		8.0

5   *Retained earnings*

	$m
Memo	360.0
Random (75% × 7.9 (W3))	5.9
Provision for unrealised profit (W8)	(0.6)
Impairment of goodwill (W4)	(2.0)
	363.3

6   *Minority interest*

	$m
Minority interest share of net assets (25% × 70.4 (W2))	17.6

7   *Exchange gains and losses in the accounts of Random*

Loan to Random (non-current liabilities)

	CRm
At 1 May 20X3 ($5 million × 2.5)	12.5
At 30 April 20X4 ($5 million × 2.1)	(10.5)
Gain	2.0

Inter-company purchases (current liabilities)

	CRm
Purchase of goods from Memo ($6 million × 2)	12
Payment made ($6 million × 2.2)	(13.2)
Loss	(1.2)

Exchange differences in income statement (retranslated to dollars)

	$m
Gain on loan (2 ÷ 2)	1.0
Loss on current liability/purchases (1.2 ÷ 2)	(0.6)
	0.4

(*Note.* This has been rounded up to $1 million.)

BPP
LEARNING MEDIA

8   Provision for unrealised profit

	$m
Sale by parent to subsidiary (6 million × 20% × ½)	0.6

9   Translation reserve

	$m	$m
Closing net assets at closing rate (W2)	70.4	
Less opening net assets at opening rate (W2)	(52.8)	
		17.6
Less reported profit (W3)		(7.9)
		9.7
Group (75%)		7.3
Exchange gain on retranslation of goodwill (W4)		1.6
		8.9

D18 Preparation question: Cash flow statement

CHARMER
CASH FLOW STATEMENT FOR THE YEAR ENDED 30 SEPTEMBER 20X1

	$'000	$'000
Cash flows from operating activities		
Profit before taxation	1,579	
Adjustments for		
Depreciation ((W1) 80 + 276)	356	
Loss on disposal of plant	86	
Amortisation of government grant	(125)	
Negligence claim previously provided	(120)	
Investment income	(120)	
Interest expense	260	
	1,916	
Increase in trade receivables (935 – 824)	(111)	
Increase in inventories (1,046 – 785)	(261)	
Decrease in trade payables (760 – 644)	(116)	
Cash generated from operations	1,428	
Interest paid (W5)	(245)	
Income taxes paid (W3)	(368)	
Net cash from operating activities		815
Cash flows from investing activities		
Purchase of property, plant and equipment ((W1) 50 + 848)	(898)	
Purchase of non-current investments	(690)	
Purchase of treasury bills (120 – 50)	(70)	
Proceeds from sale of plant (W1)	170	
Government grant received (W4)	175	
Investment income received	120	
Net cash used in investing activities		(1,193)
Cash flows from financing activities		
Proceeds from issue of share capital (W2)	300	
Dividends paid	(180)	
Net cash from financing activities		120
Net decrease in cash and cash equivalents		(258)
Cash and cash equivalents at beginning of period		122
Cash and cash equivalents at end of period		(136)

Workings

1   *Non-current assets and depreciation*

LAND AND BUILDINGS – COST/VALUATION

	$'000		$'000
Balance b/f	1,800		
Revaluation	150		
Cash purchase (bal fig)	50	Balance c/f	2,000
	2,000		2,000

PLANT – COST

	$'000		$'000
Balance b/f	1,220	Disposal	500
Cash purchases (bal fig)	848	Balance c/f	1,568
	2,068		2,068

Disposal proceeds:

	$'000
Cost	500
Accumulated depreciation	(244)
NBV	256
Loss on sale	(86)
∴ Disposal proceeds	170

LAND AND BUILDINGS – ACC'D DEPRECIATION

	$'000		$'000
		Balance b/f	680
Balance c/f	760	Depreciation (bal fig)	80
	760		760

PLANT – ACC'D DEPRECIATION

	$'000		$'000
Disposal	244	Balance b/f	432
Balance c/f	464	Depreciation (bal fig)	276
	708		708

2   *Issue of share capital*

SHARE CAPITAL

	$'000		$'000
		Balance b/f	1,000
		Bonus issue 1 for 10	100
		Conversion of loan stock*	100
Balance c/f	1,400	Issued for cash (bal fig)	200
	1,400		1,400

SHARE PREMIUM

	$'000		$'000
		Balance b/f	60
Balance c/f	460	Conversion of loan stock*	300
		Issued for cash (bal fig)	100
	460		460

∴ Total for cash = $200,000 + $100,000 = $300,000

* Conversion of loan stock:

Carrying value of loan stock = $20,000 + $380,000 = $400,000

∴ No of shares = $400,000 × $\dfrac{25}{100}$ = 100,000

Shares must be at a premium of $400,000 − $100,000 = $300,000

3 *Income taxes paid*

INCOME TAX PAYABLE

	$'000		$'000
		Deferred tax b/f	400
Income taxes paid (bal fig)	368	Current tax b/f	367
Deferred tax c/f	439	Income tax charged to I/S	520
Current tax c/f	480		
	1,287		1,287

4 *Government grant received*

GOVERNMENT GRANT

	$'000		$'000
Amortisation credited to		Balance b/f: non-current	200
cost of sales	125	current	125
Balance c/f: non-current	275	Cash receipt (bal fig)	175
current	100		
	500		500

5 *Interest paid*

INTEREST PAYABLE

	$'000		$'000
Interest paid (bal fig)	245	Balance b/f	25
Balance c/f	40	Charged to I/S	260
	285		285

D19 Preparation question: Consolidated cash flow statement

CASH FLOW STATEMENT FOR THE YEAR ENDED 31 DECEMBER 20X5

	$'000	$'000
Cash flows from operating activities		
Profit before tax	16,500	
Adjustments for:		
Depreciation	5,800	
Impairment losses (W2)	240	
	22,540	
Increase in trade receivables (9,800 – 7,500 – 600)	(1,700)	
Increase in inventories (16,000 – 10,000 – 1,600)	(4,400)	
Increase in trade payables (7,600 – 6,100 – 300)	1,200	
Cash generated from operations	17,640	
Income taxes paid (W1)	(4,200)	
Net cash from operating activities		13,440
Cash flows from investing activities		
Acquisition of subsidiary net of cash acquired (Note 1)	(600)	
Purchase of property, plant and equipment (W2)	(13,100)	
Net cash used in investing activities		(13,700)
Cash flows from financing activities		
Proceeds from issue of share capital		
(12,300 + 5,800 – 10,000 – 2,000 – (5,000 – 1,000))	2,100	
Dividends paid	(900)	
Dividends paid to minority interest (W3)	(40)	
Net cash used in investing activities		1,160
Net decrease in cash and cash equivalents		900
Cash and cash equivalents at the beginning of the period		1,500
Cash and cash equivalents at the end of the period		2,400

Notes to cash flow statement

1   *Acquisition of subsidiary*

	$'000
Cash	400
Inventories	1,600
Trade receivables	600
Property, plant and equipment	2,700
Trade payables	(300)
Income tax payable	(200)
	4,800
Minority interest (30%)	(1,440)
	3,360
Goodwill	1,640
Total purchase price	5,000
Less: cash of subsidiary	(400)
Less: non-cash consideration	(4,000)
Cash flow on acquisition net of cash acquired	(600)

Workings

1   *Additions to property, plant and equipment*

PROPERTY, PLANT AND EQUIPMENT

	$'000		$'000
b/d	25,000		
On acquisition	2,700	Depreciation	5,800
∴ Additions	13,100	c/d	35,000
	40,800		40,800

2   *Goodwill impairment losses*

GOODWILL

	$'000		$'000
b/d	0	∴ Impairment loss	240
On acquisition			
(5,000 − (4,800 × 70%))	1,640	c/d	1,400
	1,640		1,640

3   *Dividends paid to minority interest*

MINORITY INTEREST

	$'000		$'000
		b/d	0
∴ Dividends paid	40	Acquisition (4,800 × 30%)	1,440
c/d	1,600	I/S	200
	1,640		1,640

4   *Income taxes paid*

INCOME TAX PAYABLE

	$'000		$'000
		b/d	4,000
∴ Income taxes paid	4,200	Acquisition	200
c/d	5,200	I/S	5,200
	9,400		9,400

D20 Portal

Top tips. The examiner for this paper has stated that the emphasis is on advising management and on realistic scenarios. Part (b) could come under the heading of advice and Part (a), which involves using your knowledge to correct the accountant's work, could come under both headings.

Marking scheme

			Marks
(a)	Net cash inflow		8
	Taxation		3
	Sale of property, plant and equipment		4
	Minority interest		2
	Joint venture		2
	Disposal of subsidiary and cash disposed of		2
		Available	21
		Maximum	18
(b)	Subjective		7
		Available	28
		Maximum	25

(a) PORTAL GROUP

CASH FLOW STATEMENT FOR THE YEAR ENDED 31 DECEMBER 20X0

	Working	$m	$m
Cash generated from operations	1		712
Interest paid		(9)	
Income taxes paid	2	(115)	
			(124)
Net cash from operating activities			588
Cash flows from investing activities			
Disposal of subsidiary		75	
Subsidiary's cash disposed of		(130)	
Purchase of property, plant and equipment		(380)	
Sale of property, plant and equipment	3	195	
Purchase of interest in joint venture		(25)	
Interest received		26	
Dividend received from joint venture		10	
Net cash used in investing activities			(229)
Cash flows from financing activities			
Increase in short term deposits		(143)	
Dividend paid to minority interests	4	(31)	
Net cash used in financing activities			(174)
Net increase in cash and cash equivalents			185
Cash and cash equivalents at 1 January 20X0			600
Cash and cash equivalents at 31 December 20X0			785

BPP LEARNING MEDIA

Workings

1   *Cash generated from operations*

	$m
Per question	875
Add back loss on disposal	25
Adjustments for current assets/liabilities of subsidiary *	
Inventory	(60)
Trade receivables	(50)
Current liabilities (130 – 25)	105
Deduct post-tax profit on joint venture	(55)
Interest receivable	(27)
Interest payable	19
Deduct profit on sale of non current assets	(120)
	712

Note. The movements in current assets used by the accountant to calculate net cash inflow from operating activities incorrectly include amounts relating to the subsidiary disposed of.

2   *Income taxes paid*

	$m
Per question (balance sheet movement)	31
Tax on subsidiary disposed of	25
Tax on profit	(171)
Cash outflow	(115)

3   *Sale of property, plant and equipment*

	$m
Per question (carrying value)	1,585
Transferred to joint venture	(200)
Subsidiary disposed of	(310)
Sale and leaseback	(1,000)
Profit on sale	120
Cash inflow	195

4   *Dividend paid to minority interests*

	$m
Difference per question (balance sheet movement)	40
Profit for year	75
Sale of subsidiary (20% × 420)	(84)
	31

Notes

1   An investment normally qualifies as a cash equivalent only when it has a short maturity, of say three months or less from date of acquisition. It is assumed that the short term investments do not fall into this category because they have a maturity profile in excess of the suggested three months.

2   The joint venture has been accounted for, as per IAS 31, using the equity method rather than proportionate consolidation.

(b) **Cash flow statements: presentation to directors of Portal plc**

General purpose

The purpose of cash flow statements is to **provide information which is not shown in the other financial statements**. This information is important because the success and survival of every reporting entity depends on its ability to generate or obtain cash. For example, the tax authorities require an **actual cash payment**, which will differ for a number of reasons from the tax charge shown in the income statement. Some of the information, such as the purchase or sale of property, plant and equipment, is apparent or can easily be computed from the balance sheet or income statement, but the **complexity** of the financial statements may make this hard to see in respect of some items.

Group cash flow statements

Consolidated income statements and balance sheets can hide the amount of cash actually paid to acquire a subsidiary, or received on disposal, in situations where part of the consideration is in the form of shares. IAS 7 requires **cash flows relating to the consideration** to be reported under investing activities in the consolidated cash flow statement. Similarly, the dividend paid to minority interest is shown under financing activities.

However, a possible limitation of consolidated cash flow statements is that they can **obscure the cash profile of companies within the group**. For example, if there were two subsidiaries, one with a high cash flow from operations and one with high returns on investments, consolidation would obscure this. This is a limitation of consolidated accounts generally.

Accounting ratios

Useful information derived from the cash flow statement can be used in **accounting ratios** for analysis purposes. In the case of Portal plc, it might be useful to show the proportion of net cash inflow from operating activities which has been spent on purchasing non current assets:

$$\frac{\text{Purchase of property, plant and equipment}}{\text{Net cash inflow from operating activities}} = \frac{380}{588} = 64.6\%$$

It would be useful to know how much of this relates to maintenance of existing operating capacity and how much relates to increasing capacity with a view to enhancing future earnings. However, this information cannot be derived from the cash flow statement.

It would also be useful to know **how the cash flow after investment has been utilised.** This can be done by comparing the net outflow from investing with the net cash generated in the period. In the case of Portal this works out as 229/588 = 38.9%. In other words 38.9% of this net cash inflow has been used for investing purposes.

Another useful ratio is **interest cover**, based not on profit before interest and tax as in conventional ratio analysis, but on operating cash flow:

$$\frac{\text{Net cash flow from operating activities}}{\text{Interest paid}} = \frac{588}{9} = 65.3 \text{ times}$$

Further limitations

- The cash flow statement does not provide information about future cash flows.

- The reconciliation can be misinterpreted. Naïve investors may perceive the adding back of depreciation/amortisation as sources of funds.

- Some regard the cash flow statement as derivative.

- IAS 7 allows certain items (eg dividends) to be shown as either operating cash flow or a financing activity.

BPP
LEARNING MEDIA

D21 Case study question: Andash

Top tips. In tackling part (a), remember that time management is the key to cash flow questions. Set out your proforma and workings and do not spend too long on the fiddly bits. In the absence of complete information about profit earned by the associate in the period, our answer assumes that no dividend was paid by Joma. Part (b) asked you to explain the importance of the IASB's *Framework* to corporate reporting and whether this document takes into account the business and legal constraints placed on companies. The question also required candidates to explain the treatment of accounting for the decommissioning of a piece of equipment, a provision for deferred taxation and a discussion of whether the treatment of the above is consistent with the *Framework*.

Easy marks. In Part (a)These are available for basic cash flow aspects – working capital calculations, minority interest, tax and interest. Follow our order for the workings – the easy ones come first. In Part (b), though deferred tax is a difficult area generally, this particular question was fairly straightforward. Credit would be given for wide-ranging answers, so easy marks could be picked up for sensible, valid points.

Marking scheme

			Marks
(a)		Cash flows from operating activities	2
		Adjustments	4
		Cash generated from operations	3
		Interest	2
		Tax	2
		Associate	3
		Plant and machinery	3
		Sale of subsidiary	2
		Minority interest	2
		Long term borrowings	1
		Dividend paid	2
		Goodwill	3
(b)	(i)	Importance	4
		Business and legal constraints	3
	(ii)	Reasons	5
		Damage due to extraction	2
		Accounting	4
		Computation	5
		Reasons	2
	(iii)	Treatment consistent	5
		Available	58
		Maximum	50

(a) ANDASH
CASH FLOW STATEMENT FOR YEAR ENDED 31 OCTOBER 20X6

	$m	$m
Cash flows from operating activities		
Profit before taxation (400 + 1 (W3) – 78 (W7)	323	
Adjustments for:		
Depreciation	260	
Impairment of goodwill (W7)	78	
Share of profit of associate (W3)	(1)	
Gain on disposal of subsidiary	(8)	
Interest expense	148	
	800	
Increase in trade receivables (2,400 – 1,500 + 4)	(904)	
Increase in inventories (2,650 – 2,300 + 8)	(358)	
Increase in trade payables (4,700 – 2,800 + 6)	1,906	
Cash generated from operations	1,444	
Interest paid (W6)	(118)	
Income taxes paid (W5)	(523)	
Net cash from operating activities		803
Cash flows from investing activities		
Acquisition of associate	(10)	
Purchase of property, plant and equipment (W1)	(1,320)	
Proceeds from sale of subsidiary, net of cash disposed (32 – 5)	27	
Net cash used in investing activities		(1,303)
Cash flows from financing activities		
Proceeds from issue of share capital (400 + 120 – 270 – 80 – 10 – 50)	10	
Proceeds from long-term borrowings (3,100 – 2,700)	400	
Dividends paid	(50)	
Dividends paid to minority interest shareholders (W4)	(20)	
Net cash from financing activities		340
Net decrease in cash and cash equivalents		(160)

Workings

1 *Purchase of property, plant and equipment*

PROPERTY, PLANT AND EQUIPMENT

	$m		$m
Balance b/d	4,110	Disposal of subsidiary	10
Share options (10 – 1) (W8)	9	Depreciation	260
Additions	1,320	Balance c/d (5,170 – 1)	5,169
	5,439		5,439

2 *Goodwill*

GOODWILL

	$m		$m
Balance b/d	130	Disposal of subsidiary	10
		Impairment loss	78
		Balance c/d (120 – 78)	42
	130		130

3   *Share of profit of associate and dividend from associate*

INVESTMENT IN ASSOCIATE

	$m		$m
Balance b/d	–	Dividends received	–
Acquisition (50 + 10)	60	Balance c/d	61
Post-acquisition profit	1		
	61		61

Share of post-acquisition reserves:	
25% × ($32m – $20m)	3
Intragroup profit:	
25% × ($16m – $8m)	2
Profit from associate	1

As there is no information about the profit earned by the associate, the only possible assumption is that it paid no dividends.

4   *Dividend paid to minority interest*

MINORITY INTEREST

	$m		$m
∴ Cash paid	20	Balance b/d	180
Balance c/d	200	Income statement	40
	220		220

5   *Tax paid*

TAX PAYABLE

	$m		$m
Disposal	7	Balance b/d (deferred)	300
∴ Taxes paid	523	Balance b/d (current	770
Balance c/d (deferred)	400	Income statement	160
Balance c/d (current)	300		
	1,230		1,230

6   *Interest paid*

INTEREST PAYABLE

	$m		$m
∴ Interest paid	118	Balance b/d	40
Balance c/d (current)	300	Income statement	148
	1,230		1,230

7   *Impairment loss*

	$m
Net assets at 31 October 20X6	240
Goodwill (90 × 100/60)	150
	390
Recoverable amount	(260)
	130
Recognised (130 × 60%)	78

8   *Share options*

The basic rule in IFRS 2 *Share-based payment* is that when equity instruments are issued to acquire goods or services, they should be measured at the fair value of those goods and services. An adjustment is required to reduce the options and the plant by £1m to £9m.

(b)   (i)   The IASB's *Framework for the Preparation and Presentation of Financial Statements* sets out the **principles that underpin the preparation of general purpose financial statements**. The purpose of the *Framework* is to **assist the IASB in the preparation of future standards** and to **assist preparers of financial statements in applying standards** and in **dealing with topics that are not yet covered** by international accounting standards. This means that in theory, IFRSs are based on the *Framework*, which covers:

- The objective of financial statements
- Underlying assumptions
- The qualities that make the information in financial statements useful
- The elements of financial statements
- When elements should be recognised in financial statements
- Measurement in financial statements
- Concepts of capital and capital maintenance

IAS 8 *Accounting policies, changes in accounting estimates and errors* recognises the *Framework* as one of the **authoritative sources of guidance** in situations where a transaction is not covered by a specific IAS or IFRS.

The *Framework* adopts a **balance sheet based approach**. It **defines assets and liabilities** and explains the conditions that must be met before they are recognised. **Income and expenses are defined in relation to assets and liabilities**; a gain is recognised when assets increase or liabilities decrease; a loss is recognised where liabilities increase or assets decrease. There are advantages of this approach, not least that it **helps to prevent 'creative accounting'** where the economic substance of a transaction is different from its legal form. However, it is **very different from the way in which most preparers of accounts view the basis of accounting**: the allocation of transactions to accounting periods.

There are other problems. The *Framework* is a **theoretical document** and financial statements are used for **practical purposes** including determining dividend payments, tax payments and directors' remuneration. Standards based on the *Framework* are sometimes **difficult to apply**, particularly for smaller entities.

A further issue is that the IASB's work is now largely being driven by the **need to converge with US GAAP** and is in fact **moving away from the *Framework* in some respects**. For example, IFRSs make increasing use of **fair value accounting**, but arguably the *Framework* does not deal with this. The IASB is now **developing a new conceptual *Framework*** jointly with the US Financial Accounting Standards Board (FASB).

(ii)   **Situation 1**

IAS 37 *Provisions, contingent liabilities and contingent assets* states that a provision should be recognised if:

- There is a **present obligation** as a result of a **past transaction or event** and
- It is **probable** that a **transfer of economic benefits** will be required to settle the obligation and
- A **reliable estimate** can be made of the **amount** of the obligation.

In this case, the obligating event is the **installation of the facility** and it occurred before the year end. The operating licence has created a **legal obligation** to incur the cost of decommissioning the facility, the expenditure is **probable** and the **amount can be measured reliably**.

Because the entity cannot operate the facility without incurring an obligation to pay for decommissioning, **the expenditure also enables it to acquire economic benefits** (income from operating the facility). Therefore Andash **recognises an asset** as well as a provision and **depreciates the asset over its useful life of 20 years.**

Andash **recognises a provision for the cost of removing the facility**, but **does not include the cost of rectifying the damage** caused by the extraction of natural gas until it is incurred. This means that a provision for rectifying the damage caused by extraction is **recognised over the life of the facility**. The provision is **discounted** to its net present value as the time value of money is material.

The accounting treatment is as follows:

BALANCE SHEET AT 31 OCTOBER 20X7 (EXTRACTS)

	$m
Tangible non-current assets	
Extraction facility	200
Decommissioning costs (W)	40
	240
Depreciation (240 ÷ 20)	(12)
	228

	$m
Provisions	
Provision for decommissioning at 1 November 20X6	40.00
Plus unwinding of discount (40 × 5%)	2.00
	42.00
Provision for damage caused by extraction (W)	1.33
	43.33

INCOME STATEMENT FOR THE YEAR ENDED 31 OCTOBER 20X7 (EXTRACTS)

	$m
Depreciation	12
Provision for damage caused by extraction	1.33
Unwinding of discount	2

Working

	$m
Provision for decommissioning costs at 1 November 20X6 (80% × 50)	40
Provision for damage caused by extraction at 31 October 20X7	
(20% × 50 × 2.66 ÷ 20)	1.33

Situation 2

The company should **recognise a provision for deferred tax relating to the building** and there is a **deferred tax asset relating to the warranty**. Per IAS 12 *Income taxes* the calculation is as follows.

	$m	$m
Building		
Tax written down value (75% × 8)	6	
Net book value (9 – 1.8)	(7.2)	
		1.2
Other temporary differences		40.0
Total temporary differences (liabilities)		41.2
Warranty provision		4.0
Tax losses		70.0
Total temporary differences (assets)		74.0

Therefore the company **recognises a deferred tax liability of $12.4 million** (41.2 × 30%) and **can also recognise a deferred tax asset for the same amount**. It will only be able to recognise the full amount of the deferred tax asset if it can prove that **suitable taxable profits are available to offset the losses** in future.

(iii) **Treatment of the items and the *Framework***

It can be argued that some of the assets and liabilities involved are **not 'true' assets and liabilities** and therefore that they **should not be recognised**.

Under the *Framework*, the company would have to **recognise the full discounted liability** for the decommissioning costs and a corresponding asset. An **asset** is defined as a **resource controlled by the company as a result of past events** and from which **future economic benefits** are expected to flow.

The *Framework* defines a **liability** as a **present obligation arising from a past event**, the settlement of which is expected to result in an **outflow of economic benefits**. Strictly speaking, the deferred tax provision **does not meet this definition**; only an **actual liability** to the tax authorities can be an obligation at the balance sheet date. A deferred tax liability **can be avoided**, for example, with tax planning, or if a company makes future losses. Still less does the deferred tax asset meet the definition of an asset, because it **depends on the availability of future profits.**

In addition, the **grant** towards the building has been treated as a **deferred credit** and is therefore a liability. It **does not meet the definition of a liability** unless it has to be repaid.

D22 Case study question: Squire

Top tips. Part (a) of his question required candidates to prepare a group cash flow statement. There were adjustments to be made for impairment, interest on a deferred consideration, retirement benefits and the purchase of a subsidiary in the year.

You need to use a bit of imagination in (b). Try to use your own experience to think of what you can find out about resource usage, also what you would like to know and how you can obtain evidence of what you would like to know.

In (c) observation is likely to be the most useful audit technique, although if staff are being observed, they may behave differently. You may have come up with other means for informing staff.

Part (d) focuses on the impact of stakeholder views and voluntary principles-based disclosure versus compulsory rules-based disclosure.

Examiner's comment (Part (a) only. The question was quite straightforward and candidates performed very well. There are several quite easy marks to be earned in a cash flow question and many candidates gained these marks. The only major criticism of candidates' answers was that the workings were sometimes difficult to follow or were not presented at all. This latter point is critical. Many candidates simply showed a line of numbers without any narrative. This is acceptable but if these numbers are wrong or not easily recognisable then marks are difficult to award.

(a) SQUIRE
GROUP CASH FLOW STATEMENT FOR THE YEAR ENDED 31 MAY 20X2

	$m	$m
Cash flows from operating activities:		
Profit before tax	420	
Adjustments for:		
Share of profit in associate	(45)	
Exchange differences on property, plant and equipment	9	
Interest	75	
Depreciation	129	
Retirement benefit expense	20	
	608	
Decrease in inventories (1,300 – 1,160 – 180)	40	
Increase in trade receivables (1,220 – 1,060)	(160)	
Increase in trade payables (2,355 – 2,105)	250	
Cash generated from operations	738	
Interest paid (W5)	(51)	
Income taxes paid (W6)	(140)	
Contributions paid to retirement benefit scheme	(26)	
Net cash from operating activities		521
Cash flows from investing activities:		
Purchase of property, plant and equipment (W5)	(451)	
Purchase of subsidiary (200 + 30)	(230)	
Dividends received from associate (W3)	50	
Net cash used in investing activities		(631)
Cash flows from financing activities:		
Issue of shares (200 + 60 – 170 –30)	60	
Repayment of loans (1,320 – 1,270)	(50)	
Equity dividends paid (90 – 5)(W5)	(85)	
Dividends paid to minority interests (W4)	(5)	
Net cash used in financing activities		(80)
Decrease in cash and cash equivalents for the period		(190)
Cash and cash equivalents at 1 April 20X1		280
Cash and cash equivalents at 31 March 20X2		90

Workings

1
PROPERTY, PLANT AND EQUIPMENT

	$m		$m
Balance b/d	2,010	Depreciation	129
Payables balance c/d	351	Impairment losses	194
Acquisition	150	Balance c/d	2,630
Additions (balancing figure)	**442**		2,953
	2,953		

	$m
Cash flow:	
Non-current asset additions	442
Exchange difference (income statement)	9
	451

2   INTANGIBLE ASSETS: GOODWILL (PROOF)

	$m		$m
Balance b/d	65	Balance c/d	105
Acquisition (note)	40		
	105		105

Note

	$m
Goodwill on acquisition	
Purchase consideration:	
Cash	200
Deferred consideration	50
	250
Less group share of identifiable net assets acquired (70% × 300)	(210)
	40

3   DIVIDENDS RECEIVED FROM ASSOCIATE

	$m		$m
Balance b/d	550	Foreign exchange loss	10
Share of profit	45	**Dividends received (balancing figure)**	**50**
	595	Balance c/d	535
			595

4   MINORITY INTERESTS

	$m		$m
Dividend paid (balancing figure)	**5**	Balance b/d	345
Balance c/d	522	Acquisition (30% × 300)	90
		Profit for year	92
	527		527

5   INTEREST PAYABLE

	$m		$m
		Balance b/d	45
Cash paid (balancing figure)	**51**	Income statement (75 − 154 − 50)	71
Balance c/d	65		
	116		116

6   INCOME TAXES

	$m		$m
Cash paid (balancing figure)	**140**	Balance b/d:	
Balance c/d:		Current	160
Current	200	Deferred	175
Deferred	200	Income statement	205
	540		540

(b)   **The planning process**

The planning process for any investigative activity revolves around a consideration of **what information is needed,** where it **may be found** and **how to obtain it.**

Available information

In the case of an environmental audit, much information is probably already available in the form of accounting records; **heating and lighting costs,** for instance can be related to factors such as numbers employed, floor space and building volumes.

There are some fairly **standard aspects of good practice** in terms of energy conservation such as provision of wall and roof insulation; and thermostatic and time clock control of space and water heating systems. The existence and maintenance of such factors can be established from the appropriate records. In the UK, the energy utilities offer free advice on energy conservation and this should be considered. **Use of renewable**

resources should be a matter of policy and the purchasing department should be able to comment on the extent to which it is achieved.

Expert advice

Other aspects of energy consumption require expert advice. For instance, the **compressed air circuits** used in many factories to power hand and machine tools can be extremely wasteful of energy if they are leaky, since this causes the compressor to be run for excessive periods to maintain pressure. However, it is a specialised engineering task to measure the actual efficiency of a pneumatic system.

If the organisation is a manufacturer, it would be appropriate to consider the extent to which the **products themselves** were **energy efficient** in use and made use of renewable resources both in use and in their construction. These are largely matters of design and it would be necessary to take technical advice.

(c) **Testing for employee awareness**

Employee awareness could be measured by **observation, questionnaire and interview.** In a large organisation a sampling approach could be taken. Observation could be largely unobtrusive and might provide a useful control on the results of interview, since some staff might make exaggerated claims about their environmental awareness.

Involvement of employees

The techniques of **internal marketing** could be used to involve employees. Internal marketing is the use of marketing techniques that are normally associated with communications flowing out from the organisation, for internal purposes. It is a concept associated with change management and therefore may be appropriate here.

A concerted campaign could be created. This could include messages in salary advices, posters, presentations, the **formation of discussion groups**, and the creation of a **suggestion scheme** specifically aimed at environmental issues. If there are any existing empowerment schemes such as quality circles, it may be possible to introduce an environmental dimension into them.

(d) **Stakeholder interest**

Public interest in corporate social responsibility is steadily increasing. Although financial statements are primarily intended for investors and their advisers, there is growing recognition that companies actually have **a number of different stakeholders**. These include **customers, employees and the general public,** all of whom are **potentially interested** in the way in which a company's operations affect the natural environment and the wider community. These stakeholders can have a **considerable effect on a company's performance**. As a result many companies now deliberately attempt to build a **reputation for social and environmental responsibility**. Therefore the disclosure of environmental and social information is essential.

Regulatory and professional interest

Another factor is **growing interest by governments and professional bodies**. Although there are **no IFRSs** that specifically require environmental and social reporting, it may be required by **company legislation**. There are now a number of **awards for environmental and social reports** and high quality disclosure in financial statements. These provide further encouragement to disclose information.

Performance impact

There is also growing recognition that **corporate social responsibility is actually an important part of an entity's overall performance.** Responsible practice in areas such as reduction of damage to the environment and recruitment **increases shareholder value**. Companies that act responsibly and make social and environmental disclosures are **perceived as better investments** than those that do not.

Compulsory or voluntary disclosure

At present companies are normally able to disclose **as much or as little information as they wish in whatever manner that they wish**. This causes a number of **problems**. Companies tend to disclose information **selectively** and it is difficult for users of the financial statements to **compare the performance of different companies**. However, there are **good arguments** for continuing to allow companies a certain amount of freedom to determine the information that they disclose. If detailed rules are imposed, **companies are likely to adopt a 'checklist' approach** and will **present information in a very general and standardised way**, so that it is of very little use to stakeholders.

E1 IFRS AND SMEs

Top tips. This question required candidates to discuss the need to develop a set of IFRSs especially for small to medium-sized enterprises (SMEs). Do not be tempted to waffle or repeat yourself.

Easy marks. This is a knowledge-based question, so all marks are easy if you know it.

Examiner's comment. This question was generally well answered and the topic will feature in future exams.

Marking scheme

			Marks
(a)	Subjective		7
(b)	Purpose		3
	Definition of entity		4
	How to modify		6
	Items not dealt with		3
	Full IFRS		3
		Available	26
		Maximum	25

(a) Originally, International Accounting Standards (IASs) issued by the International Accounting Standards Committee (IASC) were **designed to be suitable for all types of entity**, including small and medium entities (SMEs) and entities in developing countries. Large listed entities based their financial statements on national GAAP which normally **automatically complied** with those IASs due to choices permitted in the past. In recent years, IASs and IFRSs have become **increasingly complex and prescriptive**. They are now designed **primarily** to meet the information needs of **institutional investors in large listed entities** and their advisers. In many countries, IFRSs are **used mainly by listed companies**.

There is a case for continued use of full IFRSs by SMEs. It can be argued that the **main objectives** of general purpose financial statements **are the same for all types of company**, of whatever size. Compliance with full IFRSs ensures that the financial statements of SMEs **present their financial performance fairly** and gives them greater **credibility**. It also ensures their **comparability** with those of other entities.

There are also many arguments for developing a separate set of standards for SMEs. Full IFRSs have become very **detailed and onerous** to follow. The **cost** of complying may **exceed the benefits** to the entity and the users of its financial statements. At present, an entity cannot describe their financial statements as IFRS financial statements unless they have complied with every single requirement.

SME financial statements are normally **used by a relatively small number of people**. Often, the **investors** are also **involved in day to day management**. The **main external users** of SME financial statements tend to be **lenders and the tax authorities**, rather than institutional investors and their advisers. These users have **different information needs** from those of investors. For these users, the accounting treatments and the detailed disclosures required may sometimes **obscure the picture** given by the financial statements. In some cases, **different, or more detailed information may be needed.** For example, related party transactions are often very significant in the context of SME activities and expanded disclosure may be appropriate.

In February 2007 the IASB issued an exposure draft of an *IFRS for small and medium-sized entities.* This focuses on events and conditions encountered by SMEs with about 50 employees. It is meant to be a stand-alone document with minimal cross-reference to full IFRS. It was developed by extracting fundamental concepts from the IASB *Framework* and the principles and related mandatory guidance from full IFRS.

(b) **Issues in developing IFRSs for SMEs**

(i) **The purpose of the standards and type of entity to which they should apply**

The main objective of accounting standards for SMEs is that they should provide the users of SME financial statements with **relevant, reliable and understandable information**. The standards should be **suitable for SMEs globally** and should **reduce the financial reporting burden** on SMEs. It is generally accepted that SME standards should be built on the **same conceptual framework** as full IFRSs.

It could also be argued that SME standards should **allow for easy transition** to full IFRS as some SMEs will become listed entities or need to change for other reasons. This would mean that SME standards **could not be separately developed from first principles** (as many would prefer) but instead would be a **modified version of full IFRS**. Some argue that ease of transition is not important as relatively few SMEs will need to change to IFRS in practice.

The **definition** of an SME could be based on **size** or on **public accountability** or on a combination of the two. There are several disadvantages of basing the definition on size limits alone. Size limits are **arbitrary** and **different limits are likely to be appropriate in different countries.** Most people believe that SMEs are **not simply smaller versions of listed entities**, but differ from them in more fundamental ways.

The most important way in which SMEs differ from other entities is that they are **not usually publicly accountable**. Using this as the basis of a definition raises other issues: which types of company are publicly accountable? Obviously the **definition would include** companies which have **issued shares** or other instruments **to the public**. It has been suggested that this category should also include companies **holding assets in a fiduciary capacity** (such as banks or providers of pensions), companies that provide **essential public services** (utility companies) and any entity with **economic significance in its country** (which in turn would have to be defined). This would mean that SME standards could potentially be used by a very large number of entities covering a very large range in terms of size.

There is a case for allowing **national standard setters** to **impose size limits** or otherwise **restrict** the types of entities that could use SME standards. There is also a case for allowing national standard setters to **define 'publicly accountable'** in a way that is appropriate for their particular jurisdiction.

(ii) **How existing standards could be modified to meet the needs of SMEs**

The starting point for modifying existing standards should be the most likely **users** of SME financial statements and their **information needs**. SME financial statements are mainly used by **lenders** and **potential lenders, the tax authorities** and **suppliers**. In addition, the **owners and management** (who are often the same people) may be dependent on the information in the financial statements. SME financial statements must **meet the needs** of their users, but the **costs** of providing the information **should not outweigh the benefits.**

There is considerable scope for **simplifying disclosure and presentation requirements**. Many of the existing requirements, for example those related to financial instruments, discontinued operations and earnings per share, are **not really relevant** to the users of SME financial statements. In any case, lenders and potential lenders are normally able to ask for additional information (including forecasts) if they need it.

The SME standards are likely to be a **simplified version of existing standards**, using only those principles that are likely to be relevant to SMEs. The IASB has proposed that the **recognition and measurement principles** in full IFRSs should **remain unchanged** unless there is a good argument for modifying them. Clearly the SME standards will have to be sufficiently rigorous to produce information that is relevant and reliable. However, many believe that there is a **case for simplifying** at least some of the more **complicated measurement requirements** and that it will be difficult to reduce the financial reporting burden placed on SMEs otherwise.

(iii) **How items not dealt with by SME standards should be treated**

Because SME standards are **unlikely to cover all possible transactions** and events, there will be occasions where an SME has to **account for an item that the standards do not deal with**. There are several alternatives.

(a) The entity is **required to apply the relevant full IFRS**, while still following SME standards otherwise.

(b) Management can **use its judgement** to develop an accounting policy based on the relevant full IFRS, or the *Framework*, or other IFRSs for SMEs and the other sources of potential guidance cited in IAS 8.

(c) The entity could continue to follow its **existing practice**.

In theory, the **first alternative is the most appropriate** as this is the most likely to result in relevant, reliable and comparable information. The argument against it is that SMEs may then effectively have to comply with **two sets of standards**.

Another issue is whether an SME should be able to **opt to comply** with a specific full IFRS or IFRSs while still following SME standards otherwise. There is an argument that SMEs should be able to, for example, make the additional disclosures required by a full IFRS if there is a good reason to do so. The argument against optional reversion to full IFRSs is that it would lead to **lack of comparability**. There would also need to be safeguards against entities attempting to 'pick and mix' accounting standards.

E2 Seejoy

Top tips. Do not be put off by the fact that this is a football club. These are normal accounting transactions. Sale and leaseback, in particular, should be familiar to you.

Easy marks. The sale and leaseback is actually quite straightforward if you have practised questions on this topic. The player registration is quite straightforward too, once you have identified the issues.

Marking scheme

	Marks
Sale and leaseback	10
Player registrations	5
Bond	7
Player trading	5
Available	27
Maximum	25

BPP
LEARNING MEDIA

(a) Sale and leaseback of football stadium

The proposal is for a sale and leaseback which be treated as a **finance lease**. The accounting treatment for such a transaction is dealt with by IAS 17 *Leases*. As the **substance of the transaction is a financing transaction** this would not be dealt with as a sale so the **stadium would remain on the balance sheet as an item of property, plant and equipment** and be depreciated but it will now be valued at the sales value of $15 million. The **excess of the sales value over the carrying value** will be recognised as **deferred income** and credited to the income statement over the period of the finance lease.

When the sale takes place on 1 January 20X7 the double entry will be:

		$m	$m
DEBIT	Cash	15	
CREDIT	Properties, plant and equipment		12
CREDIT	Deferred income		3

On this same date the finance lease will also be recognised:

		$m	$m
DEBIT	Properties, plant and equipment	15	
CREDIT	Finance lease payables		15

In the financial statements for the year ending 31 December 20X7 the effects will be as follows:

INCOME STATEMENT

	$'000
Depreciation of stadium ($15m/20 years)	(750)
Finance charge (($15m − $1.2m) × 5.6%)	(773)
Deferred income ($3m/20 years)	150

BALANCE SHEET

Properties, plant and equipment	
Stadium ($15m − $0.75m)	14,250
Current liabilities	
Rental payment	1,200
Non-current liabilities	
Finance lease payables ($15m − ($1.2m × 2) + $0.773m)	13,373
Deferred income ($3m − $0.15m)	2,850

There is little doubt that this form of sale and leaseback will improve the cash flow of the club as $15 million will be received on 1 January 20X7. However, the required accounting treatment by IAS 17 will mean that the sale and leaseback has **significant and detrimental affects** on the financial statements. The **profit** shown in the income statement is likely to **decrease** as the finance charge on the lease significantly outweighs the deferred income credit to the income statement. If the $15 million receipt is not used to pay off existing long term loans then the overall **gearing** of the club will **increase** as the finance lease payables are included on the balance sheet.

It might be worth investigating the possibility of a **sale and leaseback** agreement which **results in an operating lease rather** than a finance lease. In such a leaseback, as the sale is at fair value, the **profit can be recognised immediately** in the income statement and the stadium will be deemed to have been sold and removed from the balance sheet. There will also be no finance leases payables as liabilities on the balance sheet. The downside however is that any increase in the residual value of the stadium would be lost.

(b) Player registrations

The player registrations are **capitalised** by the club as intangible non-current assets under IAS 38 *Intangible assets*. This is an **acceptable** accounting treatment; the transfer fees classify as assets as it is probable that expected future benefits will flow to the club as a result of the contracts and the cost can be measured reliably at the amount of the transfer fees actually paid.

According to IAS 38, intangible non-current assets which are capitalised should be **amortised over their useful life**. Therefore on the face of it claiming a useful life of 10 years might be acceptable. However IAS 38 recommends that amortisation reflects the useful life of the assets and the pattern of economic benefits. Therefore the proposal to amortise the transfer fees over a period of **10 years is not acceptable as the contracts are only for 5 years and 3 years**.

In terms of **cash flow** this proposal regarding the amortisation would have **no effect** at all. It would simply be a bookkeeping entry which would reduce the amortisation charge to the income statement.

The potential payment to the two players' former clubs of $5 million would **not** appear to be **probable** due to the current form of the club. Therefore under IAS 37 *Provisions, contingent liabilities and contingent assets* *no provision* would be recognised for this amount. However, the possible payment does fall within the IAS 37 definition of a contingent liability which is a possible obligation arising out of past events whose existence will be confirmed only by the occurrence or non-occurrence of one or more uncertain future events not wholly within the control of the entity. Therefore as a contingent liability the amount and details would be **disclosed** in the notes to the financial statements.

(c) **Issue of bond**

What the club is proposing here is known as **securitisation**. This particular type of securitisation is often called 'future flow' securitisation. In some forms of securitisation a special purpose vehicle is set up to administer the income stream or assets involved in which case there is potentially an off balance sheet effect. However, in this case there is **no special purpose vehicle** and therefore the only accounting issue is how the bond is to be treated under IAS 39 *Financial instruments: recognition and measurement*.

The bond will be recorded as a **financial liability** and will either be classified as a financial liability at fair value through profit or loss or as a financial liability measured at amortised cost. To be a financial liability at fair value through profit or loss the bond must either be held for trading or be part of a group of financial assets, financial liabilities, or both, that are managed on a fair value basis. It is unlikely that this is the case, therefore the bond will be **classified as measured at amortised cost**.

The bond will be **initially recognised at its fair value** which is the amount for which the liability can be settled between knowledgeable and willing parties in an arm's length transaction. Fair value at inception will normally be the amount of the consideration received for the instrument. Subsequent to initial recognition the instrument will be measured using amortised cost or fair value. In this case the club does not wish to use the valuation model therefore the bond will be measured at amortised cost.

When the bond is issued on 1 January 20X7 it will be measured at the value of the consideration received of $47.5 million ($50m × 95%).

At 31 December 20X7 the valuation will be:

	$m
Initial value	47.5
Interest at 7.7%	3.7
Cash paid	(6.0)
Balance sheet value	45.2

In terms of cash flow the issue of the bond will **bring $47.5 million into the club**. The bond is effectively secured on the income stream of the future corporate hospitality sales and season tickets receipts and due to this security the coupon rate of interest is lower than the market rates. The money is to be used to improve the grounds which is an appropriate use of long-term funds. However, the proposal to pay the **short term costs of the players' wages** out of these long term funds is a **misuse of long-term capital** which is likely to lead to future liquidity problems.

(d) **Player trading**

In accounting terms there is no issue to deal with at 31 December 20X6 as the potential sale of the players will not fall to be classified as 'held for sale' non-current assets under IFRS 5 *Non-current assets held for sale and discontinued operations*. In order for these players to classify as held for sale they would need to be available for immediate sale which they are not.

However, the club must consider carrying out an **impairment review** of these assets at 31 December 20X6. If the players are sold for the anticipated figure of $16 million then the following loss will be incurred:

	$m
Carrying value at 1 May 20X7	
A Steel ($20m – ($4m + 4/12 × $4m)	14.7
R Aldo ($15m – ($10 + 4/12 × $5)	3.3
	18.0
Potential sales value	16.0
Potential loss	2.0

This potential loss of $2 million on the sale of these players may be evidence of impairment and a review should be carried out at 31 December 20X6 and the **players' value written down to recoverable amount** if necessary.

In terms of cash flow, the sale of the players would **provide much needed cash**. However, as the club is performing poorly currently the sale of the two best players **may lead to even worse performance** which is likely to have a detrimental affect on ticket sales and the liquidity of the club in future.

F1 Handrew

Top tips. This question dealt with the implications of a move to IFRS by a company. It is likely to become less frequent, though topical at the moment. Additionally, the impact of the changes of accounting policy on three key performance ratios had to be calculated and discussed. The question dealt with leases, plant and equipment, and investment properties, and the ratios to be adjusted were ROCE, gearing, and the PE ratio.

Easy marks. Marks were allocated for general principles, which candidates can easily score highly on. Additionally, marks were allocated for a report format. Marks are only given for the report if candidates set out the report in a formal way, with appendices for detailed calculations, but this is easy to do.

Examiner's comment. The question was quite well-answered although frequently the adjustments to the profit for the year and balance sheet were inaccurate, and candidates could not deal with the deferred tax implications.

Marking scheme

		Marks
Report		4
(a)	Discussion	18
(b)	Discussion and calculation	7
	Available	29
	Maximum	25

ANSWERS

REPORT

To: Directors of Handrew
From:
Subject: Impact of the move to International Financial Reporting Standards (IFRS)
Date: June 20X5

This report discusses the impact of the change to IFRS on the financial statements for the year ended 31 May 20X5, including the effect of the change on three key performance ratios. Calculations are included in an Appendix.

Leases

IAS 17 *Leases* classifies leases into finance leases and operating leases. A finance lease **transfers substantially all the risks and benefits of ownership** to the lessee while an operating lease does not. Unlike local GAAP, IAS 17 requires leases to be **separated** into **land and buildings components**. A lease of **land** is **normally classified as an operating lease**; a lease of **buildings** may be **either a finance lease or an operating lease.**

There are several indications that the company's **leases of land** *are* operating leases. **Title does not pass** at the end of the lease term. In addition, at 1 June 20X4 the **present value of the lease commitments was only 73% of the fair value of the land** (for a lease to be a finance lease the present value of the lease commitments must normally be 'substantially all' of the fair value of the leased asset). The **lessor intends to redevelop the land**, which also suggests that Handrew does not enjoy the benefits of ownership. In contrast, **title to the buildings does pass** to the company at the end of the lease term; the **present value of the lease commitments is 96% (**substantially all**) of the fair value of the buildings**; and the buildings are **leased for a period equal to their economic life**. The substance of the agreement appears to be that Handrew **has purchased the buildings** and the leases are financing arrangements, rather than rental agreements. The **leases of the buildings are finance leases.**

The buildings must be treated as assets of the company and **recognised on the balance sheet. Non-current assets will increase by $86 million at 1 June 20X4** (the inception of the lease). The buildings should be **depreciated** over 20 years and therefore there will be an **expense of $4.3 million** and the **carrying value of the buildings will be $81.7 million** at 31 May 20X5. The company should also **recognise a corresponding liability for the lease rentals**. At 31 May 20X5 this is **$81.2 million** (see Appendix)**. Current liabilities will increase by $5.1 million** (the amount due on 31 May 20X6) and **non-current liabilities will increase by $76.1 million. Interest of $5.2 million will be recognised** in the income statement. The **tax charge for the year will also be affected**, as lease rentals on the buildings will no longer be included in the income statement as a taxable expense.

Leases of land **will continue to be treated as operating leases** and lease rentals of $10 million will be recognised in the income statement.

Plant and equipment

IAS 16 *Property, plant and equipment* requires **residual values** of non-current assets **to be reviewed at each year end**. Residual value is defined as the **estimated amount** that the company **would currently obtain** from the disposal of the asset, if it were **already of the age** and **in the condition expected** at the **end of its useful life**. Any **changes in residual value** are **reflected in the depreciation charge** and are accounted for **prospectively,** as a change in accounting estimate. Depreciation is **reduced to zero** if the **residual value is equal to or greater than the asset's carrying value.**

Therefore under IAS 16 the residual value of the asset would be **$8 million** rather than $4 million. This means that the **depreciation charge** for the year ended 31 May 20X5 will be **$1 million**, rather than $2 million as at present (see Appendix).

Investment properties

IAS 40 *Investment property* allows investment properties to be measured **either at cost or at fair value**. If a property is **measured at fair value, gains and losses** on remeasurement **must be recognised in the income statement. As the company wishes to do this**, it will **adopt the fair value model**. Under IFRS, fair value is normally taken to be **market value, rather than existing use value**. Therefore the hotel should be valued at **$50 million.**

Because **the market price is obtainable** if the land is sold for redevelopment the land **should be valued at $50 million** and the **building at nil**.

Profit for the year is increased by the **revaluation gain of $15 million**. Of this amount, **$5 million has been previously recognised in equity** and would be **transferred to the income statement**. IAS 12 *Income taxes* **requires deferred tax to be provided on revaluation gains**, regardless of whether there is an actual intention to sell the property.

Impact on performance ratios

Three key performance ratios have been calculated as follows:

	Local GAAP	IFRS
Return on capital employed	$\frac{130}{520} \times 100\% = 25\%$	$\frac{151.7}{606.2} \times 100\% = 25\%$
Gearing ratio	$\frac{40}{480} \times 100\% = 8.3\%$	$\frac{120.9}{485.3} \times 100\% = 24.9\%$
Price earnings ratio	$\frac{\$6}{\$0.5} = 12$	$\frac{\$6}{\$0.552} = 10.9$

There is very **little effect on return on capital employed**. **Profit has increased** by $21.7 million, mainly because the operating lease rentals have been excluded and the gain on revaluation has been included. However, **capital employed has also increased**, due to the recognition of the finance lease liability.

Gearing has increased significantly, mainly because of the recognition of the finance lease liability.

As a consequence of the increase in profits, **earnings per share has risen** and therefore the **price earnings ratio has fallen**.

Appendix: impact of the change to IFRS on profit, taxation and the balance sheet

1   *Effect on profit*

	$m	$m
Profit before interest and tax under local GAAP		130.0
Add back operating lease rentals		10.0
Less: depreciation on building (86 ÷ 20)		(4.3)
Effect of increase in residual value: add back excess depreciation (W2)		1.0
Investment property: revaluation gain (5 + 10)		15.0
Profit before interest and tax under IFRS		151.7
Interest:		
Under local GAAP	5.0	
Add interest on finance leases (W1)	5.2	
		(10.2)
Taxation:		
Under local GAAP	25.0	
Add increase in charge under IFRS (Appendix 2)	6.2	
		(31.2)
Profit after interest and tax under IFRS		110.3

Earnings per share under IFRS: $\frac{110.3}{200} = 55.2c$

2   Effect on taxation

	Current tax $m	Deferred tax $m	Total $m
Operating lease rentals (increase in profit)	10		
Interest expense on finance lease (decrease in profit)	(5.2)		
Reduction of depreciation on plant (increase in profit)		1	
Gain on investment property (increase in profit)		15	
	4.8	16	20.8
Increase in tax charge at 30%	1.4	4.8	6.2

3   Effect on balance sheet amounts

	Share capital and reserves $m	Non-current liabilities $m	Net assets $m
At 31 May 20X5 under local GAAP	480.0	40.0	520.0
Lease (W1):			
Liability		86.0	86.0
Operating lease rentals	10.0	(10.0)	
Depreciation	(4.3)		(4.3)
Interest	(5.2)	5.2	
Current liability		(5.1)	(5.1)
Plant: depreciation (W2)	1.0		1.0
Investment property: gain	10.0		10.0
Tax (Appendix 2)	(6.2)	4.8	(1.4)
	485.3	120.9	606.2

Workings

1   Finance lease

	$m
Net present value of future lease commitments	86.0
Interest at 6%	5.2
Repayment	(10.0)
Total liability at 31 May 20X5	81.2
Interest at 6%	4.9
Repayment	(10.0)
Total liability at 31 May 20X6	76.1

Therefore $5.1 million (10 – 4.9) is included in current liabilities.

2   Excess depreciation

	$m
Cost	20
Depreciation for year ended 31 May 20X4 (20 – 4 ÷ 8)	(2)
Carrying value at 1 June 20X4	18
Residual value at 1 June 20X4	(11)
Depreciable amount	7
Annual depreciation charge (7 ÷ 7)	1

BPP
LEARNING MEDIA

F2 Guide

Top tips. This is a topical question, which required you to draft a report on the impact of a move to International Financial Reporting Standards in terms of the practical factors that a company should consider and the effects on debt covenants, performance related pay, and the views of financial analysts.

Easy marks. Part (a) gives ten easy marks for common sense. Learn our answer carefully, in case this question comes up again.

Examiner's comment. The question was generally well-answered, although some candidates wrote about the reasons why differences in national accounting practices had arisen. This type of answer obviously did not score many marks. The discussion of the practical implications of a move to IFRS was quite good, but candidates failed to see the problems relating to the recognition of debt covenants and the impact on performance related pay.

Marking scheme

		Marks	
(a)	Factors	10	
(b)	Debt covenants	5	
(c)	Performance related pay	5	
(d)	Views of analysts	5	
Report		4	
	Available	29	
	Maximum		25

REPORT

To: Directors of Guide
From:
Subject: Potential impact of the move to International Financial Reporting Standards (IFRS)
Date: December 20X3

As requested, I have set out my views on the potential impact of the move from reporting under National GAAP to reporting under IFRS.

Practical factors to consider in implementing the change to IFRS

The change to IFRS should be **planned in detail** well before the first IFRS accounts are due to be prepared. The company should consider the following matters.

(a)   Do the staff have the **relevant technical knowledge** and **experience** of IFRS? Almost certainly the company will need to **recruit IFRS experts** and to **arrange appropriate training** for everybody likely to be affected. This should include managers of subsidiaries as well as Head Office staff, because they too will need to understand the effects of the change, for example, when preparing budgets.

(b)   **Which IFRSs** will particularly affect the company? Staff need to understand the **main differences** between national GAAP and IFRS as they affect the financial statements. Because the company provides insurance and banking services, it is likely that **financial instruments** (IASs 32 and 39) and **foreign currency translation** (IAS 21) will be major issues; the standards on financial instruments are **particularly complex** and are likely to **differ considerably** from the requirements of national GAAP.

(c)   Are the **accounting systems adequate** to produce IFRS information? The finance staff will need to be clear about the nature of the **information required**, not only for the actual **accounting**, but for **disclosure**. It should be noted that IFRS **will almost certainly require more information about fair values** than the national GAAP.

(d)   Are there any **agreements** of which the terms are **defined by reference to national GAAP**? These will probably include **debt covenants** and schemes relating to **performance related pay** (discussed below) and there may be other agreements that depend on the **future financial performance** of the company.

The company will need to **keep all stakeholders in the business informed** about the **impact** that the change to IFRS could have on reported performance. Key stakeholders include investors in the form of **analysts** (discussed in more detail below), **employees** and **loan creditors**. The company should **quantify the effect** of the transition to IFRS on the financial statements **as soon as possible**.

It is also worth noting that the IASB currently has **several major projects in progress**, including projects on business combinations, revenue recognition and reporting financial performance. These will all result in **new IFRSs within the next few years**. In addition, the IASB is carrying out a short term **convergence project** with the US Financial Accounting Standards Board (FASB) which will also result in **several changes to existing IFRSs** in the near future. It is important that those responsible for the IFRS financial statements are made aware of new developments as they occur.

The company will be **required to apply IFRS 1** *First time adoption of International Financial Reporting Standards*. This requires an entity to prepare an **opening IFRS balance sheet at the date of transition** to IFRSs. All IFRSs in operation at the first reporting date are **applied retrospectively**, but a number of **exemptions** from this general requirement are available. Any accounting policy **adjustments** are recognised **directly in equity**.

Debt covenants

As noted above, debt covenants and other legal contracts **will be affected by the change** to IFRS. Because IFRS requires **extensive use of fair values** to measure assets and liabilities, **key measures** such as **interest cover** and **gearing** are likely to be **significantly affected**. **Earnings** may also change significantly. Debt covenants based on these measures may need to be **renegotiated**, otherwise the company will have to **continue to keep accounting records in national GAAP** as well as in IFRS, which would be time consuming and possibly costly.

Performance related pay

IFRS 2 *Share based payment* **will apply** to any scheme for paying directors or employees in shares or share options. Where a company makes share based payments, IFRS 2 requires it to **recognise both the additional equity (in reserves) and the related expense**. This means that employee share schemes directly affect reported earnings.

Performance criteria are normally based on measures such as **earnings per share** or **earnings before interest, tax, depreciation and amortisation (EBITDA)**. These **may no longer be appropriate**. Greater use of **fair values** and **'recycling' of gains and losses** (under IAS 21 *The effect of changes in foreign exchange rates*) mean that these measures **may become volatile**. This volatility may not be a direct consequence of staff performance and therefore it would be **undesirable** for it to trigger pay awards or executive bonuses. The company will **need to look for alternative measures** and will probably need to **redesign its incentive schemes** and methods of determining staff bonuses.

Finally, schemes are probably **based on earnings prepared under national GAAP**. Even where existing performance measures are still appropriate, the company will **need to take account of the effect of the change** to IFRS upon reported earnings and to **adjust the criteria** if necessary.

Views of financial analysts

The company should **communicate the effects of the change** from local GAAP to IFRS to the markets and to investment analysts **as soon as these are quantified**. This is necessary in order to give the analysts confidence in the finance team's ability to deal with IFRS (and therefore in the accuracy of the financial statements) and more importantly, in order **to manage the expectations of the market**. **Share prices may be adversely affected** if there are **unexpected changes in earnings** and other key performance measures.

BPP
LEARNING MEDIA

Communication about the potential impact of IFRS is normally in the form of **presentations,** but may be in other forms, such as press releases. Analysts will be particularly interested in **the effect of earnings volatility** because they need to discount future profits in order to arrive at a fair value for the business. Analysts will also need **information that is transparent** and will be assisted if **formats, disclosures and measurement bases** are, as far as possible, **comparable.**

I hope that you find this report helpful. Please do not hesitate to contact me should you require any further information or assistance.

ANSWERS

Mock Exams

ACCA

Paper P2

Corporate Reporting (International)

Mock Examination 1

Question Paper	
Time allowed	
Reading and planning	**15 minutes**
Writing	**3 hours**
This paper is divided into two sections	
Section A This ONE question is compulsory and MUST be attempted	
Section B TWO questions ONLY to be answered	

DO NOT OPEN THIS PAPER UNTIL YOU ARE READY TO START UNDER EXAMINATION CONDITIONS

SECTION A – This ONE question is compulsory and MUST be attempted

Question 1

(a) Jay, a public limited company, has acquired the following shareholdings in Gee and Hem, both public limited companies.

Date of Acquisition	Holding acquired	Fair value of net assets	Purchase Consideration
		$m	$m
Gee			
1 June 20X3	30%	40	15
1 June 20X4	50%	50	30
Hem			
1 June 20X4	25%	32	12

The following balance sheets relate to Jay, Gee and Hem at 31 May 20X5.

	Jay	Gee	Hem
	$m	$m	$m
Property, plant and equipment	300	40	30
Investment in Gee	48		
Investment in Hem	22		
Current assets	100	20	15
Total assets	470	60	45
Share capital of $1	100	10	6
Share premium account	50	20	14
Revaluation surplus	15		
Retained earnings	135	16	10
Total equity	300	46	30
Non-current liabilities	60	4	3
Current liabilities	110	10	12
Total equity and liabilities	470	60	45

The following information is relevant to the preparation of the group financial statements of the Jay Group.

(i) Gee and Hem have not issued any new share capital since the acquisition of the shareholdings by Jay. The excess of the fair value of the net assets of Gee and Hem over their carrying amounts at the dates of acquisition is due to an increase in the value of Gee's non-depreciable land of $10 million at 1 June 20X3 and a further increase of $4 million at 1 June 20X4, and Hem's non-depreciable land of $6 million at 1 June 20X4. There has been no change in the value of non-depreciable land since 1 June 20X4. Before obtaining control of Gee, Jay did not have significant influence over Gee but has significant influence over Hem. Jay has accounted for the investment in Gee at market value with changes in value being recorded in profit or loss. The market price of the shares of Gee at 31 May 20X5 had risen to $6 per share as there was speculation regarding a takeover bid.

(ii) On 1 June 20X4, Jay sold goods costing $13 million to Gee for $19 million. Gee has used the goods in constructing a machine which began service on 1 December 20X4. Additionally, on 31 May 20X5, Jay purchased a portfolio of investments from Hem at a cost of $10 million on which Hem had made a profit of $2 million. These investments have been incorrectly included in Jay's balance sheet under the heading 'Investment in Hem'.

(ii) Jay sold some machinery with a carrying value of $5 million on 28 February 20X5 for $8 million. The terms of the contract, which was legally binding from 28 February 20X5, was that the purchaser would pay a non-refundable initial deposit of $2 million followed by two instalments of $3·5 million (including total interest of $1 million) payable on 31 May 20X5 and 20X6. The purchaser was in financial difficulties at the year end and subsequently went into liquidation on 10 June 20X5. No payment is expected from the liquidator. The deposit had been received on 28 February 20X5 but the first instalment was not received. The terms of the agreement were such that Jay maintained title to the machinery until the first instalment was paid. The machinery was still physically held by Jay and the machinery had been treated as sold in the financial statements. The amount outstanding of $6 million is included in current assets and no interest has been accrued in the financial statements.

(iv) Gee is considered to be a cash-generating unit in its own right. At 31 May 20X5, Jay has determined that the recoverable amount of Gee is $64 million and that of Hem is $68 million.

(v) Group policy on depreciation of plant and equipment is that depreciation of 10% is charged on a reducing balance basis.

(vi) There are no intra-group amounts outstanding at 31 May 20X5.

Required

Prepare the consolidated balance sheet of the Jay Group as at 31 May 20X5 in accordance with International Financial Reporting Standards.

(Candidates should calculate figures to one decimal place of $ million.) **(29 marks)**

(b) In the year ended 31 May 20X6 Jay purchased goods from a foreign supplier for 8 million euros on 28 February 20X6. At 31 May 20X6, the trade payable was still outstanding and the goods were still held by Jay. Similarly Jay has sold goods to a foreign customer for 4 million euros on 28 February 20X6 and it received payment for the goods in euros on 31 May 20X6. additionally Jay had purchased an investment property on 1 June 20X5 for 28 million euros. At 31 May 20X6, the investment property had a fair value of 24 million euros. The company uses the fair value model in accounting for investment properties.

Jay would like advice on how to treat this transaction in the financial statements for the year ended 31 May 20X6. Its functional and presentation currency is the dollar.

Exchange rates	*Euro: $*	*Average rate (Euro: $)* *for year to*
1 June 20X5	1.4	
28 February 20X6	1.6	
31 May 20X6	1.3	1.5

(10 marks)

(c) Jay has a reputation for responsible corporate behaviour and sees the workforce as the key factor in the profitable growth of the business. During the year, the company made progress towards the aim of linking environmental performance with financial performance by reporting the relationship between the eco-productivity index for basic production and water and energy costs used in basic production. A feature of this index is that it can be segregated at site and divisional level, and can be used in the internal management decision-making process.

Discuss what matters should be disclosed in Jay's annual report in relation to the nature of corporate citizenship, in order that there might be a better assessment of the performance of the company. **(11 marks)**

(Total marks = 50)

BPP LEARNING MEDIA

SECTION B – TWO questions ONLY to be attempted

Question 2

The consolidated financial statements of Dietronic, a public limited company, for the year ended 30 November 20X3 areas follows.

INCOME STATEMENT		BALANCE SHEET	
	$'000		$'000
Group operating profit	13,000	Property, plant and equipment	18,500
Interest income	940	Goodwill	1,500
Profit on sale of subsidiary	100	Current assets	8,000
Profit before tax	14,040		28,000
Income tax expense	(5,000)	Share capital $1 ordinary shares	5,000
Profit after tax	9,040	Retained earnings	10,000
		Minority interest	6,000
			21,000
Attributable to: parent	6,040		
minority interest	3,000	Current liabilities	4,000
	9,040	Long term debt	3,000
			28,000

There have been a number of changes in the composition of the group during the year. The changes in the group and the accounting practices used are set out below:

(a) Dietronic had created on 1 July 20X3 a new management company in which it holds 80% of the ordinary share capital with the remainder being held by an employee share ownership trust. Dietronic had invested $160,000 in the company at the balance sheet date, and had incurred $400,000 in administrative setup costs. These costs have been treated as goodwill on consolidation as the setting up of the new company constitutes a 'notional' acquisition with the set up costs being included in the cost of acquisition. The shares held by the employee share ownership trust were issued at a price of $2 per share and are included in the consolidated balance sheet of Dietronic at this amount within current assets. The share capital of the management company is 100,000 ordinary shares of $1.

(b) Dietronic acquired 70% of the ordinary share capital of Dairy, a public limited company, on 31 October 20X2. On acquisition of Dairy, the financial assets of the company were reduced from the book value of $1·2 million to $600,000. This reduction came about as a result of the directors' assessment of the fair value of the investments after taking into account the 'marketability' of the portfolio. On 31 December 20X2, all the investments were sold for $1 million net of costs and the profit on disposal reported in 'interest income' in the consolidated income statement. The financial assets sold were wholly unquoted investments.

(c) Dietronic had a 100% owned German subsidiary which was set up in 20X0 by Dietronic. The subsidiary was sold on 1 December 20X2 for 600,000 euros ($400,000). The subsidiary is included in the holding company's accounts at a cost of $300,000 at 30 November 20X2 and the net assets at the same date included in the consolidated financial statements were 540,000 euros ($360,000). All exchange differences arising on the translation of the subsidiary's financial statements have been taken to a separate exchange reserve and the cumulative total on this reserve is $40,000 debit as at 1 December 20X2 before the receipt of the dividend. Dietronic has calculated the gain on the sale of the subsidiary as follows:

	$'000
Sale proceeds	400
Cost of investment	(300)
Gain on sale	100

The functional currency of the subsidiary is the euro. During the year to 30 November 20X2, the German subsidiary had declared and accounted for a proposed dividend of 48,000 euros. This had been included in the holding company's financial statements at the exchange rate ruling when the dividend was declared ($1 = 1.6 euros). This dividend was received on 1 December 20X2 by Dietronic and recorded in the cash book and dividends receivable account. The shareholders of the subsidiary approved the dividend on 1 October 20X2 and the exchange rate at 1 December 20X2 was ($1 = 1.5 euros).

(d)   On 1 June 20X3 Dietronic acquired a 25% share in a newly formed company, Diet, a public limited company. Diet has been classified as an associate in the financial statements but no details have been shown on the face of the balance sheet or income statement as Dietronic feels that the results and net assets of the associate are immaterial. The only amount included in the financial statements as regards the associate is the purchase consideration of $2·1 million which has been added to property, plant and equipment. The fair value of the net assets of Diet at the date of acquisition was $6·8 million. The directors are confident that Diet will be successful in future years with profits in the next financial year and dividends of 10c per share forecast for five years. If the investment in Diet were to be sold at 30 November 20X3, it is anticipated that it would realize $1·8 million.

SUMMARISED BALANCE SHEET AT 30 NOVEMBER 20X3

	$'000	$'000
Property, plant and equipment		5,000
Net current assets		2,000
		7,000
Ordinary share capital of $1		7,600
Retained earnings at 30 November 20X2	80	
Loss for year to 30 November 20X3	(680)	
		(600)
		7,000

The directors are seeking advice as to the acceptability of the accounting practices used for the above changes in the composition of the group. A discount rate of 5% should be used in any calculations.

Required

(a)   Discuss the nature of any amendments required to the consolidated financial statements of Dietronic in order to bring the accounting practices used for the changes in the composition of the group into line with International Financial Reporting Standards.   **(17 marks)**

(b)   Redraft the consolidated financial statements of Dietronic in accordance with these amendments. **(8 marks)**

(Total = 25 marks)

Question 3

Gear Software, a public limited company, develops and sells computer games software. The revenue of Gear Software for the year ended 31 May 20X3 is $5 million, the balance sheet total is $4 million and it has 40 employees. There are several elements in the financial statements for the year ended 31 May 20X3 on which the directors of Gear require advice.

(a)   Gear has two cost centres relating to the development and sale of the computer games. The indirect overhead costs attributable to the two cost centres were allocated in the year to 31 May 20X2 in the ratio 60:40 respectively. Also in that financial year, the direct labour costs and attributable overhead costs incurred on the development of original games software were carried forward as work-in-progress and included with the balance sheet total for inventory of computer games. Inventory of computer games includes directly attributable overheads. In the year to 31 May 20X3, Gear has allocated indirect overhead costs in the ratio 50:50 to the two cost centres and has written the direct labour and overhead costs incurred on the development of the games off to the income statement. Gear has stated that it cannot quantify the effect of this write off on the current year's income statement. Further, it proposes to show the overhead costs relating to the sale of computer games within distribution costs. In prior years these costs were shown in cost of sales.   **(9 marks)**

BPP
LEARNING MEDIA

(b)   In prior years, Gear has charged interest incurred on the construction of computer hardware as part of cost of sales. It now proposes to capitalise such interest and to change the method of depreciation from the straight-line method over four years to the reducing balance method at 30% per year. Depreciation will now be charged as cost of sales rather than administrative expenses as in previous years. Gear currently recognises revenue on contracts in proportion to the progression and activity on the contract. The normal accounting practice within the industrial sector is to recognise revenue when the product is shipped to customers. The effect of any change in accounting policy to bring the company in line with accounting practice in the industrial sector would be to increase revenue for the year by $500,000.   **(6 marks)**

The directors have requested advice on the changes in accounting practice for inventories and tangible non-current assets that they have proposed.

(c)   In relation to a failed acquisition, a firm of accountants has invoiced Gear for the sum of $300,000. Gear has paid $20,000 in full settlement of the debt and states that this was a reasonable sum for the advice given and is not prepared to pay any further sum. The accountants are pressing for payment of the full amount but on the advice of its solicitors, Gear is not going to settle the balance outstanding. Additionally Gear is involved in a court case concerning the plagiarism of software. Another games company has accused Gear of copying their games software and currently legal opinion seems to indicate that Gear will lose the case. Management estimates that the most likely outcome will be a payment of costs and royalties to the third party of $1 million in two years' time (approximately). The best case scenario is deemed to be a payment of $500,000 in one year's time and the worst case scenario that of a payment of $2 million in three years' time. These scenarios are based on the amount of the royalty payment and the potential duration and costs of the court case. Management has estimated that the relative likelihood of the above payments are best case – 30% chance, most likely outcome – 60% chance, and worst case – 10% chance of occurrence. The directors are unsure as to whether any provision for the above amounts should be made in the financial statements.

(7 marks)

(d)   In the event of the worst case scenario occurring, the directors of Gear are worried about the viability of their business as the likelihood would be that current liabilities would exceed current assets and it is unlikely that in the interim period there will be sufficient funds generated from operational cash flows.   **(3 marks)**

The discount rate for any present value calculations is 5%.

Required

Write a report to the directors of Gear Software explaining the implications of the above information contained in paragraphs (a) – (d) for the financial statements.   **(Total = 25 marks)**

Question 4

Autol, a public limited company, currently prepares its financial statements under local GAAP (Generally Accepted Accounting Practice). The company currently operates in the telecommunications industry and has numerous national and international subsidiaries. It is also quoted on the local stock exchange. The company invests heavily in research and development, which it writes off immediately. The local rules in this area are not prescriptive. The company does not currently provide for deferred taxation or recognise actuarial gains and losses arising on defined benefit plans for employees. It wishes to expand its business activities and raise capital on international stock exchanges. The directors are somewhat confused over the financial reporting requirements of multi-national companies as they see a variety of local GAAPs and reporting practices being used by these companies including the preparation of reconciliations to alternative local GAAPs such as that of the United States of America, and the use of the accounting standards of the International Accounting Standards Board (IASB).

The directors have considered the use of US GAAP in the financial statements but are unaware of the potential problems that might occur as a result of this move. Further the directors are considering currently the use of the accounting standards of the IASB in the preparation of the consolidated financial statements and require advice as to the potential impact on reported profit of a move from local GAAP to these accounting standards given their current accounting practice in the areas of deferred tax, research and development expenditure and employee benefits.

Required

Write a report suitable for presentation to the directors of Autol that sets out the following information.

(a)   The variety of local GAAPs and reporting practices currently being used by multi-national companies setting out brief possible reasons why such companies might prepare financial statements utilising a particular set of generally accepted accounting practices   **(7 marks)**

(b)   Advice as to whether Autol should prepare a single set of consolidated financial statements that comply only with US GAAP   **(3 marks)**

(c)   The problems relating to the current use of GAAP reconciliations by companies and whether the use of such reconciliations is likely to continue into the future   **(6 marks)**

(d)   The potential impact on the reported profit of Autol if it prepared its consolidated financial statements in accordance with the accounting standards of the IASB in relation to its current accounting practices for deferred tax, research and development expenditure and employee benefits   **(9 marks)**

(Total = 25 marks)

Answers

DO NOT TURN THIS PAGE UNTIL YOU HAVE
COMPLETED THE MOCK EXAM

BPP
LEARNING MEDIA

A PLAN OF ATTACK

If this were the real Corporate Reporting exam and you had been told to turn over and begin, what would be going through your mind?

The answer may be 'I can't do this to save my life'! You've spent most of your study time on groups and current issues (because that's what your tutor/BPP Study Text told you to do), plus a selection of other topics, and you're really not sure that you know enough. The good news is that this may get you through. The first question, in Section A, is very likely to be on groups. In Section B you have to choose three out of four questions, and at least one of those is likely to be on current issues – a new IFRS, ED or discussion paper. So there's no need to panic. First spend **five minutes or so looking at the paper**, and develop a **plan of attack**.

Looking through the paper

The compulsory question in Section A is, as a case study on groups, in this case a complex group. You also have a fairly easy bit on corporate citizenship. In **Section B** you have **four questions on a variety of topics:**

- Question 2 requires you to adjust and redraft financial statements.
- Question 3 requires a discussion about issues concerning a change in a accounting policy.
- Question 4 is about the implications of a move to IFRS.

You **only have to answer three out of these four questions.** You don't have to pick your optional questions right now, but this brief overview should have convinced you that you have enough **choice** and variety to have a respectable go at Section B. So let's go back to the compulsory question in Section A.

Compulsory question

Question 1 requires you to **prepare a consolidated balance sheet for a complex group**. This question looks daunting, partly because of the piecemeal acquisition aspects. However, there are easy marks to be gained for basic consolidation techniques such as intragroup trading. Part (c) is a good source of easy marks too.

Optional questions

Deciding between the optional questions is obviously a personal matter – it depends how you have spent your study time. However, here are a few pointers.

Question 2 requires adjustment and re-drafting. It is time-pressured and complex. Best avoided.

Question 3 has easy marks for knowledge of IAS 8, and looks worse than it is.

Question 4 is fairly straight forward if you know the topic. In our opinion, everyone should do this question.

Allocating your time

BPP's advice is always allocate your time **according to the marks for the question** in total and for the parts of the question. But **use common sense.** If you're doing Question 1 but have no idea about fair value, jot down something (anything!) and move onto Part (b), where most of the easy marks are to be gained.

Forget about it!

And don't worry if you found the paper difficult. More than likely other candidates will too. The paper is marked fairly leniently and always has a good pass rate. If this were the real thing, you would need to **forget** the exam the minute you left the exam hall and **think about the next one**. Or, if it's the last one, **celebrate**!

Question 1

Top tips. Part (a) of this question examined business combinations acquired in stages. The examiner has said that this and future questions will be structured around a core question which examines group accounting principles. Bolted on to this core will be adjustments for aspects such as accounting for financial instruments, assets 'held for sale', pensions, or maybe incorrect accounting entries. In this question, candidates had to account for the step-by-step acquisition, inter-company sales, an associate, and an impairment test. Additionally, there were some revenue recognition issues to be dealt with. Part (b) deals with foreign currency transactions. Part (c), on corporate citizenship, is the kind of question you can expect to find regularly as part of question 1.

Easy marks. There are marks for basic consolidation techniques, including setting out the proforma, adding items, and working out the group structure. Part (c) has easy marks available for any sensible points.

Examiner's comment. The step-by-step acquisition was not well-answered, with candidates unsure how to calculate the goodwill arising on the acquisitions. Similarly, the nature of the impairment testing of goodwill did not seem to be understood. Many candidates could not account for the associate, and actually used acquisition techniques instead of equity accounting to consolidate it, giving a minority interest of 75%. The elimination of the inter-company profit was quite well done but some candidates did not allocate part of the revaluation surplus arising on the fair value of the net assets at acquisition to the minority interest. Overall, the question was not particularly well-answered, mainly because of a lack of understanding of the basic technique of step-by-step acquisitions.

Marking scheme

		Marks
(a)	Property, plant and equipment	4
	Goodwill	4
	Associate	4
	Investment	1
	Current assets	1
	Share capital	1
	Revaluation surplus	1
	Retained earnings	6
	Minority interest	
	Non-current liabilities	3
	Current liabilities	
	Impairment	3
(b)	Stock, goods sold	10
(c)	Corporate citizenship:	
	Corporate governance	3
	Ethics	3
	Employee reports	3
	Environment	3
	Available	54
	Maximum	50

BPP
LEARNING MEDIA

(a)   JAY GROUP
      CONSOLIDATED BALANCE SHEET AT 31 MAY 20X5

	$m
Assets	
Property, plant and equipment	353.2
Goodwill (W2)	3.2
Investment in associate (W3)	13.0
Investment (10 – 0.5) (W8)	9.5
Current assets (120 – 6) (W10)	114.0
	492.9

	$m
Equity and liabilities	
Share capital	100.0
Share premium	50.0
Revaluation surplus (W6)	16.2
Retained earnings (W5)	130.7
	296.9
Minority interest (W4)	12.0
	308.9
Non-current liabilities	64.0
Current liabilities	120.0
	492.9

Workings

1   *Group structure*

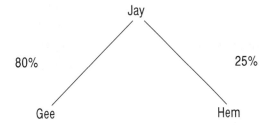

2   *Goodwill: Gee*

	1/6/X3 $m	1/6/X4 $m	Total $m
Cost of combination	15	30	
Less fair value of net assets acquired			
30% × 40	(12)		
50% × 50		(25)	
	3	5	8
Impairment (W9)			(4.8)
			3.2

3   *Investment in associate*

	$m
Cost of investment	12
Profit for year ended 31 May 20X5 (25% × 36 – 32)	1
	13

Note. the recoverable amount of the investment in the associate is $17 million (25% × 68). This is higher than the carrying amount and therefore the associate is not impaired.

4   *Minority interest*

	$m
Net assets at balance sheet date	46.00
Plus fair value adjustment	14.00
	60.00
MI share (20%)	12.00

5   *Retained earnings*

	Jay	Gee (30%)	Gee (50%)	Hem
	$m	$m	$m	$m
Per question	135.00	16.0	16.0	10
Adjustments				
PUP on machinery (W8)	(6.00)			
Add back excess depreciation of machine (W8)	0.30			
PUP on inventories (associate)				(2)
Reverse FV change in Gee (48 – 30 – 15)	(3.00)			
Impairment loss on receivable (W10)	(1.10)			
FV movement		(0.0)	(0.0)	(0)
Pre-acquisition (NA excl FV adjustments, SC & SP) (40 – 10 – 10 – 20)/(50– 14 – 10– 20)/(32 – 6 – 6 – 14)		(0.0)	(6.0)	(6)
		16.0	10.0	2

Group share:	
Gee (30% × 16)	4.80
Gee (50% × 10)	5.00
Hem (25% × 2)	0.50
Impairment loss on goodwill (W9)	(4.80)
	130.70

6   *Revaluation surplus*

	$m
Jay	15.0
Gee: after first acquisition (30% × 14 – 10)	1.2
	16.2

7   *Property, plant and equipment*

	$m	$m
Jay		300.0
Gee		40.0
Fair value adjustment (land)		14.0
Machine		
Cost	5.0	
Less depreciation (3/12 × 10% × 5)	(0.1)	
		4.9
Provision for unrealised profit (W8)		(5.7)
		353.2

Note that Jay has retained title to the machinery because the first instalment has not been paid.

BPP LEARNING MEDIA

8   *Provision for unrealised profit*

    Sales from Jay to Gee

	$m
Profit (19 − 13)	6.0
Less depreciation on machine constructed with goods: (6 × 10% × 6/12)	(0.3)
	5.7

    Sale of investments from Hem to Jay

	$m
Group share of profit (25% × 2)	0.5

9   *Impairment of goodwill: Gee*

	Goodwill $m	Net assets $m	Total $m
Carrying value at 31 May 2005	8	46	54
Fair value adjustment		14	14
Notional minority interest (20%)	2		2
	10	60	70
Recoverable amount			64
Impairment			6

    This is allocated to goodwill and the impairment loss recognised is $4.8 million (80% × 6).

10   *Impairment of receivable*

	$m
Cost of machinery	8.0
Less deposit received	(2.0)
Bad debt written off	6.0
Less net book value of machine (included in tangible assets)	(4.9)
Impairment loss deducted from retained earnings	1.1

(b)   The initial transaction of the purchase of goods from the foreign supplier would be **recorded in the ledger accounts at $5 million (€8/1.6)**. Therefore both the purchase and the payables balance would be recorded at this amount. At the **year end** the payables balance is **restated to the closing rate** but the **inventories remain at $5 million**. Therefore the payable is restated to $6.2 million (€8m/1.3) and an **exchange loss** is taken to the income statement of $1.2 million ($6.2 − 5m).

On the **sale**, the original transaction is recorded at $2.5 million (€4m/1.6) as both a sale and a receivable. When payment is made the amount actually received is $3.1 million (€4m/1.3) and an **exchange gain** is recorded in the income statement of $0.6 million ($3.1 − 2.5m).

When the investment property was first purchased it should have been recognised in the balance sheet at $20 million (€28m/1.4). At the year end the investment property has fallen in value to €24 million and the exchange rate has changed to 1.3. Therefore at 31 May 20X6 the property would be valued at $18.5 million (€24m/1.3).

The **fall in value** of $1.5 million ($20 − 18.5m) is recognised in the **income statement**. The loss is a mixture of a fall in value of the property and a gain due to the exchange rate movement. However, as the investment property is a **non-monetary asset the foreign currency element is not recognised separately**.

(c)   **Nature of corporate citizenship**

Increasingly businesses are expected to be **socially responsible as well as profitable**. Strategic decisions by businesses, particularly global businesses nearly always have wider social consequences. It could be argued, as Henry Mintzburg does, that a company produces two outputs: goods and services, and the social consequences of its activities, such as pollution.

One major development in the area of corporate citizenship is the **environmental report.** While this is not a legal requirement, a large number of major companies produce them. Worldwide there are around 20 award schemes for environmental reporting, notably the ACCA's.

Mineral plc shows that it is responsible with regard to the environment by disclosing the following information.

(i)   The use of the **eco-productivity index** in the financial performance of sites and divisions. This links environmental and financial performance

(ii) The **regeneration of old plants**

(iii) The development of **eco-friendly cars**. Particularly impressive, if successful, is the project to develop a new aluminium alloy car body. Aluminium is rust-free, and it is also lighter, which would reduce fuel consumption.

Another environmental issue which the company could consider is **emission levels** from factories. Many companies now include details of this in their environmental report.

The other main aspect of corporate citizenship where Mineral plc scores highly is in its **treatment of its workforce.** The company sees the workforce as the key factor in the growth of its business. The car industry had a reputation in the past for **restrictive practices,** and the annual report could usefully discuss the extent to which these have been eliminated.

Employees of a businesses are **stakeholders** in that business, along with shareholders and customers. A company wishing to demonstrate good corporate citizenship will therefore be concerned with **employee welfare**. Accordingly, the annual report might usefully contain information on details of working hours, industrial accidents and sickness of employees.

In conclusion, it can be seen that the annual report can, and should go **far beyond the financial statements** and traditional ratio analysis.

Question 2

Top tips. In this question you had to discuss amendments that were required to correct the group accounts of a company and to redraft the group accounts in accordance with these amendments. The amendments dealt with goodwill, fair valuation of assets, foreign subsidiaries and associated companies. The examiner did acknowledge that the amendments were quite complicated.

Easy marks. Part (a) is somewhat easier than Part (b), the easiest bit being (a)(iv), for which five marks are available.

Examiner's comment. Candidates answered this question quite poorly. Many candidates did not see the implications or the errors in the accounting practices undertaken by the company. The treatment of the overseas subsidiary was particularly badly answered. Answers to Part (b) were particularly poor.

Marking scheme

			Marks
(a)	Start-up costs	5	
	Financial assets	4	
	Overseas subsidiary	5	
	Associate	5	
	Available	19	
	Maximum		17

(b)	Start-up costs		2	
	Financial assets		3	
	Overseas subsidiary		2	
	Associate		3	
		Available	10	
		Maximum		8
		Available	29	
		Maximum		25

(a) (i) New management company

Dietronic has recognised **start up costs** of $400,000 as goodwill, despite the fact that **only a 'notional acquisition'** has taken place. In effect, the company has **recognised internally generated goodwill**, which is **prohibited** by IAS 38 *Intangible assets*. It is difficult to justify this treatment, which appears to be a way of **avoiding a charge to the income statement**. IFRS 3 *Business combinations* states that **general administrative costs cannot be included** in the cost of the combination and must be treated as an **expense**. Therefore there is an **additional expense of $400,000**.

The employee share ownership trust (ESOP trust) holds assets on behalf of employees and these should be treated as **assets of the property management company** (as the sponsoring company), but they **cannot be included in the consolidated balance sheet** because the shares are **not assets of the group**. Therefore the shares must be removed from the balance sheet. This **reduces current assets by $40,000** (20,000 × $2) and **minority interest is also reduced by $40,000**.

(ii) Dairy

The directors have carried out a **fair value exercise** that **reduced the carrying value** of the financial assets **shortly before selling them at a profit**. This appears to be a **deliberate attempt to enhance profits on disposal**. The fair value exercise took place when Dairy was acquired, so **IFRS 3 should have been applied**. Although the shares were **unquoted** it should have been **possible to arrive at a reliable valuation**. IFRS 3 states that the acquirer should use **estimated values based on price earnings ratios, dividend yields and expected growth rates of comparable entities**. It could be argued that the **subsequent sale proceeds** two months after the valuation probably provide the **most reliable evidence** of the fair value of the shares at the date of acquisition. Therefore the investments should be **valued at this amount** rather than at the directors' valuation.

Therefore:

- **Goodwill is reduced by $280,000** (1,000,000 − 600,000 × 70%).

- **Profit for the group is reduced by $280,000** and **minority interest is reduced by $120,000** (400,000 × 30%).

(iii) Sale of German subsidiary

IAS 21 *The effects of changes in foreign exchange rates* states when the financial statements of a foreign operation are translated to a presentation currency the **resulting exchange differences are recognised in equity** (reserves). On **disposal** of the subsidiary, these **exchange differences should be 'recycled'** and **recognised in the income statement**. This means that the calculation of the gain on sale should be as follows:

	$'000
Sale proceeds	400
Net assets sold	(360)
Exchange reserve	(40)
Dividend receivable (48,000 ÷ 1.6)	30
	30

Note. Because the subsidiary was set up by Dietronic, rather than acquired, there is no goodwill.

There is also an exchange gain on retranslation of the dividend:

	$'000
Dividend receivable (48,000 ÷ 1.6)	30
Dividend received (48,000 ÷ 1.5)	32
	2

(iv) **Associate (Diet)**

The results and net assets of the associate are **not immaterial** and **should be included** in the consolidated financial statements.

The carrying value of the investment at 30 November 20X3 is:

	$'000
Cost of investment	2,100
Loss for year (25% × 680 × 6/12)	(85)
	2,015

IAS 28 *Investments in associates* states that investors should account for their share of a loss making associate even though there is no obligation to make good the deficit.

The fact that the company has **incurred losses** suggests that an **impairment review** is necessary. This involves **comparing the carrying amount with the recoverable amount**, which is the **higher of fair value less costs to sell** and **value in use**. **Fair value less costs to sell** is the **anticipated selling price** of $1.8 million. **Value in use** could be calculated as the **cash flows expected from the dividends over the next five years**: $822,510 (7.6 million × 25% × 10c × 4.329). To this would need to be **added** the **fair value less costs to sell in five years time**, which is unknown. Therefore **fair value less costs to sell should be taken as the recoverable amount** and the **impairment loss is $215,000**. The investment in the associate is **written down to $1.8 million**.

(b) DIETRONIC GROUP
INCOME STATEMENT FOR THE YEAR ENDED 30 NOVEMBER 20X3

	Original $'000	(i) $'000	(ii) $'000	(iii) $'000	(iv) $'000	Amended $'000
Group operating profit	13,000	(400)				12,600
Interest income	940		(400)			540
Profit on sale of subsidiary	100			(70)		30
Impairment loss					(215)	(215)
Exchange gain				2		2
Share of losses in associate					(85)	(85)
Profit before tax	14,040					12,872
Income tax expense	(5,000)					(5,000)
Profit for the year	9,040					7,872
Attributable to						
Group	6,040					4,992
Minority interests	3,000		(120)			2,880
	9,040					7,872

BPP
LEARNING MEDIA

DIETRONIC GROUP
BALANCE SHEET AS AT 30 NOVEMBER 20X3

	Original $'000	(i) $'000	(ii) $'000	(iii) $'000	(iv) $'000	Amended $'000
Property, plant and equipment	18,500				(2,100)	16,400
Investment in associate					2,015	
					(215)	1,800
Goodwill	1,500	(400)	(280)			820
Current assets	8,000	(40)		2		7,962
	28,000					26,982
Share capital	5,000					5,000
Retained earnings	10,000	(400)	(280)	2	(85)	
					(215)	9,022
Minority interest	6,000	(40)				5,960
	21,000					19,982
Long-term debt	3,000					3,000
Current liabilities	4,000					4,000
	28,000					26,982

Question 3

Top tips. In this question you were required to discuss the issues and implications of changes in accounting practice, and accounting for provisions for a company. Make sure that you are able to distinguish between a change in an accounting policy and a change in an accounting estimate. Remember that the provision for the costs of the court case needs to be discounted.

Easy marks. In Part (a) there are easy marks for rote knowledge of IAS 8, which you should know as it has fairly recently been examined.

Examiner's comment. The question was relatively straightforward but candidates seemed to struggle to identify the fundamental issues in the case presented to them.

Marking scheme

			Marks
(a)	IASB explanation	4	
	Cost centres	6	
	Available	10	
	Maximum		9
(b)	Hardware	3	
	Revenue recognition	3	
	Available/maximum		6
(c)	Provisions	Available	8	
		Maximum		7
(d)	Going concern	Available/maximum		3
	Report		2	
		Available	29	
		Maximum		25

REPORT

To: Directors of Gear Software

From:

Subject: Implications of various transactions for the financial statements for the year ended 31 May 20X3

Date: June 20X3

As requested, I explain below the implications of several transactions for the financial statements.

(a)   **Cost centres**

The relevant standard here is IAS 8 *Accounting policies, changes in accounting estimates and errors.*

It is necessary to distinguish between changes in accounting policy and changes in accounting estimates. A change to an accounting policy involves a change in the way in which an item is recognised, measured or presented.

The indirect overhead costs are directly attributable to the two cost centres and are included in the inventory valuation in the balance sheet. The only change has been a change to the way in which the costs are allocated. There have been **no changes to the way in which they are recognised, measured or presented**. This change is **not a change in accounting policy**, but a **change in an accounting estimate**.

Direct labour and overhead costs were previously carried forward as work in progress and included in the balance sheet as part of inventories. They are now written off to the income statement as they are incurred. There has been a change in the way in which these costs are recognised and presented and therefore there is a **change in accounting policy**.

Overhead costs relating to the sale of computer games were previously included in cost of sales and are now included in distribution costs. There has been a **change in the way in which these costs are presented** and again, there has been a **change in accounting policy**.

IAS 8 states that a change in accounting policy is **only allowed if** the change is **required by a standard** or an interpretation or if it results in the financial statements providing **more reliable and more relevant information** about the effects of transactions, other events or conditions on the entity's financial position, performance or cash flows. Both accounting policy changes are voluntary, so there **must be a clear case** for them on the grounds that they do result in more useful information.

The effect of the change in accounting estimate is **included in the income statement for the current period (ie, recognised prospectively).**

IAS 8 requires the effect of changes in accounting policy to be recognised **retrospectively**, by making a **prior period adjustment**. The opening balance of retained earnings is adjusted and comparative figures are restated. IAS 8 also requires the company to **disclose the effect** of the changes, including the reason why the change provides improved information and the effect of the adjustment on the financial statements for the current period (in detail) and for each prior period presented. Therefore the company is required to disclose the effect of the write off of the development costs on the current year's income statement. It is unlikely that it is impracticable to do so.

(b)   **Computer hardware and revenue on contracts**

IAS 23 *Borrowing costs* **allows the capitalisation of interest** relating to qualifying non-current assets. The computer hardware is **likely to meet the definition of a qualifying asset** as it requires a substantial amount of time to bring it to a saleable condition. There is a change to the way in which the interest is recognised and presented and therefore there is a **further change in accounting policy.**

The change in the method of depreciation is a **change in an accounting estimate**, rather than a change in accounting policy. However, there has also been a **change in the way in which depreciation is presented** in the financial statements and this *is* a **change in accounting policy.**

BPP
LEARNING MEDIA

The requirements of IAS 8 will again apply. The accounting policy changes must be **applied retrospectively** and the effect of the changes **must be disclosed**.

It is proposed to change the way in which contract revenue is recognised. The company's current policy of recognising revenue as the contract progresses is acceptable under IAS 11 *Construction Contracts* and IAS 18 *Revenue*. However, **IASs 11 and 18 may not specifically apply to this situation.** IAS 8 states that where there is **no specifically applicable standard**, management should **select a policy** that results in information that is **relevant to the needs of users and reliable**. Management should **refer to standards dealing with similar issues** and to the **IASB** *Framework*, but it may also consider **accepted industry practice** (revenue is recognised when the product is shipped to customers). The advantage of adopting this policy is that revenue would increase and this is particularly important given that significant provisions may have to be recognised (see below). Provided that there is no conflict between the industry practice and IASs 11 and 18, the company **should change to the new policy**. Again, the **accounting and disclosure requirements of IAS 8 apply**.

(c)   **Provisions**

IAS 37 *Provisions, contingent liabilities and contingent assets* states that a provision should only be recognised if:

(i)   There is a **present obligation** as a result of a **past event**, and

(ii)   It is **probable** (more likely than not) that an **outflow of resources** embodying economic benefits will be required to settle the obligation, and

(iii)   A **reliable estimate** can be made of the **amount** of the obligation.

In the case of the disputed invoice, the company's solicitors apparently do not believe that any further sums will be payable. On this basis, **no provision should be recognised**, but the company has a **contingent liability**. Information about the contingent liability should be **disclosed** in the financial statements, including the estimated financial effects and any uncertainties relating to the amount or timing of any outflow.

In contrast, it does appear that the company has a present obligation as a result of the plagiarism case and that payment is probable. A **provision should be recognised**. IAS 37 states that the amount recognised should be the **best estimate of the expenditure required to settle the obligation at the balance sheet date**. The estimate should **take the various possible outcomes into account** and the amount should be **discounted to present value** if the time value of money is material.

The **most likely outcome** is a **payment of $1 million in two years time**, which suggests a discounted amount of **$907,000** ($1 million × 0.907). It is also possible to calculate an amount **based on expected outcomes**:

	$
Best case (500,000 × 0.952 × 30%)	142,800
Most likely (1,000,000 × 0.907 × 60%)	544,200
Worst case (2,000,000 × 0.864 × 10%)	172,800
	859,800

The difference between this amount and the most likely outcome is not material in the context of the financial statements (considering that the amounts are based on estimates) and therefore a **provision of $860,000 should be recognised**.

(d)   **Going concern**

IAS 1 *Presentation of financial statements* states that an entity **should prepare its financial statements on a going concern basis**. This assumes that management intends to continue trading for at least 12 months from the balance sheet date and that there will be no need to cease operations or to liquidate the entity during that period. IAS 1 also states that management **should assess the entity's ability to continue as a going concern** and should **disclose any uncertainties** that cast significant doubt on this ability.

Therefore it **may be necessary to disclose** the fact that there are **concerns about the viability of the business**, should the worst outcome of the plagiarism case occur.

Question 4

Top tips. This question dealt with current corporate reporting practices of multinational companies and the potential impact on financial statements of a move from local GAAP to International Accounting Standards. Candidates were also expected to discuss the potential impact of the move from local GAAP to IAS in respect of certain accounting standards. An in depth knowledge of IAS was not required but simply a general knowledge of the impact of a move to IAS on financial statements.

Examiner's comment. Candidates answered the question quite well, seemingly being well prepared for this type of question. The question asked for a report to be written but many candidates did not take into account that this was a report suitable for presentation to the directors of the company and included irrelevant technical information which was not suitable for 'presentation to the directors'. Knowledge of the use of GAAP reconciliations by companies was generally quite poor. On the move from local GAAP to IAS/IFRS, the answers seemed to indicate that candidates needed to spend more time studying the implications of the move to IAS for UK companies. Candidates again seemed to find this element of the question quite difficult. The problem seemed to be centred around the ability to compare and synthesise information about alternate GAAPs.

Marking scheme

		Marks
(a)	Introduction	2
	Dual financial statements and reconciliation	3
	Mixed GAAP	1
	Local GAAP	1
	Reconciliation with IFRS	1
	Conclusions – variety	1
(b)	US GAAP accounts	3
(c)	Reconciliations	4
	Disclosure	2
(d)	Potential impact	9
	Style etc	3
	Available	30
	Maximum	25

Note. One of the purposes of this question was to assess candidates' ability to write a report to directors in language which is easily interpreted by the directors.

REPORT

To: Directors of Autol
From:
Subject: International convergence and financial reporting practice
Date: December 20X2

I set out below the information and advice that you have requested.

(a) **Current reporting practices used by multi-national companies**

International convergence has become important largely because **business has become multi-national**. Users of financial statements (including stock exchanges and regulatory authorities) need to be able to **compare financial statements prepared in different countries**. However, a variety of different GAAPs are still in use.

In some countries, companies are required to **prepare and file financial statements under local GAAP**, but may then provide a **second set of financial statements in another GAAP** or a reconciliation to another GAAP. This may be required if the company has a foreign parent or if it is listed on a foreign stock exchange. In other countries, companies may be able to **choose between one or more GAAPs**, for example between local GAAP and IAS/IFRS.

Many multi-national companies adopt US GAAP. This is often seen as the **most rigorous system** and therefore companies believe that it will give their financial statements greater credibility than other GAAPs. **US GAAP gives access to the US capital markets, which still require a reconciliation from local GAAP to US GAAP.**

The choice of GAAP normally reflects a company's operating environment or the capital markets in which it is listed (or is seeking a listing). For example, a UK company with operations in Hong Kong may reconcile UK GAAP to US GAAP and disclose the effect of different accounting treatments under UK GAAP and Hong Kong GAAP. It is also possible for companies to mix different GAAPs. For example, a company which operates in both the UK and the Netherlands might adopt accounting policies that comply with applicable UK and Dutch GAAP.

A variety of practices are in use, but in practice US GAAP remains the most popular choice with companies seeking access to international capital markets. However, recent accounting scandals in the US have reduced the credibility of US GAAP at a time when the acceptability of IFRSs is steadily increasing.

(b)   **Preparation of US GAAP financial statements**

It might be difficult for a non-US company to prepare a single set of consolidated financial statements under US GAAP. **Most companies are required to prepare financial statements that comply with local companies legislation and to file them with the regulatory authorities**. US GAAP financial statements might not be acceptable for this purpose, although some countries may allow the use of IAS/IFRS or US GAAP. The shareholders are probably also entitled to receive a full set of financial statements prepared under local GAAP.

The best course of action would be to prepare a statement reconciling local GAAP to US GAAP. It would also be possible to prepare dual financial statements, but the cost of this might outweigh the benefits.

(c)   **Problems relating to the use of GAAP reconciliations**

Because full international convergence is unlikely in the short term, GAAP reconciliations will probably be used for many years to come. Most major national standard setters are now committed to convergence, and **from 2005 onwards IAS/IFRS will be used throughout the EU**. However, convergence of US GAAP and IAS/IFRS may be much more difficult to achieve.

The use of GAAP reconciliations is **not controlled by regulation**. For example, in many cases the auditors do not have to report on their truth and fairness. This may **reduce the credibility of the information provided.**

This also means that **companies may disclose the information in different ways**. Most companies show the reconciliation as a single note or in an Appendix, but in some cases the information appears in several different places in the financial statements and can be difficult to follow.

Some companies provide detailed information which may include summary performance statements, balance sheets, cash flow information and even non-financial disclosures and narrative discussion of the differences. Others only provide a reconciliation of profit or a reconciliation of shareholders' funds.

(d) **Potential impact of compliance with IAS/IFRS**

The change from local GAAP to international standards may have a significant effect on the company's reported profits. The three areas are discussed in turn below.

(i) *Deferred tax*

Autol does not currently provide deferred tax, while IAS 12 *Income taxes* **requires full provision**. IAS 12 **requires the calculation of the liability to be based on temporary differences.** This approach means that almost all differences between the tax base of an asset and its carrying amount in the balance sheet have a deferred tax effect. This could mean that **reported profit will be significantly reduced.**

(ii) *Development expenditure*

Autol currently writes off development expenditure immediately. IAS 38 *Intangible assets* **requires capitalisation,** provided certain stringent criteria are met. It is possible that the development expenditure may not qualify for recognition. If the development expenditure is recognised, the change will affect the timing of the charge to the income statement, rather than the amount. Expenditure will be matched with the revenue that it produces and **reported results may be less volatile.**

(iii) *Retirement benefits*

Autol does not currently recognise actuarial gains and losses arising on its defined benefit pension plan. IAS 19 *Employee benefits* **requires actuarial gains and losses to be recognised in the income statement** or **retained earnings**. However, they need not be recognised immediately if recognised in the income statement, but **may be deferred and recognised over the average remaining working lives of the employees,** using the '10% corridor' approach. The change to IAS **will reduce reported profit,** but the **degree** to which results are affected will **depend on the accounting policy adopted**.

I hope that this answers your queries. Please do not hesitate to contact me should you require any further information or assistance.

BPP
LEARNING MEDIA

ACCA

Paper P2

Corporate Reporting (International)

Mock Examination 2

Question Paper	
Time allowed Reading and planning Writing	**15 minutes** **3 hours**
This paper is divided into two sections	
Section A	This ONE question is compulsory and MUST be attempted
Section B	TWO questions ONLY to be answered

DO NOT OPEN THIS PAPER UNTIL YOU ARE READY TO START UNDER EXAMINATION CONDITIONS

SECTION A – This ONE question is compulsory and MUST be attempted

Question 1

Lateral, a public limited company, acquired two subsidiary companies, Think and Plank, both public limited companies. The details of the acquisitions are as follows:

Subsidiary	Date of acquisition	Retained earnings at acquisition	Share capital acquired $1 shares	Fair value of net assets at acquisition
		$m	m	$m
Think	1 November 20X3	150	200	400
Plank	1 November 20X3	210	300	800

The draft balance sheets as at 31 October 20X5 are:

	Lateral $m	Think $m	Plank $m
Assets			
Non-current assets			
Property, plant and equipment	700	390	780
Investment in subsidiaries:			
Think	380		
Plank	340		
Held to maturity investments	30	–	–
	1,450	390	780
Current assets			
Inventories	200	185	90
Trade receivables	170	80	100
Cash and cash equivalents	40	30	50
	410	295	240
Non-current assets classified as held for sale		15	
		310	
Total assets	1,860	700	1,020
Equity and Liabilities:			
Share capital – shares of $1	400	250	500
Retained earnings	850	280	290
Total equity	1,250	530	790
Non-current liabilities	250	60	80
Current liabilities	360	110	150
Total liabilities	610	170	230
Total equity and liabilities	1,860	700	1,020

The following information is relevant to the preparation of the group financial statements.

(i)   There have been no new issues of shares in the group since 1 November 20X3 and the fair value adjustments have not been included in the subsidiaries' financial records.

(ii)   Any increase in the fair values of the net assets over their carrying values at acquisition is attributable to plant and equipment. Plant and equipment is depreciated at 20% per annum on the reducing balance basis.

(iii)   Think sold plant and equipment to Lateral on 12 November 20X5. The transaction was completed at an agreed price of $15 million after selling costs. The transaction complies with the conditions in IFRS 5 *Non-current assets held for sale and discontinued operations* for disclosure as assets 'held for sale'. The plant and equipment had been valued at 'fair value less costs to sell' in the individual accounts of Think. At 1 November 20X4, this plant and equipment had a carrying value of $10 million and no depreciation on these assets has been charged for the year ended 31 October 20X5.

(iv) Lateral had purchased a debt instrument with five years remaining to maturity on 1 November 20X3. The purchase price and fair value was $30 million on that date. The instrument will be repaid in five years time at an amount of $37·5 million. The instrument carries fixed interest of 4·7% per annum on the principal of $37·5 million and has an effective interest rate of 10% per annum. The fixed interest has been received and accounted for but no accounting entry has been made other than the recognition of the original purchase price of the instrument.

(v) Goodwill arising on the acquisition of the subsidiaries was impairment tested on 31 October 20X4 and 31 October 20X5 in accordance with IAS 36 *Impairment of assets*. On 31 October 20X4 an impairment loss of $28 million was recognised for Plank. Plank is a cash generating unit in its own right. At 31 October 20X5, the impairment loss of $28 million had partially reversed, and the company proposed to write back to goodwill the reversal of $12 million. The goodwill arising on the acquisition of Think was not impaired at 31 October 20X4 and 31 October 20X5.

(vi) On 31 October 20X5, after accounting for the results of the impairment test, Lateral sold 100 million shares in Plank for $180 million. Lateral still maintains significant influence over Plank after the disposal of the shares. The receipt of the sale proceeds has been recorded in the cash book and as a reduction in the carrying value of the cost of the investment in the subsidiary. Goodwill associated with the shares sold is to be measured on the basis of the proportion of shares disposed of.

Required

(a) Calculate the gain or loss that would be recorded in the group income statement on the sale of the shares in Plank.
(6 marks)

(b) Prepare a consolidated balance sheet as at 31 October 20X5 for the Lateral Group in accordance with International Financial Reporting Standards.

(22 marks)

(c) In the year ended 31 October 20X6, Lateral entered into a contract to purchase plant and equipment from a foreign supplier on 30 June 20X7. The purchase price is 4 million euros. A non-refundable deposit of 1 million euros was paid on signing the contract on 31 July 20X6 with the balance of 3 million euros payable on 30 June 20X7. Lateral was uncertain as to whether to purchase a 3 million euro bond on 31 July 20X6 which will not mature until 30 June 20Y0, or to enter into a forward contract on the same date to purchase 3 million euros for a fixed price of $2 million on 30 June 20X7 and to designate the forward contract as a cash flow hedge of the purchase commitment. The bond carries interest at 4% per annum, payable on 30 June 20X7. Current market rates are 4% per annum. The company chose to purchase the bond with a view to selling it on 30 June 20X7 in order to purchase the plant and equipment. The bond is not to be classified as a cash flow hedge but at fair value through profit and loss.

Lateral would like advice as to whether it made the correct decision and as to the accounting treatment of the items for 20X6 and 20X7. The company's functional and presentational currency is the dollar.
(12 marks)

Exchange rates	Euro: $	Average rate (Euro: $) for year to
31 July 20X6	1.6	
31 October 20X6	1.3	1.5

(d) Lateral discloses the following information relating to employees in its financial statements.

Its full commitment to equal opportunities
Its investment in the training of staff
The number of employees injured at work each year.

The company wishes to enhance disclosure in these areas, but is unsure as to what the benefits would be. The directors are particularly concerned that the disclosures on management of the workforce (human capital management) has no current value to the stakeholders of the company.

Discuss the general nature of the current information disclosed by companies concerning 'human capital management' and how the link between the company performance and its employees could be made more visible. **(10 marks)**

(Total marks = 50)

SECTION B – TWO questions ONLY to be attempted

Question 2

Barking, an unlisted company, operates in the house building and commercial property investment development sector. The sector has seen an upturn in activity during recent years and the directors have been considering future plans with a view to determining their impact on the financial statements for the financial year to 30 November 20X4.

(a) Barking wishes to obtain a stock exchange listing in the year to 30 November 20X4. It is to be acquired by Ash, a significantly smaller listed company in a share for share exchange whereby Barking will receive sufficient voting shares of Ash to control the new group. Due to the relative values of the companies, Barking will become the majority shareholder with 80% of the enlarged capital of Ash. The executive management of the new group will be that of Barking.

As part of the purchase consideration, Ash will issue zero dividend preference shares of $1 to the shareholders of Barking on 30 June 20X4. These will be redeemed on 1 January 20X5 at $1·10 per share. Additionally Ash will issue convertible interest free loan notes. The loan notes are unlikely to be repaid on 30 November 20X5 (the redemption date) as the conversion terms are very favourable. The management of Ash have excluded the redemption of the loan notes from their cash flow projections. The loan notes are to be included in long term liabilities in the balance sheet of Ash. As part of the business combination Ash will change its name to Barking inc. **(9 marks)**

(b) The acquisition will also have other planned effects on the company. Barking operates a defined benefit pension scheme. On acquisition the scheme will be frozen and replaced by a group defined contribution scheme, and as a result no additional benefits in the old scheme will accrue to the employees. Ash's employees are also in a defined benefit scheme which has been classified as a multi-employer plan but it is currently impossible to identify its share of the underlying assets and liabilities in the scheme. After acquisition, Ash's employees will be transferred to the group's defined contribution scheme, with the previous scheme being frozen. **(5 marks)**

(c) As a result of the acquisition the company will change the way in which it recognises sales of residential properties. It used to treat such properties as sold when the building work was substantially complete, defined as being when the roof and internal walls had been completed. The new policy will be to recognise a sale when a refundable deposit for the sale of the property has been received and the building work is physically complete. Legal costs incurred on the sale of the property are currently capitalised and shown as current assets until the sale of the property has occurred. Further, it has been decided by the directors that as at 30 November 20X4, the financial year end, some properties held as trading properties of both companies would be moved from the trading portfolio to the investment portfolio of the holding company, and carried at fair value. **(7 marks)**

(d) The directors intend to carry out an impairment review as at 30 November 20X4 in order to ascertain whether the carrying amount of goodwill and other non-current assets can be supported by their value in use. The plan is to produce cash flow projections up to 20Y4 with an average discount rate of 15% being used in the calculations. The ten year period is to be used as it reflects fairly the long term nature of the assets being assessed. Any subsequent impairment loss is to be charged against the income statement. **(4 marks)**

Required

Draft a report to the directors of Barking, setting out the financial reporting implications of the above plans for the financial statements for the year to 30 November 20X4. **(Total = 25 marks)**

Question 3

The Gow Group, a public limited company, and Glass, a public limited company, have agreed to create a new entity, York, a limited liability company on 31 October 20X6. the companies' line of business is the generation, distribution, and supply of energy. Gow supplies electricity and Glass supplies gas to customers. Each company has agreed to subscribe net assets for a 50% share in the equity capital of York. York is to issue 30 million ordinary shares of $1. There was no written agreement signed by Gow and Glass but the minutes of the meeting where the creation of the new company was discussed have been formally approved by both companies. Each company provides equal numbers of directors to the Board of Directors. The net assets of York were initially shown at amounts agreed between Gow and Glass, but their values are to be adjusted so that the carrying amounts at 31 October 20X6 are based on International Financial Reporting Standards.

Gow had contributed the following assets to the new company in exchange for its share of the equity:

	$m
Cash	1
Trade receivables – Race	7
Intangible assets – contract with Race	3
Property, plant and equipment	9
	20

The above assets form a cash generated unit (an electricity power station) in its own right. The unit provided power to a single customer, Race. On 31 October 20X6 Race went into administration and the contract to provide power to Race was cancelled. On 1 December 20X6, the administrators of the customer provisionally agreed to pay a final settlement figure of $5 million on 31 October 20X7, including any compensation for the loss of the contract. Gow expects York will receive 80% of the provisional amount. On hearing of the cancelled contract, an offer was received for the power station of $16 million. York would be required to pay the disposal costs estimated at $1 million.

The power station has an estimated remaining useful life of four years at 31 October 20X6. it has been agreed with the government that it will be dismantled on 31 October 20Y0. The cost at 31 October 20Y0 of dismantling the power station is estimated to be $5 million.

The directors of Gow and York are currently in the final stages of negotiating a contract to supply electricity to another customer. As a result the future net cash inflows (undiscounted) expected to arise from the cash generating unit (power station) are as follows:

	$m
31 October 20X7	6
31 October 20X8	7
31 October 20X9	8
31 October 20Y0	8
	29

The dismantling cost has not been provided for, and future cash flows are discounted at 6 per cent by the companies.

Glass had agreed to contribute the following net assets to the new company in exchange for its share of the equity:

	$m
Cash	10
Intangible asset	2
Inventory at cost	6
Property at carrying value	4
Lease receivable	1
Lease payable	(3)
	20

The property contributed by Glass is held on a 10 year finance lease which was entered into on 31 October 20X0. The property is being depreciated over the life of the lease on the straight line basis. As from 31 October 20X6, the terms of the lease have been changed and the lease will be terminated early on 31 October 20X8 in exchange for a payment of $1 million on 31 October 20X6 and a further two annual payments of $600,000. The first annual payment under the revised terms will be on 31 October 20X7. York will vacate the property on 31 October 20X8 and the revised lease qualifies as a finance lease. The cash paid on 31 October 20X6 is shown as a lease receivable and the change in the lease terms is not reflected in the values placed on the net assets above. The effective interest rate of the lease is 7%.

Glass had entered into a contract with an agency whereby for every new domestic customer that the agency gained, the agency received a fixed fee. On the formation of York, the contract was terminated and the agency received $500,000 as compensation for the termination of the contract. This cost is shown as an intangible asset above as the directors feel that it represents the economic benefits related to the future reduced cost of gaining retail customers. Additionally, on 31 October 20X6, a contract was signed whereby York was to supply gas at fair value to a major retailer situated overseas over a four year period. On signing the contract, the retailer paid a non refundable cash deposit of $1.5 million which is included in the cash contributed by Glass. The retailer is under no obligation to buy gas from York but York cannot supply gas to any other company in that country. The directors intend to show this deposit in profit or loss when the first financial statements of York are produced. At present, the deposit is shown as a deduction from intangible assets in the above statement of net assets contributed by Glass.

(All calculations should be made to one decimal place and assume the cash flows relating to the cash generating unit (electricity power station) arise at the year end.)

Required

(a)   Discuss the nature and accounting treatment of the relationship between Gow, Glass and York.   **(5 marks)**

(b)   Prepare the balance sheet of York at 31 October 20X6, using International Financial Reporting Standards, discussing the nature of the accounting treatments selected, the adjustments made and the values placed on the items in the balance sheet.   **(20 marks)**

(Total = 25 marks)

Question 4

Jones and Cousin, a public quoted company, operate in twenty seven different countries and earn revenue and incur costs in several currencies. The group develops, manufactures and markets products in the medical sector. The growth of the group has been achieved by investment and acquisition. It is organised into three global business units which manage their sales in international markets, and take full responsibility for strategy and business performance. Only five per cent of the business is in the country of incorporation. Competition in the sector is quite fierce.

The group competes across a wide range of geographic and product markets and encourages its subsidiaries to enhance local communities by reinvestment of profits in local education projects. The group's share of revenue in a market sector is often determined by government policy. The markets contain a number of different competitors including specialised and large international corporations. At present the group is awaiting regulatory approval for a range of new products to grow its market share. The group lodges its patents for products and enters into legal proceedings where necessary to protect patients. The products are sourced from a wide range of suppliers, who, once approved both from a qualitative and ethical perspective, are generally given a long term contract for the supply of goods. Obsolete products are disposed of with concern for the environment and the health of its customers, with reusable materials normally being used. The industry is highly regulated in terms of medical and environmental laws and regulations. The products normally carry a low health risk.

BPP
LEARNING MEDIA

The Group has developed a set of corporate and social responsibility principles during the period, which is the responsibility of the Boards of Directors. The Managing Director manages the risks arising from corporate and social responsibility issues. The group wishes to retain and attract employees and follows policies which ensure equal opportunity for all the employees. Employees are informed of management policies, and regularly receive in-house training.

The Group enters into contract for fixed rate currency swaps and uses floating to fixed rate interest rate swaps. The cash flow effects of these swaps match the cash flows on the underlying financial instruments. All financial instruments are accounted for as cash flow hedges. A significant amount of trading activity is denominated in the Dinar and the Euro. The dollar is its functional currency.

Required

(a)   Describe the principles behind the Management Commentary, discussing whether the commentary should be mandatory or whether directors should be free to use their judgement as to what should be included in such a commentary.   **(13 marks)**

(b)   Draft a report suitable for inclusion in a Management Commentary for Jones and Cousin which deals with:

   (i)   The key risks and relationships of the business   **(9 marks)**
   (ii)   The strategy of the business regarding its treasury policies   **(3 marks)**

(Marks will be awarded in Part (b) for the identification and discussion of relevant points and for the style of the report.)

(Total = 25 marks)

Answers

DO NOT TURN THIS PAGE UNTIL YOU HAVE
COMPLETED THE MOCK EXAM

A PLAN OF ATTACK

Managing your nerves

As you turn the pages to start this exam a number of thoughts are likely to cross your mind. At best, examinations cause anxiety so it is important to stay focused on your task for the next three hours! Developing an awareness of what is going on emotionally within you may help you manage your nerves. Remember, you are unlikely to banish the flow of adrenaline, but the key is to harness it to help you work steadily and quickly through your answers.

Working through this mock exam will help you develop the exam stamina you will need to keep going for three hours.

Managing your time

Planning and time management are two of the key skills which complement the technical knowledge you need to succeed. To keep yourself on time, do not be afraid to jot down your target completion times for each question, perhaps next to the title of the question on the paper.

Focusing on scoring marks

When completing written answers, remember to communicate the critical points, which represent marks, and avoid padding and waffle. Sometimes it is possible to analyse a long sentence into more than one point. Always try to maximise the mark potential of what you write.

As you read through the questions, jot down on the question paper, any points you think you might forget. There is nothing more upsetting than coming out of an exam having forgotten to write a point you knew!

Also remember you can only score marks for what is on paper; you must write down enough to help the examiner to give you marks!

Structure and signpost your answers

To help you answer the examiner's requirements, highlight as you read through the paper the key words and phrases in the examiner's requirements.

Also, where possible try to use headings and subheadings, to give a logical and easy-to-follow structure to your response. A well structured and signposted answer is more likely to convince the examiner that you know your subject.

Your approach

This paper has two sections. The first section contains one question which is compulsory. The second has three questions and you must answer two of them.

You have a choice.

* Read through and answer the Section A question before moving on to Section B

* Go through Section B and select the two questions you will attempt. Then go back and answer the question in Section A first

* Select the two questions in Section B, answer them and then go back to Section A

You will have fifteen minutes before the start of the exam to go through the questions you are going to do.

Time spent at the start of each question confirming the requirements and producing a plan for the answers is time well spent.

Question selection

When selecting the two questions from Section B make sure that you read through all of the requirements. It is painful to answer part (a) of a question and then realise that parts (b) and (c) are beyond you, by then it is too late to change your mind and do another question.

When reviewing the requirements look at how many marks have been allocated to each part. This will give you an idea of how detailed your answer must be.

Generally, you need to be aware of your strengths and weaknesses and select accordingly.

Doing the exam

Actually doing the exam is a personal experience. There is not a single *right way*. As long as you submit complete answers to question 1 and any two from questions 2 to 4 after the three hours are up, then your approach obviously works.

Looking through the paper

The compulsory case study question is, as will always be the case, on groups, in this case, disposal of a subsidiary. You also have some foreign currency transactions and a ten marker on human capital management. In Section B you have three questions on a variety of topics:

- Question 2 a wide ranging question covering the accounting implications of various policies.
- Question 3 is a multi-standard question, covering leasing, financial instruments, impairment and revenue recognition.
- Question 4 is on the management commentary.

You only have to answer three out of these four questions. You don't have to pick your optional questions right now, but this brief overview should have convinced you that you have enough choice and variety to have a respectable go at Section B. So let's go back to the compulsory question in Section A.

Compulsory question

Question 1 requires you to prepare a consolidated balance sheet for a group in which there has been a disposal. Additional complications are presentation of non-current assets held for sale, a debt instrument and an impairment loss. The key with this question, which you cannot avoid doing, is not to panic. There is a lot of number crunching, and you might not be able to complete the question. The thing to do is to set out your proformas and then patiently, but briskly, work through the workings, doing as much as you can. By using a strategy of picking the low hanging 'fruit' you could get 80% of the group aspects right which enables you to put 22 marks in the bank!

Optional questions

Deciding between the optional questions is obviously a personal matter – it depends how you have spent your study time.

One thing is clear – the optional questions all contain a discursive element and are all based around a scenario. The Examiner has said that the emphasis in this paper is on giving advice in a practical situation.

The secret is to plan your answer; break it down into bite sized subsections, clearly labelled to help your examiner to quickly conclude you understand the problem and have a logical answer.

Allocating your time

The golden rule is always allocate your time according to the marks for the question in total and for the parts of the question. But be sensible. If (for example) you have committed yourself to answering Question 5, but can think of nothing to say about fair value, you may be better off trying to pick up some extra marks on the questions you can do.

Afterwards

Don't be tempted to do a post mortem on the paper with your colleagues. It will only worry you and them and it's unlikely you'll be able to remember exactly what you wrote anyway. If you really can't resist going over the topics covered in the paper, allow yourself a maximum of half an hour's 'worry time', then put it out of your head! Relax as it's all out of your hands now!

Question 1

Top tips. In order to do Part (a) you need to work out the net assets of the investment disposed of. It is probably best to do the two parts together with a separate sheet for workings. In part (c), try to break the transaction down into its components. The non-refundable deposit is the easiest aspect to deal with.

Easy marks. There are standard consolidation aspects in the calculation of goodwill and retained earnings. The question is constructed so that the basic consolidation calculations are not affected by the adjustments to the financial statements.

Examiner's comment. Generally speaking the performance on this question was quite good.

The main problem areas (part (a) only) were:

- Not adding back the sale proceeds of the shares to the cost of the investment in Plank. Candidates lost very few marks for this minor error. The only problem was that this error created 'negative goodwill' instead of positive goodwill.

- Candidates thought that, because Lateral still had significant influence over Plank after the disposal of shares, that Plank was still a subsidiary. Plank was in fact an associate. This error caused candidates many problems, not least the fact that they spent time consolidating an additional subsidiary.

- Candidates dealt quite well with the debt instrument. However many calculated the interest received based on the fair value and not on the principal amount. Again candidates only lost one mark for this error.

- The calculation of the group reserves was quite poor. The main reason was that this figure was dependent upon other calculations. That is the debt instrument, the post acquisition profit of the associate, the profit on the sale of shares and other adjustments. Thus errors earlier in the question would be compounded in this figure. Credit was given for the correct methodology even if the figures were inaccurate.

- The minority interest was normally calculated incorrectly as the profit and the depreciation on 'held for sale' assets was often not taken into account. Again marks were given if the principle used was sound.

Marking scheme

		Marks
(a)	Gain/loss on sale of shares	4
(b)	Plant and equipment	4
	Associate	4
	Investment	4
	Goodwill	7
	Sundry assets and liabilities	2
	Retained earnings	5
	Minority interests	2
(c)	Plant and machinery	
	Deposit	3
	Cash flow hedge	3
	Bond	3
	Forward contract	3
(d)	Nature of current information	5
	Visibility	5
	Available	54
	Maximum	50

(a) **Gain on the sale of shares in Plank**

	$m
Sale proceeds	180.0
Less net assets disposed of (20% × 847.6) (W3)	(169.5)
Less goodwill not yet written off (100/300 × 12) (W2)	(4.0)
Profit on disposal	6.5

(b) LATERAL GROUP
CONSOLIDATED BALANCE SHEET AT 31 OCTOBER 20X5

	$m	$m
Assets		
Non-current assets		
Property, plant and equipment (W6)		1,098
Investment in associate (W3)		347
Held to maturity investments (W7)		33
Intangible assets: goodwill (W2)		60
		1,538
Current assets		
Inventories	385	
Trade receivables	250	
Cash and cash equivalents	70	
		705
Total assets		2,243
Equity and liabilities		
Equity attributable to equity holders of the parent		
Share capital		400
Retained earnings (W5)		958
		1,358
Minority interest (W4)		105
Total equity		1,463
Non-current liabilities		310
Current liabilities		470
Total equity and liabilities		2,243

Workings

1   *Group structure*

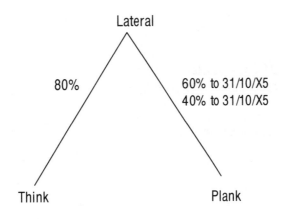

2   *Goodwill*

	Think $m	Think $m	Plank $m	Plank $m
Cost of investment per individual balance sheets		380		340
Sale proceeds				180
Cost of combination		380		520
Less net assets acquired				
Share capital	250		500	
Retained earnings	150		210	
Fair value adjustments (800 – 710)	–		90	
	400		800	
Group share: 80%		(320)		
60%				(480)
Goodwill		60		40
Impairment		–		(28)
		60		12

Note. IAS 36 prohibits the reversal of impairment losses on goodwill.

3   *Investment in associate: Plank*

	$m
Cost of associate (520 × 200/300)	346.7
Share of post acquisition retained reserves ((290 – 210 – 32.4 fair value) × 40%)	19.0
Less: impairment of investment in associate (200/300 × 28)	(18.7)
	347.0

Fair value adjustments

	At acq'n 1.11.X3 $m	Movement	$m	At b/s date 31.10.X5 $m
Plant and equipment	90	(20% × 90)	(18.0)	
		(20% × (90 – 18))	(14.4)	
	90		(32.4)	57.6

4   *Minority interests*

Net asset at balance sheet date: Think

	31.10.X5 $m
Share capital	250
Retained earnings	280
Unrealised profit on 'held for sale' assets	(5)
Depreciation on 'held for sale' assets (10% × 20%)	(2)
	523

Minority share: 20% × 523 = $104.6m

BPP
LEARNING MEDIA

5   *Consolidated retained earnings*

	Lateral $m	*Think* $m	*Plank* $m
At 31 October 20X5	850	280	290
At acquisition		(150)	(210)
		130	80
Additional depreciation on fair value adjustment (W3)			(32.4)
Profit on sale of shares in Plank in parent's books			
(180 − (100/300 × 520))	6.7		
Unrealised profit on 'held for sale' assets (15 − 10)		(5)	
Depreciation on 'held for sale' assets (10 × 20%)		(2)	
Gain on debt instrument (W7)	2.6		
	859.3	123	47.6
Share of Think (80% × 123)	98.4		
Share of Plank (40% × 47.6)	19.0		
Impairment of goodwill on Plank (200/300 × 28)	(18.7)		
	958.0		

6   *Property, plant and equipment*

The 'held for sale' assets reported in the balance sheet of Think are not 'held for sale' in the group as a whole and should therefore be included in the consolidated balance sheet at their carrying value less depreciation for the year ended 31 October 20X5.

	$m
Lateral	700
Think	390
Held for sale assets at carrying value	10
Less depreciation for year (20% × 10)	(2)
	1,098

7   *Held to maturity investment*

IAS 39 requires that this is measured at amortised cost at 31 October 20X5.

	20X3/4 $m	*20X4/5* $m
At beginning of year	30.00	31.24
Interest (10%)	3.00	3.12
Interest received (4.7%)	(1.76)	(1.76)
At end of year	31.24	32.60

Therefore the investment is carried at $32.6 million and there is a gain of $2.6 million in consolidated retained earnings.

(c)   The first part of this transaction involves a **non-refundable deposit** of €1 million paid on 31 July 20X6. As this is a non-refundable deposit it is **not a monetary item** and therefore should be **translated** and included in the balance sheet as an asset as part of property, plant and equipment at $625,000 (€1m/1.6). This will **not be retranslated** at the year end.

The company then had to make a decision about how to deal with the risk surrounding the fact that it would be required to pay €3 million on 30 June 20X7. The option that was chosen was to invest in the €3 million bond on 31 July 20X6 and to sell it on 30 June 20X7 in order to fund the purchase of the property, plant and equipment.

Initially the bond will be recognised on 31 July 20X6 at $1.9 million (€3m/1.6). This bond is classified as at fair value through profit or loss*, but as the bond has a coupon rate of 4% which is the same as the market rate then its fair value will be the same as its carrying value, ie €3 million. However as a monetary item the bond must be **retranslated at the closing rate of exchange** at 31 October 20X6 to $2.3 million (€3 m/1.3) and the exchange gain of $0.4 million ($2.3m − 1.9m) must be taken to the income statement. There will also be accrued interest on the bond of €30,000 (€3m × 4% × 3/12) which will be translated at the average rate in the income statement at $20,000 and at the closing rate as accrued income in the balance at $23,000.

In the year to 31 October 20X7 the effect of the bond will depend upon the movement in interest rates. As the bond is a fixed interest rate investment, its value will be **dependent upon the movement in interest rates**. If interest rates increase then the bond will reduce in value. Therefore by purchasing the bond the company has exposed itself to interest rate risk. To **eliminate this interest rate risk** then the company could enter into an **interest rate swap agreement** to exchange its fixed rate interest receipts for floating rate interest receipts. If this were to happen then the interest rate swap would be designated as a **hedging instrument** of the bond.

If the company had alternatively entered into a **forward contract** to purchase the €3 million for $2 million then **initially** (at 31 July 20X6) this contract would have a fair value of **zero**. At the year end (31 October 20X6) the forward contract should be revalued to its fair value:

On the open market €3m would cost
€3m/1.3 = $2.3

Under the forward contract, €3m costs= $2m

Gain on forward contract $0.3m

Under IAS 39, for hedge accounting to be applied, the hedge must be between 80% and 120% effective. Therefore we need to calculate the gain/loss on the hedged item (the purchase of the fixed asset) to test the effectiveness.

Amount expected to pay as at 31 October 20X6 : €3m/1.3 =	$2.3m
Amount expected to pay out at year end 31.10.X6 : €3m/1.6 =	$1.9m
Loss	$0.4m

Therefore effectiveness is $0.3m/$0.4m = 75%.

This falls outside the required effectiveness, which must be between 80% and 120%. Therefore the contract cannot be treated as a cash flow hedge, and should be treated as a normal financial asset at fair value through profit and loss. The gain on the forward contract should be posted to the income statement.

DEBIT	Financial asset	$0.3m
CREDIT	Income statement	£0.3m

*__BPP note__: The fair value option has been restricted and the bond could only be treated this way if it met the definition of 'held for trading'.

(d)   Although many large companies disclose information about 'Human Capital Management' the **type and level of disclosure varies**. In some countries, such as the UK, there are **legal requirements** to disclose information such as **employee numbers, policies relating to equal opportunities, information on disabled employees** and **staff remuneration**. Companies often adopt a '**checklist' approach**, often disclosing only the **minimum amount** of information required. Other companies may be more proactive. In practice, publishing information about human capital management **can enhance the reputation of a company** and **help it to recruit and retain high quality staff**.

The company wishes to help stakeholders to **understand the link** between its **performance** and **the way that it manages its employees**. As well as **information on equal opportunities** and **health and safety** at work it could disclose the following:

(i)   a **description** of the company's **policies** relating to the **recruitment, retention and motivation of employees**

(ii)   employee **numbers** and other appropriate information about the **composition of the workforce**

(iii)   details of **staff remuneration**

(iv)   details of **amounts invested** in **training** and **developing employees** and also **descriptions** of the company's **policies and practices** in this area

(v)   a description of the way in which the company ensures **management succession**.

Information should be provided **consistently** from period to period and should be **comparable with previous periods**. This means that the company will need to develop **key performance indicators.**

The most obvious vehicle for these disclosures is the **Operating and Financial Review (Management Discussion and Analysis)** as this is management's analysis of the key factors and risks affecting the company's performance. Many companies also publish **separate social or employee reports,** which can be targeted at particular stakeholder groups, such as investors or current and potential employees and the general public.

Question 2

Top tips. This was a wide ranging question, requiring you to set out the financial reporting implications of certain future plans that a company was considering. The question required quite detailed knowledge of certain accounting standards although a good mark could be attained by outlining the main areas of concern. Retirement benefits, revenue recognition, investment properties, impairment and reverse acquisitions were examined.

Easy marks. The advantage of this kind of question is that if you are on shaky ground on one area you can gain marks on another. To that extent it is easier than a question on a single topic. Easy marks were available for setting out the principles underlying the problem, for using the report format and for clarity of the report.

Examiner's comment. This question was well answered, because candidates obtained the easy marks available.

Marking scheme

		Marks
Reverse acquisition	4	
Preference capital	2	
Loan notes	3	
Retirement benefits	5	
Revenue recognition	5	
Investment properties	3	
Impairment review	4	
Report	3	
Available	29	
Maximum		25

REPORT

To: Directors of Barking

From:

Subject: Financial reporting implications of plans for the financial statements for the year ended 30 November 20X4

Date: December 20X3

I set out below my comments on the financial reporting implications of your future plans.

(a)   **Acquisition of Ash**

This type of acquisition is known as a **'reverse acquisition'**. Technically it is Ash which acquires Barking and the **legal form of the transaction is that Ash is the parent**. However, Ash will issue a large number of shares to the shareholders of Barking and the **directors of Barking will control the acquired entity**. The **substance** of the transaction is that **Barking is the acquirer.**

IFRS 3 *Business combinations* applies to the acquisition and states that **Barking will be treated as the acquirer** for the purpose of the consolidated financial statements. This means that the **assets and liabilities of Ash**, rather than the assets and liabilities of Barking are **remeasured to fair value**; the **retained earnings and equity balances of Barking are not revalued**. The **equity shares issued by Ash** must be **included in the cost of the combination** at their **fair value** at the date of exchange.

Part of the purchase consideration will be in the form of **zero rated preference shares** and **interest free loan notes. Both** of these **must be included in the cost of the combination at their fair value**. The preference shares are redeemable and therefore must be treated as **liabilities, not equity**. IAS 39 *Financial instruments: recognition and measurement* requires them to be carried at **amortised cost**. Although there is no interest charge as such **there is a finance cost**, because the shares will be **redeemed at a premium** and a **finance cost must be recognised in the income statement for the year ended 30 November 20X4**. This is **based on the effective interest rate**. The discounted redemption proceeds could be taken as the fair value of the shares if there is no market price that can be used.

The **loan rates are** convertible debt. Although it is likely that they will be converted, rather than redeemed, this does not mean they should all be included in equity. Following IAS 32 *Financial instruments: presentation*, the equity and liability components must be classified separately. This is done by deducting the value for the liability component from the value for the instrument as a whole, leaving a residual value for the equity component.

(b)   **Pension schemes**

The defined benefit pension scheme of Barking is to be frozen. Under IAS 19 *Employee benefits*, an **estimate of the present value of the scheme** is made and **recognised in the balance sheet** of the company. Because there will be **no new entrants** to the scheme, the **current service cost will probably increase** as the present members grow older and get nearer to retirement age.

The **defined contribution scheme** will present few accounting problems. The **cost** of providing pensions is the **amount of the contributions payable in the current period**. The employer has no further obligations.

Ash's defined benefit pension scheme will also be frozen. There is an added complication here because the existing scheme is a **multi-employer plan**. IAS 19 states that where (as in this case) it is **not possible to identify the company's share of the underlying assets and liabilities** in the scheme, **a defined benefit scheme can be accounted for as if it were a defined contribution scheme**. The fact that this has been done must be **disclosed** in the notes to the financial statements; the company will also have to disclose any available information about the **existence of a surplus or deficit** in the scheme that may affect future contributions; and the **basis used** to determine that surplus or deficit and the **implications, if any, for the company**. Ash will need to **determine the net assets** of the scheme in order to establish the net asset or liability that will be recognised when the employees are transferred to the new scheme.

BPP
LEARNING MEDIA

(c) **Revenue recognition and investment properties**

IAS 18 *Revenue* states that revenue for the sale of goods **cannot be recognised before** the entity has **transferred the significant risks and rewards** of ownership to the buyer. Where property is sold, this is **normally when legal title passes** to the buyer. Although the new policy will mean that revenue is recognised at a **later stage than previously** it allows revenue from the sale of a property to be **recognised before there is a legal contract**. The deposit is **refundable** and this **suggests that there is not yet a legal contract**. It is necessary to look at the various acts which have to be performed under a sales contract. It may be possible to **recognise revenue when cash is received**, but **only if there are no substantial acts still to be performed**. It is also necessary to **look at industry practice** as users of the financial statements will need to be able to **compare Barking's performance with that of other companies in the same sector**.

It is **not appropriate** to **recognise legal costs as an asset**. They **do not qualify** either as **development expenditure** or as **any other intangible asset**. They represent **expenses** of the company and should be treated as such.

IAS 40 *Investment property* states that **transfers** to or from investment property **can only be made when there is a change of use**, for example, where the company starts to lease a property under an operating lease. Assuming that this is the case, any **difference between the fair value of the property at the date of transfer and its previous carrying amount should be recognised in the income statement**.

(d) **Impairment review**

An impairment review **compares the carrying value of assets with their recoverable amount. Recoverable amount** is the **higher of fair value less costs to sell and value in use**. Because there has been an upturn in the property market, **fair value less costs to sell is likely to be higher than recoverable amount** and there will be **no impairment** and no need to calculate value in use.

However, there will be potential **problems if it is necessary to calculate value in use**. IAS 36 *Impairment of assets* states that cash flow projections should cover a **maximum of five years** unless a longer period can be justified; it is planned to use a period of ten years. The proposed discount rate of 15% appears **high**, particularly in view of the long time period to be used and it is **likely to produce inaccurate figures**. It is possible that a **shorter period and a lower discount rate will have to be used**.

Impairment losses are normally **recognised in the income statement**, but where properties have been **revalued upwards** any loss should **first be set against the revaluation surplus** in equity (the revaluation reserve) with **only the excess being taken to the income statement**.

Question 3

Top tips. As this is a multi-issue question, it is important to allocate your time sensibly between the different aspects. Do not spend too long on Gow's net assets at the expense of Glass's.

Easy marks. Part (a) is straightforward. Marks can be gained for backing up your arguments even if you come to the wrong conclusion.

Marking scheme

		Marks
(a)	Nature of relationship and accounting treatment	5
(b)	Impairment and calculation	7
	IAS 39	3
	Lease	5
	Revenue	4
	Issues with values contributed	2
	Available	26
	Maximum	25

(a) IAS 31 *Interests in joint ventures* defines a joint venture as a contractual arrangement between two or more parties that undertake an economic activity that is subject to joint control on a long-term basis. Control is defined as the power to direct the financial and operating policies of the entity with a view to gaining economic benefits from its activities. Joint control in turn is where none of the entities alone can control the joint venture but together they can do so and decisions on financial and operating policy, economic performance and financial position require each venturer's consent.

On the face of it, it would appear that York is a joint venture jointly controlled by Gow and Glass. Both venturers appear to have joint control and have contributed assets and other resources to the joint venture. The only issue however is that there is **no written contract** and the definition of a joint venture is that it is a contractual arrangement. However, the **substance of the arrangement** should be considered and with the **minutes** of the discussions about the setting up of the venture being formally approved by both companies this would certainly **imply a contractual arrangement**.

In terms of the accounting for such a joint venture it should be **either the proportionate consolidation method or the equity method** which should be used in the group accounts of both Gow and Glass.

(b) **Gow's net assets**

The loss of the only customer of the power station (a cash generating unit) would be an **indicator** of a possible impairment of that cash generating unit. Therefore according to IAS 36 *Impairment of assets* an **impairment test** must be carried out on the power station. The power station has a current carrying value of $20 million. This must be **compared to the recoverable amount** of the power station which is the higher of the power station's fair value less costs to sell and its value in use.

The fair value less costs to sell is the potential sale proceeds (offer of $16m) less the disposal costs ($1m). The value in use is the discounted value of the expected future cash flows from the power station. The future dismantling costs of $5 million must also be included in this calculation as it has been agreed with the government that this will take place therefore it is a liability.

Carrying value = $20 million

Fair value less costs to sell = $16 million – $1 million = $15 million
Value in use (W1) = $21 million

Therefore the recoverable amount is the higher of $21 million and $15 million. As this recoverable amount of $21 million is actually higher than the carrying value of the power station ($20 million) then there is **no impairment**. The discounted present value must be shown as a long term provision and as part of the cost of land and buildings.

There is however a further issue with Gow's assets and that is the debt from Race. IAS 39 *Financial instruments: recognition and measurement* states that **financial assets must be assessed at each balance sheet date for impairment**. It is highly likely that the **debt from Race is impaired** as Race has gone into receivership. The value of the amount to be received is the anticipated cash from the final settlement. As the cash is not likely to be received for a year then it should be discounted.

Value of receivable (W2) = $3.8 million

A further factor here is that the **value of the contract with Race** shown as an intangible asset will now be **zero**.

Glass's net assets

The building **remains an asset** of the joint venture and there is no reason to alter its carrying value. However, its **remaining useful life will change** and the future depreciation charges will be $2 million each year for the next two years. As this is a change in estimate it is accounted for **prospectively not retrospectively**. Therefore this **does not affect the current balance sheet**.

The lease liability must be assessed under IAS 39 to determine whether it is to be derecognised. In this case there is a change to the lease term but it **will not be derecognised**. The lease liability, however, will change and will be measured at the **present value of the future cash payments**.

Value of lease liability (W3) = $£1.1 million

The **lease receivable is also extinguished** as this is the payment of $1 million on 31 October 20X6.

IAS 38 states that if intangible non-current assets are to be recognised in the balance sheet they must give a right to future economic benefits, be capable of being disposed of separately from the business and have a readily ascertainable market value. The **payment to the agency of $0.5 million** does not meet any of these criteria and **cannot be recognised as an intangible asset** and must be removed from the balance sheet.

The terms of the contract with the overseas retailer can in fact be split into **two separate contracts** in accordance with IAS 18 *Revenue*. There is one contract to provide gas to the overseas retailer and the income from this will be accounted for in the normal way when gas is supplied. The other element of the contract is not to supply gas to any other company in that country over the four year period. Therefore the **$1.5 million deposit** received should not be taken to the income statement immediately but spread over the four year period. The deposit should not have been deducted from intangible assets but instead should be shown as **deferred income**.

Intangible assets (W4) = $3m
Deferred income (W5) = $1.5m

BALANCE SHEET OF YORK AS AT 31 OCTOBER 20X6

	$m	$m
Land and buildings (9 + 4 + 4) (W1)		17.0
Intangible assets (W4)		3.0
		20.0
Current assets		
Inventory		
Receivables (W2)	6.0	
Cash (1 + 10)	3.8	
	11.0	
Total assets		20.8
		40.8
Share capital		
Reserves (bal fig)		30.0
		4.2
Lease liability (W3)		1.1
Long-term provision (W1)		4.0
Deferred income (W5)		1.5
		40.8

Workings

1   *Value in use – power station*

	$m
Cash flow	
31 Oct 20X7 $\left(6 \times \dfrac{1}{1.06}\right)$	5.7
31 Oct 20X8 $\left(7 \times \dfrac{1}{1.06^2}\right)$	6.2
31 Oct 20X9 $\left(8 \times \dfrac{1}{1.06^3}\right)$	6.7
31 Oct 20Y0 $\left((8-5) \times \dfrac{1}{1.06^4}\right)$	2.4
	21.0

The dismantling costs must also be discounted and added into the value of property, plant and equipment $5 million $\times \dfrac{1}{1.06^4}$ 0.792 = $4 million

2   *Value of receivable – Race*

Discounted present value = $5 million $\times$ 80% $\times$ 1/1.06
                           = $3.8 million

3   *Value of lease payable*

$0.6 million $\times$ 1/1.07   = $0.56 million
$0.6 million $\times$ 1/(1.07 $\times$ 1.07) = $0.52 million
                            $1.08 rounded to $1.1 million

4   *Intangible assets in Glass*

	$m
Per balance sheet	2.0
Less agency fee	(0.5)
Add value of overseas deposit	1.5
	3.0

5   *Deferred income*

Deposit from overseas retailer = $1.5 million

BPP
LEARNING MEDIA

Question 4

> **Top tips**. In part (b), make full use of the information in the question, but do not simply regurgitate it.
>
> **Easy marks**. Part (a) is very straightforward book work. Part (b) also has easy marks for style and layout.

Marking scheme

			Marks
(a)	Principle		6
	Mandatory discussion		7
		Available/ maximum	13
(b)	Principal risks		9
	Treasury policies		3
		Available/ maximum	12
	Style and presentation		2
		Available	27
		Maximum	25

(a) In 2005, the IASB issue a discussion paper *Management Commentary*, which is the international equivalent of the UK's Operating and Financial Review. The purpose of these statements is to explain the main factors underlying a company's **financial position and performance**. The principles and objectives of a Management Commentary (MC) are as follows:

  (i) It is specifically prepared **for the shareholders of the company** not for investors in general, although it may be of interest to other parties.

  (ii) The MC **reflects the directors' view** of the business.

  (iii) It should be a **clear and balanced analysis** of the strategic position and direction of the business which should help members to assess those strategies and their potential for success.

  (iv) The MC should **be forward looking** and should identify those trends and factors that will help members to assess the current and future performance of the business.

  (v) Members should be **warned** that some information is not verifiable and of **any uncertainties** underpinning the information.

  (vi) The MC should **complement** the financial statements by providing useful financial and non-financial information which is not to be found in the financial statements.

  (vii) The MC should provide **all information** that might reasonably be expected **to influence** the shareholders.

  (viii) The MC should be **balanced and neutral** and deal equally with favourable and unfavourable information.

  (ix) The MC and key performance indicators should be comparable over time.

The arguments for a mandatory MC are largely to do with content and comparability. It is argued that a mandatory MC will make it easier for companies themselves to judge what is required in such a report and the required standard of reporting, thereby making such reports more **robust, transparent and comparable**. If an MC is not mandatory then there may be **uncertainty** as to content and the possibility of **misinformation**. There is also the risk that without a mandatory MC directors may take a **minimalist**

approach to disclosure which will make the MC less useful and the information to be disclosed will be in hands of senior executives and directors.

However, the **arguments against** a mandatory MC are that it could **stifle the development of the MC as a tool** for communication and may lead to a **checklist approach** to producing it. It is argued that a mandatory MC is not required as market forces and the needs of investors should lead to companies feeling the pressure to provide a useful and reliable report.

(b)

Jones and Cousin
Annual Report 20X6
Management Commentary

Introduction

Jones and Cousin is a public quoted company and the group develops, manufactures and markets products in the medical sector. This report is designed to assist members of the group in understanding and assessing the strategies of the group and the potential success of these strategies.

Risks

The group faces a number of risks which will be considered under the headings of:

- Market risk
- Product risk
- Currency risk

Market risk

The market in which the group operates is quite fiercely competitive and contains a number of different competitors including specialised and large international corporations. There is the risk that any technical advances or product innovations by these competitors could adversely affect the group's profits. Also this element of competition also means that there is a risk of loss of market share or lower than expected sales growth which could affect the share price.

The sector in which the group operates is heavily monitored by local governments and the group's share of revenue in a market sector is often determined by government policy. The group is therefore heavily dependent upon governments providing the funds for health care. Any reduction in funds by governments would almost certainly lead to a fall in revenue for the group.

Product risk

The products of the group are essentially a low health risk. However, there is always the possibility of a problem with products which may lead to legal action which would be costly and damage the group's reputation and goodwill. The industry is highly regulated in terms of both medical and environmental laws. Any such claims would have an adverse effect on sales, profit and share price.

There will always be innovations in this market sector and the group is careful to protect its products with patents and will enter into legal proceedings where necessary to protect those patents. There is also the problem of infringing the patents of others. If claims were brought for infringement of patents of other companies this would be costly and damaging and alternative products would have to be found.

There are constantly new products being developed by the group which is costly in terms of research and development expenditure. Product innovation may not always be successful and this highly regulated market may not always gain the regulatory approval required.

Currency risk

The group operates in twenty-seven different countries and earns revenue and incurs costs in several different currencies. Although the dollar is the group's functional currency only 5% of its business is in the country of incorporation. Therefore exchange fluctuations in the main currencies in which it trades may have a material effect on the group's profits and cash flows.

Relationships

The group has a positive ethical programme. It sources its products from a wide range of suppliers largely in the form of long term contracts for the supply of goods. The group has a policy of ensuring that such suppliers are suitable from both qualitative and ethical perspectives.

The group has a set of corporate and social responsibility principles for which the Board of Directors is responsible. The risks that the group bears from these responsibilities are managed by the Managing Director. The group operates in many geographical areas and encourages its subsidiaries to help local communities to reinvest in local educational projects. Great care is taken by the group to ensure that obsolete products are disposed of responsibly and safely. Wherever possible reusable materials are used.

Group policy is to attract and retain employees and to maintain an equal opportunities policy for all employees. To this end employees regularly receive in-house training and are kept informed of management policies.

Treasury policies

The group uses derivative products to protect against both currency risk and interest rate risk. This is done by the used of fixed rate currency swaps and using floating to fixed rate interest rate swaps. All financial instruments are accounted for as cash flow hedges which means that gains and losses are recognised initially in reserves and are only released to the income statement when the hedged item also affects the income statement.

ACCA

Paper P2

Corporate Reporting (International)

Mock Examination 3:

Pilot Paper

Question Paper	
Time allowed	
Reading and planning	**15 minutes**
Writing	**3 hours**
This paper is divided into two sections	
Section A	This ONE question is compulsory and MUST be attempted
Section B	TWO questions ONLY to be answered

DO NOT OPEN THIS PAPER UNTIL YOU ARE READY TO START UNDER EXAMINATION CONDITIONS

Pilot paper

Paper P2

Corporate Reporting (International Stream)

Time allowed

Reading and planning: 15 minutes
Writing: 3 hours

This paper is divided into two sections:

Section A – This ONE question is compulsory and MUST be attempted

Section B – TWO questions ONLY to be attempted

Do NOT open this paper until instructed by the supervisor.

During reading and planning time only the question paper may be annotated. You must NOT write in your answer booklet until instructed by the supervisor.

This question paper must not be removed from the examination hall.

Warning

The pilot paper cannot cover all of the syllabus nor can it include examples of every type of question that will be included in the actual exam. You may see questions in the exam that you think are more difficult than any you see in the pilot paper.

SECTION A: This question is compulsory and MUST be attempted

Question 1

The following draft financial statements relate to Zambeze, a public limited company:

ZAMBEZE
DRAFT GROUP BALANCE SHEETS AT 30 JUNE

	20X6	20X5
	$m	$m
Assets:		
Non-current assets		
Property, plant and equipment	1,315	1,005
Goodwill	30	25
Investment in associate	270	290
	1,615	1,320
Current assets		
Inventories	650	580
Trade receivables	610	530
Cash at bank and cash equivalents	50	140
	1,310	1,250
Total assets	2,925	2,570
Equity and liabilities		
Equity		
Share capital	100	85
Share premium account	30	15
Revaluation reserve	50	145
Retained earnings	254	250
	434	495
Minority interest	60	45
Total equity	494	540
Non-current liabilities	850	600
Current liabilities	1,581	1,430
Total liabilities	2,431	2,030
Total equity and liabilities	2,925	2,570

BPP
LEARNING MEDIA

ZAMBEZE
DRAFT GROUP INCOME STATEMENT FOR THE YEAR ENDED 30 JUNE 20X6

	$m
Revenue	4,700
Cost of sales	(3,400)
Gross profit	1,300
Distribution and administrative expenses	(600)
Finance costs (interest payable)	(40)
Share of profit in associate	20
Profit before tax	680
Income tax expense	(200)
Profit for the period	480
Attributable to	
Equity holders of the parent	455
Minority interest	25
	480

ZAMBEZE
DRAFT GROUP STATEMENT OF RECOGNISED INCOME AND EXPENSES
FOR THE YEAR ENDED 30 JUNE 20X6

	$m
Foreign exchange difference of associate	(5)
Impairment losses on property, plant and equipment offset against revaluation surplus	(95)
Net expense recognised in equity	(100)
Profit for period	455
Total recognised income and expense	355

ZAMBEZE
DRAFT STATEMENT OF CHANGES IN EQUITY FOR THE YEAR ENDED 30 JUNE 20X6

	$m
Balance at 1 July 20X5	540
Total recognised income and expense for the period	355
Change in minority interest	15
Dividends paid	(446)
Issue of share capital	30
Balance at 30 June 20X6	494

The following relates to Zambeze:

(i)   Zambeze acquired a seventy per cent holding in Damp, a public limited company, on 1 July 20X5. The fair values of the net assets acquired were as follows:

	$m
Property, plant and equipment	70
Inventories and work in progress	90
	160

The purchase consideration was $100 million in cash and $25 million (discounted value) deferred consideration which is payable on 1 July 20X6. The difference between the discounted value of the deferred consideration ($25 million) and the amount payable ($29 million) is included in 'interest payable'. Zambeze wants to set up a provision for reconstruction costs of $10 million retrospectively on the acquisition of Damp. This provision has not yet been set up.

(ii)   There had been no disposals of property, plant and equipment during the year. Depreciation for the period charged in cost of sales was $60 million.

(iii)   Current liabilities comprised the following items:

	20X6 $m	20X5 $m
Trade payables	1,341	1,200
Interest payable	50	45
Taxation	190	185
	1,581	1,430

(iv)   Non-current liabilities comprised the following:

	20X5 $m	20X6 $m
Deferred consideration – purchase of Damp	29	–
Liability for the purchase of property, plant and equipment	144	–
Loans repayable	621	555
Deferred tax liability	30	25
Retirement benefit liability	26	20
	850	600

(v)   The retirement benefit liability comprised the following:

	$m
Movement in year	
Liability at 1 July 20X5	20
Current and past service costs charged to income statement	13
Contributions paid to retirement benefit scheme	(7)
Liability 30 June 20X6	26

There was no actuarial gain or loss in the year.

(vi)   Goodwill was impairment tested on 30 June 20X6 and any impairment was included in the financial statements for the year ended 30 June 20X6.

(vii)   The Finance Director has set up a company, River, through which Zambeze conducts its investment activities. Zambeze has paid $400 million to River during the year and this has been included in dividends paid. The money was invested in a specified portfolio of investments. Ninety five per cent of the profits and one hundred per cent of the losses in the specified portfolio of investments are transferred to Zambeze. An investment manager has charge of the company's investments and owns all of the share capital of River. An agreement between the investment manager and Zambeze sets out the operating guidelines and prohibits the investment manager from obtaining access to the investments for the manager's benefit. An annual transfer of the profit/loss will occur on 30 June annually and the capital will be returned in four years time. The transfer of $400 million cash occurred on 1 January 20X6 but no transfer of profit/loss has yet occurred. The balance sheet of River at 30 June 20X6 is as follows:

RIVER: BALANCE SHEET AT 30 JUNE 20X6

	$m
Investment at fair value through profit or loss	390
	390
Share capital	400
Retained earnings	(10)
	390

BPP
LEARNING MEDIA

Required

(a) Prepare a group cash flow statement for the Zambeze Group for the year ended 30 June 20X6 using the indirect method. **(35 marks)**

(b) Discuss the issues which would determine whether River should be consolidated by Zambeze in the group financial statements. **(9 marks)**

(c) Discuss briefly the importance of ethical behaviour in the preparation of financial statements and whether the creation of River could constitute unethical practice by the finance director of Zambeze. **(6 marks)**

Two marks are available for the quality of the discussion of the issues regarding the consolidation of River and the importance of ethical behaviour.

Section B: TWO questions ONLY to be attempted

Question 2

Electron, a public limited company, operates in the energy sector. The company has grown significantly over the last few years and is currently preparing its financial statements for the year ended 30 June 20X6.

Electron buys and sells oil and currently has a number of oil trading contracts. The contracts to purchase oil are treated as non-current assets and amortised over the contracts' durations. On acceptance of a contract to sell oil, fifty per cent of the contract price is recognised immediately with the balance being recognised over the remaining life of the contract. The contracts always result in the delivery of the commodity.　　**(4 marks)**

Electron has recently constructed an ecologically efficient power station. A condition of being granted the operating licence by the government is that the power station be dismantled at the end of its life which is estimated to be 20 years. The power station cost $100 million and began production on 1 July 20X5. Depreciation is charged on the power station using the straight line method. Electron has estimated at 30 June 20X6 that it will cost $15 million (net present value) to restore the site to its original condition using a discount rate of five per cent. Ninety-five per cent of these costs relate to the removal of the power station and five per cent relates to the damage caused through generating energy.　　**(7 marks)**

Electron has leased another power station, which was relatively inefficient, to a rival company on 30 June 20X6. The beneficial and legal ownership remains with Electron and in the event of one of Electron's power stations being unable to produce energy, Electron can terminate the agreement. The leased power station is being treated as an operating lease with the net present value of the income of $40 million being recognised in profit or loss. The fair value of the power station is $70 million at 30 June 20X6. A deposit of $10 million was received on 30 June 20X6 and it is included in the net present value calculation.

(5 marks)

The company has a good relationship with its shareholders and employees. It has adopted a strategy of gradually increasing its dividend payments over the years. On 1 August 20X6, the board proposed a dividend of 5c per share for the year ended 30 June 20X6. The shareholders will approve the dividend along with the financial statements at the general meeting on 1 September 20X6 and the dividend will be paid on 14 September 20X6. The directors feel that the dividend should be accrued in the financial statements for the year ended 30 June 20X6 as a 'valid expectation' has been created.　　**(3 marks)**

The company granted share options to its employees on 1 July 20X5. The fair value of the options at that date was $3 million. The options vest on 30 June 20X8. The employees have to be employed at the end of the three year period for the options to vest and the following estimates have been made:

Estimated percentage of employees leaving during vesting period at:

Grant date 1 July 20X5	5%	
30 June 20X6	6%	**(4 marks)**
Effective communication to the directors		**(2 marks)**

Required

Draft a report suitable for presentation to the directors of Electron which discusses the accounting treatment of the above transactions in the financial statements for the year ended 30 June 20X6, including relevant calculations.

(Total = 25 marks)

Question 3

The following balance sheet relates to Kesare Group, a public limited company, at 30 June 20X6.

	$'000
Assets	
Non current assets:	
Property, plant and equipment	10,000
Goodwill	6,000
Other intangible assets	5,000
Financial assets (cost)	9,000
	30,000
Current assets	
Trade receivables	7,000
Other receivables	4,600
Cash and cash equivalents	6,700
	18,300
Total assets	48,300
Equity and liabilities	
Equity	
Share capital	9,000
Other reserves	4,500
Retained earnings	9,130
Total equity	22,630
Non-current liabilities	
Long term borrowings	10,000
Deferred tax liability	3,600
Employee benefit liability	4,000
Total non-current liabilities	17,600
Current liabilities	
Current tax liability	3,070
Trade and other payables	5,000
Total current liabilities	8,070
Total liabilities	25,670
Total equity and liabilities	48,300

The following information is relevant to the above balance sheet:

(i) The financial assets are classified as 'available for sale' but are shown in the above balance sheet at their cost on 1 July 20X5. The market value of the assets is $10.5 million on 30 June 20X6. Taxation is payable on the sale of the assets.

(ii) The stated interest rate for the long term borrowing is 8 per cent. The loan of $10 million represents a convertible bond which has a liability component of $9.6 million and an equity component of $0.4 million. The bond was issued on 30 June 20X6.

(iii) The defined benefit plan had a rule change on 1 July 20X5. Kesare estimate that of the past service costs of $1 million, 40 per cent relates to vested benefits and 60 per cent relates to benefits that will vest over the next five years from that date. The past service costs have not been accounted for.

(iv)   The tax bases of the assets and liabilities are the same as their carrying amounts in the balance sheet at 30 June 20X6 except for the following:

(1)

	$'000
Property, plant and equipment	2,400
Trade receivables	7,500
Other receivables	5,000
Employee benefits	5,000

(2)   Other intangible assets were development costs which were all allowed for tax purposes when the cost was incurred in 20X5.

(3)   Trade and other payables includes an accrual for compensation to be paid to employees. This amounts to $1 million and is allowed for taxation when paid.

(v)   Goodwill is not allowable for tax purposes in this jurisdiction.

(vi)   Assume taxation is payable at 30%.

Required

(a)   Discuss the conceptual basis for the recognition of deferred taxation using the temporary difference approach to deferred taxation.   **(7 marks)**

(b)   Calculate the deferred tax liability at 30 June 20X6 after any necessary adjustments to the financial statements showing how the deferred tax liability would be dealt with in the financial statements. (Assume that any adjustments do not affect current tax. Candidates should briefly discuss the adjustments required to calculate deferred tax liability.)   **(18 marks)**

(Total = 25 marks)

Two marks will be awarded for the quality of the discussion of the conceptual basis of deferred taxation in (a).

Question 4

A significant number of entities and countries around the world have adopted International Financial Reporting Standards (IFRS) as their basis for financial reporting, often regarding these as a means to improve the quality of information on corporate performance. However, while the advantages of a common set of global reporting standards are recognised, there are a number of implementation challenges at the international and national levels if the objective of an improved and harmonised reporting system is to be achieved.

Required

(a)   Discuss the implementation challenges faced by the International Accounting Standards Board (IASB) if there is to be a successful move to International Financial Reporting Standards.

(18 marks)

(b)   The International Accounting Standards Board recently issued Exposure Drafts of *Proposed Amendments to IFRS 3 Business combinations* and IAS 27 *Consolidated and separate financial statements.* The proposals radically change the basis of reporting business combinations and transactions with minority interests.

Discuss how the above exposure drafts will fundamentally affect the existing accounting practices for business combinations.   **(7 marks)**

(Total = 25 marks)

Two marks will be awarded for the quality of the discussion of the ideas and information.

Answers

DO NOT TURN THIS PAGE UNTIL YOU HAVE
COMPLETED THE MOCK EXAM

A PLAN OF ATTACK

Managing your nerves

As you turn the pages to start this exam a number of thoughts are likely to cross your mind. At best, examinations cause anxiety so it is important to stay focused on your task for the next three hours! Developing an awareness of what is going on emotionally within you may help you manage your nerves. Remember, you are unlikely to banish the flow of adrenaline, but the key is to harness it to help you work steadily and quickly through your answers.

Working through this mock exam will help you develop the exam stamina you will need to keep going for three hours.

Managing your time

Planning and time management are two of the key skills which complement the technical knowledge you need to succeed. To keep yourself on time, do not be afraid to jot down your target completion times for each question, perhaps next to the title of the question on the paper.

Focusing on scoring marks

When completing written answers, remember to communicate the critical points, which represent marks, and avoid padding and waffle. Sometimes it is possible to analyse a long sentence into more than one point. Always try to maximise the mark potential of what you write.

As you read through the questions, jot down on the question paper, any points you think you might forget. There is nothing more upsetting than coming out of an exam having forgotten to write a point you knew!

Also remember you can only score marks for what is on paper; you must write down enough to help the examiner to give you marks!

Structure and signpost your answers

To help you answer the examiner's requirements, highlight as you read through the paper the key words and phrases in the examiner's requirements.

Also, where possible try to use headings and subheadings, to give a logical and easy-to-follow structure to your response. A well structured and signposted answer is more likely to convince the examiner that you know your subject.

Your approach

This paper has two sections. The first section contains one long case study question which is compulsory. The second has three questions and you must answer two of them.

You have a choice.

- Read through and answer the Section A question before moving on to Section B
- Go through Section B and select the three questions you will attempt. Then go back and answer the question in Section A first
- Select the three questions in Section B, answer them and then go back to Section A

You are allowed 15 minutes before the start of the exam to go through the questions you are going to do.

Time spent at the start of each question confirming the requirements and producing a plan for the answers is time well spent.

Question selection

When selecting the two questions from Section B make sure that you read through all of the requirements. It is painful to answer part (a) of a question and then realise that parts (b) and (c) are beyond you, by then it is too late to change your mind and do another question.

When reviewing the requirements look at how many marks have been allocated to each part. This will give you an idea of how detailed your answer must be.

Generally, you need to be aware of your strengths and weaknesses and select accordingly.

Doing the exam

Actually doing the exam is a personal experience. There is not a single *right way*. As long as you submit complete answers to question 1 and any two from questions 2 to 4 after the three hours are up, then your approach obviously works.

Looking through the paper

The compulsory question is a case study. It starts with a group cash flow statement, then draws on your knowledge of criteria for consolidation, and finally goes into ethical matters. In Section B you have three questions on a variety of topics:

- Question 2 is a multi-standard question dealing with environmental provisions, leasing, EABSD and share-based payment.
- Question 3 is all about deferred tax. Nasty.
- Question 4 is a nice practical question on implementing IFRS with a current issues aspect thrown in.

You only have to answer two out of these three questions. You don't have to pick your optional questions right now, but this brief overview should have convinced you that you have enough choice and variety to have a respectable go at Section B. So let's go back to the compulsory question in Section A.

Compulsory question

Part (a) requires you to prepare a consolidated cash flow statement for a group in which there as been an acquisition. Additional complications include a few misclassifications. Work through Part (a) systematically, but leave plenty of time for parts (b) and (c), where easy marks may be gained.

Optional questions

Deciding between the optional questions is obviously a personal matter – it depends how you have spent your study time.

In our opinion, unless you love deferred tax, avoid question 3. It is easier to pick up marks when the question is on a variety of topics.

One thing is clear – the optional questions all contain a discursive element and are all based around a scenario. The Examiner has said that the emphasis in this paper is on giving advice in a practical situation.

The secret is to plan your answer; break it down into bite sized subsections, clearly labelled to help your examiner to quickly conclude you understand the problem and have a logical answer.

Allocating your time

The golden rule is always allocate your time according to the marks for the question in total and for the parts of the question. But be sensible. If (for example) you have committed yourself to answering Question 5, but can think of nothing to say about fair value, you may be better off trying to pick up some extra marks on the questions you can do.

Afterwards

Don't be tempted to do a post mortem on the paper with your colleagues. It will only worry you and them and it's unlikely you'll be able to remember exactly what you wrote anyway. If you really can't resist going over the topics covered in the paper, allow yourself a maximum of half an hour's 'worry time', then put it out of your head! Relax as it's all out of your hands now!

Question 1

Top tips. Some students don't like group cash flow statements, but they really are a gift. You can simply ignore any complications – at least to start off with – and concentrate on getting the easy marks (see below). Set out your proforma, and, if you can, try to set out your workings in the order shown in our answer. This order has been designed so that the easy workings come first. Part (b) requires straightforward bookwork knowledge of the criteria for consolidation, but also application of this knowledge to the matter of River. Part (c) requires a general discussion of ethical behaviour, but also, more specifically, how these general principles may be applied in the case of River.

Easy marks. Look at the marking scheme for Part (a). There are six marks for operating activities – most of which you know from your non-group cash flow studies at earlier levels. The property plant and equipment working has a few complications, but the same complications come up regularly, so if you learn our working you can't go too far wrong. Tax, interest and dividends are all straightforward. Turning to parts (b) and (c), as indicated above, there are easy marks for a more general discussion, as well as trickier marks for specific application. And write clearly, so you earn those extra two marks for communication.

Marking scheme

		Marks
(a)	Operating activities	6
	Retirement benefit	3
	Associate	3
	Subsidiary treatment	4
	Property, plant and equipment	3
	Goodwill	2
	Minority interest	3
	Taxation	3
	Dividend paid	3
	Interest	2
	River	2
	Issue of shares	1
		35
(b)	Issues	9
(c)	Ethical discussion	3
	River	3
		50

BPP
LEARNING MEDIA

(a)   ZAMBEZE
GROUP CASH FLOW STATEMENT FOR THE YEAR ENDED 30 JUNE 20X6

	$m	$m
Cash flow from operating activities		
Profit before tax	690	
Adjustments for		
Share of profit in associate	(30)	
Depreciation	60	
Impairment of goodwill (W7)	8	
Interest	40	
Retirement benefit expense	13	
	781	
Decrease in inventories (650 – 580 – 90)	20	
Increase in trade receivables (610 – 530)	(80)	
Increase in trade payables (1,341 – 1,200)	141	
Cash generated from operations	862	
Interest paid (W3)	(31)	
Income taxes paid (W4)	(190)	
Contributions paid to retirement benefit scheme	(7)	
Net cash from operating activities		634
Cash flows from investing activities		
Purchase of property, plant and equipment (W1)	(251)	
Purchase of subsidiary	(100)	
Dividends received from associate (W2)	35	
Investment in River	(400)	
Net cash used in investing activities		(716)
Cash flows from financing activities		
Issue of shares	30	
Increase in loans (621 – 555)	66	
Dividends paid (W6)	(46)	
Dividend to minority interest (W5)	(58)	
Net cash used in financing activities		(8)
Decrease in cash and cash equivalents		(90)
Cash and cash equivalents at 1 July 20X5		140
Cash and cash equivalents at 30 June 20X6		50

Workings

1   *Purchase of property, plant and equipment*

PROPERTY, PLANT AND EQUIPMENT

	$m		$m
Balance b/fwd	1,005	Depreciation	60
Payable c/d	144	Impairment losses	95
Acquisition: Damp	70	Balance c/fwd	1,315
Additions (balancing figure)	251		
	1,470		1,470

2   *Dividend received from associate*

INVESTMENT IN ASSOCIATE

	$m		$m
Balance b/fwd	290	Foreign exchange loss	5
Share of profit after tax	20	Dividend received (balancing figure)	35
		Balance c/fwd	270
	310		310

3   *Interest paid*

INTEREST PAYABLE

	$m		$m
Unwinding of discount on purchase (29 – 25)	4	Balance b/fwd	45
		Income statement	40
Cash paid (balancing figure)	31		
Balance c/fwd	50		
	85		85

4   *Income taxes paid*

TAX PAYABLE

	$m		$m
Cash paid (balancing figure)	190	Balance b/fwd	
Balance c/fwd		Current	185
Current	190	Deferred	25
Deferred	30	Income statement	200
	410		410

5   *Dividend paid to minority interests*

MINORITY INTERESTS

	$m		$m
Dividend paid (balancing figure)	58	Balance b/fwd	45
		Acquisition: 30% x 160	48
Balance c/fwd	60	Profit for year	25
	118		118

6   *Dividend paid*

	$
Per SOCIE	446
Less investment in River	400
Dividend paid	46

7   *Impairment of goodwill*

INTANGIBLE ASSET: GOODWILL

	$m		$m
Balance b/fwd	25	Impairment (balancing figure)	8
Acquisition (note)	13	Balance c/fwd	30
	38		38

BPP LEARNING MEDIA

Note: Goodwill on acquisition

	$
Purchase consideration	
Cash	100
Deferred	25
	125
Less group share of identifiable net assets acquired: 70% x 160	(112)
Goodwill	13

(b) The requirement to consolidate an investment is determined by **control**, not merely by ownership. Both IFRS 3 *Business combinations* and IAS 27 *Consolidated and separate financial statements* state that control can usually be assumed to exist when the parent **owns more than half (ie over 50%) of the voting power** of an entity *unless* it can be clearly shown that **such ownership does not constitute control** (these situations will be very rare).

However, IFRS 3 and IAS 27 also list the certain situations where control exists, even when the parent owns only 50% or less of the voting shares of an entity. Control exists if any one of the following apply:

(i) The parent has power over more than 50% of the voting rights by virtue of **agreement with other investors**

(ii) The parent has power to **govern the financial and operating policies** of the entity by statute or under an agreement

(iii) The parent has the power to **appoint or remove a majority of members of the board of directors** (or equivalent governing body)

(iv) The parent has power to cast a **majority of votes at meetings of the board of directors**

Control exists by virtue of having certain powers, regardless whether those powers are actually exercised. Control of decision making is not enough, however: the reporting entity must control the decision making with a view to **obtaining benefits** from the entity over which it has control.

Applying the above criteria to Zambese's relationship with River:

Zambese has power to govern the financial and operating policies of River, through its **operating guidelines.**

The control is exercised with a view to **obtaining financial benefits** from River. Zambese receives 95% of the profits and 100% of the losses of River.

Zambese therefore **controls** River, and **River should be consolidated.**

(c) **Ethical behaviour** in the preparation of financial statements, and in other areas, is of **paramount importance**. This applies equally to preparers of accounts, to auditors and to accountants giving advice to directors. Accountants act unethically if they use "creative" accounting in accounts preparation to make the figures look better, and they act unethically if, in the role of adviser, they fail to point this out.

The creation of River is **a device to keep activities off Zambese's balance sheet**. In hiding the true nature of Zambese's transactions with River, **the directors are acting unethically.** Showing the payment of $400 to river as a dividend is **deliberately misleading,** and may, depending on the laws that apply, be illegal.

The creation of River, and the failure to disclose and account for the transactions properly, puts Zambese's directors **in breach of three important principles** which must apply to the preparation of financial statements:

Compliance with generally accepted accounting principles (GAAP). IAS 27 is not complied with.

Fair presentation, sometimes called the principle of **substance** over form. River is an example of off balance sheet finance, where the form does not reflect the economic substance of the transaction.

Transparency of disclosure. Disclosure must be sufficient for the reader of financial statements to understand fully the nature of the transaction.

The directors must correct this unethical behaviour by consolidating River, and by disclosing the true nature of the payment to River.

Question 2

Top tips. This is a multi-standard question on environmental provisions, leases, proposed dividend and a share option scheme. The good thing about this kind of question is that, even if you don't know all the standards tested, you can get marks for the ones you do know. The question on the power station is similar to one you will have already met in this kit, and you have come across longer, more complicated questions on share-based payment, a favourite topic with this examiner.

Easy marks. The proposed dividend is straightforward, as is the explanation (if not the calculations) for the provision. The treatment of share options provides 4 easy marks for nothing much in the way of complications.

Marking scheme

	Marks
Oil contracts	4
Power station	7
Operating leases	5
Proposed dividend	3
Share options	4
Effective communication	2
Available/Maximum	25

REPORT

To: The Directors, Electron
From: Accountant
Date: July 20X6

Accounting treatment of transactions

The purpose of this report is to explain the accounting treatment required for the following items.

- Oil trading contracts
- Power station
- Operating lease
- Proposed dividend
- Share options

Oil trading contracts

The first point to note is that the contracts always result in the delivery of the commodity. They are therefore correctly treated as normal sale and purchase contracts, **not financial instruments.**

The adoption of a policy of **deferring recognising revenue and costs is appropriate** in general terms because of the duration of the contracts. Over the life of the contracts, costs and revenues are equally matched. However, there is a mismatch between costs and revenues in the early stages of the contracts.

In the first year of the contract, 50% of revenues are recognised immediately. However, costs, in the form of amortisation, are recognised evenly over the duration of the contract. This means that **in the first year, a higher**

BPP
LEARNING MEDIA

proportion of the revenue is matched against a smaller proportion of the costs. It could also be argued that revenue is inflated in the first year.

While there is no detailed guidance on accounting for this kind of contract, IAS 18 *Revenue* and the IASB *Framework* give general guidance. IAS 18 states that revenue and expenses that relate to the same transaction or event should be recognised simultaneously, and the *Framework* says that the "measurement and display of the financial effect of like transactions must be carried out in a consistent way".

It would be advisable, therefore, to match revenue and costs, and to **recognise revenue evenly** over the duration of the contract.

Power station

IAS 37 *Provisions, contingent liabilities and contingent assets* states that a provision should be recognised if:

- There is a present obligation as a result of a past transaction or event and
- It is probable that a transfer of economic benefits will be required to settle the obligation
- A reliable estimate can be made of the amount of the obligation

In this case, the obligating event is the **installation of the power station**. The **operating licence** has created a **legal obligation** to incur the cost of removal, the expenditure is **probable,** and a **reasonable estimate** of the amount can be made.

Because Electron cannot operate its power station without incurring an obligation to pay for removal, **the expenditure also enables it to acquire economic benefits** (income from the energy generated). Therefore Electron correctly **recognises an asset** as well as a provision, and **depreciates this asset over its useful life of 20 years.**

Electron should recognise a provision for the cost of removing the power station, but should not include the cost of rectifying the damage caused by the generation of electricity until the power is generated. In this case the cost of rectifying the damage would be 5% of the total discounted provision.

The accounting treatment is as follows:

BALANCE SHEET AT 30 JUNE 20X6 (EXTRACTS)

	$m
Tangible non-current assets	
Power station	100.0
Decommissioning costs (W)	13.6
	113.6
Depreciation (113.6 ÷ 20)	(5.7)
	107.9
Provisions	
Provision for decommissioning at 1 July 20X5	13.6
Plus unwinding of discount (13.6 × 5%)	0.7
	14.3
Provision for damage (0.7(W)÷20)	0.1
	14.4

INCOME STATEMENT FOR THE YEAR ENDED 30 JUNE 20X6 (EXTRACTS)

	$m
Depreciation	5.7
Provision for damage	0.1
Unwinding of discount (finance cost)	0.7

Working

	$m
Provision for removal costs at 1 July 20X5 (95% × (15 ÷ 1.05))	13.6
Provision for damage caused by extraction at 30 June 20X6	
(5% (15 ÷ 1.05))	0.7

Operating lease

One issue here is the **substance** of the lease agreement. IAS 17 *Leases* classifies leases as either finance leases or operating leases. A finance lease **transfers substantially all the risks and rewards of ownership to the lessee**, while an operating lease does not. The company **retains legal ownership of the equipment** and also **retains the benefits of ownership** (the equipment remains available for use in its operating activities). In addition, the **present value of the minimum lease payments is only 57.1% of the fair value of the leased assets** ($40 million ÷ $70 million). For a lease to be a finance lease, the present value of the minimum lease payments should be **substantially all** the fair value of the leased assets. Therefore the lease **appears to be correctly classified as an operating lease**.

A further issue is the **treatment of the fee received**. The company has recognised the whole of the net present value of the future income from the lease in the income statement for 30 June 20X6, despite the fact that only a deposit of $10 million has been received. In addition, the date of inception of the lease is 30 June 20X6, so **the term of the lease does not actually fall within the current period**. IAS 17 states that **income from operating leases should be recognised on a straight line basis over the lease term** unless another basis is more appropriate. IAS 18 *Revenue* and SIC 27 *Evaluating the substance of transactions involving the legal form of a lease* also apply here. Neither of these allows revenue to be recognised **before an entity has performed under the contract** and therefore **no revenue should be recognised** in relation to the operating leases for the current period.

Proposed dividend

The dividend was **proposed after the balance sheet date** and therefore IAS 10 *Events after the balance sheet date* applies. This **prohibits the recognition of proposed dividends** unless these are declared before the balance sheet date. The directors **did not have an obligation** to pay the dividend **at 31 October 20X5** and therefore there **cannot be a liability**. The directors seem to be arguing that their past record creates a constructive obligation as defined by IAS 37 *Provisions, contingent liabilities and contingent assets*. A constructive obligation may exist as a result of the proposal of the dividend, but this had **not arisen at the balance sheet date**.

Although the proposed dividend is not recognised it was **approved before the financial statements were authorised for issue** and should be **disclosed** in the notes to the financial statements.

Share options

The share options granted on 1 July 20X5 are **equity-settled transactions**, and are governed by IFRS 2 *Share based payment*. The aim of this standard is to recognise the cost of share based payment to employees over the period in which the services are rendered. The options are generally **charged to the income statement** on the basis of their **fair value at the grant date**. If the equity instruments are traded on an active market, market prices must be used. Otherwise an option pricing model would be used.

The conditions attached to the shares state that the share options will vest in three years' time provided that the employees remain in employment with the company. Often there are other conditions such as growth in share price, but here **employment is the only condition**.

The **treatment** is as follows:

- Determine the fair value of the options at grant date.

- Charge this fair value to the income statement equally over the three year vesting period, making adjustments at each accounting date to reflect the best estimate of the number of options that will eventually vest. This will depend on the estimated percentage of employees leaving during the vesting period.

For the year ended 30 June 20X6, the charge to the income statement is $3m × 94% × 1/3 = $940,000. Shareholders' equity will be increased by an amount equal to this income statement charge.

BPP
LEARNING MEDIA

Question 3

Top tips. To state the obvious, this is a question best avoided unless you like deferred tax. However, if you do, or if you dislike other topics more, the question may be broken down into components where you can get a foothold. Layout is important to avoid getting muddled.

Easy marks. For those not fond of high speed number-crunching, there are some fairly easy marks in Part (a) available for a general discussion about concepts and the framework. In addition there are some easy marks for adjustments to the financial statements, most of which do not relate to the deferred tax aspects. In generally, however, this is not a question that lends itself to easy marks.

Marking scheme

			Marks
(a)	Quality of discussion		2
	Framework		1
	Temporary difference		2
	Liability		1
	Weakness		1
			7
(b)	Adjustments:	Available for sale assets	2
		Convertible bond	2
		Defined benefit plan	2
		Property, plant and equipment	1
	Deferred tax:	Goodwill	1
		Other intangibles	1
		Financial assets	1
		Trade receivables	1
		Other receivables	1
		Long-term borrowings	1
		Employee benefits	1
		Trade payables	1
	Calculation		3
		Available	19
		Maximum	18
		Available	26
		Maximum	25

(a)   IAS 12 *Income taxes* is based on the idea that **all changes in assets and liabilities** have **unavoidable tax consequences.** Where the recognition criteria in IFRS are different from those in tax law, **the carrying amount of an asset or liability in the financial statements is different from its tax base** (the amount at which it is stated for tax purposes). These differences are known as **temporary differences.** The practical effect of these differences is that a transaction or event occurs in a different accounting period from its tax consequences. For example, depreciation is recognised in the financial statements in different accounting periods from capital allowances.

IAS 12 requires a company to make **full provision** for the tax effects of temporary differences. Both **deferred tax assets**, and **deferred tax liabilities** can arise in this way.

It may be argued that deferred tax assets and liabilities **do not meet the definition of assets and liabilities** in the IASB *Framework.* Under the *Framework* an asset is the right to receive economic benefits as a result of past events, and a liability is an obligation to transfer economic benefits, again as a result of past events. Under IAS 12, the tax effect of transactions are recognised in the same period as the transactions themselves, but in practice, tax is paid in accordance with tax legislation when it becomes a legal liability. There is a **conceptual weakness** or inconsistency, in that only one liability, that is tax, is being provided for, and not other costs, such as overhead costs.

(b)

	$'000	Adjustments to financial statements $'000	Tax base $'000	Temporary difference $'000
Property, plant and equipment	10,000		2,400	7,600
Goodwill	6,000		6,000	
Other intangible assets	5,000		0	5,000
Financial assets (cost)	9,000	1,500	9,000	1,500
Total non-current assets	30,000			
Trade receivables	7,000		7,500	(500)
Other receivables	4,600		5,000	(400)
Cash and cash-equivalents	6,700		6,700	-
Total current assets	18,300			
Total assets	48,300			
Long term borrowings	10,000	(400)	10,000	400
Deferred tax liability	3,600		3,600	-
Employee benefits	4,000	520	5,000	480
Current tax liability	3,070		3,070	-
Trade and other payables	5,000		4,000	(1,000)
Total liabilities	25,670			13,080
Share capital	9,000			
Other reserves	4,500	1,500		
		400		
Retained earnings	9,130	(520)		
Total equity	22,630			

Deferred tax liability	$'000
Liability b/fwd	3,600
Charge (bal fig)	324
Deferred tax liability c/fwd	
14,980 x 30%	4,494
Deferred tax asset – c/fwd	
1,900 x 30%	(570)
Net deferred tax liability	
13,080 x 30%	3,924

Notes on adjustments

(i)   The financial assets are shown at cost. However, per IAS 39, since they are classified as 'available for sale', they should instead be valued at fair value, with the increase ($10,500 – $9,000 = $1,500) going to equity.

(ii)   IAS 32 states that convertible bonds must be split into debt and equity components. This involves reducing debt and increasing equity by $400.

(iii)   The defined benefit plan needs to be adjusted to reflect the change. The liability must be increased by 40% × $1m + (60% × $1m ÷ 5) = $520,000. The same amount is charged to retained earnings.

BPP LEARNING MEDIA

(iv) The development costs have already been allowed for tax, so the tax base is nil. No deferred tax is recognised on goodwill.

(v) The accrual for compensation is to be allowed when paid, ie in a later period. The tax base relating to trade and other payables should be reduced by $1m.

Question 4

Top tips. Part (a) of this question is topical and practical, and you should have been prepared for this topic to come up. If you weren't, learn our answer carefully – you may be able to apply it to some variant of the question in an exam. Part (b) is on current issues, specifically the changes proposed to accounting for business combinations in recent exposure drafts. The examiner has specifically stated that he will not set a whole question on an exposure draft, or test the detail. The focus will be on the main implications for the financial statements, as here.

Easy marks. As you can see from the marking scheme, much of the mark allocation is 'subjective'. Thus does not mean you can say anything you want or waffle, but it does mean that credit is given for any valid points, provided you can back them up with arguments. So keep writing and stay calm and logical. A quick answer plan will help.

Marking scheme

		Marks
(a)	Subjective	18
(b)	Subjective	7
		25

(a) **Practical matters**

Changing from local GAAP to IFRS is **likely to be a complex process** and should be **carefully planned**. Even if local GAAP and IAS/IFRS follow broadly the same principles there are still likely to be **many important differences** in the detailed requirements of individual standards.

The company will also need to ensure that its overseas subsidiaries comply with any local reporting requirements. This **may mean that subsidiaries will have to prepare two sets of financial statements**: one using local GAAP; and one using IFRS (for the consolidation).

The process will be affected by the following.

(i) The **differences between local GAAP and IFRS** as they affect the group financial statements in practice. The company will need to carry out a **detailed review of current accounting policies,** paying particular attention to areas where there are significant differences between local GAAP and IFRS. These will probably include deferred tax, business combinations, retirement benefits and foreign currency translation. It should be possible to estimate the effect of the change by preparing pro-forma financial statements using IFRS.

(ii) The **level of knowledge** of IFRS of current finance staff (including internal auditors). It will probably be necessary to **organise training** and the company may need to recruit additional personnel with experience of IFRS.

(iii) The group's **accounting systems**. Management will need to assess whether computerised accounting systems **can produce the information required** to report under IFRS. They will also need to produce new consolidation packages and accounting manuals.

There should be a **detailed plan** for the project, including timetables, management teams and resource requirements.

Lastly, the company **should consider the impact of the change** to IFRS on investors and their advisers. For this reason management should **try to quantify the effect** of IFRS **on results** and other key performance indicators as early as possible.

Problems of enforcement

The success of implementation of IFRS depends on how rigorously they are enforced. In turn, this depends on the **robustness of the regulatory framework** of the country in which standards are being implemented. In the EU, this is less of an issue, since endorsement is required as part of the implementation process. However, even here there are problems, since the endorsement process could **create standards** that are **different from those of the IASB**.

Enforcement of IFRS requires an **international mechanism**. IOSCO has an infrastructure for listed companies and has put forward proposals for regulatory interpretation and enforcement of IFRS. However, the situation is by no means uniform and is in a **state of flux**.

Potential problems and challenges

(i)   The **legal framework** may present difficulties in adopting IFRS. In some countries, this will be more apparent than in others, such as the UK, where the legal framework and accounting standards – and UK FRS and IFRS – are a better fit.

(ii)   **Small and medium entities** (SMEs) present particular problems. In recent years, IFRS have become **increasingly complex and prescriptive.** They are now designed **primarily** to meet the information needs of **institutional investors in large listed entities** and their advisers. In many countries, IFRS are **used mainly by listed companies.** There are arguments for the use of full IFRS and for the development of a separate IFRS for SMEs, as with the FRSSE in the UK.

(iii)   There may be problems with **enforcement.** In the EU this is less of an issue for listed companies, which must, in its consolidated accounts, comply with IFRS.

(iv)   **Translation** of IFRS could cause difficulty where it gives rise to ambiguity.

(v)   The **complexity and volume** of IFRS add to the difficulties of implementation, especially in countries where there is less expertise. There will be a tendency, where a choice is available, to choose the treatment most like existing local GAAP, rather than the best treatment.

(vi)   All of the above have **cost and time implications**.

(b)   Under current accounting practice the objective of acquisition accounting is to reflect the **cost of the acquisition.** To the extent to which it is not represented by identifiable assets and liabilities (measured at their fair value), goodwill arises and is reported in the financial statements. The **EDs** adopt a different perspective and requires the financial statements to reflect the **fair value of the acquired business.**

To date, accounting has been based on the 'parent entity concept'. Under the **parent entity concept** the extent of **non-controlling interests** and transactions with non-controlling interests are **separately identified** in the primary financial statements.

The proposals treat the group as a **single economic entity** ('entity concept') and any outside equity interest in a subsidiary is treated as part of the overall ownership interest in the group. As a consequence of this **changes in a parent's ownership interest, that do not result in a change of control, are to be recognised as changes in equity. No gain or loss will be recognised in profit or loss.**

IFRS 3 requires that goodwill arising on acquisition should only be recognised with respect to the part of the subsidiary undertaking that is attributable to the interest held by the parent entity. Under the proposals, **goodwill is to be recognised in full**; that is 100% of goodwill is recognised even if less than 100% is acquired. In other words, goodwill is to be shown **gross of non-controlling (minority) interest.**

BPP
LEARNING MEDIA

Under IFRS 3, **costs incurred in connection with the acquisition** are accounted for as part of the investment. Under the proposals, they **will be charged in the income statement.**

Business combinations must be measured and recognised as of the acquisition date **at the fair value of the acquiree, even if the business combination is achieved in stages or if less than 100 per cent of the equity interests in the acquiree are owned at the acquisition date**. The current version of IFRS 3 requires a business combination to be measured and recognised on the basis of the accumulated cost of the combination.

ACCA
Examiner's answers

BPP
LEARNING MEDIA

Part 3 Examination – Paper 3.6(INT)
Advanced Corporate Reporting (International Stream)   December 2006 Answers

1   Andash, public limited company, Group Cash Flow Statement
                                           for year ended 31 October 2006

	$m	$m
Cash flows from operating activities		323
Profit before taxation		
Adjustments for profit on sale of subsidiary	(8)	
Depreciation	260	
Impairment of goodwill	78	
Associate's profit	(1)	
Finance costs	148	
		477
		800
Increase in trade receivables (2,400 – 1,500 + 4)	(904)	
Increase in inventories (2,650 – 2,300 + 8)	(358)	
Increase in trade payables (4,700 – 2,800 + 6)	1,906	
		644
Cash generating from operations		1,444
Interest paid (40 + 148 – 70) (w (vi))		(118)
Income taxes paid (w (vi))		(523)
Net cash from operating activities		803
Cash flows from investing activities		
Purchase of associate (w(iii))	(10)	
Purchase of property, plant and equipment (working ii)	(1,320)	
Sale of subsidiary (32 – 5)	27	
		(1,303)
		500
Cash flows from financing activities		
Proceeds of issue of share capital (working vii)	10	
Dividend paid to minority interest (180 + 40 – 200)	(20)	
Proceeds from long term borrowings	400	
Dividends paid	(50)	
		(340)
Net decrease in cash and cash equivalents		(160)
Cash and cash equivalents at 1 November 2005		300
Cash and cash equivalents at 31 October 2006		140

Workings

		$m
(i)	Profit before tax	400
	Associates profit (iii)	1
	Impairment of goodwill (iv)	(78)
	Profit before tax	323

(ii) **Property, plant and equipment**

IFRS2 says that the fair value of the goods and services received should be used as the value of the share options issued. Therefore, the plant should be valued at $9 million and the share options at the same amount. There is no need to adjust depreciation because of the date of purchase, but other reserves will fall by $1 million.

	$m
Plant, property and equipment – balance 31 October 2005	4,110
Purchases – non-cash } above	9
Over valuation }	1
Depreciation	(260)
Sale of subsidiary	(10)
Purchases in period (balancing figure)	1,320
Plant, property and equipment per balance sheet	5,170

The balance sheet figure for property, plant and equipment will be $5,169 million.

(iii) Associate – Joma

The investment in the associate should be measured using the equity method

	$m	$m
Cost of investment		60
Share of post-acquisition reserves (25% × ($32 – $20)m)	3	
Inter company profit eliminated (25% × ($16 – $8)m)	(2)	
		1
		61

(iv) Impairment of Goodwill-Broiler

	Goodwill $m	Net assets $m	Total $m
Carrying amount	90	240	330
Unrecognised minority interest (90 × 40/60)	60	—	60
	150	240	390
Recoverable amount			260
Impairment loss			(130)

Goodwill will be reduced by 60% of 130, i.e. $78 million. The income statement will be charged with this amount.

(v) Sale of subsidiary

The sale of the subsidiary should be taken into account in the cash flow statement as follows:

	DR	CR
Plant, property and equipment		10
Inventory		8
Trade receivables		4
Cash and cash equivalents		5
Trade payables	6	
Current tax payable	7	
Cash proceeds	32	
Goodwill disposed of		10
Profit on sale		8
	45	45

(vi) Income taxes paid

	$m	$m
Current tax payable 31 October 2005	770	
Deferred tax payable 31 October 2005	300	
		1,070
Income statement		160
		1,230
Cash paid (balancing figure)		(523)
Sale of subsidiary		(7)
Current tax payable 31 October 2006	300	
Deferred tax payable 31 October 2006	400	
		700

(vii) Shares issued

Cash flow from the issue of shares is $(30 + 30 – 50) i.e. $10 million (from statement of changes in equity). The shares issued for the purchase of Joma are taken out of the issue proceeds set out in the statement of changes in equity.

BPP LEARNING MEDIA

2 (a) **Foreign subsidiary, Chong**

The following computation sets out the accounting treatment of the sale of the foreign subsidiary, Chong.

	31 October 2005		31 October 2006	
	€m			€m
Share capital	100			100
Retained earnings	40			60
Shareholders' equity	140			160
Net assets	140			160
Translated into dollars:				
Net assets (140 ÷ 1·4)	100	(160 ÷ 1·3)		123
Share capital (100 ÷ 1·1)	91			91
Retained profits (40 ÷ 1·2)	33		33	
		(20 ÷ 1·5)	13	46
Exchange reserve	(24)		(24)	
			gain 10	(14)
	100			123

Gain/loss on sale	Mission	Group
	$m	$m
Sale proceeds (195 ÷ 1·3)	150	150
Cost of investment	(91)	
Net asset value		(123)
Exchange losses		(14)
Gain on sale	59	13

IAS21, 'The Effects of Changes in Foreign Exchange Rates', requires the cumulative exchange losses of $14 million to be recognised in profit or loss for the year ended 31 October 2006. IAS27 requires the exchange losses to be included as part of the gain on disposal. As a result the gain on sale is reduced to $13 million. The gain on sale is effectively the gain on sale in the parent company's financial statements ($59 million) less the cumulative profits already taken to the group income statement of $46 million.

(b) **Inventory, Goods sold and Investment property**

The inventory and trade payable initially would be recorded at 8 million euros ÷ 1·6, i.e. $5 million. At the year end, the amount payable is still outstanding and is retranslated at 1 dollar = 1·3 euros, i.e. $6·2 million. An exchange loss of $(6·2 − 5) million, i.e. $1·2 million would be reported in profit or loss. The inventory would be recorded at $5 million at the year end unless it is impaired in value.

The sale of goods would be recorded at 4 million euros ÷ 1·6, i.e. $2·5 million as a sale and as a trade receivable. Payment is received on 31 October 2006 in euros and the actual value of euros received will be 4 million euros ÷ 1·3, i.e. $3·1 million.

Thus a gain on exchange of $0·6 million will be reported in profit or loss.

The investment property should be recognised on 1 November 2005 at 28 million euros ÷ 1·4, i.e. $20 million. At 31 October 2006, the property should be recognised at 24 million euros ÷ 1·3, i.e. $18·5 million. The decrease in fair value should be recognised in profit and loss as a loss on investment property. The property is a non-monetary asset and any foreign currency element is not recognised separately. When a gain or loss on a non-monetary item is recognised in profit or loss, any exchange component of that gain or loss is also recognised in profit or loss. If any gain or loss is recognised in equity on a non-monetary assets, any exchange gain is also recognised in equity.

(c) **Plant and equipment**

Where a deposit is paid, the treatment depends upon whether the amount is refundable. If the deposit is refundable, then the amounts should be treated as monetary items and retranslated at the balance sheet date. In this case the deposit is not refundable and it should be recorded as plant and equipment at a value of 1 million euros ÷ 1·6, i.e. $625,000.

IAS39 governs the accounting for the two instruments.

A cash flow hedge is a hedge of the exposure to variability in cash flows that:

(i)   is attributable to a particular risk associated with a recognised asset or liability or a highly probable forecast transaction, and

(ii) could affect profit or loss

Cash flow hedge accounting involves the following accounting treatments:

(i) changes in the fair value of the hedging instrument attributable to the hedged risk are deferred as a separate component of equity to the extent the hedge is effective (rather than being recognised immediately in profit or loss)

(ii) the accounting for the hedged item is not adjusted

(iii) if a hedge of a forecast transaction subsequently results in the recognition of a non-financial asset or non-financial liability (or becomes a firm commitment for which fair value hedge accounting is applied), the entity has an accounting policy choice of whether to keep deferred gains and losses in equity or remove them from equity and include them in the initial carrying amount of the recognised asset, liability, or firm commitment (a so-called 'basis adjustment')

(iv) when the hedged item affects profit or loss (for instance through depreciation or amortisation), a corresponding amount previously deferred in equity is realised from equity ('recycled') and included in profit or loss.

(v) If the hedge is not 100% effective, the ineffectiveness is recognised in profit or loss.

Bond

The bond would be initially recognised on 31 July 2006 at 3 million euros ÷ 1·6 i.e. $1·9 million. As current market rates are 4%, the fair value and carrying value of the bond will be $1·9 million. On 31 October 2006, the value of the bond will have changed to $2·3 million (3 million euros/1·3) and the exchange gain will be recognised in profit or loss ($0·4 million). The bond is classified as at fair value through profit or loss and therefore changes in fair value are recognised in profit or loss. At present interest rates are the same as the interest rates on the bond. However, because the interest rate on the bond is fixed, the company has exposed itself to the risk of decline in the market value of the bond. If interest rates rise then the value of the bond will fall because the bond will pay a lower interest rate than equivalent investments in the market. Thus this method of hedging risk would lead to a risk in the decline in the value of the bond itself. To eliminate such a risk, the company would need to enter into an interest rate swap agreement to exchange fixed interest payments for floating interest rate payments. Such an agreement would be designated as a hedging instrument of the bond. At 31 October 2006, the bond will have accrued interest which will be accrued in the balance sheet and be translated at average rate in the income statement and closing rate in the balance sheet.

Forward contract

At inception, the forward contract has a fair value of zero. On 31 October 2006, the dollar has depreciated, such that three million euros for delivery on 30 June 2007 costs 2·3 million dollars on the market. Therefore, the forward contract has increased in fair value by 0·3 million dollars. Since the hedge is fully effective, the entire change in the fair value of the hedging instrument is recognised directly in equity. The following entry is made:

CR Equity	$300,000	
DR	Forward contract	$300,000

The deferred gain or loss remaining in equity on 30 June 2007 should either remain in equity and be released from equity as the machine is depreciated or otherwise affects profit or loss, or be deducted from the initial carrying amount of the machine.

If the company purchases a bond then it will tie cash up in the bond until its maturity date and will leave itself vulnerable to changes in the value of the bond unless a hedging instrument is created. The simplest and most effective way is to use the forward contract.

3 (a) Sale and leaseback

A sale and leaseback agreement releases capital for expansion, repayment of outstanding debt or repurchase of share capital. The transaction releases capital tied up in non liquid assets. There are important considerations. The price received for the asset and the related interest rate/rental charge should be at market rates. The interest rate will normally be dependent upon the financial strength of the 'tenant' and the risk/reward ratio which the lessor is prepared to accept. There are two types of sale and leaseback agreements. One utilising a finance lease and another an operating lease.

The accounting treatment is determined by IAS17, 'Leases'. The substance of the transaction is essentially one of financing as the title to the stadium is transferred back to the club. Thus a sale is not recognised. The excess of the sale proceeds over the carrying value of the assets is deferred and amortised to profit or loss over the lease term. The leaseback of the stadium is for the remainder of its economic and useful life, and therefore under IAS17, the lease should be treated as a finance lease. The stadium will remain as a non-current asset and will be depreciated. The finance lease loan will be accounted for under IAS39 'Financial Instruments: Recognition and Measurement' in terms of the derecognition rules in the standard.

The transaction will be recognised by the club as follows in the year to 31 December 2007:

	DR $m	CR $m
Receipt of cash 1 January 2007		
Cash received	15	
Stadium		12
Deferred income		3
	15	15

	DR $m	CR $m
Assets held under finance lease	15	
Finance lease payable		15
Depreciation (15 ÷ 20 years)	0·75	
Assets held under finance lease		0·75

Year ended 31 December 2007
Income Statement

	$ 000
Deferred income ($3m ÷ 20 years)	150
Depreciation	(750)
Finance charge ($15m – $1·2m) × 5·6%	(773)

Balance sheet
Non-current assets

Stadium ($15m – $750,000)	14,250

Non-current liabilities

Deferred income ($3m – $150,000)	2,850
Long term borrowings (15 – (1·2 × 2) + 773)	13,373
Current liabilities – rental payment	1,200

This form of sale and leaseback has several disadvantages. The profit for the period may decrease because of the increase in the finance charge over the deferred income. Similarly the gearing ratio of the club may increase significantly because of the increase in long term borrowings although the short term borrowings may be reduced by the inflow of cash. Unsecured creditors may have less security for their borrowings after the leasing transaction. It may be worth considering a sale and leaseback involving an operating lease as in this case the profit on disposal can be recognised immediately because the sale price is at fair value. The stadium will be deemed to be sold and will be removed from the balance sheet. Similarly a long-term liability for the loan will not be recognised in the balance sheet, and the sale proceeds could be used to repay any outstanding debt. This form of sale and leaseback would seem to be preferable than the one utilising a finance lease although any increase in the residual value of the stadium would be lost.

(b)   Player Registrations

The players transfer fees have been capitalised as intangible assets under IAS38, ' Intangible Assets' because it is probable that expected future benefits will flow to the club as a result of the contract signed by the player and the cost of the asset can be measured reliably, being the transfer fee. The cost model would be used because the revaluation model has to use an active market to determine fair value and this is not possible because of the unique nature of the players. IAS38 requires intangible assets such as the player contracts to be amortised over their useful life. Intangible assets with indefinite useful lives should not be amortised and should be impairment tested annually. If the player is subsequently 'held for sale' i.e., becomes available for sale to other clubs and satisfies the criteria in IFRS5, 'Non-current assets held for sale and discontinued operations', then amortisation ceases.

The amortisation method should reflect the pattern of the future economic benefits. The amortisation of the contracts over ten years does not fit this criterion. IAS38's recommends an amortisation method which reflects the useful life of the asset and the pattern of economic benefits and, therefore, the current method over ten years cannot be used as an accounting policy. The current amortisation level should be maintained and a charge of $9 million would be shown in the income statement for the year ended 31 December 2007. This proposal in any event would only mask the poor financial state of the club. It is a book entry which may help prevent negative equity but will not give a cash benefit. The fundamental strategy for the club should be to contract players which it can afford and to spend at levels appropriate to its income.

There does not appear to be any probability that the contingent liability will crystallise. Under IAS37, 'Provisions, Contingent Liabilities and Contingent Assets', a contingency is a possible obligation arising out of past events and whose existence will be confirmed only by the occurrence or non-occurrence of one or more uncertain future events not wholly within the control of the entity. At present the club is performing very poorly in the league and is unlikely to win the national league. Therefore, the contingent liability will not become a present obligation but will still be disclosed in the financial statement for the year ended 31 December 2007.

(c)   Issue of bond

This form of financing a football club's operations is known as 'securitisation'. Often in these cases a special purpose vehicle is set up to administer the income stream or assets involved. In this case, a special purpose vehicle has not been set up. The benefit of securitisation of the future corporate hospitality sales and season ticket receipts is that there will be a capital injection into the club and it is likely that the effective interest rate is lower because of the security provided by the income from the receipts. The main problem with the planned raising of capital is the way in which the money is to be used. The use of the bond for ground improvements can be commended as long term cash should be used for long term investment but using the bond for players' wages will cause liquidity problems for the club.

This type of securitisation is often called a 'future flow' securitisation. There is no existing asset transferred to a special purpose vehicle in this type of transaction and, therefore, there is no off balance sheet effect. The bond is shown as a long term liability and is accounted for under IAS39 'Financial Instruments: Recognition and Measurement'. There are no issues of derecognition of assets as there can be in other securitisation transactions. In some jurisdictions there are legal issues in assigning future receivables as they constitute an unidentifiable debt which does not exist at present and because of this uncertainty often the bond holders will require additional security such as a charge on the football stadium.

The bond will be a financial liability and it will be classified in one of two ways:

(i)   Financial liabilities at fair value through profit or loss include financial liabilities that the entity either has incurred for trading purposes and, where permitted, has designated to the category at inception. Derivative liabilities are always treated as held for trading unless they are designated and effective as hedging instruments. An example of a liability held for trading is an issued debt instrument that the entity intends to repurchase in the near term to make a gain from short-term movements in interest rates. It is unlikely that the bond will be classified in this category.

(ii) The second category is financial liabilities measured at amortised cost. It is the default category for financial liabilities that do not meet the criteria for financial liabilities at fair value through profit or loss. In most entities, most financial liabilities will fall into this category. Examples of financial liabilities that generally would be classified in this category are account payables, note payables, issued debt instruments, and deposits from customers. Thus the bond is likely to be classified under this heading. When a financial liability is recognised initially in the balance sheet, the liability is measured at fair value. Fair value is the amount for which a liability can be settled between knowledgeable, willing parties in an arm's length transaction. Since fair value is a market transaction price, on initial recognition fair value will usually equal the amount of consideration received for the financial liability. Subsequent to initial recognition financial liabilities are measured using amortised cost or fair value. In this case the company does not wish to use valuation models nor is there an active market for the bond and, therefore, amortised cost will be used to measure the bond.

The bond will be shown initially at $50 million × 95%, i.e. $47·5 million as this is the consideration received. Subsequently at 31 December 2007, the bond will be shown as follows:

	$m
Initial recognition	47·5
Interest at 7·7%	3·7
Cash payment	(6)
Amount owing 31 December 2007	45·2

(d)   Player trading

The sale of the players will introduce cash into the club and help liquidity. The contingent liability will be extinguished as the players will no longer play for Seejoy. The club, however, is not performing well at present and the sale of the players will not help their performance. This may result in the reduction of ticket sales and, therefore, cause further liquidity problems. The proceeds from the sale of players may be difficult to estimate at present as the date of sale is significantly into the future. Also the sale of the players will not constitute 'held for sale' non-current assets under IFRS5 'Non-current assets held for sale and discontinued operations' at 31 December 2006 as the players are not available for immediate sale.

If the sale proceeds are $16 million, then a loss on sale will be recorded of $2 million.

	Transfer fee $m	Amortisation $m	Carrying amount $m
A. Steel	20	4 + 4/12 of 4	14·7
R. Aldo	15	10 + 4/12 of 5	3·3
			18
Sale proceeds (estimate)			16
Loss			2

As a loss on sale is anticipated on the players, an impairment review should be undertaken at 31 December 2006.

BPP
LEARNING MEDIA

4 (a) IAS31, 'Interests in Joint Ventures' says that a joint venture is a contractual agreement between two or more parties that undertake an economic activity that is subject to joint control. Joint control is the contractually agreed sharing of control and it exists when the strategic decisions relating to the activity require the unanimous consent of the parties involved. Control is the power to govern the financial and operating policies of the entity. In this case York has been formed by two companies each with a 50% share and having equal representation on the Board of Directors. Thus there is joint control. This type of joint venture normally involves the setting up of a company or partnership or other entity in which each of the joint venturers has an interest. The key thing about this type of entity is that there will be a contractual arrangement which establishes the joint control over it. Each venturer would normally contribute assets and other resources to the jointly controlled entity which would be included in the accounting records of the venturer and recognised as an investment in the jointly controlled entity. IAS31 allows two accounting treatments for an investment in the jointly controlled entity:

(a) proportionate consolidation
(b) the equity method of accounting

If the venturer ceases to have joint control over a jointly controlled entity then the use of proportionate consolidation should be discontinued. The only issue is the fact that there is no written contract. The substance of the arrangement is important. The existence of a contractual arrangement can be shown in a number of ways, one of which is the minutes of discussions between the companies. In this case the minutes of the discussions have been formally approved, and this establishes the joint control over the venture. Therefore, York is a jointly controlled entity and will be accounted for using proportional consolidation or equity accounting in the accounts of the venturers.

(b)

York
Balance Sheet at 31 October 2006

	$m
Assets:	
Property, plant and equipment	17
Intangible assets	3
	20
Current assets:	
Inventories	6
Trade receivables	3·8
Cash	11
	20·8
Total assets	40·8
Equity and liabilities:	
Share capital	30
Reserves (capital)	4·2
Deferred income	1·5
Total equity	35·7
Long term provision	4
Lease payables	1·1
Total equity and liabilities	40·8

Gow's net assets

IAS36 'Impairment of Assets', sets out the events that might indicate that an asset is impaired. These circumstances include external events such as the decline in the market value of an asset and internal events such as a reduction in the cash flows to be generated from an asset or cash generating unit. The loss of the only customer of a cash generating unit (power station) would be an indication of the possible impairment of the cash generating unit. Therefore, the power station will have to be impairment tested.

The recoverable amount will have to be determined and compared to the value given to the asset on the setting up of the joint venture. The recoverable amount is the higher of the cash generating unit's fair value less costs to sell, and its value-in-use. The fair value less costs to sell will be $15 million which is the offer for the purchase of the power station ($16 million) less the costs to sell ($1 million). The value-in-use is the discounted value of the future cash flows expected to arise from the cash generating unit. The future dismantling costs should be provided for as it has been agreed with the government that it will be dismantled. The cost should be included in the future cash flows for the purpose of calculating value-in-use and provided for in the financial statements and the cost added to the property, plant and equipment ($4 million). The value-in-use based on a discount rate of 6 per cent is $21 million. Therefore, the recoverable amount is $21 million which is higher than the carrying value of the cash generating unit ($20 million) and, therefore, the value of the cash generating unit is not impaired when compared to the present carrying value of $20 million.

Additionally IAS39, 'Financial Instruments: recognition and measurement', says that an entity must assess at each balance sheet date whether a financial asset is impaired. In this case the receivables of $7 million is likely to be impaired as Race is going into administration. The present value of the estimated future cash flows will be calculated. Normally cash receipts from trade receivables will not be discounted but because the amounts are not likely to be received for a year then the anticipated cash payment is 80% of ($5 million × 1/1·06), i.e. $3·8 million. Thus a provision for the impairment of the trade receivables of $3·2 million should be made. The intangible asset of $3 million would be valueless as the contract has been terminated.

Glass's Net Assets

The leased property continues to be accounted for as property, plant and equipment and the carrying amount will not be adjusted. However, the remaining useful life of the property will be revised to reflect the shorter term. Thus the property will be depreciated at $2 million per annum over the next two years. The change to the depreciation period is applied prospectively not retrospectively. The lease liability must be assessed under IAS39 in order to determine whether it constitutes a de-recognition of a financial liability. As the change is a modification of the lease and not an extinguishment, the lease liability would not be derecognised. The lease liability will be adjusted for the one off payment of $1 million and re-measured to the present value of the revised future cash flows. That is $0·6 million/1·07 + $0·6 million/(1·07 × 1·07) i.e. $1·1 million. The adjustment to the lease liability would normally be recognised in profit or loss but in this case it will affect the net capital contributed by Glass. Thus the carrying value of the lease liability will be $(3 − 1 − 0·9) million i.e. $1·1 million.

The termination cost of the contract cannot be treated as an intangible asset. It is similar to redundancy costs paid to terminate a contract of employment. It represents compensation for the loss of future income for the agency. Therefore it must be removed from the balance sheet of York. The recognition criteria for an intangible asset require that there should be probable future economic benefits flowing to York and the cost can be measured reliably. The latter criterion is met but the first criterion is not. The cost of gaining future customers is not linked to this compensation.

IAS18 'Revenue' contains a concept of a 'multiple element' arrangement. This is a contract which contains two or more elements which are in substance separate and are separately identifiable. In other words, the two elements can operate independently from each other. In this case, the contract with the overseas company has two distinct elements. There is a contract not to supply gas to any other customer in the country and there is a contract to sell gas at fair value to the overseas company. The contract has not been fulfilled as yet and therefore the payment of $1·5 million should not be taken to profit or loss in its entirety at the first opportunity. The non supply of gas to customers in that country occurs over the four year period of the contract and therefore the payment should be recognised over that period. Therefore the amount should be shown as deferred income and not as a deduction from intangible assets. The revenue on the sale of gas will be recognised as normal according to IAS18.

There may be an issue over the value of the net assets being contributed. The net assets contributed by Glass amount to $21·9 million whereas those contributed by Gow only total $13·8 million after taking into account any adjustments required by IFRS. The joint venturers have equal shareholding in York but no formal written agreements, thus problems may arise if Glass feels that the contributions to the joint venture are unequal.

Workings

Value-in-use

	$m 31 October 2007	$m 31 October 2008	$m 31 October 2009	$m 31 October 2010	$m Total
Net inflows	6	7	8	8	
Dismantling cost				(5)	
Discount factor	$1/1·06$	$1/1·06^2$	$1/1·06^3$	$1/1·06^4$	
	5·7	6·2	6·7	2·4	21

Contributed by Gow $(20 − 6.2)$m i.e. **$13.8 m**
Contributed by Glass $(12 + 1.9)$m i.e. **$21.9 m**
Provision for decommissioning is $(5m × $1/_{1.06}^4$) i.e. **$4 m**

York
Balance Sheet at 31 October 2006

	Gow	Adjustment	Glass	Adjustment	Total
Cash	1	—	10		11
Trade receivables	7	(3·2)	—		3·8
Inventory			6		6
Intangible assets	3	(3)	2	(0·5)	
				1·5	3
PPE	9	4	4		17
Provision for decommissioning		(4)			(4)
Lease receivables			1	(1)	
Lease payables			(3)	1·9	(1·1)
	20	(6·2)	20	1·9	35·7
Share capital					30
Reserves − capital (difference)					4·2
Deferred income				1·5	1·5
					35·7

BPP LEARNING MEDIA

5 (a) The purpose of the Management Commentary (MC) is to present a balanced and comprehensive analysis of the development position and performance of the entity in the year. Additionally, it deals with the main trends and factors behind the development, position and performance of the entity during the financial year and those factors which are likely to affect the entity in the future. The MC should enable users to assess the strategies adopted by the entity and the potential success of those strategies. The key principles are as follows:

- The MC should be seen through the eyes of the directors and should focus on those matters relevant to the members of the company.
- The review should look forward, identifying trends and factors relevant to the assessment of the current and future performance of the entity.
- The MC should supplement and complement the financial statements so as to improve disclosure by providing additional financial and non-financial information.
- The review should be comprehensive, understandable, reliable, relevant and represent faithfully the underlying strategies and trends.
- Both good and bad aspects of the position of the entity should be discussed in a balanced and neutral way.
- The MC should be comparable over time, and the information should be supportable and consistent with the financial statements to which it relates.

The increase in transparency and accountability improves the links between strategy, performance and risk, and the evaluation of directors, and how they are paid.

A mandatory MC would make it easier for companies to judge the content of the reports and the necessary standard of reporting, and would mean that the reports may be more robust and comparable. If the MC is not mandatory then this could lead to uncertainty, risks of non compliance and possible mis-information being shown in the review. Directors may adopt a review policy of stating the minimum amount of disclosure which will frustrate the significant benefits to be gained from using financial reporting as a strategic communication tool. 'Necessity to report' decisions will become subjective with possible legal outcomes. The minimalist approach may also prove problematic if directors' insurers reject claims because of 'non-disclosure' of information. Senior executives and the company board will play a more prominent role in deciding upon matters of MC content than will be the case with mandatory reporting practice. Influential factors driving MC disclosure practice may become those expected to have short-term financial impact, whether shareholder decisions may be influenced, and issues of risk management rather than the broader issues.

However, it can be argued that a mandatory MC could produce stereo-typed reports which would be based on a checklist approach. Thus innovation in corporate reporting would be stifled. The power of market forces could be enough to ensure that entities produce relevant and reliable information. Every company is different as are their challenges and risks and in a non-mandatory environment, companies could produce individual MC's to reflect those challenges and risks.

(b)

Jones and Cousin, a public quoted company
Annual Report 2006
Management Commentary

(i) Introduction

Jones and Cousin is a global company engaged in the medical products sector. This report provides information to assist the assessment of strategies adopted by the company and the future potential of those strategies.

Principal risks and relationships

Trends:

Expenditure in the medical sector is often controlled by governments and is, therefore, affected by government policy. Thus the Group is largely dependent on governments providing funds for health care. Product innovation and the resultant increase in competition could lead to downward pressure on the price of goods and a decline in the Group's market share which could affect the operational results and hinder the growth of the Group.

Currency fluctuations:

The Group reports its results using the dollar as its functional currency. As there is only five per cent of the business in the country of incorporation, fluctuations in exchange rates may have a material effect on the Group. If the exchange rate of the dollar strengthens against the Dinar and Euro, then group turnover and operating profit would be lower on translation into dollars. As the manufacturing base is worldwide, the finished products when sold to the Group's selling operations could expose the Group to fluctuations in exchange rates.

Product liability claims and loss of reputation:

Although the products are not inherently high risk, there is a possibility of malfunction which could entail risk of product liability claims or recalls on the product. Both these events could be costly and harmful to the Group's reputation which is dependent upon product safety. Any product liability claims or product recalls would have a negative effect on cash flow and profit, and are likely to adversely affect sales of the product.

Highly Competitive markets:

The principal business units compete across many diverse geographic and product markets. Technical advances and product innovations by competitors could adversely affect the operating results. Some of the Group's competitors could have greater resources and may be able to sell products on more competitive terms. If the Group were to lose market share or have lower than expected sales growth, there could be an adverse impact on the Group's share price and future strategies.

Patents and Products;

The Group protects its intellectual rights in its products and opposes third parties where there is a conflict with the group's patents. The Group may itself be subject to patent infringement claims. If the Group failed to protect its position, its competitive position could suffer and operating results be harmed. Similarly if any claims are successful then damages may have to be paid, or non patent infringing products developed, both of which would adversely affect results.

Product innovations will occur constantly in the sector and, therefore, the Group has to continually develop products to satisfy consumer needs and to provide cost and other advantages. Not all products will be brought to the market for several reasons, including failure to receive regulatory approval or infringement of patents. Thus there is a significant cost implication in the research and development of products. However, if new products do not remain competitive with competitors' products, then Group sales revenue could decline.

Relationships:

The Group has developed a set of corporate social responsibility principles which is the responsibility of the Board of Directors, and the Managing Director in particular. The Group contributes to the treatment and recovery of patients within its product range by providing solutions to health care needs. Although having a relatively minor impact on the environment compared to some companies, any obsolete products are disposed of in an environmentally friendly way so as not to potentially compromise the health of its customers. Reusable materials are used in the manufacture of products.

The Group fosters ethical relationships with its suppliers and encourages them to share the same social and environmental standards. In this way a long term relationship is expected to be developed with suppliers.

The Group's employment policies are based on equality of opportunity and the performance standards and goals are communicated to the employees. Jones and Cousin is committed to the provision of continuous training and development and open communication with its employees. Additionally the group encourages its subsidiaries to reinvest profits in local educational projects.

(ii) **Strategy of the business regarding its treasury policies**

Treasury policies are reviewed regularly by the Board. It is group policy to account for all financial instruments as cash flow hedges. As a result, changes in the fair values of financial instruments are deferred in reserves to the extent the hedge is effective and released to profit or loss in the time periods in which the hedged item impacts profit or loss.

The Group contracts fixed rate currency swaps and issues floating to fixed rate interest rate swaps to meet the objective of protecting borrowing costs. The cash flow effects of the interest rate swaps match the cash flows on the underlying instruments so that there is no net cash flow effect from movements in market interest rates. If the interest rate swaps had not been transacted there could have been an increase in the annual net interest payable to the Group. The strategy of the group is to minimise the exposure to interest rate and fluctuations.

BPP LEARNING MEDIA

Part 3 Examination – Paper 3.6(INT)
Advanced Corporate Reporting (International Stream)

December 2006 Marking Scheme

			Marks
1	Cash flows from operating activities		2
	Adjustments		4
	Cash generated from operations		3
	Interest		2
	Tax		2
	Associate		3
	Plant, property and equipment		2
	Sale of subsidiary		3
	Minority interest		2
	Long term borrowings		1
	Dividend paid		1
	Goodwill		3
	Forward Contract		1
		AVAILABLE	29
		MAXIMUM	25

				Marks
2	**(a)**	Foreign subsidiary		9
	(b)	Inventory, goods sold, investment property		8
	(c)	Plant and equipment deposit		2
			cash flow hedge	3
			bond	3
			forward contract	3
			AVAILABLE	28
			MAXIMUM	25

			Marks
3	Sale and leaseback		10
	Player registrations		5
	Bond		7
	Player trading		5
		AVAILABLE	27
		MAXIMUM	25

				Marks
4	**(a)**	Nature of relationship and accounting treatment		5
	(b)	Impairment and calculation		7
		IAS39		3
		Lease		5
		Revenue recognition		4
		Issues with values contributed		2
			AVAILABLE	26
			MAXIMUM	25

				Marks
5	(a)	Principles		6
		Mandatory discussion		7
			AVAILABLE/MAXIMUM	13
	(b)	Principal risks		9
		Treasury policies		3
			AVAILABLE/MAXIMUM	12
		Style and presentation		2
			AVAILABLE	27
			MAXIMUM	25

BPP LEARNING MEDIA

P2 Pilot Paper (INT)
Corporate Reporting (International)

1   (a)   Zambeze Group
         Group Statement of Cash Flows for the year ended 30 June 2006

	$m	$m
Cash flows from operating activities:		
Net profit before taxation		690
Adjustments for:		
Share of profit in associate	(30)	
Depreciation	60	
Impairment of goodwill (Working 2)	8	
Interest expense	40	
Retirement benefit expense	13	
		91
Operating profit before working capital changes:		781
Increase in trade receivables	(80)	
Decrease in inventories (650-580-90)	20	
Increase in trade payables	141	
		81
Cash generated from operations:		862
Interest paid (Working 5)	(31)	
Income taxes paid (Working 4)	(190)	
Cash paid to retirement benefit scheme	(7)	
		(228)
Net cash from operating activities:		634
Cash flows from investing activities		
Acquisition of subsidiary	(100)	
Purchase of property, plant and equipment (Working 1)	(251)	
Dividends received from Associate (Working 3)	35	
Investment in River	(400)	
Net cash used in investing activities		(716)
Cash flows from financing activities:		
Proceeds from issue of share capital	30	
Increase in long-term borrowings	66	
Dividends paid (Working 6)	(46)	
Minority interest dividends (Working 2)	(58)	
Net cash used in financing activities		(8)
Net decrease in cash and cash equivalents		(90)
Cash and cash equivalents at beginning of period		140
Cash and cash equivalents at the end of period		50

Working 1

	$m
Tangible non-current assets	
Balance at 1 July 2005	1,005
Impairment losses	(95)
Depreciation	(60)
Purchases (by deduction)	395
Acquisition – Damp	70
Closing balance	1,315

Cash flow is $395 million minus the liability for Property, plant and equipment of $144 million, ie $251 million.

10

333

Working 2

	$m
Purchase of subsidiary:	
Net assets acquired	160
Group's share of net assets (70%)	112
Goodwill	13
Purchase consideration (100 + 25)	125

	$m
Goodwill:	
Balance at 1 July 2005	25
Goodwill on subsidiary	13
Impairment	(8)
Balance at 30 June 2006	30

	$m
Minority interest:	
Balance at 1 July 2005	45
Acquisition of Damp (160 x 30%)	48
Profit for year	25
Dividend	(58)
Balance at 30 June 2006	60

Working 3

	$m
Dividend from associate:	
Balance at 1 July 2005	290
Income (net of tax) (30-10)	20
Foreign exchange loss	(5)
Dividends received (difference)	(35)
Balance at 30 June 2006	270

Working 4

		$m	$m
Taxation:			
Balance at 1 July 2005	Income tax		185
	Deferred tax		25
Income statements (210–10)			200
Tax paid (difference)			(190)
Balance at 30 June 2006	Income tax	190	
	Deferred tax	30	
			220

Working 5

	$m
Interest paid:	
Balance at 1 July 2005	45
Income statement	40
Unwinding of discount on purchase	(4)
Cash paid (difference)	(31)
Closing balance at 30 June 2006	50

Working 6
The cash payment to River should be shown as "investing activities" of $400 million and the dividend paid will then be $(446-400) million, ie $46 million.

(b) The definition of "control" underpins the definition of the parent and subsidiary relationship. IAS27 *Consolidated and separate financial statements* states that control is presumed when the parent acquires more than half of the voting rights of the enterprise. Even when more than one half of the voting rights is not acquired, control may be evidenced by power (IAS27, para 13)

(i)   over more than one half of the voting rights by virtue of an agreement with other investors; or

(ii) to govern the financial and operating policies of the other enterprise under a statute or an agreement; or

(iii) to appoint or remove the majority of the members of the board of directors; or

(iv) to cast the majority of votes at a meeting of the board of directors.

11

IAS27 emphasises that the reference to power in the definition of "control" means the ability to do or affect something. As a result an entity has control over another entity when it has the ability to exercise that power, regardless of whether control is actively demonstrated or passive in nature. Further SIC12, *Consolidation – Special Purpose Entities* says that special purpose entities (SPEs) should be consolidated where the substance of the relationship indicates that the SPE is controlled by the reporting enterprise. This may arise even where the activities of the SPE are predetermined or whether the majority of voting or equity are not held by the reporting enterprise.

Under IAS27 control of an entity comprises the ability to control the entity's decision making with a view to obtaining benefits from the entity. The ability to control decision making alone is not sufficient to establish control for accounting purposes but must be accompanied by the objective of obtaining benefits from the entity's activities. If a company obtains the benefits of ownership, is exposed to the risks of ownership, and can exercise decision making powers to obtain those benefits, then the company must control the third party.

Zambeze should consolidate River as Zambeze controls the it through the operating guidelines. Zambeze also receives 95% of the profits and suffers all the losses of River. The guidelines were set up when River was formed and, therefore, the company was set up as a vehicle with the objective of keeping certain transactions off the balance sheet of Zambeze. The investment manager manages the investments of River within the guidelines and incurs no risk and receives 5% of the profits for the management services.

(c) Ethics in accounting is of utmost importance to accounting professionals and those who rely on their services. Accounting professionals know that people who use their services, especially decision makers using financial statements, expect them to be highly competent, reliable, and objective. Those who work in the field of accounting must not only be well qualified but must also possess a high degree of professional integrity. A professional's good reputation is one of his or her most important assets.

There is a very fine line between acceptable accounting practice and management's deliberate misrepresentation in the financial statements. The financial statements must meet the following criteria:

(i)   Technical compliance: A transaction must be recorded in accordance with generally accepted accounting principles (GAAP).
(ii) Economic substance: The resulting financial statements must represent the economic substance of the event that has occurred.
(iii) Full disclosure and transparency: Sufficient disclosure must be made so that the effects of transactions are transparent to the reader of the financial statements.

In the case of River it could be argued that the first criterion may be met because the transaction is apparently recorded in technical compliance with IFRS, but technical compliance alone is not sufficient. The second criterion is not met because the transaction as recorded does not reflect the economic substance of the event that has occurred.

Accounting plays a critical function in society. Accounting numbers affect human behaviour especially when it affects compensation, and to deliberately mask the nature of accounting transactions could be deemed to be unethical behaviour.

River was set up with the express purpose of keeping its activities off the balance sheet. The Finance Director has an ethical responsibility to the shareholders of Zambeze and society not to mask the true nature of the transactions with this entity. Further, if the transaction has been authorised by the Finance Director without the authority or knowledge of the Board of Directors, then a further ethical issue arises. Showing the transfer of funds as a dividend paid is unethical and possibly illegal in the jurisdiction. The transfer should not be hidden and River should be consolidated.

2   Report to directors of Electron

Terms of reference
This report sets out the nature of the accounting treatment and concerns regarding the following matters:
* Oil contracts
* Power station
* Operating leases
* Proposed dividend
* Share options.

Oil Contracts

The accounting policy adopted for the agreements relating to the oil contracts raises a number of concerns. The revenue recognition policy currently used is inflating revenue in the first year of the contract with 50% of the revenue being recognised, but a smaller proportion of the costs are recognised in the form of depreciation. Over the life of the contract, costs and revenues are equally matched but in the short term there is a bias towards a more immediate recognition of revenue against a straight line cost deferral policy. Additionally oil sales result in revenue whilst purchases of oil result in a tangible non-current asset. IAS18 *Revenue* states that revenue and expenses that relate to the same transaction or event should be recognised simultaneously and the "Framework" says that the "measurement and display of the financial effect of like transactions must be carried out in a consistent way". Accounting policies should provide a framework to ensure that this occurs. The current accounting practice seems to be out of line with IAS18 and the *Framework*.

However, the election of the company to use some form of deferral policy for its agreements is to be commended as it attempts to bring its revenue recognition policy in line with the length of the agreements. The main problem is the lack of a detailed accounting standard on revenue recognition. The result is the current lack of consistency in accounting for long-term agreements. However, it may be advisable to adopt a deferral policy in terms of this type of revenue. The contracts always result in the delivery of the oil in the normal course of business and are not, therefore, accounted for as financial instruments as they qualify as normal sale and purchase contracts.

Power Station

Under IAS37 *Provisions, Contingent Liabilities and Contingent Assets*, a provision should be made at the balance sheet date for the discounted cost of the removal of the power station because of the following reasons:

(i)   the installation of the power station creates an obligating event
(ii) the operating licence creates a legal obligation which is likely to occur
(iii) the costs of removal will have to be incurred irrespective of the future operations of the company and cannot be avoided
(iv) a transfer of economic benefits (ie the costs of removal) will be required to settle the obligation
(v)   a reasonable estimate of the obligation can be made although it is difficult to estimate a cost which will be incurred in twenty years time (IAS 37 says that only in exceptional circumstances will it not be possible to make some estimate of the obligation)

The costs to be incurred will be treated as part of the cost of the facility to be depreciated over its production life. However, the costs relating to the damage caused by the generation of energy should not be included in the provision, until the power is generated which in this case would be 5% of the total discounted provision. The accounting for the provision is shown in Appendix 1.

Operating Leases

SIC27 *Evaluating the substance of transactions involving the legal form of a lease* considers whether a leasing agreement meets the definition of a lease in IAS17 *Leases* and how a company should account for any fee that it might receive. A lease is classified as a finance lease if it transfers substantially all the risks and rewards "incident" to ownership. All other leases are classified as operating leases. In this case, the beneficial and legal ownership remains with Electron and Electron can make use of the power station if it so wishes. Also for a lease asset to be a finance lease the present value of the minimum lease payments should be substantially all of the fair value of the leased asset. In this case this amounts to 57.1% ($40 million ÷ $70 million) which does not constitute "substantially all". Thus there does not seem to be any issue over the classification of the lease as an operating lease. The immediate recognition as income of the future benefit at net present value is a little more problematical. IAS17 says that lease income from operating leases should be recognised on a straight line basis over the lease term unless another systematic basis is more representative. If a fee is received as an "up front" cash payment then IAS18 *Revenue* (para 20) and SIC27 should be applied. If there is future involvement required to earn the fee, or there are retained risks or risk of the repayment of the fee, or any restrictions on the lessor's use of the asset, then immediate recognition is inappropriate. The present policy of recognising the total lease income as if it were immediate income which it is not, would be difficult to justify. Similarly, as regards the deposit received, revenue should only be recognised when there is performance of the contract. Thus as there has been no performance under the contract, no revenue should be accrued in the period.

Proposed dividend

The dividend was proposed after the balance sheet date and the company, therefore, did not have a liability at the balance sheet date. No provision for the dividend should be recognised. The approval by the directors and the shareholders are enough to create a valid expectation that the payment will be made and give rise to an obligation. However, this occurred after the current year end and, therefore, will be charged against the profits for the year ending 30 June 2007.

The existence of a good record of dividend payments and an established dividend policy does not create a valid expectation or an obligation. However, the proposed dividend will be disclosed in the notes to the financial statements as the directors approved it prior to the authorisation of the financial statements.

Share options

Equity-settled transactions with employees would normally be expensed on the basis of their fair value at the grant date. Fair value should be based on market prices wherever possible. Many shares and share options will not be traded on an active market. In this case, valuation techniques, such as the option pricing model, would be used. IFRS2's objective for equity-based transactions with employees is to determine and recognise compensation costs over the period in which the services are rendered. In this case, the company has granted to employees share options that vest in three years' time on the condition that they remain in the entity's employ for that period. These steps will be taken:

(i) the fair value of the options will be determined at the date on which they were granted
(ii) this fair value will be charged to the income statement equally over the three year vesting period with adjustments made at each accounting date to reflect the best estimate of the number of options that eventually will vest

Shareholders' equity will be increased by an amount equal to the income statement charge. The charge in the income statement reflects the number of options that are likely to vest, not the number of options granted or the number of options exercised. If employees decide not to exercise their options because the share price is lower than the exercise price, then no adjustment is made to the income statement. Many employee share option schemes contain conditions that must be met before the employee becomes entitled to the shares or options. These are called vesting conditions and could require, for example, an increase in profit or growth in the entity's share price before the shares vest. In this case the vesting condition is the employment condition. $940,000 ($3 million x 94% x 1/3) will be charged in the income statement and to equity at 30 June 2006.

13

LEARNING MEDIA

Recommendations and conclusion

The above report sets out the recommendations regarding the accounting treatment of the items specified. It is imperative that the recommendations are followed as non-compliance with a single IFRS constitutes a failure to follow International Financial Reporting Standards for reporting purposes.

Appendix 1

	$m	$m
Present value of obligation at 1 July 2005 (15 ÷ 1.05)	14.3	
Provision for decommissioning (95% x 14.3)	13.6	
Provision for damage through extraction (5% x 14.3)		0.7

Balance Sheet at 30 June 2006

	$m	$m
Tangible non current assets:		
Cost of power station	100	
Provision for decommissioning	13.6	
	113.6	
less depreciation (113.6 ÷ 20 years)	(5.7)	
Carrying value	107.9	
Other provisions:		
Provision for decommissioning 1 July 2005	13.6	
Unwinding of discount (13.6x5%)	0.7	
		14.3
Provision for damage (0.7 ÷ 20 years)		0.1
		14.4

Income Statement

	$m
Depreciation	5.7
Provision for damage	0.1
Unwinding of discount (finance cost)	0.7

A simple straight line basis has been used to calculate the required provision for damage. A more complex method could be used whereby the present value of the expected cost of the provision is provided for over 20 years and the discount thereon is unwound over its life.

3　(a)　Under IFRS, an asset or liability is recognised if it meets the definition of such in the Framework document. The definitions refer to the right to receive or the obligation to transfer economic benefits as a result of a past event. The accounting model used to account for deferred tax is based on the premise that the tax effects of transactions should be recognised in the same period as the transactions themselves. The reality is, however, that tax is paid in accordance with tax legislation when it becomes a legal liability. There is an argument, therefore, that deferred tax is neither asset nor liability.

The temporary difference approach is based on the assumption that an asset will ultimately be recovered or realised by a cash inflow which will enter into the determination of future taxable profits. Thus the tax payable on the realisation of the asset should be provided for. It is argued that it would be inconsistent to represent that the asset can be recovered at its balance sheet value whilst ignoring the tax consequences.

Similarly for a liability carried in the balance sheet, there is an implicit assumption that the liability will ultimately be settled by a cash outflow. The outflow will enter into the determination of tax profits and any tax deduction allowable will effectively be an asset. As above, it would be inconsistent to recognise the liability whilst ignoring the tax consequences of its recognition.

Conceptually there is a weakness in this approach as only one of the liabilities that is tax, is being provided for and not other costs which will be incurred, such as overhead costs. The principal issue in accounting for deferred tax is how to account for the future tax consequences of the future recovery or settlement of the carrying amounts of the assets and liabilities.

14

(b)

	$'000	Adjustment to financial statements $'000	Tax base $'000	Temporary difference $'000
Property plant, and equipment	10,000		2,400	7,600
Goodwill	6,000		6,000	
Other intangible assets	5,000		0	5,000
Financial assets (cost)	9,000	1,500	9,000	1,500
Total non-current assets	30,000			
Trade receivables	7,000		7,500	(500)
Other receivables	4,600		5,000	(400)
Cash and cash equivalents	6,700		6,700	–
Total current assets	18,300			
Total assets	48,300			
Long term borrowings	10,000	(400)	10,000	400
Deferred tax liability	3,600		3,600	–
Employee benefits	4,000	520	5,000	480
Current tax liability	3,070		3,070	–
Trade and other payables	5,000		4,000	(1,000)
Total liabilities	25,670			13,080
Share capital	9,000			–
Other reserves	4,500	1,500		
		400		
Retained earnings	9,130	(520)		
Total equity	22,630			

	$000
Deferred tax liability 14,980 @ 30%	4,494
Deferred tax asset (1,900) @ 30%	(570)
Net deferred tax liability 13,080 @ 30%	3,924
Less existing liability	(3,600)
Adjustment to deferred tax	(324)

(i) The available for sale investments should be valued at fair value with the increase going to equity ($1.5 million).

(ii) The bond should be split into its equity and liability elements as per IAS39.

(iii) The defined benefit plan should recognise 40% of $1 million + (60% of $1 million ÷ 5) ie $520,000 as an increase in the liability. Retained earnings will be charged with the same amount.

(iv) As the development costs have been allowed for tax already, it will have a tax base of zero. Goodwill is measured as a residual and, therefore, the impact is not measured under IAS12.

(v) The accrual for compensation will not be allowed until a later period and, therefore, will reduce the tax base relating to trade and other payables.

4   (a) International Financial Reporting Standards (IFRS) were initially developed for the preparation of group accounts of listed companies. The use of IFRS is growing such that in some countries that are building or improving their accounting regulatory framework, IFRS based corporate reports are deemed to be more reliable and relevant than local GAAP reports. In many of these countries IFRS are the statutory requirement for legal entities and, therefore, an implementation issue that has arisen is that the national law has to be reconciled with the requirements of IFRS.

Another implementation issue relates to small and medium-sized enterprises (SMEs) in terms of whether a separate set of standards should be developed and what should be the underlying conceptual and methodological basis for such standards. Effective implementation requires continuous interaction between the International Accounting Standards Board (IASB) and national regulators. The IASB has issued a draft Memorandum of Understanding on the role of Accounting Standard Setters and their relationship with the IASB. It identifies responsibilities that the IASB and other standard setters should adopt to facilitate the ongoing adoption of or convergence with IFRS.

With the increase in the number of entities applying IFRS, the demand for implementation guidance is growing. The International Financial Reporting Interpretations Committee (IFRIC) has been given the task of meeting this demand but there may be a need for additional coping mechanisms as a limited number of interpretations have been issued since the inception of IFRIC.

15

BPP LEARNING MEDIA

Variations in translation of IFRS could introduce inconsistency. In some countries the capacity for highly technical translation is low and there may be a conflict with existing national terminology and legislation. Additionally, time lags in the local "endorsement" process and in translating new IFRS could mean that financial reports may not be consistent with the latest body of standards. Additionally the successful implementation of IFRS will depend upon the robustness of the local regulatory framework. Effective corporate governance practices, high quality auditing standards and practices, and effective enforcement or oversight mechanisms will be required to underpin the IFRs. Often endorsement of the standards is required as part of the implementation process. For example, in the European Union, after IFRS have been issued by the IASB, they must go through an endorsement process before companies listed in the European Union are required to apply them. This process could create standards that differ from those of the IASB.

Implementation of IFRS can have implications for a number of legislative areas. The more complex the regulatory framework, the more problems will arise. There can be tax, price control and company law implications, and certain sectors, such as banking and insurance, may be subject to additional regulation that may require special reporting requirements. Entities may find that they are in breach of existing covenants with lenders where the provision of funding is based on national GAAP ratios. Similarly corporate law may set out the requirements on distribution of dividends and unless the necessary corporate law amendments are made then dividend distributions would be based on national GAAP which might create confusion.

An international mechanism for the co-ordination of enforcement of IFRS is required. IOSCO provides an infrastructure for enforcement with respect to publicly listed companies. IOSCO has put forward proposals for the regulatory interpretation and enforcement of IFRS. On a more local level, the European Union has established the Committee of European Securities Regulators whose role is to improve co-ordination among securities regulators and ensure implementation of legislation in the European Union.

The complex nature of IFRS and the sheer volume of standards make the task of implementation difficult. The standards are deemed to be "principles based" and this may lead to inconsistencies of application, particularly in countries without a critical mass of experienced accountants. Most accountants will have been trained to apply domestic accounting standards, and where there are options in IFRS, then it is likely that the accounting practice closest to their National GAAP will be chosen. Similarly IFRSs utilise fair value measurement extensively and market information is required to more accurately reflect the value. The nature of this market information will vary around the world. If market information is not available, an alternative source can be obtained by simulating a hypothetical market or by using mathematical modelling. Experience of such techniques will vary worldwide, and this experience will be variable in such areas as actuarial estimation, impairment testing, and valuing share based payments. The concepts set out in IFRS may be new to some accounting professionals and may be difficult to grasp.

(b) Under current accounting practice the objective of acquisition accounting is to reflect the cost of the acquisition. To the extent to which it is not represented by identifiable assets and liabilities (measured at their fair value), goodwill arises and is reported in the financial statements. These exposure drafts adopt a different perspective and require the financial statements to reflect the fair value of the acquired business. The recognition of the acquired business at fair value will mean that any existing interest owned by the acquirer before it gained control will be remeasured at fair value at the date of acquisition with any gain or loss recognised in the income statement.

The proposals treat the group as a single economic entity and any outside equity interest in a subsidiary is treated as part of the overall ownership interest in the group. As a consequence, transactions with minority shareholders are to be treated as equity transactions. No gain or loss will be recognised in the income statement. Accounting for business combinations has to date been based on the "parent entity" concept where the extent of non-controlling interests and transactions with non-controlling interests are separately identified in the primary financial statements.

It is also proposed that goodwill is to be recognised in full even if control is less than 100%. IFRS3 currently requires that goodwill arising on acquisition should only be recognised with respect to the part of the subsidiary undertaking that is attributable to the interest held by the parent entity.

Costs incurred in connection with an acquisition are not to be accounted for as part of the cost of the investment but will be charged in the income statement. There will also be changes to the way in which some assets and liabilities acquired in a business combination are recognised and measured. The draft IFRS requires assets and liabilities acquired to be measured and recognised at fair value at the acquisition date. Currently estimated fair values are used and guidance was given as to how to measure 'fair value' in the current standard. This guidance often resulted in the measurement of assets and liabilities in a manner which was inconsistent with fair value objectives.

16

P2 Pilot Paper (INT)
Corporate Reporting (International)

Marking Scheme

1	**(a)**	Operating activities	6
		Retirement benefit	3
		Associate	3
		Subsidiary treatment	4
		Property, plant and equipment	3
		Goodwill	2
		Minority interest	3
		Taxation	3
		Dividend paid	3
		Interest	2
		River	2
		Issue of shares	1
			35
	(b)	Issues	9
	(c)	Ethical discussion	3
		River	3
		AVAILABLE/MAXIMUM	**50**

2	Oil contracts	4
	Power station	7
	Operating leases	5
	Proposed dividend	3
	Share options	4
	Effective communnication	2
	AVAILABLE/MAXIMUM	**25**

3	**(a)**	Quality of discussion		2
		Framework		1
		Temporary difference		2
		Liability		1
		Weakness		1
				7
	(b)	Adjustments:	Available for sale assets	2
			Convertible bond	2
			Defined benefit plan	2
			Property, plant and equipment	1
		Deferred tax:	Goodwill	1
			Other intangibles	1
			Financial assets	1
			Trade receivables	1
			Other receivables	1
			Long-term borrowings	1
			Employee Benefits	1
			Trade payables	2
		Calculation		3
			AVAILABLE	**19**
			MAXIMUM	**18**
			AVAILABLE	**26**
			MAXIMUM	**25**

4	**(a)**	Subjective	18
	(b)	Subjective	7
		AVAILABLE/MAXIMUM	**25**

17

BPP LEARNING MEDIA

Review Form & Free Prize Draw – Paper P2 Advanced Corporate Reporting (International Stream) (6/07)

All original review forms from the entire BPP range, completed with genuine comments, will be entered into one of two draws on 31 July 2007 and 31 January 2008. The names on the first four forms picked out on each occasion will be sent a cheque for £50.

Name: _____   Address: _____

_____

_____

How have you used this Kit?
(Tick one box only)

☐ Home study (book only)

☐ On a course: college _____

☐ With 'correspondence' package

☐ Other _____

Why did you decide to purchase this Kit?
(Tick one box only)

☐ Have used the complementary Study text

☐ Have used other BPP products in the past

☐ Recommendation by friend/colleague

☐ Recommendation by a lecturer at college

☐ Saw advertising

☐ Other _____

During the past six months do you recall seeing/receiving any of the following?
(Tick as many boxes as are relevant)

☐ Our advertisement in *Student Accountant*

☐ Our advertisement in *Pass*

☐ Our advertisement in *PQ*

☐ Our brochure with a letter through the post

☐ Our website www.bpp.com

Which (if any) aspects of our advertising do you find useful?
(Tick as many boxes as are relevant)

☐ Prices and publication dates of new editions

☐ Information on product content

☐ Facility to order books off-the-page

☐ None of the above

Which BPP products have you used?

Text	☐	Success CD	☐	Learn Online	☐
Kit	☑	i-Learn	☐	Home Study Package	☐
Passcard	☐	i-Pass	☐	Home Study PLUS	☐

Your ratings, comments and suggestions would be appreciated on the following areas.

	Very useful	Useful	Not useful
Passing ACCA exams	☐	☐	☐
Passing 3.6	☐	☐	☐
Planning your question practice	☐	☐	☐
Questions	☐	☐	☐
Top Tips etc in answers	☐	☐	☐
Content and structure of answers	☐	☐	☐
'Plan of attack' in mock exams	☐	☐	☐
Mock exam answers			

Overall opinion of this Kit   Excellent ☐   Good ☐   Adequate ☐   Poor ☐

Do you intend to continue using BPP products?   Yes ☐   No ☐

The BPP author of this edition can be e-mailed at: katyhibbert@bpp.com

Please return this form to: Nick Weller, ACCA Publishing Manager, BPP Learning Media Ltd, FREEPOST, London, W12 8BR

Review Form & Free Prize Draw (continued)

TELL US WHAT YOU THINK

Please note any further comments and suggestions/errors below.

Free Prize Draw Rules

1 Closing date for 31 July 2007 draw is 30 June 2007. Closing date for 31 January 2008 draw is 31 December 2007.

2 Restricted to entries with UK and Eire addresses only. BPP employees, their families and business associates are excluded.

3 No purchase necessary. Entry forms are available upon request from BPP Learnng Media Ltd. No more than one entry per title, per person. Draw restricted to persons aged 16 and over.

4 Winners will be notified by post and receive their cheques not later than 6 weeks after the relevant draw date.

5 The decision of the promoter in all matters is final and binding. No correspondence will be entered into.